THE GOVERNOR'S HOUNDS

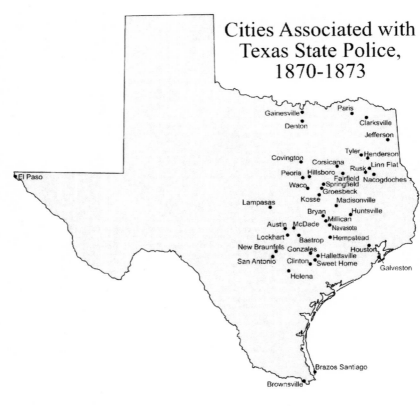

Cities Associated with Texas State Police, 1870-1873

Charles D. Grear

NUMBER THIRTY
JACK AND DORIS SMOTHERS SERIES IN
TEXAS HISTORY, LIFE, AND CULTURE

THE
GOVERNOR'S
HOUNDS

THE TEXAS STATE POLICE, 1870–1873

Barry A. Crouch & Donaly E. Brice

To Al Mc Cutchan
Best Wishes
Donaly E. Brice

UNIVERSITY OF TEXAS PRESS ⋎ AUSTIN

Publication of this work was made possible in part by support from the J. E. Smothers, Sr., Memorial Foundation and the National Endowment for the Humanities.

Requests for permission to reproduce material
from this work should be sent to:
Permissions
University of Texas Press
P.O. Box 7819
Austin, TX 78713-7819
www.utexas.edu/utpress/about/bpermission.html

The paper used in this book meets the minimum requirements of
ANSI/NISO Z39.48-1992 (R1997) (Permanence of Paper). ∞

Library of Congress Cataloging-in-Publication Data

Crouch, Barry A., 1941–
The governor's hounds : the Texas State Police, 1870–1873 /
by Barry A. Crouch and Donaly E. Brice.
p. cm. — (Jack and Doris Smothers series in
Texas history, life, and culture ; no. 30)
Includes bibliographical references and index.
ISBN 978-0-292-74770-8
1. Texas State Police—History. 2. Police, State—Texas—History—
19th century. 3. Law enforcement—Texas—History—
19th century. I. Brice, Donaly E. II. Title.
HV7571.T4C76 2011
363.209764—dc22
2011005076

ISBN 978-0-292-73538-5 (E-book)

To the memory of Bear

Contents

Acknowledgments

Researching and writing *The Governor's Hounds* required much more than the efforts of these authors; bringing this book to fruition required the assistance and support of a tremendous number of individuals. After many years of research and writing, our work is complete. Unfortunately, the untimely death of Barry A. Crouch prevented him from enjoying the final production of our work. Barry brought to this project a sense of dedication, a fountain of knowledge of the subject, and a discipline in writing that would be difficult to match. Barry's vast knowledge of Reconstruction instilled in me an enthusiasm for that exciting and misunderstood period of history. This is the second book that I have had the privilege to research and write with Barry. Our first book was *Cullen Montgomery Baker: Reconstruction Desperado*. After completing that book, Barry had originally set his sights on writing a general history of Reconstruction in Texas. I had become quite interested in the Texas State Police during the administration of Governor Edmund J. Davis and persuaded Barry to set aside his general history to work on a history of this unique and controversial constabulary force. Until 1969, little had been written about the Texas State Police that had portrayed them in a positive light. In that year Ann Patton Baenziger's article "The Texas State Police During Reconstruction: A Reexamination" was published in the *Southwestern Historical Quarterly*. Having read her article, I realized that the State Police had accomplished much good in spite of what had previously been written about them. I decided that a balanced history of the State Police was needed to show the positive results of their actions as well as the negative things that had been written about them. Thanks, Ann, for opening my eyes to the positive contributions made by this constabulary force that struggled to combat the violence in Reconstruction Texas.

In acknowledging the following persons, I am confident that I am also expressing the appreciation and gratitude that Barry would have extended for all the assistance and support we received in this project.

Two people who deserve a very special recognition for their warm friendship and untiring support in our endeavor are Charles and Pat Spurlin of Victoria. When they first met Barry and me, I am not sure what they made of us. I am sure that they thought we were "different." However, from the beginning they expressed a warm friendship and accepted us both as part of their family. Their kindness, generosity, and support have been unconditional. Barry appreciated their friendship, and I will always be in their debt for all their help and encouragement. Pat, there are not enough "thank yous" in the world to express my gratitude for your assistance that compensated for my lack of computer knowledge in this endeavor.

A number of institutions have provided invaluable information and assistance to us in the course of writing our book. First and foremost I would like to thank the patient and knowledgeable staff of the Texas State Library and Archives Commission in Austin. Jean Carefoot, Bill Simmons, Sergio Velasco, and John Anderson, in particular, were always there to help and put up with a great deal of Barry's wry sense of humor during his extended stays in Texas during the summer months. Although the lion's share of State Police records was found in the Texas State Archives, we did visit a number of other institutions and libraries where we obtained valuable information. We both owe a debt of gratitude to the staffs at the Austin History Center and the Dolph Briscoe Center for American History in Austin, the Texas Collection at Baylor University in Waco, the Ralph W. Steen Library at Stephen F. Austin State University in Nacogdoches, the National Archives and Records Center in Washington, D.C., and the Indiana State Archives in Indianapolis. We also appreciated the courteous and helpful personnel at the many county courthouses that we visited during our numerous research trips around the state.

Special thanks must be extended to Sheron Barnes and Greg Garcia of the Regional History Center at the Victoria College/University of Houston–Victoria Library for their computer expertise and helpful assistance.

For assisting us in acquiring a number of photographs and images for this project, I would like to thank John Anderson and Liz Clare of the Texas State Archives; Christina Stopka of the Texas Ranger Museum and Hall of Fame in Waco; the staffs of the Austin History Center and the Dolph Briscoe Center for American History; Richard Banks of Lockhart; Bryan Davis of Nacogdoches; Caroline Anderson of Houston; Anne Watkins of Viveash, Western Australia; Malford Ackermann of Schertz; and Harriett and David Condon of Middleburg, Virginia.

To Carl H. Moneyhon of the University of Arkansas–Little Rock and Walter L. Buenger of Texas A&M University–College Station, I owe a debt of gratitude for your sage advice and constructive recommendations that helped us improve our manuscript tremendously.

To Theresa May, Leslie Tingle, Teri Sperry, Nancy Bryan, and all the staff of the University of Texas Press, I want to acknowledge your encouragement, guidance, and long-suffering patience in helping to bring our book into reality. Your assistance has been greatly appreciated.

Although I never had the opportunity to meet Erik Larsen, a friend of Barry's, I appreciate the statistical analysis that he provided us regarding the composition and makeup of the Texas State Police force. This information was gleaned from incomplete data in the State Police records and has added greatly to our book. Barry was impressed with his analysis and felt that it would lend much to our book.

I would also like to express my appreciation to Charles D. Grear of Prairie View A&M University for providing the maps that will help the reader to understand the logistics and place-names associated with the Texas State Police.

Some others who have offered valuable information and insight into our work include Kenneth W. Howell of Prairie View A&M University, Chuck Parsons of Luling, Harold Weiss of Leander, Jeff Jackson of Lampasas, James M. Smallwood of Gainesville, Rick Miller of Harker Heights, Dave Johnson of Zionsville, Indiana; Larry Madaras of Lake Worth, Florida; Patrick Williams of Fayetteville, Arkansas; and Lynne Payne of Gallaudet University in Washington, D.C. All the many friends of Barry's and mine who have offered their support and encouragement in this project are too numerous to mention by name. I hope that each of you know how much your support meant to both of us.

Last, but not least, I must acknowledge my wife, Clare, and Barry's family, his daughter Jennifer Crouch and his sister Patsy Conn. Without the love, support, and encouragement of our families, it would have been a much more difficult task to complete *The Governor's Hounds*.

THE GOVERNOR'S HOUNDS

Introduction

One of the most hated organizations—and one of the most misunderstood—in the history of Texas is the State Police, created under the administration of the Radical Republican Governor Edmund J. Davis. Often described as "snakes, wolves, and other undesirable things," they were opposed from their 1870 inception by Democratic newspapers and much of the populace.[1] The State Police have been maligned, excoriated, vilified, and discredited by almost everyone. Yet, no extended serious investigation of the agency or its members has ever been undertaken. This adverse characterization began in the nineteenth century and has continued into the twenty-first. Not until 1969 was the prevailing perspective about the State Police challenged. Until now, no full-scale study of the force existed.

The denigration of the state constabulary follows three major themes. Two of the criticisms of the police involve its members. The first is that a majority of the personnel were desperadoes and criminals who had served terms in the state penitentiary and committed crimes of a heinous nature. The second is that due to their background, they attempted to destroy democracy by fraudulent practices, interfering in elections, costing the taxpayers exorbitant sums of money, and supporting a military dictatorship under Governor Davis. They used their official status to legally murder prisoners who attempted to escape from their custody, and oppressed Texans. The third theme is that a significant portion of the force (generally estimated at about 40 percent) was African American. (This, as we will later see, is simply untrue.)[2]

More than four decades ago, Ann Patton Baenziger dissented from this jaundiced view of the State Police, positing that the organization did indeed have some problems but nowhere near what previous writers had suggested. The force was created for a legitimate purpose, namely, to reduce the level of violence within the Lone Star State. And, for all the previous condemnation, they were a necessary element in Texas history. Moreover, violence was so pervasive that local areas needed assistance from a statewide directed mobile unit which could legally enter any jurisdiction. The policemen could move in and out of areas, where necessary and when needed, to reduce upheaval in local communities across the state. In short, they were created to suppress crime.[3]

What aroused the most opposition was the fact that many mistakenly believed the State Police were staffed with a high percentage of African Americans. (Some may have confused them with Special Policemen.) Policemen had the authority of the state behind them, but the idea that blacks could be endowed with police powers angered and simultaneously frightened many. Moreover, they carried weapons. As Matthew Gaines, one of two black state senators during Reconstruction declared, the real hostility was not in the "idea of placing such a great power in the hands of the executive," but by the "idea of gentlemen of my color being armed and riding around after desperadoes." African American State Policemen were often accused of "being the vanguard of a black insurrection," and as outlaws who desired to impose a new order upon the populace through coercion.[4]

In the wake of Reconstruction, African Americans joined city police departments across the South. From Raleigh, North Carolina, to Galveston, Texas, black men saw service, no matter how briefly, in and among urban constabularies. And, not surprisingly, they performed adequately. It will amaze no one that these "colored" members faced daunting obstacles and a storm of censure in carrying out their responsibilities. But only in Texas was a State Police cadre envisioned. As Frederick Nolan, a noted biographer of Billy the Kid, remarked, until that time "there had never been any such force in any American state." One historian has contended that the organization "could well have served as a model for other southern states."[5]

Even after redemption black policemen continued to perform in Texas (Houston, Austin, Galveston, and Bryan) and elsewhere across the South. But in the later period, after the fervor of Reconstruction had waned, according to W. Marvin Dulaney, "racial proscriptions were placed on the police powers of African Americans: black police could not arrest whites and they patrolled only areas and communities inhabited by other African Americans." At the end of the first decade of the twentieth century, blacks had "literally disappeared" from Southern police forces. Only five Southern cities continued to employ African American police officers: Houston, Austin, Galveston, San Antonio, and Knoxville, Tennessee. None served in the "Deep South" states.[6]

Certainly, the State Police had its share of unsavory personnel. Some men were dishonest; others unscrupulous; a few, including officers of color, acted in haste. And they occasionally murdered individuals for seemingly no reason. Yet, there is but one example of a State Policeman being sentenced to the penitentiary. Republicans sometimes used the police for electioneering purposes, but mostly the Special Police performed this task as elections were of short duration. Even opponents of the State Police conceded its success in curtailing crime and apprehending criminals. When Democrats dissolved the organization in 1873, one Southern historian remarked that "brigands and assassins roamed freely once again."[7]

As they can be the cause of some confusion, an explanation of the different statuses of State and Special Policemen is in order. At the urging of Governor Davis, the State Police were established as a state-sponsored permanent organization in mid-1870. As violence continued to plague the Lone Star State, in 1871 Davis convinced the legislature to create a subsidiary group of policemen. These Special Policemen (a maximum of twenty for each county) served at the behest of the state and were only paid when summoned in an emergency. Many historians of Texas have confused these two groups. In this case terminology is significant. Neither force performed in a manner described by previous writers, but the State Police are the major focus herein.

Another myth associated with Governor Davis, the State Police, and Reconstruction, is the number of times the chief executive declared martial law during his tenure. Discussing the problems in Lampasas County, not long before the demise of the police, Frederick Nolan contends that the Chief of Police contemplated imposing martial law in the county. This was not an option, he continues, because it had already been tried without success in Bastrop, Brown, Nacogdoches, and Smith counties. Pauline Buck Hohes wrote that Davis prescribed the same sanction for Palestine, in Anderson County, and dispatched an armed force to the area.[8] None of this is true. Martial law was declared only in Hill, Walker, and Limestone/Freestone counties.

Violence in the antebellum years, throughout the Civil War, and during Reconstruction led state authorities to rely upon the militia, or some other citizen organization, to reduce the mayhem. Until the advent of Republican

control in 1870, the majority of these efforts focused upon the Mexican border or the Indian frontier. Internal upheaval was ignored, with various administrations believing that county law enforcement officials could contain those
who committed illegal actions. The establishment of the State Police was the
first attempt in Texas history to decrease this non-border and non-frontier
eruption. Within the state itself, although often dismissed as inconsequential,
is where the vast number of confrontations occurred.

The State Police was indeed a unique organization. For the first time in
American history, perhaps whether local, county, district, or state, police officers employed were black, white, and brown. The agency has been caught
between old and new interpretations of Reconstruction history, but there has
never been a full-scale history of this constabulary based upon the massive
archival records in the Texas State Archives. With the exception of one historian, the manuscripts have remained relatively untouched. Numerous writers
have condemned the policemen based on nothing more than hearsay or vile
diatribes in opposition newspapers. What the sources do reveal is an entirely
different story than previously presented.

The State Police have often been compared to the Texas Rangers in accounts of Texas history. Of course, the police come off as second best in these
accounts. What most historians have failed to realize is that the police under
Davis and the Rangers under Richard Coke discharged many of the same duties. Indeed, the charges leveled at the "governor's hounds" were similar to
those aimed at the Rangers in the late nineteenth and early twentieth centuries. They murdered prisoners who attempted to escape their custody, violated personal and private rights, and had no concern for individual civil liberties. (The major difference between the two organizations is that the State
Police employed African Americans. The Texas Rangers did not do so until
late in the twentieth century.) And yet, until the past two decades, few, if any,
historians condemned the Rangers for their course of action; the State Police
have always been castigated.[9]

Myths, memory, and false newspaper stories have damned the State Police
of Governor Davis to a rung below that of the unspeakable, somewhat similar
to the Freedmen's Bureau, the United States Army, and carpetbaggers in the
Reconstruction South. Most of the history of the police has been invented
from pro-Southern attitudes and repugnance to what happened in the aftermath of war, when Republican administrations attempted to integrate blacks
into the body politic. Later, this was not an issue when the Texas Rangers became the official force of Democratic governors and the populace supported

their efforts, even if they violated personal rights at every turn. The Rangers captured criminals and attempted to excise crime, as did the State Police during their tenure.[10]

Because the Reconstruction era is still such a controversial period in Texas history, the State Police have been tarnished with a negative brush. Amateur and professional historians alike have been guilty of this depiction. With little research and an overreliance on newspapers that were neither reliable nor factually correct, they proceeded to paint a picture of the postwar years as a time of betrayal, lost cause apostasy, and a violation of the rights of the common citizens, when, in fact, most of the stories and reminiscences were highly exaggerated. Reliance on memory and oral accounts has not served Texas history very well.

This book is a comprehensive history of the State Police during its three-year existence. It examines the reasons why Governor Davis proposed such an organization and why he selected his original Chief of Police, James Davidson. It gives extensive treatment to the selection of policemen and how they performed their myriad duties, discussing and interpreting their conduct in every area where they were actively involved. This is a venture at an even-handed history, neither ignoring the faults, peccadilloes, or even murderous ways of individuals on the force, nor failing to point out those policemen who served honorably and carefully discharged their obligations. This is a necessary correction of past accounts.

Murder

AN INALIENABLE STATE RIGHT

Violence has ever been associated with Texas. When it was controlled by Spain and Mexico, officials commented about the area's outrageousness. The causes for individual Texans' propensity toward brutality, especially after the arrival of immigrants from the United States until the twenty-first century, have often attracted the attention of writers. Texas violence has been characterized as extensive, and the state's "reputation for lawlessness" has been repeatedly chronicled. The frontier milieu, reinforced by both a Southern and a Western heritage, "produced a habit of self-redress more deeply ingrained" than anywhere in the country, claimed C. L. Sonnichsen. The early Texan moral code propagated the belief that "*'revolvers make all men equal.'*"[1]

To attempt an explanation of the level of mayhem and its causes in Texas from the entrance of the first Anglo settlers through the Reconstruction period is an almost insurmountable challenge. Texas was truly a vast frontier region where law and order, although important, never seemed to be adequately enforced. Violence fluctuated with the changing political and geographical environment. Before the Civil War, lawlessness functioned through a code of Southern honor.[2] Weapons were commonplace, and to be armed was to be ready for any contingency. Outlaws and gangs infested the region, but local residents would occasionally band together with lawmen to eradicate these too frequent pests.

One nineteenth-century traveler came as close as anyone to explaining why Texas experienced so much violence. He discovered the citizens to be like the weather, "a perpetual enigma, a tissue of contradictions." When the other members of the Confederacy surrendered, Texans wanted to fight. An individual would jeopardize his life for a friend, but would immediately turn around and defraud another of six months' wages. Texans did "everything for honor," "nothing for justice," and broke more laws than anyone else. Fervent believers in six-gun equality, they frequently resorted to its judgment. This Texas was a "land which has spilled so much blood for the *gusto picaresco* literature of the million."[3]

The Civil War, emancipation of the slaves, and the subsequent upheaval that characterized Reconstruction irrevocably altered violence patterns. Although the Democrats complained that the real necessity was the protection of settlers on the Indian frontier to the north and west (internal outrages would be disposed of by local authorities), in actuality those inhabitants facing the Native Americans were safer than a black individual living in East Texas. Those who vocalized their unionism in the postwar years also became the subject of dishonorable intentions. But to explain why the level of violence became so outlandish is a Sisyphean task. The complexity and diversity of confrontations between all classes and races in Reconstruction Texas boggle the mind.

The Lone Star State had been widely touted for its wayward ways long before the Civil War. After all, the Republic had been born through revolution. The isolation of the frontier and its attendant culture perpetuated the idea of self-defense and "no duty to retreat."[4] The new majority of the inhabitants, many of whom transported slaves, were of a similar cultural background, which tended to be violent, honor-driven, and thus tumultuous. The legacy of the South's defeat and the destruction of slavery added fuel to an already lawless reputation.

Throughout its history as a colony, a Republic, and a state, the central authority that controlled Texas sanctioned a citizen force of soldiers to combat violence, particularly against the Native Americans, but occasionally to pursue criminals. The leaders of Texas, under whatever flag, almost always focused upon external and not internal upheaval. Texans sporadically concerned themselves with the inner turmoil that afflicted their society, but it never received the same attention as those who threatened the borders of the state or the protection of those who desired to extend the frontier. Even though lawlessness and crime might become a serious concern, only rarely was a special force created to combat its deleterious effect.

Under Spanish rule, the idea of organizing citizens on the *frontera* to combat Indian incursion originated in 1713. These military units evolved into "flying squadrons" or *compañía volante*, which defended Texas and adjacent provinces. Members of these frontier regiments enjoyed a special status, but service was demanding. Individuals were required to possess a musket, two pistols, a saddle, blanket, spurs, hat, and various horses. Their duties increased from fighting Indians to preventing illegal immigration from the United States to pursuing fugitives from civil jurisdiction. The *compañía volante* eventually declined, but this quasi-organization had pursued "civilian criminals as well as external enemies."[5]

American immigrants to Texas brought a similar heritage as part of their cultural baggage, which confronted a Hispanic tradition of a force that served "primarily a police function." Mexico followed the latter pattern in order to reduce the expense of a large standing army. Stephen F. Austin received approval to establish a "National Militia" (a "rigid and active police") to engage the Indians and taxed the settlers to maintain the unit. They were authorized to sustain the constitution, guard the legislative hall, preserve public tranquility, and apprehend "all deserters, vagabonds, thieves, or other evil-doers or criminals." Texans later proposed that they have their own regular volunteer army, ranger corps, and militia.[6]

After 1832, Texans developed a type of military squadron that proved to be a "highly efficient and formidable type of ranging cavalry." As they preserved the "basic principles of the old compañía volante, the militia flying squadrons had as their objective the security and protection of their own *vecindario* [community] from any harmful threat." The types of local military organization encouraged and practiced, first by the Spanish authorities, then by Mexican officials, and finally by the Texans during independence and as a state, owe much to the Hispanic influence. Later, the Texas Rangers, and even the State Police, "represented something of a connecting link between the Tejano flying squadrons of the 1830s and the Rurales of the 1890s."[7]

During its Republic phase and continuing into statehood, Texas attempted to reduce violence on the frontier and occasionally in the interior, when the state authorized a militia and the Texas Rangers. The Rangers, who had powers similar to those later awarded the State Police, patrolled the Mexican border and attempted to keep the Indians in check. Many of the Rangers fought as United States soldiers in the war with Mexico. But it would not be until the last quarter of the nineteenth century that the Rangers would focus upon internal violence. (After the demise of the State Police, the Rangers would gain their reputation for apprehending and killing criminals.)[8]

When the Civil War ended, much changed. In July 1865, John C. Gill, a surgeon in the 114th Ohio Volunteer Infantry, negatively characterized Texans in letters to his sister and mother. Captured in the 1864 Red River campaign, he was imprisoned for six weeks. He was treated well, and Dr. Gill's attitude did an about-face once the war ended. Describing his experiences in Galveston, Houston, and Millican, he found the latter place to be a "miserable cut throat hole" where "every one carries a large bowie knife and revolver strapped to him" as they also did in Houston. Gill wrote that "this seems very little like times of peace." Texas was "an outlawed state" and the army should have "gone through the entire state, and laid it in waste."[9]

Gill's comments were neither unique nor unusual. Before and during the Civil War, Texas had been plagued with violence. A Texan told Albert D. Richardson that "'if you want to obtain distinction in this country, kill somebody.'" The most famous antebellum visitor, Frederick Law Olmsted, observed that there were "as many revolvers as male adults" in Texas. A northern traveler, Thomas North, wrote that a man was "a little nearer death" in Texas "than in any other country." James Arthur Fremantle of the English Coldstream Guards claimed Texas to be the "most lawless state in the Confederacy" and "much frequented by desperadoes." The execution of forty-two Unionists at Gainesville in 1862 received national attention.[10]

Perhaps the most cited and frequently quoted of all the refugees who fled to Texas during the Civil War and made intensive notations of its unsavory culture and characteristics was Kate Stone, a Louisiana escapee. In March 1863, the family and slaves moved from the "Brokenburn" plantation (thirty miles northwest of Vicksburg, Mississippi, in Madison Parish, Louisiana) and finally settled in Tyler, Smith County, Texas. Stone did not like Texas or Texans. (They apparently did not like her either.) To be sure, her family had been uprooted and forced to live in an alien and unsettled environment. Stone confided to her diary that "nothing seems more common or less condemned [in Texas] than assassination." Boys wore pistols to school.[11] Little changed in the aftermath of war.

Two months after General Robert E. Lee surrendered at Appomattox, the occupation army arrived in Texas. The commander, Major General Gordon Granger, stripped the state government of its power and implemented a program of national sovereignty. He emancipated the slaves, disbanded the Texas militia, and "voided the legislative acts of 1861 and 1863 that had given the militia legality." As state conditions worsened, citizens approached General Philip H. Sheridan about forming a militia or local constabulary, but he stated that he wanted it "distinctly understood that no home guards or armed bands for self-protection" would be permitted. Sheridan mistakenly believed the army "competent to protect individuals and their property."[12]

On June 17, two days before Granger's emancipation decree and militia disbandment order, President Andrew Johnson issued his Texas proclamation, outlined the necessary requirements which had to occur before readmission would be granted, and appointed the Unionist Andrew Jackson Hamilton as provisional governor. A year later the insurrection would be declared ended in Texas. By that time Congress had tired of the failed Johnsonian program and made plans to reinstitute military control. Moreover, although the military and the Hamilton government had reasonably equitable relations, this relationship was sundered once the Conservatives assumed control of the state political machinery in the fall of 1866. Violence mounted.[13]

During the course of the Civil War, Texas had never been successfully invaded. Isolated from the fighting, Texans evinced a feeling of invincibility at the conclusion of the conflict. A northerner stated that "Texas was never whipped in spirit, only nominally whipped." They considered themselves to simply have been "found in bad company." Thomas North observed that white Texans seriously considered the proposition that the state "could carry on the war by herself, and alone win what the whole South failed to achieve together." Those who believed this foolish notion (a mixed class of the lower sort), North wrote, "did not accept the situation in good faith, have not yet, and never will so long as they can keep the waters muddy."[14]

Observers of Texas violence and lawlessness during Reconstruction reiterated the same themes about Texans that characterized previous descriptions. A Freedmen's Bureau official headquartered in Clinton summarized many complaints about the lack of legal observance among the denizens when he wrote that there was, and "always has been, and probably will be, difficulty in controlling these people by civil law" as "they have never been educated to respect it." Many others emphasized that civil law in the state was a "farce." A Bureau agent in Paris, who had been chased and assaulted by desperadoes, voiced the perspective of insiders and outsiders alike when he wrote that the "revolver rules the day."[15]

With the cessation of hostilities, mounting evidence from a variety of sources suggested that Texas was a violent place. Writing five weeks after the slaves were emancipated, Provisional Governor Hamilton informed President Andrew Johnson that "we have here" the "most painful accounts of the shooting and hanging of Negroes by the half dozens at a time, for the crime

of leaving their former Masters." Hamilton admitted that some of these stories "may be exaggerated as such things generally are, but there is too much
evidence that such things have occurred." Former owners who had taken the
amnesty oath and swore to recognize black freedom simultaneously talked of
the "*gradual emancipation* of the slaves as the proper policy for Texas."[16]

Hamilton also alerted the head of the Freedmen's Bureau, E. M. Gregory,
to the situation in Texas. Evidence had been accumulating for some weeks,
the governor wrote Gregory, "all tending to prove that the freedmen in every
portion of the state not occupied with troops are being badly treated, in many
instances, murdered." Scarcely a day passed that he was not informed of "a
homicide committed upon a freedman." Hamilton realized that it was impossible to "prevent entirely the abuses" he had mentioned, but if the military
would manifest an aggressive stance to "promptly punish such offenses by a
few examples," he thought it would have a "most happy effect."[17]

Race relations continued to deteriorate. Many of the "late owners" of
slaves "seem to be disposed to vent upon the poor Negro, all the bitterness
which they feel towards the Government, for making him free; and in districts remote from military forces openly deny the Negroes freedom," Hamilton informed the president. Freedmen had been killed by the previous
masters and "many more greatly abused." Hamilton reported persecution so
fierce that "human life in Texas is not to day worth as much so far as law or
protection can give value to it, as that of domestic cattle." Letters poured into
Hamilton's office recounting scenes of terror and anarchy. There can be little
doubt that violence abounded in the Lone Star State.[18]

In January 1866, after traveling over part of Texas, Brigadier General W. E.
Strong described a "fearful state of things" and declared blacks, who had only
been free a few months, to be "in a worse condition than they ever were as
slaves." Beaten "unmercifully, and shot down like wild beasts, without any
provocation," they were "maltreated in every possible way," Strong informed
the commissioner of the Freedmen's Bureau, Oliver Otis Howard. To Strong,
there was more cruelty "in Texas than any southern State" he had visited. He
believed that "one campaign of an army through the eastern part of the State,
such as was made by General Sherman in South Carolina, would greatly improve the temper and generosity of the people."[19]

In February 1866, an important Johnsonian sympathizer visited Texas just
as the new constitutional convention was about to convene. (He later viewed
the proceedings.) Writing for the *New York Times*, Benjamin C. Truman was
not an impartial observer. He had served as the president's private secretary
during the war and favored his plan for restoring the Union. Loyalty aside

(and Truman was about the only outside visitor to support Texan faithfulness to the Union), his characterization of Texans was unflattering. "There never has been a time," he wrote in his front-page column for the *Times*, "when a man's life was ever safe in Texas." Everyone, he noticed, went about "armed, and shoot and cut each other upon the least provocation."[20]

Truman depicted (often with tongue in cheek) Galveston as the "commercial capital" of Texas, with about 14,000 inhabitants, "of which at least two thousand are murderers, vagabonds and thieves." Here was a city where they shot "cross-eyed men and red-headed women at sight," and where they drank whiskey that would "kill at twelve paces, go home blind drunk every night and get up ditto every morning." The "full programme of a high-toned ranger is to get full of bad whisky, like some small boy," then "fire off his revolver three or four times, kill a Mexican, and beat his wife, and d_ _n the Yankees—this last being set to music." All men carried "Bowie-knives and pistols in their belts" in addition to a "Mexican cane, which is nothing more or less than a sword-cane."[21]

Others agreed with Truman's rendering of a typical Texan; all carried "a large bowie knife" with a "revolver strapped" to them. Desperadoes and gangs of outlaws infested many areas of the state. Some claimed to be regulators attempting to restore law and order but exploited the turbulent condition of postwar society for their own advantage. Livestock, agricultural produce, and the recently emancipated were favorite targets of these bands. They "roamed unchecked" because communities lacked even a semblance of government. "Thieves and cutthroats attacked and killed law enforcement officers with impunity." Nobody was safe, and those who had supported the Union during the war were clearly in danger.[22]

Edward King, the famous journalist, defended Texans against the onslaught of so much criticism. "The people of the North and of Europe have been told that the native Texan was a walking armament, and that his only argument was a pistol-shot or the thrust of a bowie-knife." He had been "paraded on the English and French stages as a maudlin ruffian, sober only in savagery; and the vulgar gossipings of insincere scribes have been allowed to prejudice hundreds of thousands of people." The state had been "duly maligned; has been made a by-word and reproach," King contended. To him it was a "region of strange contrasts in peoples and places" with the "great mass of the citizens" determined to "maintain law and order."[23]

In February 1866, Texans held a constitutional convention and reluctantly accepted the war's outcome. In August, the president declared the rebellion in Texas at an end. But it was external, not internal problems that received attention from the state government. Frontier defense became the immediate focus. Governor James W. Throckmorton requested that the military send more forces to the new settlements to end Indian resistance. If the army failed to honor this requirement, the governor said, then the legislature would have to "devise some means by which we can protect the frontier ourselves." (A similar plan had been promoted in 1863.) "Money should not weigh against the blood and lives of our people," he said when asked about financing the organization.[24]

Although the Eleventh Legislature authorized the recruitment of three battalions of Texas Rangers to engage the Indians, the national administration refused to yield on this point. Sheridan bluntly informed Throckmorton that these volunteers would "not be accepted." When the army procrastinated in sending the promised troops to the frontier, the governor advertised in newspapers for individuals to man the Ranger forces. Sheridan told Throckmorton that there was "no excuse for the employment of a voluntary state force since double the number" of soldiers "which the legislature had thought necessary had been ordered to the frontier." The governor temporarily gained his objective, but it led to his removal as violence continued unabated in the interior.[25]

William H. Sinclair, a Freedmen's Bureau inspector, who later became a prominent Texas legislator, also disliked Throckmorton. After a sojourn through eastern Texas, he wrote sarcastically that he thought the "war was over." But, Sinclair exclaimed, he had been "dreaming. It isn't." The official added in a farcical vein: "Is it true that the yankee gun boats are coming up Red River? They have such rumors here and many think it will be the cause of demoralizing their *slave* labor and perhaps set them free. Run to the yankee lines you know," he declared in 1867. Had that "Political demagogue," Throckmorton, been relieved yet? Sinclair believed the governor lied about conditions in Texas, representing that "civil law reigneth." Instead, "rebels rule and criminals stalked boldly throughout every county."[26]

The legislature, apparently trying to deflect settlers' criticism from the frontier about doing nothing and ignoring Sheridan's admonitions, attempted to establish a legal militia on November 13, 1866. Encompassing all white males between the ages of eighteen and forty-five (obviously it did not include the freedmen), it would comprise eight divisions (fifteen brigades) in sixteen districts to be commanded by a major and brigadier general. A historian of the Texas militia stated that Throckmorton "never appointed the full roster of general officers" because Congress assumed Reconstruction leadership. In fact, the organization existed only on paper.[27]

As violence increased, relations between the state government and the military collapsed. Throckmorton wrote Benjamin H. Epperson that "like the helpless female who has been violated, we have already lost our chastity." He knew that Charles Griffin, the head of the Freedmen's Bureau and chief military officer in Texas, and Sheridan were "looking for an excuse" to remove him. In August 1867, because of the increasing hostility of Griffin to Throckmorton, and, of course, Sheridan's disgust with the governor's antics and obstructionist tactics, he removed Throckmorton in his famous Special Order Number 105 as "an impediment to the reconstruction of that state under the law." E. M. Pease became the provisional governor.[28]

When Congress assumed the reins of Reconstruction policy in 1867, it explicitly declared that it would neither allow the organization nor the establishment of a militia, rangers, or any other type of volunteer enforcement group. One Reconstruction act stated that "all militia forces now organized or in service" in Texas would "be forthwith disbanded." To make certain no more efforts would be made in this direction without their consent, Congress added that the "further organization, arming, or calling into service of the said militia forces, or any part thereof, is hereby prohibited under any circumstances whatever, until the same shall be authorized by Congress."[29]

Writing to the Radical Republican senator Benjamin P. Wade in mid-1867, O. D. Barrett informed the Ohioan that he had just completed an extensive interview with Abner Doubleday, of mythical baseball fame. Doubleday had recently arrived from Galveston, where he had served in the Texas Freedmen's Bureau. He told Barrett that no white man had been punished in the Lone Star State for murder since Texas had gained its independence from Mexico. Barrett declared that this "murdering propensity must be put down." Congress should frame its new military laws so that the proceedings of a military commission would be enforced at the local level. "Murder," Barrett wrote Wade, "is considered one of their inalienable state rights."[30]

This portrayal of Texans' murderous disposition was not unusual or even unique. Everyone, it seemed, whether visitor or governmental official, along with state and national newspapers, commented upon the quite violent nature of Texas postwar society. Even residents of the region remarked upon what the war and emancipation had wrought. Mrs. L. E. Potts, a native Tennessean who lived in Paris, Texas, implored President Johnson to aid the freedpeople as whites were perpetrating disgusting acts of violence upon them. The goal: "to persecute them back into slavery." Often "run down by blood hounds" and "shot because they do not do precisely as the white man says," Potts contended that killing them was not considered a crime.[31]

When the delegates to the Constitutional Convention of 1868–1869 assembled in Austin on June 1, 1868, the majority were Republicans, which included a few carpetbaggers and ten black delegates. Future governor E. J. Davis desired an in-depth investigation into the disorderly nature of the state. A movement soon developed among a few members, noticeably Hamilton, for the creation of a "loyal militia force" to assist the army in curtailing lawlessness. The Republicans realized sooner than the Democrats/Conservatives that a state-directed organization, with power over local jurisdictions and officials, was a necessity. Clashes over how to control and perhaps limit the violence went to the heart of each party's beliefs.[32]

Heirs to a governmental philosophy that believed centralization of state power was a necessity to bring order to the state's social and economic affairs, the Republican convention agenda was twofold. First, the leaders moved to establish a body of statistics that would irrevocably prove that loyal whites and blacks were being eliminated at an alarming rate. Second, they would use the compiled numbers to demonstrate the necessity for the establishment of a state constabulary and various other local militia-type units that would assist in enforcing law and order. The participation of citizens in quelling violence throughout the state was essential for the Republican program.[33] They would be sorely disappointed.

The Democrats/Conservatives opposed Hamilton's resolution. They believed that the reports about lawlessness and crime were "greatly exaggerated, and many of them [had] no foundation in fact." If Congress granted such power, "owing to the existence of much excitement and unfounded fears, the result" would be "unfavorable to the promotion of peace and order." The "organization of such a force by a political party" would "exasperate the public mind" and "produce conflicts of races." If the provisional government and the military did their duty, all transgressors could be punished. The "masses of [white] people" would "lend any needful assistance." Clearly, the Democrats shuddered at any state group that might include African Americans.[34]

Throughout the convention proceedings, members focused upon violence, lawlessness, and the establishment of a militia. George T. Ruby, a black delegate from Galveston, resolved that a special committee be appointed to study the militia. Colbert Caldwell, representing Bowie, Davis (Cass), and Marion counties, a former Arkansas state legislator and future Texas Supreme Court justice, recommended that a group of five be appointed who would consider the upheaval occurring in the state. Albert J. Evans, a Mississippi-born lawyer and former Freedmen's Bureau agent who resided in Waco and represented McLennan, Falls, and Bell counties, declared that "there now exists in the State of Texas an unparalleled degree of lawlessness and violence, and to such an extent as to render property and life alarmingly insecure."[35]

The delegates accepted the motion and Davis selected eight men, headed by Caldwell, to compose a Special Committee on Lawlessness and Violence. The Radicals on the committee included George H. Whitmore, from Smith County, a former district attorney who had previously served in the legislature, and John H. Lippard, from Freestone County. One moderate Republican, Albert A. Bledsoe, a Dallas judge, served, as did two conservatives, W. H. Mullins, a Cherokee and Angelina County lawyer, and D. Washington Cole, a former Hopkins County judge. Fred W. Sumner, a watchmaker from Grayson County, and Evans, later a district court judge, were also members who tended to support the Republican view.[36]

Rather quickly, a majority of the committee recommended passage of a resolution requesting Major General J. J. Reynolds to "call to his aid" a "sufficient number of loyal men" to quell the violence. It existed to "such an alarming extent" in the state that the convention should do all in its power to "protect life and property," along with suppressing crime. Former provisional governor Hamilton added a different twist when he concluded that permission should be obtained from Congress to organize a militia, which would act under Reynolds's command. M. L. Armstrong from Lamar County, a former state representative, district and county clerk, and election registrar, proposed that $25,000 in rewards be set aside to apprehend desperadoes.[37]

The Republicans persevered in their quest for a centralized police organization. As long as the "State government" was "without any militia or police whatever," violence would continue to run amok. The Republicans argued that "either the citizens themselves must keep the peace, or the military must interfere and compel obedience, or there will be no peace." Contrary to the popular belief in Texas Reconstruction history, the Republicans did not yearn for continued army occupation. They desired to transfer these responsibilities to a variety of state forces that would be under the governor's control. In short, the Republicans, unlike the Democrats, did not trust those who wielded power at the local level.[38]

Even newspapers entered the fray and called for serious measures to reduce the unceasing violence. A month after the convention began its deliberations, the editor of the *San Antonio Daily Express* asked his readers: "How much longer will these atrocious crimes be permitted in our midst?" Invoking a religious theme, he declared that the "blood of innocent victims cries out to heaven." The newspaper and, by implication, the people looked toward the convention and congress for "relief from these murderers and assassins." The state needed a "militia, or give us troops," the editor pleaded, "so that we shall not be given up entirely to midnight murderers and prowling assassins."[39]

J. Warren Bell, a friend of President Andrew Johnson, appraised the Texas situation during the deliberations of the constitutional convention. After traveling over much of the interior of the state, Bell concluded that "there is much lawlessness and disregard of what is right, based perhaps upon the hope, that something will come to pass, to relieve the pressure felt in consequence of the attempt of Congress to put the ballot into the hands of the Negro." He believed that if it were not "for the military authority exerted[,] a *very bad* state of things would exist." The citizens did not seem eager to have murderers or reckless individuals punished, "but rather to a great extent encourage such violence."[40]

The Republicans believed they were under siege. The hypocrisy of blaming the violence on thieves or Indians served to "expose the guilty to the minds of reflecting men" and could not change the fact "that loyal men [white and black] are murdered by rebels." Conservative newspapers openly advocated assassination. One example was the *Houston Daily Telegraph* of July 14, 1868, which stated that individuals such as Morgan C. Hamilton and C. Caldwell "ought to die." C. C. Gillespie, the editor, believed the reports of violence were inflammatory and would plunge Texas into a "war of races," the result being the "extermination of the blacks and ruin of the State." Some convention members wanted him arrested and the paper suppressed.[41]

While the convention members debated a course of action, racial confrontations occurred in Washington, Falls, and Freestone counties, and in the towns of Houston, Hempstead, and Millican. The Millican affray, the first race riot of 1868, initiated by the Ku Klux Klan, left the black population of this Brazos County village leaderless. George W. Brooks and two of his lieutenants were either slain in the imbroglio or later found dead. The convention determined to investigate, but nothing ever came of it. In addition, George W. Smith, a delegate, was killed in Jefferson on October 4, and the East Texas desperado Cullen Montgomery Baker and his cohorts murdered a Freedmen's Bureau agent and harassed the military.[42]

In two reports to the 1868 Constitutional Convention, the violence committee quantified the number of murders committed between mid-1865 and mid-1868, attempted to determine who perpetrated them, and assessed the general causes of this mayhem. Stating that "there is much bad blood in the land," they affirmed "that multitudes who participated in the rebellion, disappointed and maddened by their defeat," were "intensely embittered against the freedmen on account of their emancipation and enfranchisement, and on account of their devotion to the Republican party." They also detested "loyal whites" and desired to "create such a state of alarm and terror" to negate any changes the war had wrought and feared no "retribution."[43]

In spite of Democratic opposition, the Special Committee conveyed its findings to the convention. Although Betty J. Sandlin believed their conclusions to be "of an incendiary nature," they clearly have the ring of authenticity. What the members found was a "frightful story of blood" that consumed the state. The majority of committee members traced the reigning political and racial "hostility" to former rebels who "entertained" feelings of outrage against "loyal men of both races." They believed that their statistical compilation demonstrated conclusively that the "war of the races" was "all on the part of the whites against the blacks." In addition, a "large portion of the whites murdered were Union men."[44]

Although bandits "infested" the highways and desperadoes roamed the countryside along with "combinations of lawless men," horse thieves, and other detestable characters, a majority of the violence, the committee concluded, definitely had political overtones. The atmosphere which resulted from this set of circumstances was not conducive to democracy. The "dominant rebel element" would not "tolerate free discussion," and blacks were "wantonly maltreated and slain, simply because they are free, and claim to exercise the rights of freemen." Discriminated against, blacks "despaired of securing their rights by law" since they believed the courts were "employed as engines" of oppression.[45]

The committee declared that a "spirit of lawlessness" reigned in Texas. The legal system had collapsed and the rights of those who had opposed the rebellion had been made a mockery. Citizens were intimidated in many areas and would not support law enforcement officials, taunting them with the admonition to "'call on your nigger friends.'" Two commanders of the Fifth Military District had not been supportive in reducing the vast amount of violence and ignored the upheaval taking place within the state. Without the military's cooperation, "no government under the sun could preserve the peace of society." Since the "State Government [was] without any militia or police whatever," such an organization needed to be established.[46]

In a supplementary report the committee deflected the Conservative criticism of their findings by stating that individuals of this persuasion had testified before them, which resulted in "flagrant outrages" being committed upon them. They emphasized that they had never stated "that *all* of these murders were committed by rebels for political ends." Although they admitted that their tally "came far short of representing the actual number" of the murders, they doubted that "such a record of blood can be exhibited in any Christian or civilized State in the world in a time of peace." According to the compiled statistics, since 1860, Texas had a yearly average of *forty-five times* more homicides than New York.[47]

The figures compiled by the Special Committee, along with its supplementary report, revealed the "insecurity of human life in Texas." Disloyal whites had now become "desperate" and formed organizations such as the Ku Klux Klan to thwart the war's result. "Bad men," in whatever posture, disguised or openly feared neither the law nor its personnel. And, in most communities everyone knew who committed these depredations but feared for their life if they reported them to the proper authorities. The recognizable ones, such as Cullen Montgomery Baker, Elisha Guest, Benjamin F. Bickerstaff, Bob Lee, "Wild" Bill Longley, Ben Griffith, and a host of others, left a body count of blacks and whites wherever they operated.[48]

Without going into a detailed analysis of the statistics produced by the Special Committee, or the compilation of all acts of violence that could be documented by the Freedmen's Bureau, it does not require a sophisticated interpretation to understand the ramifications of these numbers. And, even presuming a wild inflation, the committee was obviously onto something, whether the Democrats/Conservatives wanted to admit it or not. Blacks, if calculated from their proportion of the population (30 percent) or simply the number of murders, were clearly being dispatched at a considerable rate. (One percent of all black males between fifteen and forty-five years of age died between 1865 and 1868.) The Democrats accepted the figures but disputed the causes.[49]

Although the Democrats endeavored to ignore its existence, the Ku Klux Klan had made its Texas appearance as early as 1866. The white-hooded organization had established local groups in Anderson, Collin, Hays, Panola, Robertson, Tarrant, and Travis counties. Black men had not as yet been enfranchised, so the Klan terrorized the social and cultural institutions of the black community, along with chastising (sometimes permanently) black laborers, ministers, and teachers. They also persecuted local Unionists. Elated at the response of the Throckmorton administration to the imposition of national sovereignty, the Klan burgeoned throughout 1867, and, by the meeting of the convention in mid-1868, had become aggressive and vicious.[50]

By 1867 the number of counties where the Klan existed had nearly qua-
drupled from seven to twenty-seven. The Klan rapidly spread its tentacles
across the eastern portion of the Lone Star State. By 1868, the number had
skyrocketed, with at least 54 of the 136 counties in the state, or almost 40 percent, reporting various forms of Klan deviousness. By the latter date the Klan
had focused upon the political, social, and economic dealings of the freedpeople and kept a close watch on Unionists and members of the Republican
Party. The Klan terrorized the black population and intimidated whites who
supported the "new order." In Texas, desperadoism, outlawism, and the Klan
joined hands, which engendered even more violence.[51]

In November 1868 the commander of the Fifth Military District, Brevet
Major General Joseph J. Reynolds (who was being replaced), assessed the
condition of Texas. He confirmed the existence of the Klan. These "armed
organizations" existed "independently or in concert with other armed bands,
in many parts of Texas" and were "most numerous, bold and aggressive east
of the Trinity River." Reynolds said that the precise object of the group could
not be "readily explained," but their method could. It was to "disarm, rob, and
in many cases murder Union men and negroes, and, as occasion may offer,
murder United States officers and soldiers, also, to intimidate every one who
knows anything of the organization, but will not join them."[52]

In some counties, civil officers were all, or at least a portion of them, members of the Klan. When they refused to join the "Klan or some other armed
band," they were compelled to leave the county. And, where they were not
forced to leave, their influence was "scarcely felt." Reynolds could not define
the Klan's political ends but he did know these groups attended "in large bodies the political meetings (barbecues) which have been and are being held in
various parts of the State, under the auspices of the Democratic clubs of the
different counties." In several counties men had been targeted by name from
the speaker's stand as "elected for murder." They either had to leave or be
murdered "on the first convenient opportunity."[53]

Reynolds declared that the "civil law east of the Trinity river is almost
a dead letter" and, in an oft-quoted remark, stated that the "murder of negroes is so common as to render it impossible to keep an accurate account of
them." Reynolds believed that the "official reports of lawlessness and crime,
so far from being exaggerated, do not tell the whole truth." Some were simply
afraid to report outrages. Many members of bands of outlaws "are transient
persons" and "countenanced" by a "majority of the white people" in areas

where the bands were the "most numerous" or "they would not otherwise exist." Even Secretary of War Edwin M. Stanton characterized the internal condition of Texas as "peculiarly anarchic."[54]

Any remedy would have to be "gradually applied, and combined with the firm support of the army" until the outlaws were "punished or dispersed." This would also necessitate the establishment of military commissions because "perpetrators of such crimes have not heretofore, except in very rare instances, been punished" in Texas. Free speech and free press, as understood in other states, had "never existed in Texas." Towns such as Jefferson, where George W. Smith had recently been murdered, required additional soldiers. If this weakened the frontier posts it was a necessity because the "bold, wholesale murdering in the interior of the State seems at present to present a more urgent demand for troops than Indian depredations."[55]

Reynolds was not without compassion for those Texas citizens who resided in sparsely settled areas. The frontier posts needed to be reinforced because of the recent defeat of the Indians in the northwest, who would now begin migrating to Texas and "make heavy incursions" into the state. To restore internal "peace and quiet" would require, for a "long time, that troops be stationed at many county seats, until, by their presence, and aid, if necessary, the civil law can be placed in the hands of reliable officers, and executed." This process would take many years and be "fully accomplished only by an increase of population." Citizens of other states could not "appreciate the state of affairs in Texas without actually experiencing it."[56]

On December 7, 1868, the convention again convened. Lawlessness seemingly prevailed throughout the state. Citizens complained to Provisional Governor Pease of the activities of horse thieves, murderers, rioters, desperadoes, outlaws, and the Ku Klux Klan. The rebel element enveloped society. A Hempstead black man, Robert Standfield, told the governor that he had "witnessed so much barbarity and cruelty from whites to Blacks" that he confirmed it in writing. Speaking for the "masses of the freedmen" in his vicinity, Standfield requested that some official investigate the brutal murder of blacks "so that we the fried [sic] people can enjoy the freedom that was intended for us[.] We ask for nothing more." Although conditions had improved throughout the state, a "deep-seated hostility to the policy and laws of the government" still lingered and frequently exhibited "itself in violence and terrorism toward loyal white and colored citizens."[57]

The second session of the constitutional convention was characterized by debates over whether Texas should be divided into three or four states,

Edmund J. Davis served as colonel of the First Texas Cavalry Volunteers (U.S.)
during the Civil War and, in 1870, was elected governor of Texas. During his tenure as
governor, Davis established the State Police to help combat violence and lawlessness
in Texas. *Courtesy of the Texas State Library and Archives Commission.*

who should be disenfranchised, a call for a state election in July 1869, and a pronounced split between moderate and radical Republicans. The members unceremoniously adjourned on February 8, 1869. Both Republican factions sent delegations to Washington to curry favor with President-elect Ulysses S. Grant and congressional leaders. The Radicals stressed the extent of violence and lawlessness within Texas, and the moderates emphasized the obstructive tactics of their opponents. Congress ignored both petitions, empowered the president to call elections in the state, and then adjourned.[58]

Once he became president, Grant reappointed General Reynolds commander of the Texas district, but his Reconstruction policy remained vague. For seven months the two Republican factions trekked between Texas and Washington attempting to influence the national administration. Finally, in mid-July President Grant issued a proclamation establishing November 30, 1869, the date for the Texas election. By this time E. J. Davis, the radical, and Andrew J. Hamilton, the moderate, had declared for the governorship. In September, General Reynolds wrote a widely circulated letter in support of Davis and condemning the anti-conciliatory tactics of the Hamilton group. This event also coincided with the Democrats' endorsement of Hamilton.[59]

In early October, Reynolds set the election dates for November 30 through December 3. A tumultuous campaign ensued with the radical wing labeled as the "black man's party" and the moderate/Democratic faction stigmatized as the "white man's party." Although fraud, intimidation, and chicanery characterized the 1869 gubernatorial race, Davis clearly won the election. Moreover, the constitution was approved. Thousands of whites failed to cast ballots. This apathy destroyed any opportunity the conservatives had of winning. The Republicans, but not the Radicals, won a majority in both houses of the legislature. The balance of power would belong to the moderates, who had consistently opposed Davis and his group.[60]

By early 1870, the Republicans had assumed control of the state government. The army began to formally end its occupation and station troops on the frontier. In fact, less than three hundred men, all infantry, remained on duty in the interior of the state, concentrated in Austin, San Antonio, and Jefferson. Although a few soldiers had been stationed at polling places during the 1869 election, they were few and far between.[61] In summary, Davis would have to move quickly to provide some assistance for local and county law enforcement officials to stem the tide of violence and lawlessness. Once officially endowed with gubernatorial powers, he was ready with a comprehensive plan. Davis needed one. In that same year, Texas led the nation in homicides.

An "Untiring Enemy to All Evil-Doers"

THE FORMATION OF THE STATE POLICE

In January 1870, the commander of the Fifth Military District, Major General Joseph J. Reynolds, acting for President Ulysses S. Grant, appointed the 1869-elected officials as a provisional government and ordered the legislators to meet in February. They ratified the Fourteenth and Fifteenth Amendments and chose Morgan C. Hamilton and J. Winwright Flanagan to serve in the United States Senate. Texas was readmitted to the Union on March 30, 1870, and Governor E. J. Davis called the Twelfth Legislature into special session. Although the Republicans were rent by factionalism, most members of the party believed that steps had to be taken to reduce the carnage throughout the state.[1]

Davis needed time to implement his program. In early May, he believed that Texas still required the presence of the United States Army. He wrote to President Grant asserting that it was inadvisable to withdraw troops from the state at that time. Moreover, Davis hoped that General George P. Buell would remain as the Jefferson post commander and retain his troop contingent. In addition, the governor requested the army's cooperation in arresting desperadoes in "Nacogdoches and adjoining counties." The legislature was discussing a "Militia Bill and other measures necessary to the maintenance of order," but Davis told President Grant that "some little time must elapse before a [state] system can be perfected and put in operation."[2]

In his inaugural address on April 28, 1870, Governor Davis claimed that after "ten years of war and civil disorganization" a "fresh departure in political affairs" was necessary. "While the general government was restrained from all violation of the right of life, liberty and property," Davis averred, "it was conceded that the local government had no such restraint, and accordingly local despotisms often flourished under the name of State government." Although the coercion of Southern citizens may have been an "unpleasant necessity," the military had been "defenders of freedom" and created a "supervisory power over all" that would not be implemented on the state level through a rejuvenation of a "fair-minded political process."[3]

Law enforcement was uneven in Texas, and where weakest, offenders congregated. Because most crimes were committed by individuals and not groups, it was necessary to provide a state police force that would enable law officers to arrest offenders. It would assist in bringing criminals to justice and destroy lawless organizations. To be directed by one individual (a chief of police), all the local sheriffs, constables, and their deputies would be "made a part of that general police, to act in concert with" them, all subject to the orders of the chief, who might double as the state's adjutant general. To incarcerate the felons, the governor requested permission to levy a special tax on each county to erect jails and courthouses.[4]

Davis considered these measures "necessary to the intimidation of the lawless, and the punishment of offenders." The primary duty of the state government was to see "that crime is quelled at once." Davis also recommended that the legislature take a bold step and limit the wearing of arms by an individual. "There is no doubt," Davis exclaimed, "that to the universal habit of carrying arms is largely to be attributed the frequency of homicides in this State." He wanted to see this privilege "placed under such restrictions as may seem" to the legislators' "wisdom best calculated to prevent the abuse of it." Other than in a few frontier counties there was "no good reason why deadly weapons should be permitted to be carried on the person."[5]

Davis ended his law-and-order plea on a controversial note. Concerned about protecting the "majority of the people" in communities where "mobs of lawless men" operated "in disguise" against the recently enfranchised, Davis felt the criminal code should be modified to punish such action with "special severity." He also required power that would "enable him in any emergency to act with authority of law." The possibility that "combinations of lawless men" could be organized to resist local authorities, "due caution" advised preparation. He desired the power to temporarily establish "martial law under certain contingencies, and within limited districts." Such authority would go far "toward obviating the necessity for its exercise."[6]

In late June 1870, as part of Davis's program for mobilizing the state against internal disturbances and before the creation of the State Police, the Twelfth Legislature enacted a statute establishing a State Guard, a Reserve Militia, and the office of adjutant general to direct all these forces, and provided the governor with authority to declare martial law. All "able-bodied" males between the ages of eighteen and forty-five, with certain exemptions, were subject to military duty. Those individuals liable for service in the Reserve Militia could avoid activation by paying $15 a year, later reduced to $5. Whenever mobilized, the men would receive the same pay as commissioned and noncommissioned officers of the United States Army.[7]

On May 10, 1870, State Senator P. W. Hall, of Robertson County, introduced a bill entitled "An Act to establish a State Police, and provide for the regulation and government of the same." After being read, it was referred to the Committee on Militia. The House simultaneously began debating its purpose. Following several weeks of political infighting, wrangling, charges, and countercharges, in late June the legislature enacted the law creating the State Police. Davis signed the bill on July 1, 1870.[8]

Because the proposed legislation contained no discriminatory clause as to who could join, black Senate and House legislators unanimously supported Davis's effort to create such an organization. George T. Ruby from Galveston believed such a force necessary to protect black Texans. He did not think these measures totally satisfactory but felt whites would go no further. Blacks in the House thought the police necessary to protect blacks against the widespread violence.[9]

The Twelfth Legislature thus created a State Police organization along with a militia system. Its regulation and supervision would be directed by the state's adjutant general, who would be the "Chief of State Police." The force would comprise 257 men, which included 4 captains, 8 lieutenants, 20 sergeants, and 225 privates. The latter would receive $60 a month, sergeants $75, lieutenants $100, and captains $125. The adjutant general did not receive additional pay for performing his role of chief. All received four-year appointments but could be removed by the governor, the chief, or both for "malfeasance, misfeasance, incompetency or disobedience of orders."[10]

Under the law, the governor and the adjutant general wielded considerable power. The chief, with the governor's approval, made "all needful rules and regulations for the government of the State Police." He also, again with the chief executive's permission, formed the rules and regulations for the "government and direction" of the local constabulary "in matters looking to the maintenance of public peace, preventing or suppressing crime, and bringing to justice offenders." If an individual refused "prompt obedience" to these guidelines or to the orders of the governor or the chief, he would be "removed from office, and suffer such other punishment as may be prescribed by law."[11]

In May 1871, the legislature amended and revised the original statute. The force would now comprise a chief, 6 captains, 12 lieutenants, 30 sergeants, and 210 privates. Base pay remained the same, but each officer received an additional $30 per month, noncommissioned officers $25, and privates $20 as compensation for use of their horses and arms and in lieu of all traveling expenses. The chief was paid an extra $50 per month for the same purpose, which also covered all expenses he incurred while traveling under orders. The chief, through a voucher and with the governor's approval, could make requisition for the money necessary to pay salaries out of any funds in the treasury appropriated for that purpose.[12]

The 1871 supplementary police law also created a category of "Special Policemen." A number of these individuals, not to exceed twenty in each county, might be appointed by the governor and could not be sent out of the county, unless ordered by the chief executive. These Special Policemen would be paid at three dollars per diem, in lieu of traveling expenses and all other allowances, and for the use of their horses and arms, when they actually served. Their compensation would be paid out of the county treasuries of the counties where they were employed through vouchers certified by the chief of police. Thus, declared Governor Davis, "an inexpensive force may always be relied on to assist the local authorities." They mostly served during elections, observing the polls.[13]

Even before Governor Davis initiated legislation to establish the State Police, he proposed to select James Davidson of Company H of the Eleventh Infantry as his adjutant general. Davidson desired the position but wished, if it were at all possible, to remain in the regular army. Davis thought this would be the "better for him" as Davidson had been raised from "infancy as a soldier." The governor requested that the Texas congressional delegates "procure an indefinite leave of absence, or at least one for four years unless he should sooner desire to return to the line of his duty." Davis declared that he was *particularly* anxious to have" Davidson "with me." Davidson, however, had to resign his regular army commission.[14]

On June 24, 1870, Davis appointed Davidson as adjutant general. He was about five feet six inches, square built, with grey eyes and a sunburnt complexion. His dark brown hair was slightly drawn over his eyes, and he sported a coarse and heavy brown mustache. Thirty-two years old, Davidson was brusque in manner with a deep, rough voice, who talked loudly when excited. He walked with his hands in his pockets, eyes to the ground. Davidson wore heavy boots made of alligator skin and carried a gold watch with a photograph of himself and his wife on the dial-plate, adorned with a valuable seal (oval-shaped) and other trinkets on the chain. His ring was a Texas topaz with his monogram, *J* imposed over *D*, encrusted with diamonds and set in gold.[15]

Davidson was born on April 22, 1838, in Kelso, Roxburgh, Scotland. He served in the British Army in the 6th Heavy Dragoons and later with the Cape Mounted Rifles in India and Australia. Beginning as an ensign, he was promoted to an officer from the ranks and received citations for meritorious conduct. He migrated to America and in March 1865 enlisted as a second lieutenant in the Nineteenth Maine Infantry Volunteers. Viewed as "zealous, energetic, and competent," Davidson later joined the regular army as a private in Company D, Corps of Engineers. Rising to the rank of first sergeant, he passed examinations in 1867 for a second lieutenancy. Assigned to the Twenty-ninth Infantry, in 1869 he transferred to the Eleventh Infantry.[16]

As adjutant general, Davidson automatically became chief of police when the legislature established that body. The *Daily State Journal* praised Davidson as being "widely known for his thorough, energetic, and executive talent in Eastern Texas during the reign of Loughery and the Ku Klux." He would "make his office anything but a sinecure" and advised "felons, assassins, desperadoes, and *their abettors*, to act, if they are wise, upon the theory that if peace is not thoroughly kept, somebody will get hurt." The State Police would make the rascals "running loose" seek a "cooler region than Texas." The editor thought it the "best measure ever adopted to secure the enforcement of law in our state."[17]

As the state legislature finalized his appointment, Davidson organized the Adjutant General's Office, sought recommendations for appointments for members of the State Police, and attempted to ascertain just how many criminals inhabited the state. In a July 1 circular, he requested county sheriffs to furnish lists of criminals evading justice, the nature of their crime, and when and where they committed their deeds. After consolidating the reports from 108 counties (29 did not respond), Davidson discovered 2,790 criminals

James Davidson was selected by Governor E. J. Davis to serve as adjutant general of Texas in 1870. Davidson served as chief of the State Police and head of the State Militia until he resigned his commission in 1872.
Courtesy of Caroline D. Anderson and Anne G. Watson.

at large. In the first month of operation the State Police arrested 44 murderers and felons, 5 of whom they killed "resisting arrest." By the end of 1870 the arrest number totaled 978.[18]

Sheriff George D. Kelley of Anderson County was typical of those who responded to Davidson's circular. Originally appointed by General Joseph J. Reynolds in 1867, he won election in 1869. Kelley attempted to be as comprehensive as possible in his report to the chief but encountered incomplete files or incompetent officials. The district court criminal records showed "no less" than sixty-eight cases that had not been prosecuted as the parties were fugitives, two-thirds of them white and most charged with murder. This did not include eight or ten other whites. These individuals had rioted on the streets and public square of Palestine against the loyal people who assembled to celebrate the Declaration of Independence.[19]

Kelley recommended individuals for the State Police. He believed there to be four or five reliable white men competent in "every way" to discharge the duties required of a policeman. Specifically, he mentioned Joel A. Lufkin, late of Company G, 6th U.S. Cavalry, who, during the war, was a member of detective service under General John J. McCook in Kentucky. Kelley thought he would make an efficient and brave lieutenant or sergeant. The sheriff's appraisal: "worthy in every respect." Lufkin, a New York City native, was young, over six feet tall, enjoyed excellent health, and practiced sobriety. His loyalty had been demonstrated in his military record and had been "fully corroborated by his conduct" since living in the county.[20]

The Bastrop mayor, James E. Brady, informed Chief of Police Davidson that Thomas Hodges, a thirty-eight-year-old freedman, desired a privacy in the State Police and also wanted to be designated as "representative at large" for the freedmen in his area. Brady asserted that Hodges was one of the "most influential colloured men in Bastrop County. A man of responsibility and confidence integrity courteous sober and brave to a fault." For evaluations of Brady's private and public character the mayor referred Davidson to two representatives of the state legislature, Julius Schutze and Jeremiah J. Hamilton (a black). Hodges was commissioned a private on August 9, 1870, and served the organization until December 1871.[21]

Letters poured into Davidson's office seeking appointments in the State Police. Davidson admitted that he at first experienced "much difficulty in procuring the names and securing the services of reliable, energetic and efficient men." In a measure, Davidson had to be "guided" in his selections by the "recommendations of parties of well-known loyalty and good standing."

Justifying his actions, Davidson reported that these choices had "proven" the best "that could possibly have been made under the circumstances." If individuals were found wanting, they were "promptly removed, and men well known to be peculiarly suited to the discharge of the duties devolving upon them appointed to the vacancies thus caused."[22]

Davidson searched for two overriding characteristics in the men he selected for the police; courage and nerve. In a state "overrun with desperadoes and refugees from justice, these qualities [were] absolutely essential." Many criminals, Davidson claimed, were known persons of a "desperate character," so, in picking individuals, he had to be satisfied that they possessed the two important attributes of courage and nerve for duty in the field. Moreover, he required individuals who were useful, efficient, and would willingly render aid and assistance to local law officials and the law-abiding population in order to ensure a feeling of security. They had to be always vigilant and, as he phrased it, the "untiring enemy to all evil-doers."[23]

In an additional proclamation on July 4, 1870, Chief of Police Davidson outlined the guidelines and requirements of the newly created State Police. Because of its immense size, Texas was divided into four police districts, each to be under the supervision of a captain. Each district was assigned a specific contingent of State Police members. The First,[24] Second,[25] and Third District[26] would each comprise a captain, two lieutenants, five sergeants, and fifty-six privates. The Fourth would have one captain, one lieutenant, and five privates.[27] The subdistricts of El Paso and Presidio counties in the far western portion of the state would have but one lieutenant and five privates.[28]

The four captains initially named by Davidson included E. M. Alexander of Clarksville (Red River County), John Jackson "Jack" Helm of Concrete (DeWitt County), Leander H. McNelly of Brenham (Washington County), and M. P. Hunnicutt of Waco (McLennan County). Alexander and McNelly served until 1872 and 1873 respectively, but Helm and Hunnicutt lasted less than six months. Later captains included George W. Ballantine of Waco, Francis Cusack of Jefferson (Marion County), George W. Farrow of Bryan (Brazos County), Robert F. Haskins of Helena (Karnes County), A. C. Hill of Denton (Denton County), Emil Kellner of New Braunfels (Comal County), Thomas G. Martin of Mountain City (Hays County), and Thomas G. Williams of Lockhart (Caldwell County).[29]

There is some confusion surrounding Edward M. Alexander's birth date, but he was apparently born September 14, 1826, in Arkansas. His father was a Virginian and his mother a Missourian. Alexander served in the Mexican

War as a private in Sims's Company of the First Texas Mounted Volunteers. Before the Civil War he fought against the Indians on the frontier. A farmer in Red River County, by 1870 he had amassed $3,600 worth of real estate and $1,000 of personal property, primarily the accumulation of his parents' hard work. Chief of Police Davidson commissioned him a captain on July 7, 1870, placing him in charge of the Second Police District, which essentially comprised northeast Texas. He died in 1901.[30]

One major reason the State Police have fared so disastrously at the hands of historians has been the focus upon such individuals as John Jackson "Jack" Helm. Helm brought approbation upon the police because of his outrageous activities. He was born in Missouri in 1837. Helm's father, George W., had migrated from Virginia to Missouri and finally to Texas in 1838 or 1839. They settled in the Charleston community in Lamar County (later Hopkins and

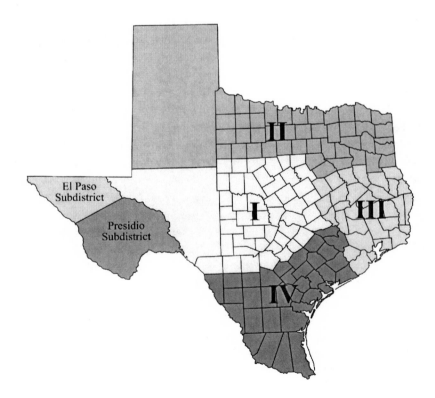

Configuration of the State Police districts when the organization was established in July 1870. *Courtesy of Charles D. Grear.*

now Delta) in the northeast section of the state in an area often referred to as the Sulphur Forks. Jack Helm came from a rather prominent family, his father having served in various local judicial and political positions. Helm was also an inventor and patented two devices: a cotton cultivator and a cotton worm destroyer.[31]

During the Civil War Helm served in Captain L. D. King's company. Later, he was a member of the 9th Texas Cavalry, but when this unit was converted to infantry, Helm, along with several others, deserted and returned home. (One local story has it that he returned because he learned his wife had committed adultery.) For the remainder of the conflict he may have been a member of the Texas militia. Helm soon became involved in a controversy when five deserters were court-martialed and subsequently hanged. Later, Helm and his father, who had been a freighter for the Confederacy, were arrested for murder, tried, and found not guilty. Local legend also relates that Helm murdered a black man for whistling "Yankee Doodle" in his presence.[32]

To avoid prosecution, Helm left the area and emerged in Matagorda County, where he labored for the famous cattleman Abel Head "Shanghai" Pierce as a "captain" of vigilantes to end the widespread practice of rustling and illegal branding. Although there is some dispute about what role Helm played under military rule and Provisional Governor E. M. Pease, he apparently operated under orders from the Fifth Military District commander, Major General J. J. Reynolds, to stem the tide of banditry, cattle rustling, and outlawry. He published a "card" in the *Victoria Advocate* claiming his group acted under orders from the "highest authority in the State" and that his men were kept under control and "no citizen can complain of the least injury at our hands."[33]

Before Jack Helm became a captain in the State Police, the events that led to his downfall and death had already been set in motion. The major players in this drama—the Taylors, the Suttons, the Pridgens, and the Tumlinsons, and later John Wesley Hardin—began their feuding in the aftermath of the Civil War and would continue into the 1870s, after the State Police had been disbanded. The conflict ranged over a considerable area but primarily centered in DeWitt, Gonzales, Lavaca, Goliad, and Victoria counties. Although much controversy exists about why and how the imbroglio began, it was rooted in the animosities that emerged from the Civil War. The whole panorama of death and destruction became known as the Sutton-Taylor Feud.[34]

Helm's tactics were questionable. C. S. Bell, with whom Helm worked, wrote that the Helm/Tumlinson band had "caused a stampede of criminals and bad men of every shade" from the area. Unfortunately, the Helm/Tumlinson Group failed to "capture, or even seek a single *desperado*." Eleven had died at their hands, most while "attempting to escape." Little control could be exerted over men such as Helm. "It is to be feared also that the effect of the killing of these men (*even though* they were desperadoes) by the Helm party," wrote Captain T. M. K. Smith, "will not cease with the dismemberment of the band, but on account of the well known clannishness of the Texas people it will be a fruitful source of bloodshed and murder for years to come."[35]

As deputy sheriff of Lavaca County, Helm received the support of several citizens who desired that Governor Pease confer authority upon Helm to pursue a gang of horse thieves and robbers who infested the area. Described as an "energetic industrious young man," Helm was deemed "prudent and cautious." In 1870, after Helm became DeWitt County sheriff, he was often identified with Bell. He told Governor Davis that he had received disturbing reports from "bad men" questioning Bell's veracity. Helm admitted that he liked Bell. In fact, they had worked together and "encountered difficulty and hardship Togeather [sic] that places us almost like brothers." To Helm, Bell was a "gentleman" and "strictly honest."[36]

After his State Police appointment, Helm visited the town of Gonzales, where the *Gonzales Inquirer* obtained an interview. Referring to him as "redoubtable," the editor did not fail to inform Helm of the *Inquirer*'s "utter abhorrence" of the police law and the "vindictive spirit of those who passed that law." But Helm assured the interviewer that he would receive "none but good men," as the paper's publisher feared the ranks would be filled with "ignorant negroes." Helm contended he would accept recommendations for policemen only from "old citizens of known probity." No pretext for violence should be given, the newspaper concluded, as this would only lengthen the "tyranny which the law was designed to perpetuate, but which is now in its last gasp."[37]

Leander H. McNelly was born in Brooke County, Virginia, on March 12, 1844. He arrived in Texas with his family in 1860. During the war he participated in Sibley's New Mexico campaign and the defense of Galveston, served with Colonel Tom Green's cavalry brigade in southern Louisiana, and helped arrest Texas deserters at war's end. McNelly was cited for his "daring gallantry," "meritorious conduct," and for remaining "true to his colors to the very last." His determination and other soldierly qualities made him an outstanding company leader, declared Major General James P. Major. In fact, Colonel Green remarked that, because of McNelly's courage and "consummate skill," he was "one of the best soldiers and the most daring scout in the cavalry service."[38]

McNelly joined the State Police in early July 1870, shortly after its organization. Davis and Davidson wanted to hire reputable men, and McNelly, although a former Confederate soldier, brought an irreproachable character. The *Galveston News* described McNelly as a "brave, frank," and honest official, "with strong Democratic tendencies." Whatever his political affiliation, he asserted that he "only knew the intention of the authorities at Austin by the instructions," orders, and personal interviews supplied by Governor Davis and Chief of Police Davidson. Both had "cautioned" McNelly to be "prudent and courteous" in discharging his duties. He would later dismiss any policeman reported for doing otherwise.[39]

Mordecai P. Hunnicutt was born in Ohio between 1827 and 1830. His parents were Alabama natives. Nothing is known of his early life. In November 1862 he joined Company I, 73rd Ohio Infantry Volunteers, and attained the rank of sergeant. Discharged in 1864, Hunnicutt came to Texas with Major General E. R. S. Canby. A professional detective, he served in that capacity as a civilian and in the military. He settled in Waco, where he served as the head of the city's police force. Appointed a State Police captain, he quickly ran afoul of Chief of Police Davidson. In August 1870, Hunnicutt was suspected of killing a boy named Eugene Carter in Waco. Found guilty and sentenced to the penitentiary, an appeal overturned the verdict. He died in Waco in 1891.[40]

In selecting men for the State Police, Davidson could be unusually blunt at times. Wallace Rogers of La Grange had received an appointment to the organization in August. But as more information surfaced about his infirmity, Rogers was discharged because "none but able-bodied men can belong to the force." Rogers, "being a cripple, cannot have a position in it." But Davidson could be proven wrong and change his mind. He informed William M. Speights of Milam (Sabine County) that because he was a "cripple and could not properly perform the duties" of a policeman, his appointment had been canceled. But Judge Speights later qualified for the organization in 1871 and served until his death on May 18, 1872.[41]

Within three months, Davidson decided to change his policy about vacancies and promotions. Having difficulties in finding suitable men who were willing to sacrifice their private lives, he felt that circumstances required modification to stabilize the force and maintain a consistent coterie of men who would travel over the state. Although appointees would not necessarily be confined close to their residences, many believed they could do better service in areas where they lived. He declared that "all vacancies will hereafter be filled by promotions from the ranks." The *Daily State Journal* thought this the "true Republican method, and will serve as an additional stimulus to good service and meritorious effort."[42]

Appointments to the State Police also received the scrutiny and tirades of hostile administration newspapers such as the *Democratic Statesman.* They initiated the myth of the unsavory character of State Policemen. The newspaper editorialized that the "acting Chief of Police or Adjutant-General would pick up some poor devil in the street, who wasn't worth a dime and fit him with mount and gear." A policeman's necessities, in their jaundiced eyes, matched his sorry state. A "broken down horse," worth maybe ten or twenty dollars, would be charged to the recruit at fifty or one hundred fifteen dollars. For a "shoddy" twelve-dollar uniform, the individual paid thirty, and for ten dollars more he could buy a Winchester carbine that sold for thirty dollars. For his badge, which should have cost but a dollar, he paid five.[43]

The *San Antonio Daily Herald* followed the viewpoint of the Austin *Democratic Statesman.* The two newspapers took shots at the organization at every turn. Speaking of recruitment, denigrating those who joined the force, and adding a strong touch of racism, the *Daily Herald* nastily remarked that "Meredith, a nigger, shot and killed an old man by the name of Billingsly at Austin recently." Meredith, the newspaper snidely predicted, "will no doubt have an appointment on the Police force." The *Democratic Statesman* suggested that many policemen had served in prison or were about to be confined there, suppressed free speech, and were from the lowest class; in short, "ruffians," who frequently murdered innocent people.[44]

Although Chief of Police Davidson has been roundly criticized for his administration of the State Police, according to observers his office was a model of efficiency. One individual, writing in 1871, remarked that he doubted that "if a more thorough and better disciplined organization of the kind exists in the [United] States today." Davidson's chief clerk, Henry Orsay, possessed all the qualifications and brains necessary to oversee the internal workings of the agency. A better regulated, systematized, and managed office could not be imagined. Statistics were readily available on the current status of the police, and one could easily learn "how effectually and efficiently this corps" performed their duties.[45]

As part of his responsibilities, Davidson decided to become "more thoroughly acquainted, by personal observation," with the men who had been commissioned as policemen and visit the "disorderly sections of the State, and ascertain the evils that actually exist, and apply the proper remedy." This could only be done by traveling through the various police districts. Accordingly, from August until November 1870, he traversed thirty-six counties, which encompassed over one thousand miles. He examined "different detachments at their respective stations," removed "objectionable appointees," and replaced them "with suitable men, thus rendering the force reliable and efficient in case of an emergency."[46]

The first test of the collective power, flexibility, and effectiveness of the State Police as an organization centered on Madison County. Davis was compelled to order a contingent of policemen into the area, but he did not, as is often thought, declare martial law.[47]

Named for President James Madison and carved out of Grimes, Leon, and Walker counties in 1853, Madison County's existence dates from August 1854. The climate, warned the 1871 *Texas Almanac*, was "changeable." One hundred miles northwest of Houston and comprising 473 square miles, Madison County numbered 4,049 inhabitants in 1870, of whom 1,470 were black (about one-third). Although the area had not contained a large slave population (there were only 902 in 1864), following the war the black populace became active, especially after their enfranchisement in 1867. During the Civil War decade, the county experienced an 80 percent increase in the number of residents, which exacerbated race and class tensions.[48]

An unsettled judicial system and weak law enforcement officials, hampered by the lack of court proceedings, allowed desperadoes to roam the area. However, arrest attempts were made. Sheriff James W. Neighbors jailed Neal McMillan, who had been indicted for murdering John Longbotham. McMillan presented a writ of habeas corpus before Judge Davis, who refused to grant bail. On the night of July 21, 1870, a disguised mob of undetermined numbers surrounded the jail, "forced the keys from the sheriff," and released McMillan and W. L. Berryman, who was charged in another killing. The jailbreak was led by the "notorious" Bill McIver, who had killed a Bryan policeman. Accessories to the jailbreak were the Gardners and Poney Stephens, who had slain a Leon County doctor.[49]

Sheriff Neighbors was compelled by "brute force" to release McMillan and Berryman, according to a county inhabitant, who also remarked that the "only wonder is that [Neighbors] kept them in custody so long." Chief of Police Davidson contacted the Bryan City Marshal, George W. Farrow (who later became a captain in the State Police), requesting that he make every attempt to recapture the escapees and also the parties responsible for releasing them. Following the jailbreak, efforts were soon made to remove Neighbors. A member of the Davis ticket who had received both white and black support, Neighbors was described as efficient in some matters. Unfortunately, he often ignored and neglected his subsidiary duties.[50]

A prominent Madison County politico, J. D. McMahon, criticized the citizens for their lack of support for law and order. The verbal attack drew an immediate response. In a letter to the governor, twenty-eight Madison County residents admitted that their county had experienced occasional murders and lynchings between the end of the war and the adoption of the 1869 Constitution. However, the "good people" of the county deprecated these acts. They refused to accede to the fact that anything serious enough had occurred within the county limits to justify the published charges. Attempting to forestall a declaration of martial law, they maintained that in the previous six months there had not been a "more quiet and law abiding people" within Texas. In defense of what occurred, the citizens stated: "And pray sir what county is it that does not afford us instances of escapes of prisoners from their jails even when jails are considered safe and where the laws are said to be most rigorously executed."[51]

Individuals connected to the state administration also precipitated the entrance of the State Police into Madison County. One of the key men was John H. Patrick, a State Policeman. Patrick was a twenty-eight-year-old Georgia-born farmer. His wife, Sarah J., was from Alabama. They had two daughters born in Texas. Patrick joined the State Police in August 1870. He soon experienced difficulties with Chief of Police Davidson because of his unprofessional conduct. Before his clash with Davidson, Patrick organized a company of State Guards, primarily comprised of African Americans, and became its captain. Neither these activities nor his demeanor endeared him to several county residents.[52]

Patrick confirmed to Davidson that one company of State Guards, "every one of them Colored men," had been formed in Madison County. Patrick and his cohorts were "carrying things through." The company was anxious for a Davidson visit, as Patrick believed it would do the Chief of Police "no harm." A committed Republican, Patrick also wished to expand the party's influence by formally joining the Union League. He planned to visit Austin, where he hoped to receive authorization to initiate such a cell in Madison County. In addition to his political activities, Patrick desired to reduce chances for violence and requested information about the law in regard to carrying six-shooters, which he would subsequently misinterpret.[53]

Patrick ran afoul of Davidson's wrath. The Chief of Police learned that on a visit to Bryan, Patrick had behaved "disgracefully, being nearly all the time intoxicated, getting into difficulty with livery stable keepers, taking pistols from persons who were by law allowed to carry them," and representing himself as a captain in the State Police (he was a mere private). The adjutant general gave Patrick an opportunity to provide evidence that the reports were false or, failing that test, that he had been unjustly libeled. Patrick's shenanigans were confirmed, and he was dismissed from the force in December, but not until after Governor Davis sent a force of State Police into Madison County.[54]

After the July 1870 jailbreak, unrest continued in the county. The precise nature of what actually occurred is contradictory, but Patrick's actions in forming the State Guard and illegally disarming individuals, along with the violence aimed at the freedpeople, led to more outrages. An unidentified deputy sheriff organized a "posse" composed of Jack Rogers and others to arrest Patrick on a robbery charge (confiscating weapons). This group believed the State Police used excessive force and "undue authority over criminal and civil matters." This anti-police and anti-administration band swore they intended to "kill every G_d_ _ _d Radical in Madison County." They also contended that blacks had joined the State Guard to murder whites.[55]

In November 1870, the gang entered Madisonville to take Patrick into custody but found that he was in Austin attempting to resolve his difficulties with Davidson. After slaying Edward W. Tinsley, who had declined a position in the State Police but was a second lieutenant in the State Guard, they surrounded the Patrick home. Mrs. Patrick sent a messenger to warn her husband that he was in danger. The vigilantes discovered John Copeland and four freedmen in front of the Patrick house, where the latter took refuge. The "posse" fired into the house but ceased when Mrs. Patrick exclaimed that there were children inside. Copeland tried to escape but died in a fusillade of bullets. A freedman may also have been killed, but the evidence is ambiguous.[56]

The attack compelled State Representative C. Duval Harn to write from Navasota (Grimes County), where Madison County refugees appeared seeking relief from the carnage, that its neighbor was in a "terrible condition." Patrick's life had been threatened, and Harn requested that three companies of the State Guard be activated to "quiet things." State Guard members, including Tinsley and Private Sam Walton, had been killed; Corporal George Washington was wounded. One of the two Perkins brothers (either J., a fifth sergeant, or W., a second corporal), along with a man named Black, was beaten. Harn desired protection for the "best men." He also reported that McIver had returned to the county with one hundred men.[57]

Amidst the confusion, J. R. Burnett, who had been born in Georgia in 1843, arrived in Texas in 1860, served in the Confederate Army, and became

District Judge of the 30th Judicial District, kept the governor partially informed of Madison County events. Disguised whites had whipped two black men, and a warrant was issued for Patrick's arrest, charging him with robbery for disarming people. In the exchange of gunfire at Patrick's house, two were killed, one white and one black. Various parties intended to "whip or drive out of the county all the negroes who belonged to Patrick's company of State Guard and the negroes must have supposed that the sheriff and posse were after them to carry out their threats." (This was not a far-fetched assumption.) When challenged by the mob, they naturally believed their lives in danger and responded accordingly, seriously wounding one white man. Great indignation ensued, but no further casualties occurred. The whites dispersed. Although seriously shaken by the attack and concerned about their safety, those blacks in the area where the disruption occurred returned home.[58]

Burnett mistakenly felt that the "great body of the white people" was "disposed to cooperate with the authorities in establishing perfect good order," and the judge claimed that before the adjournment of his court this result would be attained. He thought the individuals who whipped the blacks would soon be apprehended and "every means" in his power would be used to see that the laws were rigidly enforced. Burnett had two policemen with him (whether state or local was not specified, but probably state), "both good men," and felt confident the laws could be enforced. He recommended that Patrick be removed from the State Police as he had disarmed several citizens of the county contrary to law and never restored their arms.[59]

Governor Davis decided to act even though conflicting reports emanated from Madison County. Led by Davidson, Davis ordered forty State Policemen and three hundred State Guards into the county. The "disorder and bloodshed are alarming," concluded the *Journal*, which proclaimed the hope that this force would "promptly insure the restoration of peace and order, the protection of the innocent, and the arrest of the guilty." The newspaper's editorial board felt that under Davis's "energetic and discreet" action such "manifestations of violence and ferocity" were "continually growing more rare, and that soon they will be numbered among the things that were."[60]

On November 17, 1870, Chief of Police Davidson addressed a crowd of approximately 150 whites and 50 blacks at Lookout in Sand Prairie in Madison County. Davidson condemned the deplorable condition of the section where armed mobs raided homes at night, treated the freedmen brutally, and threatened to hang them if they supplied any information to the State Police. Citizens lived in danger, officers of the law had been abused and cursed, and rumors circulated that armed freedmen, congregating in the woods, planned to burn houses and murder whites, "causing devastation and pillage wherever they might go." These baseless stories led armed whites to "parade through the county" intending to "exterminate the niggers."[61]

Davidson emphasized that the residents should allow the courts to deal with the "bad men" who infested the county and not take the law into their own hands. The State Police could arrest these lawbreakers if only the "good citizens would aid them with the necessary information." Davidson was aware that the police had been "misrepresented to them by some few of the opposition papers," but they were "required in Texas." In five months of operation they had arrested 350 criminals, which included 100 murderers, 125 horse thieves, and assorted felons. These accomplishments were not the work of a "band of secret spies," but the dedicated endeavors of an organization designed to assist local law enforcement officials to do their duty.[62]

Davidson declared that within a "short period of time" eighteen homicides had been committed in Madison County and yet no one had been arrested. Dastardly cowards called men out of their homes at night and shot them down. Although the good citizens of the county were "terror-stricken," no one had come out boldly and "denounced this midnight assassination." On the morning of his speech, Davidson observed a man and his family in a buggy. By his side the man had a double-barrel shotgun and an undetermined number of pistols. He was escorted by two other men, one of whom was armed with a cavalry seven-shooter, the other with a double-barrel shotgun. A man could not even travel to his cornfield without an "armed escort."[63]

To supplement police efforts, the State Guard had also been organized in Madison County, with Patrick elected captain. He would remain in that capacity until "proven to be a bad man," Davidson asserted. Although the company would be armed and perform drills, as provided by law, the citizens should neither be alarmed at its presence nor attempt to interfere with its activities. Governor Davis, observed Davidson, was "working for the peace and quiet of Texas, and for the proper enforcement of the civil laws." The Chief of Police assured the inhabitants, however, that unless those who desired to destroy law and order became "too strong for the civil authorities to manage," the guard would not be called into service.[64]

Davidson concluded that all should join together to repress lawless bands and bring them to justice. A small contingent of the State Police would remain, and all parties arrested for the recent outrages would be "turned over and dealt with by the courts." Whites should treat blacks fairly to secure the benefit of their labor and goodwill, rather than using "threats and bad usage." The freedmen had to avoid misleading advice and whiskey offered by immoral men and ignore those who claimed they would be paid $60 a month for their State Guard services. All should return home, lay aside their arms, and begin work. In the future Davidson wanted to congratulate everyone upon the peace and prosperity of the section, not have to "quell disturbances."[65]

After Davidson's speech, State Police Lieutenant Thomas Sheriff, the commander of the force stationed in Madison County, declared that the outbreaks were of "such a strange and startling character, and grew to be of such huge and monstrous proportions," that the circulated reports about their origins were "but little if at all exaggerated." Sheriff found the county in "a deplorable condition" and observed that the mob who created the frenzy "embraced almost all the citizens." He believed it grew out of the whipping of some freedmen by a party of whites under the leadership of Jack Rogers. Sheriff had made seventy arrests and felt that the excitement had, "in great measure, subsided," and he hoped to soon leave the county.[66]

But Madison County problems did not cease with the presence of Lieutenant Sheriff. Unfortunately for the governor, Patrick reentered the picture. Although he would soon be removed from the State Police, before his dismissal he would become the subject of various jibes by anti-administration newspapers. The *Galveston News* took particular delight in poking malicious fun at his plight. "One Patrick, of the State Police, after cutting up a terrible row in Madison," stated the newspaper, "reported the county in a state of insurrection." But when a group of the State Police arrived under the command of Captain L. H. McNelly, they "couldn't see the insurrection and Patrick mourneth the loss of a commission."[67]

Information is sketchy, but Patrick stated that in late November, he, Lieutenant Sheriff, and members of the State Police were attacked by eighty men, who threatened Patrick's life. Forced to retreat, Patrick had to abandon his family and asked for protection. The state militia, under J. M. Gibbs, proceeded to Madison County. One murder had been committed by a man named Barry Rankin, but he escaped to Navarro County. Captain McNelly also arrived but reported no trouble. He did request two hundred rounds of ammunition. The crisis was brief. By early December quiet returned. Patrick wanted to return to duty and received support from Representative Harn, but he was subsequently arrested and charged with assault with intent to murder. Patrick left Madison County, but his attempt to be reinstated in the State Police failed.[68]

After the "Madison outrage," Governor Davis received a summary and assessment of what had occurred in the area from a Methodist Episcopal Church missionary. According to Richard Sloan, "several good Loyal citizens have been brutally murdered by a set of desperadoes" who violated law-abiding people and especially those men whom the "Government had placed in authority to execute the law which they are all hostile to, as they were when the Rebel cannon boomed." Both black and white left their homes "in the dead hours of night," leaving everything they possessed, along with their crops, to the mercy of their "Rebel enemies" because of these depredations.[69]

Sloan believed Davidson's conduct seriously injured the Republican Party. He should have dealt with these miscreants in a harsh fashion. People complained they could not be protected or their wrongs and grievances righted, and thus they distrusted the Republicans. The common opinion among Madison Countians, related Sloan, was that too much "laxity" had been shown to the "enemies of freedom," and they desired the removal of these individuals. Since he labored as a missionary among the freedpeople, Sloan was influenced by their request to lay their situation before the governor in "its true light." As their professed protector, they believed Davis would provide them with the necessary protection that they required.[70]

Until the end of Governor Davis's administration, Madison County continued to be a trouble spot. On the eve of the 1873 election, the registrar who had been sent to supervise the polling was conversing with various people when a man rode up and with no provocation stabbed him. The assailant was arrested and bail established at $2,000. In default, Sheriff M. W. Burney took charge and placed the perpetrator with men "in sympathy with such lawlessness." Citizens told the governor that the assailant was permitted to go anywhere he pleased, which allowed his friends time to procure a horse so that he could escape. He now walked the street every day, although he had never been tried or posted bond, seemingly the "best friend" of the sheriff-elect.[71]

Finally, a group of citizens, tired of the upheaval, the violence, and constant disruption of county government, requested assistance from the chief executive. After the burning of the county courthouse, they wrote: "Our county is in a state of lawlessness" and the "peaceable and law abiding citizens no longer" felt "safe either in life or property." The law was a "farce." The only individuals "free from danger" and who could openly express their opinions were outlaws, gamblers, and rioters. A large number of criminals in the county were allowed to "go where they please, seemingly free of any dread of arrest, and menacing the lives and property of good and quiet citizens." Before irrevocably making the decision to abandon their homes so they would not be left to the "mercy of outlaws," they believed one more effort to redeem their county was worthwhile.[72]

Governor Davis complied with the request of the Madison County petitioners. On January 31, 1873, he forwarded the document to the legislature for their consideration. Although he listed no specifics, Davis asserted that "in regard to the disturbances in that county" he had sent in a body of police and had "taken other measures to secure peace, and arrest the offenders." Davis informed the new Chief of Police, F. L. Britton, a Davis in-law, of the violence and the desire of the citizens for state action. Britton ordered the State Police into Madison County once again, but their stay was limited. They would soon be disbanded by the predominantly Democratic Thirteenth Legislature, who believed the force unnecessary.[73]

The *Daily State Journal* referred to the Madison County troubles as a "carnival of blood and horror."[74] Surely this was an exaggeration of the events. Nevertheless, Madison County was representative of several regions in the Lone Star State that experienced upheaval and violence once Davis assumed power. Although much of the controversy centered upon Patrick and his disarming of individuals, postwar hatred of black participation in politics and state-sponsored militia units engendered hostility. As the Madison County controversy subsided, another involving State Police Captain Jack Helm flared anew, forever tainting the reputation of the "governor's hounds." While a policeman, Helm also maintained his position as DeWitt County sheriff. Why he was allowed to serve in both offices is unclear because Davis and Davidson were normally careful about refusing such a practice. Whatever the reason for his dual employment, Helm aggressively performed his duties, although he occasionally raised Davidson's ire for addressing his letters to the governor and not the chief. He and his group dispersed the Lum gang of Matagorda County, who had been killing stolen cattle for their hides at the rate of one hundred per day. Helm counted 1,014 carcasses.[75]

Although he was never convicted of any crime, what finally led to Helm being ousted from the State Police were his heavy-handed and probably illegal activities in his district. Helm also continued to be a participant in the Sutton-Taylor Feud, which led to his murder in 1873. Helm received praise from Chief of Police Davidson in August 1870 for his arrest of fifty-four men in Lavaca County, but he was later admonished by Davidson that he would be held "strictly accountable" for "every man killed by your party." Boards of inquiry would be instituted to investigate any murders. "There is no reason," asserted Davidson, "in taking the life of a man without any cause or circumstances." He would act "more discreetly in the future."[76]

The specific incident that raised a storm of protest and charges that Helm acted like a tyrant and a murderer was the killing of William and Henry Kelly in DeWitt County on August 26, 1870. Although the initial confrontation is unclear, the four Kelly brothers, William, Henry, Wiley, and Eugene, shot up a circus performance in Sweet Home (Lavaca County), apparently wounding some of the performers and the audience. Davidson "highly commended" Helm's action in the matter. Precisely what transpired after the circus incident is murky and muddled. Whether the Kellys were arrested, fined, and released is uncertain. What is known is that William and Henry were slain a few days later.[77]

About sunrise on August 26, 1870, a party of three men consisting of Doc White, John Meader (a friend of William Kelly), and C. C. Simmons, a State Police private, appeared at the home of Henry Kelly and informed him he would be taken to Hallettsville, presumably about the circus incident. The group then met William Sutton, who had charge of William Kelly. Taking the two Kellys into the brush, Sutton killed William and White shot Henry, after which a general firing commenced. (Meader was not present at the death scene.) Much of the information about the murders is based upon testimony from Amanda Kelly, daughter of Pitkin Taylor and wife of Henry; and Delilah Kelly, the mother of the two slain men. They did not provide any statements until seven weeks after the killing.[78]

There is no evidence that Jack Helm was involved in the murders (he was not present), although it is possible that he ordered the men's execution. One State Policeman, Simmons, participated. In addition, Helm and his band killed Henry Westfall and also forced a group of citizens to pay for a dinner of forty-five men under his command at Sweet Home in Lavaca County. The political repercussions from the dual slaying, along with the murder of Westfall and the allegedly forced dinner, were dramatic and played out in some of the major newspapers in the state. Helm had indeed disgraced the State Police, and his obsessive pursuit of either personal or political enemies in the DeWitt County area marred the organization's history forever.[79]

Bolivar J. Pridgen, a state senator from the region, became the spokesman for the Kellys and denounced Helm and the State Police at every opportunity. Pridgen was allied with the Taylor faction in the feud, and his brother Wiley W. Pridgen, who had an unsavory reputation, had run afoul of Helm. The senator admitted that the Kellys "may have been *bad men*," but the law provided a "proper mode of disposing of *bad men*." Nothing could be more revolting to "civilization and good morals," Pridgen exclaimed, "than for an officer to wantonly murder prisoners in his charge, and then without calling on the neighbors to take charge of the dead and have them decently buried," but "suddenly disappear and leave the bodies to be devoured by the hogs or wolves."[80]

Helm was summoned to Austin to answer the charges levied against him and was relieved from further duty. Simultaneously, the district attorney for the 22nd Judicial District, J. A. Abney, empanelled a sixteen-member grand jury to investigate the murder of the Kellys. After patiently examining Amanda and Delilah Kelly, along with other witnesses, the panel decided that the circumstances would not justify a bill of indictment, to which Abney concurred. Chief of Police Davidson assured Senator Pridgen, who desired guarantees from Governor Davis, that certain named individuals would not be molested in any way and that they need not fear "private persecution or bodily injury." Helm, however, remained sheriff of DeWitt County.[81]

By early December 1870, the saga had almost run its course with the announcement that Robert F. Haskins had been promoted to a captaincy in the State Police to replace Helm. The *Weekly Austin Republican* praised Chief of Police Davidson for delivering "Western Texas" from the "rule of the most noted brigand that has appeared upon the stage since the days of Quantrill and Bill Anderson." Even though Helm was indicted for robbery in Bee County, he served as sheriff and collected taxes, keeping Davis informed of his activities. But Helm could not escape his past, his notorious reputation, or the continuing Sutton-Taylor Feud. In July 1873, at his blacksmith shop, Helm was killed in a hail of gunfire by John Wesley Hardin and Jim Taylor.[82]

By the close of 1870, the composition of the State Police stood at 4 captains, 8 lieutenants, 12 sergeants, and 172 privates; a total of 196 men. To make them more effective, Davis claimed the arrangement found best adapted to Texas, where mail and telegraph facilities were limited, was to split the police districts into a number of subdivisions under officers who were made directly responsible for the activity and efficiency of the police in their respective areas. Because of poor communication facilities Davis desired to increase the number of officers (but not the overall force, 257) by adding two additional captains, four lieutenants, and ten sergeants. Thus, the subdivisions could be better policed.[83]

Davis provided a candid overview of the State Police after six months of operation. He admitted that the authorized number of policemen granted by

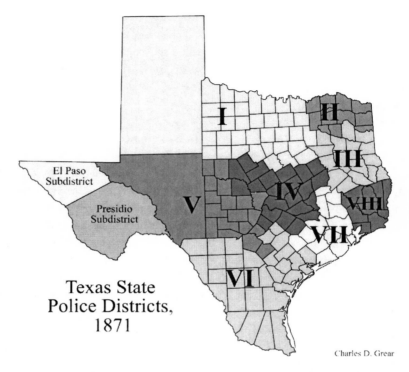

Texas State
Police Districts,
1871

Charles D. Grear

Reconfiguration of the State Police districts after
May 1871. *Courtesy of Charles D. Grear.*

the legislature had not been reached, because "many of those appointed, have
been found incompetent or otherwise objectionable, and removed." Only
the "highest standard of efficiency" would suffice. The danger and required
equipage of the position demanded that Davis request the state grant them
a raise as "good government and law and order, cannot be maintained without an efficient military or police force to sustain the civil authority, and this
we cannot have without paying liberally for it." Its expenditure would not be
"unprofitable."[84]

The State Police had, in a short time, accomplished considerable inroads
in "suppressing lawlessness and arresting offenders." This inspired a "feeling
of safety and of confidence both at home and abroad, in the future stability"
of Texas and had already increased the value of property and promoted immigration into the state. This more secure condition of affairs offset the future
cost of "these forces." In its first six months of existence the State Police had

arrested 978 offenders, although its numbers had not "averaged more than half that allowed by law." Included in the 978 arrests were 109 charged with murder, 130 with assaults with intent to kill, and 394 with various other felonies, as well as the recovery of $30,000 worth of stolen property.[85]

Davis made one suggestion and one recommendation to the legislature in order to reduce further "violence and bloodshed (a class of crimes which, you will notice, occupies a large space on our criminal calendar)." He returned to a theme that he had emphasized in his inaugural address to the legislature, the wearing of six-guns. The carrying of deadly weapons should be further restrained and regulated. Although the lawmakers had previously forbidden carrying weapons in "public places," the governor believed that this was only a "partial remedy" and that further limitations needed to be implemented. A "general and stringent law against the practice would avoid loss of life or bloodshed." Thus, it required the assemblymen's attention.[86]

The problems that Governor Davis encountered with Madison County and Jack Helm were only a prelude of what was to come. Texas remained a violent place, and blacks, who comprised only 30 percent of the population, were often murdered for no apparent reason. Davis's commitment to protect

Although the date of death is incorrect, the epitaph on this tombstone of Thomas J. Smith is worth a thousand words in describing how many people felt about the State Police: "Killed by W. W. Davis and his nigger police." *Courtesy of Richard Banks.*

their lives and property infused his administration and his philosophy. Although the State Police were a mobile force, they could not be everywhere at once. When emergencies arose, personnel had to be co-opted from various districts in order to form a sizeable contingent. Such an occurrence presented itself in Hill County in December 1870, where two black people were savagely murdered. Davis responded by establishing martial law when local citizens directly interfered with and thwarted the efforts of the State Police.

Once the State Police began their field operations, clashes between the "Governor's Hounds" and local citizens would test Governor Davis's mettle, demonstrate the extent of the new powers conferred on the head of state, and reveal how much some Texas residents detested blacks and the State Police, doubly so in the latter's case since the organization had been staffed with a large number of freedmen. Davis finally became so frustrated with the inaction of local officials and unfulfilled promises to aid in the enforcement of the law that he was compelled to resort to the extreme measure of martial law.

"An Affair Only Equalled by the Exploits of the Comanches"

THE HILL COUNTY IMBROGLIO

In March 1871, after having declared martial law in Hill County and disgusted at the lack of citizen action, Governor E. J. Davis related to the residents that if he had one object closer to his heart than any other, it was to "leave Texas at the end of my term of office a quiet and peaceable and law respecting State." He proposed to "devote to this purpose all the authority and appliances given me."[1] Davis had this goal in mind when he encouraged the Twelfth Legislature to establish a State Police organization, along with a host of other state-sanctioned local guards, reserves, militias, and Special Policemen. What the governor attempted was to marshal all citizens, no matter their political persuasion, in the war against violence.

Almost simultaneously with its creation, Hill County earned a reputation for being a brutal section. Feuds erupted over timber rights along with the advent of rings of horse and cattle thieves. Before Governor Davis focused his attention upon the doings in Hill County, the infamous gunfighter (and indeed one of the most proficient of all time) John Wesley Hardin, in early 1870 gunned down Benjamin F. Bradley in Hill County. Bradley had humiliated and embarrassed the young Hardin in a card game. Although Davis may not have been aware of Hardin's exploits, the evidence clearly points to the fact that Hill County was a troublesome place and that he would have to carefully monitor its internal political and social divisions.[2]

Located in the blacklands of north central Texas, Hill County is 130 miles north of Austin and 60 miles south of Dallas. Named either for its founder George W. Hill (an army surgeon in the Texas Revolution) or for the "mountain" which served as a watershed and divided the waters of the Brazos and Trinity rivers, it was detached from Navarro County in 1853. Part of the Upper Brazos Valley, the Brazos River is its western boundary with Bosque County. Hill originally contained 1,030 square miles, slightly smaller than Rhode Island. At Texas's geographical center, its topography encompassed the Cross Timbers, rich river valley bottoms, and excellent grazing land. In short, the western half of the county was timbered; the eastern half prairie.[3]

Major crops included cotton (which yielded one bale per acre in 1870), corn (forty bushels per acre), wheat, rye, and oats. In the area grew abundant native grasses, watered by numerous springs. Timber everywhere dotted the landscape and composed a variety of woods: post oak, hickory, ash, elm, and blackjack, interspersed with swamp timbers. In this environment existed Hill County, where Lexington first served as the county seat. Hillsboro became the official center in September 1853. Although Hillsboro maintained its official status, three efforts were made to effect a change of the county seat, two of which occurred during Reconstruction and exacerbated tensions among all citizens.[4]

During the antebellum era the area was dominated by agriculture basically without slavery (the county only produced 171 bales of cotton in 1860). Pro-Southern, the citizens overwhelmingly supported the secession ordinance (376 to 63) and provided four companies of soldiers for the Confederate Army. Before the end of the Civil War the slave population increased considerably. From 1860 to 1864 the number of bondspeople more than doubled in the county, undoubtedly due to slaveholders bringing in their chattels from other, war-ravaged states for safekeeping. With few exceptions, the county maintained its prewar political stance into the postwar years.[5]

Migration from adjoining counties and other defeated Confederate states doubled the population in the decade after the Civil War began. By 1870, 7,453 residents made Hill County their home, 11 percent of them black. At least 75 percent of the inhabitants labored on the land on small farms (fifty acres or less). Manufacturing encompassed one sawmill employing three people. Two towns vied for the chief political and commercial center, and both lay in the central part of the county. Hillsboro (with 313 citizens in 1876) was challenged for its political supremacy in 1870 by not so neighborly Peoria (213 people in 1876). Peoria was "rabid" in its rebel element. But Hillsboro, too, was under the domination of the conservatives.[6]

Although several residents would later deny the fact, Hill County had experienced at least twelve murders from 1868 until mid-1870, of which half of the victims were black men. (Subsequently, more killings would occur which would bring down the governor's wrath.) There were also robberies and attempted murders committed upon various individuals, both black and white. In only one of the acts of violence, a robbery and murder, did black men participate, and these two individuals seemingly formed part of a small gang with two white men. In short, Hill County blacks, although they composed but a fraction of the total population, found themselves on the receiving end of outrageous acts. Murder did not abate. In July 1870, a prominent white man was shot.[7]

A major reason for the initial State Police presence in Hill County was the desperado Kinch West, born around 1843. His background is murky, but at war's end he was a member of Quantrill's Missouri guerrillas and participated in outlawry with these marauding miscreants in Grayson County. Due to his unsavory character, West established no permanent residence but appeared again (if indeed he had ever left) in northern Texas in 1867–1868, where Lamar County officials desired his apprehension on a murder charge. West eventually drifted off to Kansas but returned to Texas and was killed in Fort Worth by Sheriff John R. Cox. One observer summarized West's life as "daring, reckless," and without remorse.[8]

Writing in June 1870 about violence-prone Hill County and praising the governor for proposing a State Police, Judge William Chambers (who was defeated by Democrat Richard Coke in the 1876 gubernatorial race) urged Davis to include in his policy a stipulation that county "officers must be forced to do their full duty, and the people must be required to assist the officers." Chambers mistakenly believed that those under the "old influences" were "ready to cooperate." Hill County had a long history of violence, and Chambers pleaded for the governor to pursue his plan to create a state constabulary with wide-ranging law enforcement power. Davis was in the process of doing precisely as Chambers envisioned.[9]

Chambers wrote from Waco, approximately thirty-five miles from Hillsboro (the county seat of Hill County). He described recent turmoil. On June 18, 1870, Thomas Tanner, "a colored citizen," had been murdered by Edward and Benjamin Majors and Bill Williams. Six other black men, Tanner's neighbors, fled to Waco. They declared that no protection was afforded to blacks by the Hill County officers and they were afraid to return to their homes without some kind of assurance against further violence. Local authorities dismissed their fears and refused to take action. Chambers characterized the idea of applying the law equally as fruitless, as "everyday *decreases* the fact" (emphasis added) that it would "afford even comparative protection, as it is now administered."[10]

A desperate element infested Hill County. Violence mounted. After the Tanner murder, which occurred nine miles north of Hillsboro, Governor Davis offered a $900 reward for the delivery of the two Majors and Williams "inside the jail door" to the sheriff. For whatever reason, a description of Williams was not supplied, but Edward and Benjamin Majors received specific attention. Benjamin was said to be twenty-one years old, five feet ten inches to six feet tall, with brown hair, grey eyes, and by trade a carpenter. Edward, a farmer, was two years younger, five feet eight, and had light hair and blue eyes. Like many others who inhabited Hill County during this era, they were not established community members.[11]

The sheriff of Hill County, Evin Beauchamp, around whom much controversy swirled before his removal in December 1870, was Tennessee born, married, with two children. A resident of the county since at least 1864, after the war Beauchamp served as a county commissioner and chief justice. He was then elected sheriff in the Republican victories of 1869. M. J. Morrow was his deputy; there was no marshal. The sheriff had two major complaints: he received no citizen assistance in capturing the outlaws who remained in the county, and he could garner no additional manpower. To be sure, the sheriff had limited resources and support, but his heavy drinking and questionable integrity bothered many of the inhabitants.[12]

A letter to the governor from an individual identified only as "Justice," appeared in the *Daily State Journal* in July 1870, which gave a synopsis of Hill County unrest. On July 17, A. D. Martin, who "Justice" claimed bore "an irreproachable character," was murdered three miles from Hillsboro. The killer was well known in the vicinity for his "dissolute, profligate character" and had the strange name of Kinch West. West had won a horse from a black man in a card game, but Martin claimed the horse belonged to him and appeared at West's house to reclaim it. The two men exchanged words, West drew his pistol, and Martin died instantly when shot in the temple. West escaped as several men stood by and let him ride off.[13]

Some writers have attempted to portray Martin as a character similar to Kinch West, the man who murdered him. This is nonsense. Martin, a thirty-eight-year-old Tennessee-born farmer, was a long-standing Fort Graham community member. His wife, who was thirteen years younger, was North Carolina born. The household also included two girls and a boy (4, 3, and 1 years of age), the two girls being born in North Carolina and the boy in Texas.

The (1860) census taker assessed Martin's worth as $3,000 in personal possessions and his land value at a rather large $5,215. Martin, who did not achieve his status through rash actions, was a responsible citizen who met his death at the hand of a man who had no scruples.[14]

William C. "Bill" Atchison, who often appears in the literature in connection with Kinch West, the State Police, and Sheriff Beauchamp, was South Carolina born. He came to Hill County after 1860 although he had lived in Texas as early as 1854. Married to a Tennessee woman, with four children, his land was valued at $1,500 and his personal property at $200. (He did have a farm hand living in the household.) Atchison may have been a family man, but he is described as being profligate. H. W. Young, who knew him for a decade, depicted Atchison as dissipated, inoffensive, and peaceable when sober, but a completely different individual when drinking (sometimes with Sheriff Beauchamp).[15]

Atchison was not always inoffensive. John J. Gage, a Peoria resident, had known him for four years. He informed the district judge that Atchison had murdered a freedman in Waco, had been arrested, posted bail, but later forfeited his bond. Gage concurred with Young's assessment; he was not a desperado or outlaw, and the Peorian believed he could have been arrested without any difficulty. Although Atchison may have been a "dissipated man," he was by no means a "desperate" one according to H. Harvick, another Peorian. He was never arrested because Sheriff Beauchamp drank with him, during which time they talked extensively. Those who made statements about Atchison contended that he could easily have been apprehended at any time.[16]

Although the Cox brothers are difficult to pin down (in past writings about Hill County only general reference was made to them as part of West's gang), they apparently were farmers with few possessions. Both George W. (twenty-two years old) and his brother William (twenty-one) had been born in Missouri. The 1870 census taker listed George as having $500 worth of real estate, a wife born in Indian Territory, and two children (a four-year-old girl and a one-year-old boy) who were Texas born. William's situation was somewhat different. Although younger, he had a Missouri-born wife, with two children (a two-year-old girl and an eleven-month-old boy), but in addition he had a farm laborer living in the household. Nothing else is known about these scoundrels.[17]

After Kinch West murdered A. D. Martin, the State Police, still in the process of organization, stationed a contingent in a central location at Waco, the McLennan County seat. Commanded by Captain M. P. Hunnicutt, he found only two men on duty when he arrived on July 19, 1870. Several others were scattered throughout a large district. Hunnicutt did not specify how many who reported to him were black, but his letters suggest that they comprised a significant portion of his immediate personnel and that they were penniless. (Policemen had to pay expenses out of pocket and were later reimbursed.) Hunnicutt believed the freedmen "good efficient men," but he had to give them verbal orders which were less satisfactory "than if they could read and write."[18]

Hunnicutt soon ran afoul of Chief of Police James Davidson's wrath. Hunnicutt believed Davidson had an "overbearing and domineering manner." A Waco newspaper reported that Hunnicutt stated he would arrest no one and disagreed with the governor's militia policy. When Davidson read these comments he told Hunnicutt that others in the organization of similar rank had "done good service" and he was to demonstrate himself "worthy" of his responsible position. Hunnicutt was admonished not to make such future statements, and Davidson wanted West captured "dead or alive." In Hunnicutt's defense, he was awaiting information from an ongoing investigation in Hill County which would assist him in capturing West, the Coxes, Atchison, Frazier, and others.[19]

Davidson, already displeased with Hunnicutt's behavior, continually inquired about what action had been taken by the State Police captain to apprehend West. He wanted a report from Hunnicutt, including names of the policemen who had reported for duty at the Waco office. Contrary to Davidson's incessant communications and queries, Hunnicutt was not inactive. He initiated twenty-nine arrests within a fifty-mile radius of Waco and declared that he would not be "behind any officer" in making arrests and "securing the conviction of criminals." On September 1, 1870, Davidson relieved Hunnicutt. Hunnicutt attempted to enlist the governor's intervention, but he was not reinstated. Lieutenant W. S. Pritchett became the new Waco commander.[20]

Pritchett had no more success in eliminating the West gang than previous efforts had. Chief Davidson, through the telegraph and the mail, ordered Pritchett to assist the Hill County authorities in their attempt to capture West and his cohorts. The lieutenant did not comply with the adjutant general's demand to furnish Sheriff Evin Beauchamp with five men. Having delivered a letter from Davidson to the sheriff, Pritchett made the offer of five men to accompany Beauchamp back to Hill County. The sheriff lingered in Waco for days and then "refused to take the men" because the "number was not sufficient to accomplish that which was to be done," claiming it would take "at least forty or fifty" men to "do the work in his county."[21]

The initial incident, in addition to the numerous outrages already committed in Hill County, which triggered the full-scale intervention of the State Police, occurred on Saturday evening, August 27, 1870. Private Pierce Nagle, while serving writs of attachments in Hill County, was shot and badly wounded either by Burcon, a Louisiana desperado, or by the fourteen-member Kinch West gang. At Waco, State Police Private L. J. Hoffman claimed that the West band had declared they would not be arrested. Sheriff Beauchamp allegedly had also been shot by Burcon, but this proved to be false. Nevertheless, Beauchamp only had four men, and the county refused assistance. A shortage of manpower limited the effectiveness of the local constabulary and the State Police.[22]

Continuing difficulties in Hill County forced Adjutant General Davidson to order L. J. Hoffman, on September 20, 1870, to keep the majority of his force at his station because in a few days they would be required as part of a larger squad to move into Hill County. Sergeant George E. Haynie and privates E. Heinz, G. W. Campbell, William Gibson, Joseph Hoseman, S. E. McFarland, William J. Mitchell, and Anthony Rucker were to present themselves fully armed, mounted, and equipped. Haynie, on his arrival at Belton, and then at Waco, would take police at these stations with him, specifically Sergeant William E. Evans and four Waco privates. He would confer with the sheriff and hunt down the desperadoes.[23]

On September 20 Davidson mobilized the State Police for a Hill County expedition. On the same day he wrote Sheriff Beauchamp that the police would soon be on their way and they had been ordered to aid him in making the necessary arrests. They were to be used "for no other purpose," Davidson emphasized. It had earlier been reported by Captain Hunnicutt that Beauchamp and his deputy, Morrow, "refused to have anything to do with colored policemen" and would not accompany any unit sent if it included blacks. Davidson wished to apprise the sheriff of the fact that he was himself a policeman under the law, "and as such you are supposed to give your aid as well as be aided in arresting and securing criminals."[24]

Interestingly enough, on the same day that Davidson wrote Beauchamp, the sheriff wrote him. He asserted that a small detachment (twenty-five to thirty men) of the State Police was required in his county to assist him in arresting all the desperadoes infesting the area. Beauchamp claimed he could not secure sufficient assistance from the locals. Postwar Texas sheriffs had a multitude of duties to perform. Between serving numerous capiases and visiting the "various sections of the country to collect the annual tax," which he believed the outlaws would endeavor to prevent him from collecting, he did not have enough support to secure their arrest. Only the State Police could accomplish these ends.[25]

To command the Hill County State Police force Davidson selected one of his best and most versatile men, Lieutenant Thomas G. Williams of Lockhart. Williams was to consult with the legal and civil officers and then proceed to arrest the desperadoes infesting that section and in adjoining counties. "If absolutely necessary," Williams had the authority "to summon citizens" to assist his group in tracking down the bad guys. Williams also had the right to call upon law enforcement officials in the counties surrounding Hill, and all those in Hill itself, to assist in the capture of these disruptive elements. After making the arrests, Williams would return to his station and leave Sergeant Haynie at Waco.[26]

Lieutenant Williams, along with two sergeants and thirteen privates, arrived at Hillsboro on the morning of September 28, 1870. The Williams force remained several hours, during which time they consulted with the sheriff and other officers of the county, seeking information about the names of the desperadoes and the places to which these outlaws might retreat within the area. Contrary to what some of the citizens would later declare, Williams received little assistance. Sheriff Beauchamp relayed to Williams his knowledge about the West gang. The State Police detachment, along with the sheriff, proceeded to Peoria, where they expected to find the fourteen-member Kinch West clan, as the desperadoes had been seen in the village the previous day.[27]

The Williams group scouted Peoria, but the West gang had disappeared. On September 29 they located the residence of West and the Cox brothers. While searching the premises, West, the two Coxes, and a man named May-field attacked the State Police and Sheriff Beauchamp. The outlaws shouted epithets at the police and began to fire upon the five men present, the remainder having gone to another field in search of the criminals. The police returned the gunfire, but upon the approach of the other policemen, West and his cronies fled to the Cross Timbers. The police chased them for four miles, but knowing the region and with fresh horses, West and his gang soon disappeared. Williams returned to Waco, and the others went back to their proper stations.[28]

After Williams left Hill County, an Austin newspaper interviewed the "accomplished and efficient officer." The lieutenant contended that the outlaws numbered about fifteen men and operated in squads of four or five but could "always concentrate when necessary." Well mounted and well armed with guns and revolvers, the desperadoes successfully defied the "civil authorities and have, in connection with their sympathizers, produced a reign of terror in Hill county" where anyone affiliated with the Davis regime excited the "ire of these men and their allies." Although Williams had about the same number in his group, only a portion of them were equipped with rifles.[29]

Although a State Police force was sent to Hill County in an effort to arrest Kinch West, the Coxes, Mayfield, Oliver, Atchison, and their accomplices, this endeavor proved unsuccessful because, claimed the police, the citizens either sympathized with these specific parties or were "under intimidation by the outlaws." The locals, complained Governor Davis, "did not co-oper-ate with the police, but on the contrary furnished the outlaws information, and aided them in evading arrest." Davis was outraged at the conduct of Hill County residents and demanded certain actions from Beauchamp. It has rarely been pointed out, but Davis informed the citizens of what they could expect if they did not end the desperado menace.[30]

Spurred by Williams's verbal report, Davis required Sheriff Beauchamp to call a meeting of the county citizens and tell them "publicly that these des-peradoes" had so far evaded capture, "either by the sympathy of the citizens, or because of their intimidations." At the end of thirty days, if the citizens had not "arrested and delivered" the outlaws to the civil officers, Davis would send in a sufficient force of the militia and state guard to secure their appre-hension and also declare martial law. (They would be quartered in the county at citizen expense.) The Peoria village residents had been the "most conspicu-ous in this lawlessness," and they should be specifically notified of the penal-ties they would incur.[31]

Davis's letter of October 3 to Beauchamp did not receive public notice for three weeks, but it eventually led to two meetings of county residents. The first resulted in a petition signed by eighty-three inhabitants that claimed a desire to see "law and order reign supreme." They avowed that in no other county in Texas did "good order and harmony prevail among the people" more than in Hill County. The lives, liberty, and property of every person were "safe and as well protected." Individuals had misrepresented events and newspapers had printed "notoriously false" accounts of attacks on the jail by the Atchison and West party. The stories were "fabricated for the purpose of misleading" the governor into declaring martial law.[32]

The citizens defended Atchison, who had apparently left the county. The Cox brothers, after escaping from Private William Hooper, associated with Kinch West. These "three lawless characters" (the only refugees from justice) remained in the county during which time the Coxes gathered their crops and collected their stock but did not commit any violence. Critical of Lieutenant Williams and Sheriff Beauchamp, the petitioners believed if the former had been on the lookout, he could have arrested the parties by remaining in the county. The sheriff, by his own "intoxication[,] prevented" the capture of West, "wholly failed" to perform his duties, and neglected to arrest the outlaws or to call upon the citizens to assist.[33]

To underscore the seriousness of the situation and force citizens to feel that such interest was the only motive that would ever compel Davis to establish martial law at their expense, he emphasized that this drastic action would not be implemented "anywhere except as the last resort." He did believe that this necessity might exist in Hill County and contemplated taking prompt measures, but only after giving the citizens a "fair opportunity" to declare themselves. Their promptness in coming forward induced Davis to think that they proposed to "act in good faith in support of the officers of the law." Thus, he had temporarily suspended preparations to send state troops into the county.[34]

Nevertheless, Davis refused to do nothing and directed a detachment of the State Police into Hill County "with orders to hunt down those outlaws." The governor had recently received information that the desperadoes had fled the confines of Hill County, but Davis did expect the citizens to assist local and state authorities in ascertaining their whereabouts. The chief executive emphasized that "they must be brought to justice, and efforts are not to cease till they are." Hill County citizens had clearly demonstrated that they preferred the ravages of the outlaws rather than have the State Police or any other group patrol the area against future depredations. The governor would not allow lawlessness to go unchecked.[35]

Although the State Police monitored the Hill County situation, internal personnel problems made the situation even more unstable. Davidson assured Mrs. J. C. Martin (the wife of A. D.) that every effort was being made to arrest West for the murder of her husband. This did not deter West and his associates, who continued to make their presence known. When a detachment of State Police delayed pursuit, the adjutant general became enraged. Davidson was furious at the inaction of Lieutenant Pritchett. His lack of decisiveness met with the "*disapprobation*" of the chief of police. Even if the civil authorities refused to assist, it was Pritchett's duty to go there and make the arrests himself.[36]

After receiving orders from Lieutenant Pritchett through Chief Davidson, State Police Sergeant William E. Evans, with a supporting cast of five men, departed from Waco on October 29, 1870, for Hillsboro. Upon their arrival, the detachment arrested William Hutchinson and had him conveyed to Waco, where he had committed his crime. After this initial success more followed, some imbued with tragedy. They apprehended Henry Mayfield for "aiding and abetting" outlaws in criminal activities and lawlessness; Mitchell H. Ferguson for murder; Jack Mitchell for the same offense; Payton Bevins for assisting prisoners to escape; and Joseph Elliott for wearing arms at a public assembly, which the law forbade.[37]

Ferguson and several others (their names were not listed) had been indicted for the killing of two brothers, Union men, by the name of George. Ferguson, Evans maintained, resisted arrest. The policeman called upon him to surrender. Ferguson refused and drew his revolver. The State Policeman fired and wounded him, whereupon he continued to resist, attempting to shoot the state officers, at which point they proceeded to "riddle him with bullets." After the Ferguson killing, Evans did not have enough men to arrest the accomplices of this particular gang. He proposed remaining with Lieutenant Pritchett until they could be attended to and the depredations ended, but he was ordered to return to his original post at Belton.[38]

Lieutenant Pritchett assisted Sheriff Beauchamp and established a post in Hill County. He kept the policemen he had brought from Waco with him, along with Private Hooper. This force, Davidson believed, would be sufficient to assist the legal and civil authorities in attempting to arrest the desperadoes that had so disrupted county life. If it became necessary to procure more men, Pritchett could summon those stationed in counties adjoining Hill. Later, Davidson contemplated adding fourteen more men to Pritchett's group, "but they did not report." The men that did arrive could be kept as part of Pritchett's Hill County group or sent to other counties where they might be needed. By late November, the detachment returned to Waco. In addition, District Judge F. P. Wood removed Beauchamp for "malfeasance, misfeasance and nonfeasance of office, of gross inefficiency and of conduct unbecoming an officer."[39]

This violence disease, Wood contended, had grown maniacal and required "desperate appliances." One remedy, Wood reminded the Hill County citizens, included martial law, which was about to be imposed if matters were not righted. The "condition of things" must change, Wood told the citizens, and in his declarations he had attempted to offer the inhabitants a warning rather than a threat. It was up to all county residents, not only those sitting in the courtroom, who had to diligently inquire into the manner in which county officers discharged their official duties and executed the law. If they failed this scrutiny, then indictments would be forthcoming.[40]

Wood painted a different picture than the inhabitants and observed the tense situation when men were allowed to wear weapons within the town limits. He attended a performance, along with approximately 1,200 other people, of "Robinson's Circus." At least one hundred men wore six-shooters. This was in singular contrast to his experience in Navarro County (especially Corsicana, part of his judicial district) where arms were not allowed inside the town. At the term meeting of the district court, Wood ordered the sheriff, his deputies, and the State Police to arrest anyone wearing a weapon. He asserted that in Hill County the law had been ignored and the officials made no effort to enforce its provisions.[41]

During the circus, Sergeant Evans had several pistols drawn on him, and "desperate men" assaulted him. Evans sought out Wood for protection. The sheriff, three deputies, and the chief justice, all of whom were present, made no effort to assist Evans. Wood requested the assistance of the county officials, but the group with weapons openly defied them. The judge informed Joe Abbott and W. H. Turner in "plain terms" that if Evans were injured or any other disturbance occurred, he would apply to the governor to send troops into the county and declare martial law. Action had to be taken to suppress the threatened lawlessness or Wood would refuse to hold court. Finally, order was restored and Wood disgustedly left the circus.[42]

Shortly before Christmas 1870, the voters of Hill County once again traipsed to the polls to decide on the permanent location of the county seat. The 515 individuals who had registered for this poll included 89 blacks. A two-thirds vote was necessary for changing the county seat. In this 1870 election, Peoria received 285 votes and Hillsboro, 55 fewer. Since Peoria required a total of 344 votes, the change failed. Although Peoria did not become the county seat, the entire county vote seems to suggest that many of the other residents sympathized with the political outlook of Hillsboro's rival. After all, the county seat, if not a hotbed of Republicanism, contained the two major factions of that party.[43]

Two days after the election, an innocent black man and woman were slain by two members of a prominent Hill County family. On December 26, 1870, the Willinghams, according to one source, were "foully murdered" on a public highway near Clifton, in Bosque County. (Davis referred to it as an "atrocious murder" and not "surpassed in atrocity by any similar deeds of the Savages on the frontier.") The coroner's inquest concluded that James Gathings and Solloela Nicholson committed the slaying. Both were tied to the wealthiest individual in the county, James J. Gathings, the father of James and the guardian of Nicholson. This incident (an affair only "equaled by the exploits of the Comanches") so exasperated Davis that he took action.[44]

The two slain African Americans were Joe Willingham and the wife of Lewis Willingham. Both were longtime residents of Meridian, "quiet persons" who were passing through Clifton on their way to Waco to celebrate Christmas. Joe had stopped at a grocery store to make a purchase. While there, he was whipped by some "drunken men." When their bodies were discovered, the woman, whose corpse was by the roadside, had been shot through the head and heart. Joe Willingham was found a day later, some three miles down the road. He had been shot several times through the body. The editor of the *Houston Daily Union* stated that he did not believe that "lawless himself [sic] was capable of committing so fiendish an act."[45]

One of the central characters in the confrontation between Governor Davis, the State Police, and Hill County citizens was unquestionably James J. Gathings. Although much folklore and misinformation exists about Gathings and his part in the Hill County confrontation, apparently Gathings was not quite as revered as past writers would like us to believe. His background and status have been delineated in various ways by previous writers, who have been generally reluctant to question his participation in precipitating the declaration of martial law in the county. Some denied the fact that it was Gathings's son who participated in the murder that led Davis to assume military control of the county, but the evidence is conclusive that he was one of the killers.

With South Carolina roots where he was born in 1817, James J. Gathings migrated to North Carolina and married Martha W. Covington, a native, in 1838. The Gathings (there were thirteen children) moved to Mississippi, where they amassed a large number of slaves. Around 1849, the family became Texas residents, bringing with them a considerable number of bondspeople and a caravan of twenty wagons. Gathings's first Texas home was on Richland Creek in Navarro County about 1850. The family later moved to an area that became Hill County and around 1852 established the one hundred acre town of Covington (obviously named after Gathings's wife), where Gathings had acquired 10,000 acres of land. Here they financially flourished.[46]

Although there may be some doubt as to precisely what date Gathings and his entourage arrived in Texas, by 1854, the first year in which he appeared upon the tax rolls, his property was assessed at $15,494. For that time, it was a rather considerable amount and included 31 slaves worth $13,500; 10 horses valued at $750; 123 head of cattle estimated at $752; and wagons and sheep added another $492. His taxes were minimal. Gathings paid the state $23.74; the county $11.87; and a poll tax of $.75. His property and apparently his influence would continue to grow through the decade of the Civil War. In 1870 the value of Gathings's real estate was placed at $26,910 and his personal property at $32,925.[47]

Gathings's financial empire suffered a major blow with emancipation. In 1860 the total value of his possessions was $44,160. By 1870 this figure had declined to $19,242. During this decade, Gathings lost 57 percent of his wealth but still maintained his status as the "richest" man in Hill County. Not surprisingly, such an individual aimed his postwar wrath at the representatives of the new order. Although almost every prominent individual complained about the high taxes under the Davis administration, they, in effect, were wrong. In 1860, Gathings paid a total of poll, state, and county taxes of $112.40. Under the hated and detested Republicans, his bill was a grand total of $28.86.[48]

After the Willinghams's inquest, a small force led by State Police Lieutenant W. T. Pritchett "hotly pursued" the murderers to the Gathings household in Covington, fourteen miles from Hillsboro. Pritchett had information that the two killers were concealed in the Gathings home. Pritchett, two other officers, and four black State Policemen approached and requested permission to search the premises. Gathings refused and told Pritchett, "You cannot search my house with your damned negro police." If they entered, their lives would be in danger. He supposedly seized a shotgun and announced that a white man could go in but "no 'nigger,'" while he cursed the state officers "in the severest terms."[49]

Although some claimed that Gathings was but a "distant relative of one of the refugees," or refused to believe that one of his sons participated in the killing of a black couple, the evidence is clear: his offspring was a murderer. Allegedly, the State Police appeared before sunrise demanding the "opportunity to search the house for 'little Jim' Gathings." When the elder Gathings refused to permit the State Police to search his home, except by force of arms, two of the policemen drew their pistols and exclaimed that they intended to do that very thing. Pritchett ordered the "negroes to go in and search." Not surprisingly, they found no one. Gathings's stalling tactics proved successful.[50]

This initial encounter between Gathings and the State Police allowed the criminals (who had been seen entering the premises an hour earlier) time to escape. The father's obstruction of justice and display of outrageousness hampered the State Police in performing their assigned duties. Gathings did not have to stand alone against the hated police. Many of his neighbors (of course he originally owned the town) supported his viewpoint. His influence was deep and abiding. (After this incident, Gathings would aid a killer of a former State Policeman, L. J. Hoffman, who had become the Waco marshal.) Gathings used his political, economic, and social power to hide his questionable character. An incensed governor proclaimed martial law.[51]

Pritchett and his men proceeded about a mile from the Gathings home, where they ate breakfast. He sent four men ahead to continue the search. Shortly after, a party of twelve to fifteen citizens, ostensibly under Gathings's leadership, secreted themselves behind a house and a fence on the roadway. When Pritchett and the two remaining policemen approached, the citizens, who represented themselves as officers of the law, "rushed across the road in front" of the state officers, "leveled their guns and demanded their surrender." Pritchett and his subordinates were held captive for two hours until a magistrate could arrive. A warrant was issued for their arrest, returnable before Justice of the Peace A. M. Lawrence.[52]

By this time, Pritchett and his men were "thoroughly convinced" that they were "in possession of an infuriated *mob*, and were arrested by irresponsible persons, who were neither officers of the law and without any authority or writ for our arrest." Believing this, he submitted an affidavit that "justice could not be done me in that precinct." They responded with a writ returnable before Justice R. R. Booth of Hillsboro where the State Policemen were taken under guard of "some twenty men." On arriving in Hillsboro, the four men Pritchett had sent ahead were overtaken and also arrested. A trial soon commenced. Pritchett and his subordinates were charged with forcibly entering the "premises of J. J. Gathings without a search warrant."[53]

As news spread of the policemen's arrest, armed men entered Hillsboro while the trial was in progress. The courtroom quickly filled with individuals *"armed with shot-guns and six-shooters,"* which created "intense excitement" during the proceedings. Pritchett described the trial scene: "more armed men were coming in; whiskey freely drank, and myself and men threatened and insulted." Justice Booth placed Pritchett under a $500 bond to appear in court in one week. Gathings, the armed leader of the "mob," "walked up to the justice's stand, and with anger and clenched fist, swore to the court that 'by God, if the bond is not made strong and substantial, I will re-arrest him and hold him until the date of his trial.'"[54]

Although he was released, subsequent warrants were issued upon the same charge for the re-arrest of Pritchett. When the State Police endeavored to leave the county, a group of citizen vigilantes re-arrested the state troopers, but they managed to escape. Pritchett was of the impression that he and his detachment were originally apprehended in order to provide the two criminals, Nicholson and Gathings, an opportunity to escape. The two fugitives were but a short distance in front of their pursuers, and Pritchett believed they would undoubtedly have been captured but for the timely intervention of the elder Gathings and his associates. If fact, the State Police were probably lucky to leave the county still alive.[55]

After the arrest of the State Police, Davis reached the limits of his patience. The total disregard of the law as evinced by Hill County inhabitants induced him to believe that the situation was completely beyond the control of local forces. Therefore, on January 10, 1871, he proclaimed martial law. Davis announced that there existed a "combination of lawless men, who have been guilty of various outrages against the peace and dignity of said State, and that said combination is too strong to be controlled by the civil authorities of said county." He suspended the laws in Hill County "until such time as the legislature shall take such action in the premises as it may deem necessary or until [the] proclamation [was] revoked."[56]

The governor ordered Chief of Police Davidson to go to Hill County and issue the proclamation of martial law, which had been signed and placed in his hands. But Davidson had the option of forestalling its issuance after he surveyed the scene. Any expenses incurred would be assessed upon the county or the implicated parties, Davidson to choose the most expedient method. Permitted to convene a General Courts Martial if justice could better be "subserved in that manner than by trial before civil courts," Davidson's action was expected to be prompt and the matter disposed of without delay. Davis suggested a strong squad of police be left in the district "with orders to hunt down and bring to justice all offenders."[57]

The outrageous murder of two black people and the interference by local citizens with the State Police, exclaimed Chief of Police James Davidson, "taken in connection with the previous disregard of law evinced by the citizens of Hill county," was reprehensible. He concluded that the "state of affairs in that section" was "totally beyond the control of the civil officers of the law." Upon entering the area, Davidson observed the condition of the county to be "confused," and he added, "officers intimidated, authority resisted, and a spirit of defiance to law extant, which the civil officers were utterly powerless to control."[58]

In addition, Davidson ordered Captain E. H. Napier, head of Company H of the Sixth Regiment of State Guards, which numbered about fifty men, to proceed to Hill County. Napier's group marched into Hillsboro after Davidson's arrival. Davidson found county affairs in complete disarray. The hostility to the presence of Davidson and the governor's minions was everywhere evident. Davidson felt that he had no choice but to declare martial law. Colonel J. M. Gibbs of the reserve militia was placed in command and a provost marshal appointed to oversee the necessary regulatory procedures. Although the State Police were present, they played a subsidiary role due to manpower shortage. Actually, they were no longer needed.[59]

Orders were immediately issued for the arrest of James J. Gathings, James Gathings Jr., Philip Gathings, James Denmember, William L. Towner, David Gathings, George Gathings, and Dr. Astyanax M. Douglass, as they had been the leaders in the "outrage" against Lieutenant Pritchett and his men. Promptly apprehended, the parties were brought before Davidson. They acknowledged their participation in preventing the police from arresting the two men who had murdered the black man and woman and were fined $3,000. Of this sum, $2,765 ($1,000 in gold) was promptly paid by the parties and was estimated "as sufficient to cover all expenses incident to the declaration of martial law in that county."[60]

All expenditures from the collected fund had been made through certified vouchers. Davidson deemed this method, instead of a general assessment, more beneficial to Hill County inhabitants, which the parties who paid the fine confirmed. Booth said that he had rendered the decision in Pritchett's case out of "fear of murder by the infuriated mob in the court room at the trial." The county remained under martial law for only two days, when it became "sufficiently quiet" to return power to the civil authorities and the troops left. The application of martial law, Davidson reported, had the effect of rendering Hill County "as peaceable and subservient to the laws as any other portion of the State." His observation was delusional.[61]

On February 7, 1871, after the Hill County excitement had ended, the Texas Senate adopted a resolution calling upon Davis to provide information "respecting acts of lawlessness and crime which may have occurred" in Hill County and what action "if any," had been taken by the governor. Davis complied with the Senate's wishes. He forwarded to Don Campbell (President of the Senate) Davidson's report and various other materials which document-ed his reasons for taking such drastic action. Davis believed this would "pres-ent to the Senate a complete statement of the causes which led to the procla-mation of martial law in Hill county, and the proceedings that have been had thereunder."[62]

Two weeks after the conclusion of martial law, Davidson observed a change in the attitude of Hill County citizens, but the "lies" and misstatements of the *Waco Examiner*, vehemently anti-administration, concerned him. He was sat-isfied that the people had decided to "abide by the Laws, and any protection" the state could afford "in so laudable an undertaking will be cheerfully and promptly extended." Davidson planned to send Sergeant Martin and a suf-ficient body of policemen as desired by the citizens. But the *Examiner*'s sto-ries of the Hill County affair were being copied extensively by other papers throughout the state. The Chief of Police felt that the misinformation should be "publicly corrected" by the county's citizens.[63]

The citizens assured Wood of their "readiness to support law and order." He desired to give them an opportunity of "having their professions tested by their works and action." He believed it expedient the policemen did not testify because public sentiment suggested that any action would have sus-tained the Gathings party and would have censured the action of the police authorities. The grand jurors had consulted with Wood on the declaration of martial law in Hill County and had heard his public charge. Wood had no private advice for them but expected the jurors to respect their oath to inquire into the outrages and bring to trial those who had been the immediate cause of defeating the authorities in their efforts to enforce the law.[64]

Six weeks after Davis imposed martial law, a Hill County grand jury be-lieved the "earnestness" of the subject demanded the governor's attention to the "late troubles" in their county. They were aware of the difficulties between the citizens, the State Police, and Gathings. The grand jurors requested that Davis use his influence in bringing these matters to a just, proper, and "equi-table" settlement by having a committee composed of members of the legis-lature, "irrespective of party," come to the county and "investigate the matter thoroughly." In conclusion, they pledged to Davis their "hearty co-operation and support in the fair just and proper administration and execution of the law." Davis had heard all this before.[65]

It took Davis two weeks to compose his response to the Hill County grand jury, but he favored them with a tongue-lashing, described his philosophy of government, and defended the rights of all citizens. Legislative committees had been established in both houses to "bring all facts and circumstances to light" concerning the imposition of martial law and the assessment of the cost for this state action, which was levied upon James J. Gathings and his accomplices. In the Senate, a majority of the militia committee filed their report on February 17. Although some of the members had doubts about Davis's action, they concluded that they neither desired to scrutinize his decision nor believed in the "propriety" of such an inquiry.[66]

Nevertheless, Davis had informed the appropriate legislative officials that he willingly supported the idea that a committee should be appointed to inquire into the situation in Hill County. Although he had no objection to any investigation, he did not want Hill Countians to suppose that he was "under any doubt as to the substantial justice of what had been done." If the case had been treated differently, he thought that the penalty should have been "more severe." What disturbed the governor so much, and which is clear from his response, is that black and white Unionists seemed to be the targets of open hostility and they were denied justice. This type of political and social controversy the governor attempted to prevent.[67]

Old patterns prevailed. On December 8, the governor reminded the grand jury that, by Sheriff John P. Grace's own testimony, the jail had been broken into and Samuel Stults, charged with murder, had escaped. Davis desired to know the number of citizens who turned out to hunt down and arrest the jail breakers. The governor felt the people had "not interested" themselves. This pattern reversed itself when the State Police became involved and the citizens aroused themselves when two black people were murdered. Unfortunately, they arrested the State Police instead of pursuing the Willingham killers. How many citizens, Davis asked, searched for the "young scoundrels" Gathings and Nicholson, the slayers, and what measures had been taken to locate them?[68]

But the murderers went unmolested. Davis established martial law, sent in troops, and the cost, approximately $3,000, was charged to Gathings and his followers because of their "assault on the police." The citizens considered the assessment upon Gathings and his abettors inappropriate and encouraged the grand jury to address the governor for redress, but they said "not a word" about the killing of the "colored man and [his] wife," or even the jail breakers, which included the failure of the citizens to punish such offenses. Nothing was said about the "murder of this pair of poor blacks, or the credit of your people as supporters of the law of less consequence in your minds than a money assessment on your right neighbor Gathings."[69]

Davis, in his final comments, became particularly snide, as he should have. After all, blacks had been murdered in Hill and adjoining counties and nothing had been done by the local law enforcement officials. When the governor found "Mr. J. J. Gathings as vigorous in the pursuit and arrest of the young murderer who bears his name (and for whose worthless character he may be largely responsible) as he was the State Police, and when he becomes an active and earnest supporter of law and order and an enemy of jail breakers and other disturbers, it will be time to talk of his relief." Davis, as he closed his letter, somewhat disingenuously added, it is by "no means a pleasure" to "have to use such severity towards any one of my fellow citizens."[70]

In a series of letters published in July 1871, the writers, either friends of Gathings who participated in arresting the State Police or local Hill County officials, excoriated Davis for his action. None of the individuals mentioned the savage killing of a black man and woman that had initially precipitated the clash between Davis and Gathings. Dr. A. M. Douglass referred to the incident as a "robbery perpetrated upon" Gathings and claimed that the governor's "vindictive reply" to the grand jury wherein he indulged in "opprobrious epithets against" Hill Countians and Gathings only proved that a "man never denounces crime in stronger terms than when fresh from its commission." For what Davis had done he should be consigned to the penitentiary.[71]

Douglass, along with statements from Hill County justices of the peace A. M. Lawrence and R. R. Booth, attempted to disprove that the decision in the case of Lieutenant Pritchett had been due to intimidation by Gathings and that Davidson never signed an affidavit to that effect. Sheriff Grace provided the most pathetic (in fact, dishonest) account. He said that no intimidation of county officers existed during the crisis and there had been "no organized defiance to the laws." Grace claimed he had arrested the Gathings group with no assistance and turned them over to Davidson. Moreover, he stated that martial law had not been instituted and that Gathings was "one of our best citizens—strictly honorable and law abiding."[72]

Brutal murders continued to dot the Hill County landscape. In White Rock, a man was savagely killed on October 20, 1871. Two more died by hanging, both of them described as "bad men," who "no doubt got their just reward." Unfortunately, the crowd that dispatched them was as bad as the victims. As in the past, the Hill County jail once again became the focus of attention as it was broken open and all the prisoners released, two whites and one black. (One of the men returned and surrendered.) In late 1871, three cattle drovers were murdered (they had a considerable amount of cash with them after driving their beeves to Kansas). Little seems to have been done to ascertain who did the killing. And the upheaval continued.[73]

In the 1872 election, Hill County Democrats decided to use Gathings as a focal point for its opposition to Governor Davis. One newspaper contended that the Democrats selected Gathings "in order to show the powers that be that an innocent man cannot be outraged in his district with impunity." The paper declared that Gathings was "robbed by a negro State Policeman of $3,000 in gold." With 989 listed voters in 1872, 109 of them black, the Democrats easily won. In the state Senate contest for the 20th District, Gathings finished fourth, 100 votes behind the third place finisher. R. R. Booth came in fifth. This was merely the denouement. In the 1873 gubernatorial race, the Wacoan Richard Coke polled almost ten times more votes than Davis.[74]

In April 1873, as the State Police were about to be disbanded by the Thirteenth Legislature, the new adjutant general, Frank L. Britton, was urged by Hill County residents to send a detachment of the State Police to protect their lives. A number of persons had been murdered at night. The clan who committed the deeds, "still thirsting for more blood," sent a missive (signed "death to thieves") to certain "law-abiding" citizens ordering them to leave the county within thirty days or suffer the consequences. But the legislature continued to withhold the pay of the State Police, which made it impossible for Britton to provide the assistance "prayed for" by this long-suffering community.[75]

The Hill County clash had four ironic circumstances. This irony began in September 1870 and would not be completed until January 1874. First, Chief of Police Davidson refused to pay a bill for services rendered by Hillsboro attorneys George L. Hart and Booth in defending Lieutenant Pritchett and Sergeant Evans, after they had been brought before a justice of the peace by the Gathings vigilantes. These two officers, Davidson wrote, who allowed themselves to be arrested (actually they had no choice in the matter if they valued their lives) and held to trial by a mob, were "guilty of disobedience of expressed orders." The state, therefore, could not allow the bill, so the officers themselves had to be looked to for payment.[76]

By early 1873, the Democrats, once again in control of the legislature, inquired about the "large sum of money" which Adjutant General Davidson had compelled Gathings to pay for the costs of declaring martial law in Hill County and mobilizing a unit of the State Guard. The legislature considered the propriety of reimbursing Gathings. That Hill County citizens had interfered with the capture of two murderers and had taken vigilante action against a duly constituted state authority bothered the Democrats not at all. Their attempt to curry the favor of Gathings was more important than appeasing Texas African Americans. Their relations with the Texas black community were abysmal anyway, and they simply made them worse.[77]

Second, the man who precipitated the confrontation with state authorities emerged as a "hero" of the legislators. In 1874, the 14th State Legislature came to Gathings's aid, as if he needed it. Claiming that the State Police under Davidson had extorted $1,000 in gold coin (worth $1,150 in currency) and also took from him $1,765 in currency, the aggregate amounting to $2,915 in currency, the members determined to repay Gathings for this outrage. Thus, they confirmed the repayment of the money Gathings had earlier given the state and reimbursed him for that amount.[78]

Third, Gathings's son and Native American ward were never indicted or charged for killing the black man and woman. But this obstruction of justice did not end with his own family.

For the fourth irony we must return to September 1870 when L. J. Hoffman was a member of the State Police, involved with attempting to capture the infamous Kinch West and his gang. Hoffman resigned when he accepted the position of Waco marshal. George Tomason, alias Wild George, and his "clan of desperadoes," which consisted of fourteen or fifteen "of the worst characters in Texas," murdered Hoffman. Although the precise circumstances of the encounter are unclear, Wild George was wounded and it was reported that he had died. Such was not the case, and he was later observed in Shreveport. His escape had been made possible by Gathings himself, who had provided George with a horse and money to flee the county.[79]

The discord in Hill County caused by Gathings and his sons was not their first attempt to violate the law. In fact, the *Daily State Journal* claimed they were "old and notorious offenders." In 1866, a man named Burnett, married to Gathings's niece, stole a mule from A. M. Arnold, who lived in Cleburne. Arnold arrested him but was prevented by the thief from taking him to Hill County for trial. Gathings "rescued" Burnett, who had been indicted in Ellis County for theft. Gathings should have answered for aiding Burnett when caught with stolen property. These jail birds and lawless Democrats were always ready to oppose the police and play the role of "Quantrill, of [Cullen Montgomery] Baker, and of [Elisha] Guest in defiance of civilization and peaceful rule."[80]

From the time Davidson assessed the military tax upon Gathings and his associates in January 1871 to the final reimbursement to Gathings by the legislature in January 1874, controversy swirled around Davidson's actions and the money he collected. Public charges of misappropriations, misapplication, and embezzlement were aimed at the adjutant general. Although Davidson may have later absconded with a considerable sum of money from the Texas state treasury (it was suspected but never proven he took the funds), in this instance his accounts were in order. The comptroller, Albert A. Bledsoe, detailed the expenditures and disposition of the Gathings money, supported by the record of Alfred D. Evans, the paymaster of Texas. There is simply no evidence the money was mismanaged.[81]

In the power clash between Governor E. J. Davis and the wealthy, prominent, and politically connected power of Hill Countian J. J. Gathings, Davis clearly lost. The governor did the right thing in declaring martial law, but he seemed unwilling to commit considerable force to support his beliefs. But if Davis had attempted to severely punish Gathings and his associates, many of whom were notable men of the county (and, of course, Democrats), he may have invoked a full-scale rebellion. Even after this confrontation, Hill County continued to be racked by turmoil and killings. The saddest commentary on the affair is that the son of Gathings and his Indian ward were never punished for the wanton killing of a black man and woman.

Governor Davis confronted opposition in other counties which required the intervention of the State Police. In the Piney Woods area in the southern and eastern portion of the state, another test of wills between the administration and local citizens emerged. In a facsimile scenario, the question was: Who murdered an elderly black man after his testimony before a grand jury? The response of many Walker County residents to apprehending and protecting the killers of an old freedman was similar to Hill County attitudes. The bitter hatred of the Republicans, the State Police, and black equality forced Davis to declare martial law in Walker County.

"The Dark Recesses of Their Hearts"

THE STATE POLICE AND MARTIAL LAW IN WALKER COUNTY

In late 1870, almost concurrently with the troubles in Madison and Hill counties, along with the controversy over Captain Jack Helm, the murder of an elderly black man in Walker County forced Governor E. J. Davis to declare martial law in that county. A similar set of circumstances faced Davis in Hill and Walker counties as citizens rebelled at the presence of the State Police. When the police attempted to apprehend the murderers, they were stymied by the interference of residents. After a Walker County grand jury no-billed the culprits accused of slaying a Huntsville freedman, a district judge later arraigned them before his court. This attempt to ensure justice resulted in a shoot-out in his courtroom. No one was killed, but the confrontation further polarized the citizens against the administration of Governor Davis.

As Davis proclaimed martial law and prepared to dispatch troops into Walker County, he stated that a black man had been "foully murdered" and described the altercation in Burnett's courtroom as a "high handed act." The incident had no parallel in "any country where the English language is spoken" for "overbearing lawlessness." Davis asserted that the citizens deprecated the violence, but they all "stood by supinely, or actively aided the attack upon the judge and officers of the law" while the latter "engaged in the exercise of their legitimate authority and sworn duty." The governor regretted that the people of Texas "do not see that it is [in] their true interest, without regard to the question of duty, to put a stop to such lawlessness."[1]

Some seventy miles north of Houston, Walker County was created from Montgomery County in 1846 by the first legislature of the newest member of the United States. Originally named after the Mississippian Robert J. Walker, who introduced the Texas annexation resolution, the 1863 state legislature rejected honoring the county after Walker, who had become a Unionist. Instead, they claimed its title for Samuel H. Walker, a Texas Ranger killed in the war with Mexico, who had fittingly introduced the Walker Colt into the fighting. Located among the Piney Woods, Walker County is bounded on the north by the Trinity River and by the San Jacinto in the west. During the antebellum era its cotton production expanded as did its slave population.[2]

With an economy based upon corn, cotton, cattle, and slaves, the region burgeoned. Manufacturing appeared; by 1870 a cotton ginning industry employed over one hundred people, along with three lumber mills, and a wool refining factory. When created, the county had 720 slaves. Within fourteen years, this number increased to 3,766 and another 2,000 were added by 1864. Of the 646 white families, 376, or 58 percent, owned slaves in 1860; most had fewer than 20. Joshua A. Thomason, a forty-nine-year-old Georgia-born slaveholder, topped the list with 128 slaves. By 1860, blacks were a majority of the population. Walker County supported secession by a vote of 490 to 61, thus one of the characteristics of Deep South culture.[3]

Before the war, Huntsville's black denizens had comprised about one-quarter of the town's residents. By 1870 the percentage had risen to almost 40 percent. Wartime immigration increased the black county population percentage from 50 to almost 60 percent. With emancipation, the former slaves celebrated in Huntsville, the county seat and one of the "most flourishing inland towns" of the state. Andy McAdams remembered they were "plum thick hollering and shouting cause they were free, but that merriment did not last long, as there was a white man came down through that bunch of people on a horse fast as he could with rag tied over his face and rode by a negro woman, just leaned over in his saddle and cut that negro woman nearly half" in two. Former Freedmen's Bureau agent James P. Butler declared that among the inhabitants the "old spirit of slavery is so deeply engraved into the dark recesses of their hearts that nothing but death can ever eradicate their animosity against the colored man."[4]

In October 1870, tensions between Walker County Democrats and Republicans were further exacerbated by the formation of two Reserve Militia companies and a State Guard unit. Those who opposed the Davis administration joined companies A and B of the 21st Reserve Militia. These two groups enrolled almost all the major players in the later courtroom drama, in particular Nat Outlaw, John M. Parish, John Wright, and Fred Parks, the four who later would be charged with murdering a freedman. In addition, the militia contained almost all the prominent county Democrats. On the other side was the organization of Company B of the 1st Regiment of the State Guard, led by Mortimer H. Goddin as captain and other important Republicans, along with a host of freedmen.[5]

The killing of a freedman precipitated state action. Sam Jenkins, a Tennessee native, arrived in Texas in 1852, probably as a slave. By 1870, he was sixty-eight years old, with a wife born in Mississippi and a son born in Louisiana, who, like his father, was a farm hand. Jenkins became involved in a dispute over the division of a crop he and Fred Parks had cultivated. Parks ordered Jenkins to leave. Jenkins unsuccessfully attempted to recover his portion of the crop or receive a satisfactory settlement. Jenkins was also an active member and major booster of the Union League. A resident described him as "one of the leaders under 'Carpetbagism' rule," who "made himself obnoxious to white people generally."[6]

Two friends of Parks, John Wright and Nat Outlaw, disgusted at Jenkins's economic demands and political activities, met him some two or three miles outside of Huntsville and declared they would either shoot him or whip him. He could take his choice. Wright and Outlaw battered Jenkins "unmercifully" with sticks, almost to the point of death. The night after the beating it was believed that Jenkins would die. Additionally, Wright and Outlaw threatened to kill Jenkins if he testified against them before a grand jury. Another Parks friend, John M. Parish, mistakenly shot Parks through the neck because he thought he was shooting at Jenkins. One newspaper claimed that Jenkins had "several times been waylaid and beaten" on visits to Huntsville.[7]

Who were John M. Parish, John Wright, Nat Outlaw, and Fred Parks, around whom so much controversy swirled? Parish, in 1870, was a twenty-year-old Texas-born farmer with $1,100 worth of real estate and $500 worth of personal property. His household was composed of a Eulein Wynne, a black domestic servant born in Alabama, and her two children, Richard, age eleven, and Arthur, age eight. Also born in Texas was John Wright, a sixty-nine-year-old farmer with a thirty-four-year-old wife and three children. Two women, an eighteen- and a thirty-three-year-old, also resided with them. Nat Outlaw was a twenty-six-year-old Mississippi-born watch smith who lived with the Thomas B. Harding family. A native Tennessean, Parks was twenty-four years old, with no real or personal property.[8]

On December 5, 1870, Jenkins testified before a grand jury (which included seven or eight blacks) on several indictments of assault and battery against Parks, Parish, Outlaw, and Wright. The district attorney, W. E. Horne, examined the case. With the assistance of Horne and the local freedpeople, for five days the grand jury "gave the matter a very thorough investigation." After exploring "all the sources of information," the panel "refused to find a bill against" Wright, Outlaw, Parish, and Parks. They argued that the evidence was insufficient for an indictment. When the proceedings finished, Jenkins left the courtroom about four o'clock, followed by four men, three of whom were identified as Outlaw, Parish, and Wright.[9]

Between sundown and dark, three miles from Huntsville, Jenkins was "cowardly and brutally murdered." Shot in the head and body, the wounds suggested he attempted to escape. Although more than a half-dozen witnesses allegedly observed four white men murder Jenkins, one riding a "black" horse, two on "grays," and one astride a bay, they refused to give any testimony. Governor Davis offered a reward of $500 for the arrest of Jenkins's killers. The *Huntsville Item* attempted to convey the impression that Jenkins "*might* have lost his life in trying to rob somebody," but Jenkins's corpse "presented unmistakable signs that he had been foully murdered." Horne labeled it "a cold-blooded murder and assassination of a poor old freedman."[10]

Local officials needed to take action. Writing to J. P. Burnett, District Judge of the 30th Judicial District, Governor Davis had heard many unfavorable reports in regard to the county sheriff, William H. Stewart. He had earlier been connected with the killing of a prisoner or prisoners whom he attempted to arrest. The murder of Jenkins after his grand jury appearance was "a very flagrant affair" in Davis's eyes, and he would accept no excuse that Stewart could not discover the murderer. "He *must* find out who did it," Davis emphasized, "or be removed." Burnett proposed Stewart's removal and the governor thought it should be immediately done. He had to have "men in the office beyond suspicion" or he could not "enforce the laws."[11]

Two weeks after the Jenkins murder, Judge Burnett removed the Irish-born Stewart, who had also served as town marshal. Although Stewart possessed an "animal force," he was "mentally incompetent," a "rebel" sympathizer, could barely read and write, and spent too much money on liquor and cigars. Stewart frightened many of the local residents. Burnett planned to make the change earlier but needed to find a solid successor. Several applicants did not belong to the party, and only Goddin was a member. He was a "good man," but he had neither the judgment nor discretion to be sheriff. Cobb Butler had spoken of his brother, Michael, for the job, but he had not yet arrived and there was no assurance he would move to the county.[12]

Burnett recommended Cyrus R. Hess, a Pennsylvania native, to be interim sheriff. Hess, an old citizen, a thorough Republican, and a competent man, with an "irreproachable character for honesty" and integrity, would make an "excellent and impartial officer." One resident regarded him as solid and trustworthy. Another claimed his character was that of a "correct and upright man." Previously promoted for the board of aldermen by the Union League, Hess served briefly as Huntsville mayor. His selection would give "satisfaction to the law abiding citizens of all classes, especially to the Republicans," but a permanent appointment was necessary as the special road, school, and indebtedness taxes required collection.[13]

On January 4, 1871, a complaint was lodged before Judge Burnett over the unsolved murder of Sam Jenkins. (James M. Maxey stated it was made by a Colonel Jones, who was not examined as a witness at the subsequent hearing.) Based on Jones's affidavit Burnett issued an arrest warrant, executed by Captain L. H. McNelly and five compatriots who had been ordered to the area by Chief of Police Davidson on Burnett's request. On January 6 McNelly apprehended the four men and placed them in the custody of Sheriff Hess. On January 9 they were arraigned before Burnett and charged with killing Jenkins. Notable local attorneys James M. Maxey, James A. Baker, and Lewis B. Hightower Sr. represented the defendants. District Attorney Horne argued the case for the state.[14]

The *Daily Union*, quoting the *Huntsville Union Republican*, best summarized the arguments for prosecuting the killers of Jenkins: "The truth is too plain—it was a little too much to commit white men to jail for killing a negro." They say Sam Jenkins was a "quarrelsome, bad old man. Well, if so, were the laws too weak to protect society against a bad old freedman of seventy years? But, notwithstanding all his difficulties, poor old uncle Sam always came out second best, and no grand jury has ever yet indicted him for any offense whatsoever." Reflecting negatively on the county, "these things cannot exist in a government of laws, and, unless the laws are obeyed and observed, justice will depend upon the whims or caprices of a mob."[15]

The evening before the trial began, a meeting was held where Maxey gave, in Burnett's words, "a very inflammatory argument" intended to intimidate the judge before a packed room, in which several men were armed. Maxey argued that if Burnett committed the men to jail he could not have the "moral support of the community" and that such a course of action was fraught with pitfalls. Burnett perceived this as a threat. The judge considered dismissing Maxey as one of the defendants' counsel but decided it would be unwise and lead to violence. Neither Baker nor Hightower followed Maxey's reasoning. Burnett condemned Maxey's argument, who contended the impending trial was a "political prosecution," which the judge denounced as a falsehood.[16]

During the proceedings, in addition to Sheriff Hess and the five State Policemen, at least two other guards assisted in detaining the prisoners. An older man named William McElroy, whose responsibility was Parish and whom McElroy had known for ten or twelve years, served for four or five days at Hess's request. A younger man named Smith was also involved in overseeing the prisoners both in the jail and in the courtroom. The Huntsville jail was in horrendous shape, so Outlaw, Parish, and Wright were confined with Hess in a room in the jail. Wright remained at home at night under guard because his wife was ill. Judge Burnett had authorized Hess to summon as many citizens as he thought proper to make it relatively safe and to guard the prisoners.[17]

As the trial progressed, Burnett became apprehensive about the friends of the prisoners but not from the citizens in general. His decision in *The State vs. Nat Outlaw et al.* created considerable controversy. "That Sam Jenkins, a poor old freedman," was "most cowardly and brutally murdered" on December 5, 1870, could not be controverted. Unquestionably, the perpetrators of this "horrid assassination" were guilty of a capital offense and the proof showed "no alleviation or excuse whatever for the damnable deed." Under Texas law they could not be allowed bail. The evidence failed to connect Parks to the murder and he was discharged. For the other three defendants, the allegation demonstrated to Burnett with a "moral and reasonable certainty, that they are guilty."[18]

Burnett found "nothing inconsistent in the main body of the testimony" of the defendants' witnesses "with their guilt; and the facts and circumstances detailed by the State's witnesses" completely satisfied him that they participated in the killing. An "onslaught" had been made "on the State" through the defense counsel, which had asserted that "if the court desires the moral support of the community" then the parties should not be jailed on the evidence. It was fortunate, however, Burnett contended, for the "administration of public justice that the conscience of the Judge is not in the hands of paid advocates or any part of the community at large." If they desired a remedy, the case could be appealed to the Supreme Court.[19]

Burnett concluded that if he was to be "cowardly assassinated" because of his "honest decision," and if the law was to be "outraged by a mob and the prisoners set free in defiance of the law, be it so." Whatever transpired, he would do his duty. Burnett apprehended "no such violations of the law on the part of the good citizens" since everyone had been "outraged by the horrible murder," and "all classes, if they should feel aggrieved" at his decision, "will resort for redress to the due process of the law of the land." Thus, Outlaw, Parish, and Wright would be incarcerated until the next term of the district court to answer for the murder of Jenkins.[20]

Baker and Maxey, defense counsel members, attempted to discredit Burnett's decision in the case. In a *Galveston News* article, written by Maxey, the Davis administration was charged with undertaking the prosecution of the four men for political purposes. Maxey found freedmen testimony unreliable, ignored the violence the defendants had perpetrated upon Jenkins, and implied that many strangers had congregated in Huntsville for a horse race on the day Jenkins was killed, of which anyone could have been responsible for the murder. He believed the "whole thing was fixed up in Austin and the dark room at the Penitentiary, where schemers met to plot the destruction of these young men."[21]

Burnett defended himself against this "garbled statement" and "wholly deceptive" account. He denied being influenced by Davis or Davidson, or by any other consideration than "a conscientious desire" to do his duty. That the prosecution was initiated for political effect he called a "miserable slander." Prosecutor Horne admitted that the defendants' "learned, zealous, and overactive counsel" inflamed the spectators. Baker and Hightower joined in the incitement. Burnett wrote a portion of his opinion the night before, but only after closing speeches on each side. He concluded that the "*persecution of the officers who faithfully discharged their duties is for political effect*," and it would "recoil on the heads of the persecutors and slanderers."[22]

After announcing the decision, Burnett handed McNelly the warrant and ordered him, along with Sheriff Hess, to escort the prisoners to jail. The judge told Hess that if he expected any difficulties he could summon as many citizens as necessary to enforce the order, but the sheriff anticipated no problems. As Burnett left, he met Cal Watkins and a Mr. Hopkins, who also foresaw no danger. As Burnett neared the Brown Hotel, pistol shots rang out from the courtroom and gunfire emanated from the streets. One man emptied his six-shooter at the judge and Horne. Another man discharged a bullet into the ground near Burnett's feet. The next night an attempt was made on Burnett's life.[23]

McNelly, not realizing that Burnett would conclude the trial so quickly, had sent two policemen to get their weapons and had but three men with him inside. McNelly and Sheriff Hess searched the men, and the captain discovered Outlaw had a gun and, with the assistance of McElroy and J. H. Whitehead, disarmed him. Hess asked Wright if he too had arms. Wright said no, but then drew a revolver and fired at McNelly, as did Parish. State Policemen McNelly, Tom Keesee, L. E. Dunn, and Joseph L. Martin returned the gunfire, severely wounding Parish in the right arm and Wright in the leg and the body. McElroy jumped into the window to avoid the bullets. Aided by "friends outside and inside the court room," each prisoner had concealed two six-shooters.[24]

McNelly was also shot in the leg, and Keesee received a ball in the jaw that passed around the neck. (These wounds would temporarily incapacitate the two men.) Even though wounded, both men continued to fire until Wright and Parish escaped from the courtroom and down the steps where their "benefactors" awaited them. For "about one or two minutes an incessant firing was kept up," Horne wrote, with perhaps forty or fifty shots fired. Outlaw seemed to have been grazed on the arm with the skin hardly broken, accidentally shot by Wright. Outlaw immediately surrendered and was later taken to the penitentiary for safe-keeping. It was surmised that no attempt would be made to rescue Outlaw while in the secure confines of the prison.[25]

Two additional State Policemen, Hugh Pennington and Val Lemmons, were stationed at the base of the courtroom stairs when the shooting began. Preventing the two officers from rendering any assistance, the prisoners' supporters had pistols presented and cocked and threatened the two State Policemen with "immediate death" if either "attempted to move." As Wright and Parish exited the courtroom, bleeding from their wounds, the twenty or thirty confederates who had held Pennington and Lemmons at bay had horses ready and were armed with shotguns. When Wright and Parish appeared, they were greeted "with cheers." Mounting their horses, shooting and "yelling like savages," the band rode out of Huntsville.[26]

McNelly immediately ordered Sheriff Hess to summon a posse, but only two citizens volunteered. It was well known that the fugitives were well protected and it would be difficult to capture them. (McNelly claimed he could have reasoned with the crowd and gathered one hundred men to pursue the fugitives.) Initially wounded in the thigh, McNelly, while in the street, had three balls pass through his coat. He told Chief Davidson that he and Keesee

Leander H. McNelly served as an officer in the Confederate Army, was appointed as one of the first four captains in the State Police, and served in that position until the organization was disbanded in 1873. He later served as captain of the Washington County Volunteer Militia, a ranger unit created in 1874.
Courtesy of the Texas Ranger Hall of Fame and Museum, Waco, Texas.

would be ready for duty in a few days. Both escapees had been wounded and were hiding somewhere in the county. McNelly promised to use every means to recapture them, dead or alive. They had already cut the telegraph line so he had to communicate through an intermediary.[27]

Very quickly, the anti-administration forces in Walker County mounted a propaganda campaign to discredit the State Police and Davis appointees, in addition to promoting the innocence of Wright, Parish, and Outlaw. The friends and supporters of the escapees were "industrious in circulating reports" that attempted to denigrate the efforts of the court and the State Police by claiming Burnett had written his opinion before he heard any evidence and had treated the defense counsel with disrespect. "Everywhere it was said that the prisoners were innocent," editorialized the *Daily State Journal*, "but that the Radical court wanted a *victim*; a negro had been killed and somebody must be punished."[28]

The state government did not respond quickly, undoubtedly because Governor Davis was involved with difficulties in Hill County. By January 17 "no reinforcements have arrived," Burnett informed Davis, and he regretted to "say the civil authorities are still unable to cope with the lawless men in our midst." If additional men were forthcoming, the State Police would be able to arrest the parties who aided the prisoners and re-arrest the prisoners. McNelly would assume his duties again in a day or two, but he had kept the men alert and determined to break up the "lawless element here, and bring the offenders to justice." From prudent considerations, it was deemed best not to call out the State Guard, who were primarily black. Burnett thought if it became necessary, "this force will be called in aid."[29]

When Governor Davis received Burnett's account of the Huntsville clash, he had already heard something of what occurred by telegraph. He was preparing to regulate affairs in the county, as Burnett would soon learn. Davis supported Burnett's course and intended to sustain him. These outrages would bring upon the residents "severe expense and retribution as well as injury to the reputation and prosperity of the county." On January 20, 1871, Davis placed Walker County under martial law because there existed a "combination of lawless men" who had committed depredations against the "peace and dignity" of the state. Too strong to be controlled by the civil authorities, Davis ascertained they needed outside assistance.[30]

Although Governor Davis proclaimed martial law in Walker County, the failure of Colonel J. M. Gibbs of the State Guard to muster enough men to accompany him from Grimes County to impose the governor's order delayed the full implementation of Davis's wrath. In fact, it was not until February 15 (again, due to the Hill County mess) that he ordered Chief of Police Davidson to Walker County. Upon his arrival Davidson was instructed to issue and publish the governor's declaration and enforce it "rigidly." As the state's agent, Davidson would assess the amount of expenses incurred, either upon the county or the parties implicated in the recent disruption, whatever was most expedient. He was also directed to convene general courts martial or military commissions.[31]

If Davidson determined that justice could better be served in that manner than by the trial of individuals before the civil courts, these tribunals would include at least three officers, of which one had to be a field officer. Davidson's action should "be as prompt as possible, and the whole matter disposed of without delay, so that the troops may return to their homes." A squad of State Police would remain in the county. If there were not enough police to spare, then a detachment of the militia or State Guard would hunt down and "bring to justice all offenders." A board of three for general courts martial was also to be established in Grimes County to try the militiamen who refused service in Walker county.[32]

Walker County political upheaval, along with the failure of individuals to respond to the call to march on Huntsville, delayed the implementation of martial law. Colonel J. M. Gibbs of the 4th Regiment, Reserve Militia in Navasota, Grimes County, was ordered to bring a force to the county seat. He appeared on February 5, but had been able to raise only five men to support the governor's proclamation. Although Gibbs worked diligently to procure reliable men sufficient to carry out his instructions, the situation, claimed Burnett, was "considerably demoralized from false reports of the affairs at Huntsville and in some cases from a sympathy with the lawless bands." In addition, Judge Burnett had moved on to Anderson County to hold court there.[33]

When Chief Davidson proceeded to Walker County, Burnett suggested he procure men from Washington County or some other section if he could not obtain the assistance of United States troops. Davidson needed a contingent of fifty troops, but a larger force would be better. The escapees remained in the county, badly wounded, protected by their armed friends until they were well enough to travel. Captain McNelly had also left Walker County. Currently at Crockett, he was accompanied by two or three other policemen but believed he could recruit others if necessary. He thought the fugitives might have gone to Arkansas or Louisiana, or at least in that direction, and contended he would pursue them to the "jumping off" place, meaning the state line.[34]

Almost three weeks after Davis declared martial law, Senator E. Petit, on February 6, introduced a resolution in the state senate that the governor communicate to that body "any information in his possession, respecting acts of lawlessness and crime" which occurred in Walker County and any action he had taken in the matter. Two days later Davis submitted a lengthy report. A little over a week later, on February 17, the Committee on Militia (George T. Ruby, J. S. Mills, P. W. Hall, and Henry Rawson), declared that martial law was "imperatively demanded." They had no further opinion as a special Senate committee had been appointed to visit the county and investigate the disturbances.[35]

Even before the Committee on Militia approved Davis's action in Walker County, the Senate, on February 15, at the urging of Senator E. B. Picket resolved that a committee of two from the Senate and three from the House be selected to proceed to Huntsville to examine and fully report on "all the facts connected" with the upheaval and to ascertain the "present condition of affairs." The House was reluctant to challenge the governor's decision and simply wanted to approve what Davis had done. They desired to permit him to "pursue such course in the premises as he may deem necessary." On February 23, the House took cognizance of the Senate resolution to investigate the Huntsville fracas, but nothing further came from this matter.[36]

A month after Governor Davis imposed martial law, sixty-six Walker County residents questioned his declaration and attempted to deflect certain misrepresentations which had been made about their section. Although some claimed that there existed "a combination of lawless men too strong to be controlled by the civil authorities" and that certain officers "expressed an apprehension that it would be unsafe for them to perform their official duties," the citizens contended this was untrue. No such gang ravaged the area and the local officials could amply "preserve order and enforce the laws in this county." The petitioners only desired the "impartial *enforcement of the laws against all offenders without distinction of race or color.*"[37]

When Davidson left for Walker County, he ordered Captain McNelly to Huntsville to take charge of the State Police detachments. McNelly was to "go to work and have all parties arrested who assisted the prisoners to escape." In addition, Davidson summoned some of his best policemen: Captain George W. Farrow from Kosse, Lieutenant W. T. Pritchett from Waco, Sergeant W. C. Slade from Richmond, and Sergeant J. T. Browning from Hempstead. Colonel Gibbs was also present with forty men. Once all the State Police converged in Huntsville along with the Reserve Militia, a semblance of order was restored. A military tax would pay their upkeep. On February 22 a general courts martial was convened, its members selected by Davidson.[38]

Rather surprisingly, W. E. Horne, also a member of the 8th Regiment of the State Guard, was named Judge Advocate. (He served only temporarily.) Captain George W. Farrow and First Lieutenant B. F. Boldridge, both State Policemen, and First Lieutenant George H. Stacy, who belonged to the 8th Regiment, State Guard, along with Colonel Gibbs, First Lieutenant S. C. Graves, and First Lieutenant G. W. Jones, all of the 4th Regiment, Reserve Militia, and finally, the controversial Captain Goddin of the 1st Regiment, State Guard, completed the panel. All the selectees were Republicans of assorted stripes. Their commitment to the goals of the Davis administration varied considerably. They would deliberate for a little over a week.[39]

Once empanelled, the court martial proceedings began. Immediately, defense counsel James A. Baker, assisted by Abercrombie, Banton, Randolph, and McKinney, filed a "plea to the jurisdiction of the court." The lawyers contended the tribunal had limited powers and received its authority, life, and jurisdiction from statutes, orders from superior officers, or both, and the martial law declaration. Even though Governor Davis received the right to impose martial law from the Twelfth Legislature, this directly contradicted the Bill of Rights of both the State and United States Constitutions. Specifically, it violated the right of the accused to be indicted by a grand jury, to have a speedy public trial decided by an impartial jury, and not to be compelled to give evidence against himself. Any law contrary to these basic rights was inviolate and therefore void, especially as decided by the United States Supreme Court in the Milligan case. The state government might believe its action was necessary because the civil officers were powerless, but this was the plea "offered by every tyrant who seeks to rob a free people of their liberties."

The lawyers, however, emphasized the right of trial by jury. Even if the governor had the power to suspend the writ of habeas corpus and imprison individuals without assigning a cause for their detention, the law did not abrogate being tried by one's peers. This type of action could not even be taken from the people by a tyrannical commander of a military department in time of war. But even if the plea of the attorneys failed to convince the court, the defense insisted that their client had not been charged with any offense against the law, "written or unwritten, human or divine." In short, it was not a crime either in the civil or military code to aid a prisoner to escape from a state or county officer, even if he was legally held in custody. The tribunal rejected this argument.[40]

The majority of cases involved individuals accused of aiding, abetting, and facilitating the escape of John Wright on January 11. A few citizens were also charged with failing to assist and refusing aid to Sheriff Hess in pursuing the fugitives, Wright and Parrish. The initial trio, George W. Rather, Thomas Walker, and Willie Parrish, tried under the escape charge, produced a parade of black and white witnesses who presented conflicting testimony. Rather and Walker were found guilty and fined, but the fines were remitted. Parrish was acquitted of all charges.[41]

One of the two most significant cases decided by the court martial panel was that of Cyrus Hess, the much beleaguered former Walker County sheriff. Hess was charged with being an accessory in attempting to murder officers of the district court and in negligently permitting the prisoners to escape. He pleaded not guilty. The court found Hess not guilty on the accessory and complicity charge. Even though Hess had lived in Huntsville for many years and knew all the defendants in the original case, there was simply no evidence whatsoever he conspired to murder the officers of the district court or the State Policemen. Hess was a respectable man and highly thought of, but as sheriff he was out of his element. On the charge of negligently permitting the prisoners to escape, the court ruled Hess guilty and fined him $250. Although Adjutant General Davidson stated that the "sentence will be duly inflicted," he did not consider it "adequate to the offence of which the prisoner has been convicted."[42]

Nat Outlaw, who failed to escape on January 11, became the showcase defendant for the military court. Since that time he had been held in the state penitentiary. Outlaw was charged with the murder of Sam Jenkins, to which he pleaded not guilty. Represented by Baker, Maxey, Hightower, Abercrombie, and Banton, they filed a "plea to the jurisdiction of the court," but as in the other cases it was immediately overruled. Both sides agreed that the written evidence taken before District Judge Burnett in the January examination would be used, subject to all legal exceptions. The prosecution reserved the right to introduce further oral testimony as deemed necessary, and defense had the right to adduce evidence in rebuttal.[43]

Rather strangely, no testimony or witnesses were called in the Outlaw case. At least the records do not indicate a parade of individual statements. Nevertheless, the court found him guilty and sentenced him to five years in prison. Although Davidson approved the findings of the court, in his capacity as the reviewing officer he expressed his "unqualified disapprobation" of their action. The adjutant general reprimanded the six-member panel for the "uncalled for leniency" which they "extended towards a murderer, whose hands as proven, were red with the blood of a fellow being." His final admonishment was that "when the juries of the country fail to punish the assassin— Courts-Martial must fill the full measure of their duties."[44]

On March 11, 1871, in a move that must have shocked many, Governor Davis remitted the five-year sentence imposed upon Outlaw by the general court martial on March 4 and directed his release from the penitentiary. Davis argued that the evidence in Outlaw's alleged participation in killing Jenkins was "altogether circumstantial in its character." However, it did seem to the governor that the facts pointed to Outlaw as one of the parties engaged in the murder. If believed by the court, Davis observed, they should have declared him guilty of murder and sentenced him to the "extreme penalty of the law." But Davis concluded that the court disbelieved the testimony in full and proposed their initial sentence as a compromise.[45]

Amidst all the turmoil, Chief Davidson and Captain George W. Farrow became embroiled in a brief squabble. As of March 3, Farrow tendered his resignation as captain of the First Police District. He received a telegram from his wife, Anna Caroline, who lived in Kosse in Limestone County, stating that she was "very sick." Farrow requested a leave of absence for a few days to visit her. His request was denied. Farrow told Davidson that he was "satisfied that my wife would not have sent me a message" that she was quite ill, "unless she was actually in a *dying condition*." Farrow believed he owed it to his "wife and family to visit them at all hazards." Davidson relented and Farrow went to his wife, remaining a captain in the State Police.[46]

Even after Farrow's reinstatement, the relationship remained strained. The fact that the State Policeman sent bills to the head office for settlement rankled the chief. This practice would not be tolerated in the future, exclaimed Davidson, and if policemen persisted in doing this they would be dismissed. In addition, the *Houston Union* had reported that some of the military forces "behaved badly" toward Huntsville citizens. This was unacceptable. Complaints had reached Davidson that Farrow had been drunk and had abused a Huntsville resident by beating him over the head with a six-shooter. Finally, nearly every petition from Huntsville for remission of fines for individuals implicated in the courtroom affair bore Farrow's signature.[47]

The drunkenness and beating charge disturbed the adjutant general. "This conduct is unbecoming a police officer and will not be tolerated by the Department," Davidson wrote Farrow. He suspended the captain from his rank and pay until Farrow rendered a "full explanation exculpating yourself from these charges." Farrow complied, but Davidson was not happy. "When an officer has to appeal to his men for a certificate of good character it is considered that said character is strongly in need of support," stated the chief. He expected his officers to "maintain the same rigid discipline as that which is enforced in the regular army of the United States." Farrow received a reprimand and was sent back to Waco to assume command of that district.[48]

Although Davidson did not specifically plan for their examination, the State Police stationed in Huntsville after the martial law declaration came under the scrutiny of Dr. W. H. Webb. In late December 1870, Davidson appointed State Police Sergeant B. F. Boldridge as inspector. He would immediately proceed to various judicial districts, one of which was Walker County, to make a thorough investigation of the State Policemen in those particular areas. Boldridge was to report on their efficiency or inefficiency, and condition of their horses and arms, instruct them in their duties, and suggest ways to improve the organization. Webb scrutinized eighteen members of the force, including one captain and two sergeants; all was fine.[49]

Governor Davis kept abreast of the Huntsville situation and maintained a constant contact with Chief Davidson. He made certain that Davidson had enough men, although the chief of police complained that two of his officers had resigned and left. In addition, one private had quit the force and another was dismissed for leaving his post and conveying prisoners contrary to orders. Moreover, the adjutant general wanted to appropriate some of the fines the general courts martial levied to pay the troops. Proceeds from the military tax had not reached expectations. With the completion of the courts martial proceedings, all was quiet, and Davidson assured the governor that Judge Burnett could now hold his court with safety.[50]

As Davidson left Huntsville, he named Goddin as post commander to replace J. M. Gibbs. He would retain this position until all the assessed military tax was collected and he could determine the condition of affairs in Walker County. Then, martial law would be lifted. Goddin could not call out his company unless there was resistance to collecting the military tax or interference with military authority. If in doubt, Goddin would communicate with Davidson. Davidson concluded with the hope that Walker County citizens would not again "give cause for the inauguration of martial law and that when it is abrogated they will act in conformity with their promises" in "fearlessly sustaining the enforcement of the laws."[51]

After the brouhaha had subsided in Walker County, McNelly was interviewed by the editor of the *Galveston News*, a self-proclaimed Democratic supporter. The newspaper wondered why the captain's report of the occurrence had never been published. Although McNelly did not know why it had not appeared in print, he asserted that he had actually made two reports: one from Navasota and the second by mail eight or ten days after the courtroom shootout. The reporter asked the captain if he had recommended that martial law be imposed. McNelly believed "there was no occasion for it." Sheriff Hess was responsible for the disturbance as it was his duty to make certain the prisoners were disarmed when he had them in custody.[52]

McNelly mistakenly believed the prisoners had been searched. Otherwise he would have acted differently and could have taken the men to jail "without firing a shot." Although McNelly suspected he would have been stopped by the friends of Outlaw, Parish, and Wright (remember, Parks had been released) outside the courtroom, he confidently knew he could have overcome the opposition through reason. (His gift of gab must have overpowered his sense of writing. There is little correspondence from McNelly in the State Police records.) Even after the prisoners' escape, although other evidence does not support McNelly's view, he reiterated the belief that he could have enlisted the support of a hundred volunteers to pursue them if he had not been wounded.[53]

The reporter asked McNelly if martial law was declared because of money. "Possibly," he responded. Queried about a "determination on the part of the Austin authorities to force the people of Texas into resistance of authority," McNelly refused to reply. The reporter's opinions had been confirmed. The assertions made by McNelly indicated that no necessity existed for martial law, there were no Ku Kluxers in the district, and the governor used martial law as a guise to collect money. Moreover, state officials sought to disturb the public peace in order to force resistance from the people. Thus, claimed the News, a high-ranking State Policeman charged his superiors with the "blackest and most unmitigated villainy."[54]

With the publication of the interview, McNelly telegraphed Davidson that his words had been "garbled." Not anticipating the distribution of his comments, McNelly admitted his statements were "less guarded" than they should have been and he had failed to protect against the possibility that he might be misunderstood. McNelly was ordered to place the prisoners in the penitentiary for safekeeping while the preliminary examination took place, but the captain had already turned them over to the sheriff. He asserted that he intended to have all the parties who refused to obey the sheriff's orders indicted.[55]

McNelly would have been the first to denounce Davis and Davidson if he felt that they had been guilty of any crime. But the newspaper wrote that Mc-Nelly's correction was "lame, evasive and inadequate." If he made remarks impugning the "honesty, honor and political morality of his superiors," he was duty bound to stand by the admission. If not, he should have issued a denial and left the impression of the "substantial correctness" of the original conversation. Additionally, the *Daily State Journal*, the administration newspaper, believed McNelly's reply was not as "clear and able a defense" as the newspaper had expected. He should not have attempted to defend himself "unless he could have done so in a more pointed manner."[56]

In his favorite forum, the *Galveston News*, Maxey levied a tirade against Judge Burnett, District Attorney Horne, the Davis administration, and anything remotely connected to the Republican Party or its philosophy. He viewed the persecution of Outlaw, Parish, Wright, and Parks as a vast conspiracy and labeled Burnett a "political partisan judge," along with his numerous "dirty coadjutors," who plotted the "destruction of these young men" to "deprive them of their life and liberty." Burnett disregarded the testimony of "unimpeached white men, men of the highest standing," but gave full credit to the declarations of blacks; "albeit, those who testified to the identity" of two of the defendants "were shown to be perjured villains."[57]

As martial law continued, the animosity and bitterness which led to the killing of Jenkins and the courtroom gunfight carried over into personal grudges. On the morning of March 16, Judge Burnett and Maxey encountered each other in the post office. Burnett and some policemen stood in the door when Maxey came in to purchase a money order. Sympathetic to the Democrats, the *Galveston Daily News* wrote that Burnett called Maxey a liar and a scoundrel, which, in fact, he was. Maxey lunged at Burnett, and "they used their sticks freely on each other." Captain Farrow separated the two men with a drawn six-shooter to Maxey's head. Maxey and others believed that "there was a regular plot on the part of Burnett and the police to assassinate him."[58]

Democratic newspapers continued to rail at Davis throughout March 1871 for placing Walker County under martial law and having "citizens tried by self constituted Courts-martial, and upon mere exparte testimony arresting numbers" of them, "imprisoning, fining and dealing out vengeance through his willing satraps, whose only legal excuse would be that of incompetency to judge right and wrong." *Flake's Daily Bulletin* screamed that the "annals of oppression, nowhere, for centuries past, can furnish a more wanton abuse of authority" than exhibited in Walker County. The *San Antonio Daily Herald* referred to the affair as a "reign of force" and Davis as a "modern Caligula," and asserted that he was making "slaves" of Texans.[59]

William H. Sinclair, a former inspector for the Freedmen's Bureau and one of the ablest men that agency employed, announced in September 1871 an investigation of the money collected during martial law in Walker County. It had been publicly charged, Sinclair declared, that monies paid in both Hill and Walker counties had been "misappropriated, misapplied and embezzled" by Adjutant General Davidson. The chief of police was required to furnish the House a statement of all the funds he had collected by way of fines, taxes, and penalties. He was to submit a statement of all expenditures and how he disposed of them. The comptroller also had to furnish the House a list of all the vouchers filed by Davidson. Davidson was exonerated.[60]

In one month martial law was lifted. Walker County returned to a semblance of tranquility, but there was little Davis could do to stem the tide of violence. Outlaw had been pardoned, and there is no record that John Parish and Wright were ever punished for their role in the courthouse shooting. The area remained hostile to the police and the Republicans. This did not prevent them from requesting assistance, however. Even as late as 1872, Edward T. Randle desired the appointment of State Policemen for Walker County. He told Davidson that "we are having a hard fight of it and are entitled to whatever assistance you can give us." Randle directed Davidson to make the selection immediately or he would "conclude you do not intend to aid us *at all*."[61]

Tensions ran high during the summer of 1871, with martial law previously having been declared almost simultaneously in Hill and Walker counties. The citizens were restless, and a coalition of members of both political parties met in a Tax-Payer's Convention in Austin in September. The gathering denounced the state military system which Davis had established as "pets, favorites, and tools of the Governor." This anti-militia and anti–State Police sentiment pervaded the state.[62] The Walker County altercation had barely subsided when within six months trouble arose again in the blackland prairie section of central Texas, where a congressional election was in the offing. Strained race relations and the appearance of Special Policemen to ensure a fair election led to violence.

A Shamelessly Disloyal Community

THE STATE POLICE AND LIMESTONE/FREESTONE COUNTIES

During E. J. Davis's administration the blackland prairie region of Texas caused him considerable difficulties. Along with the earlier confrontation in Hill County, Limestone/Freestone counties presented the governor with additional trouble. In 1871, an impending tumultuous congressional election forced Davis to appoint several Special Policemen, a force created in the same year to oversee political activities, to make certain all voters were fairly registered, to maintain order at the polls in counties where they might be necessary to ensure an honest election, and to prevent a local crisis. No more than twenty of these policemen could be appointed for any county, and they were paid three dollars per diem by the county only for the time served.[1] It was the actions of the Special Policemen in this charged political atmosphere that led to the declaration of martial law. Throughout these events the State Police were also intimately involved.

In 1870 the Freestone County clerk, James King, despaired over the condition of affairs in his section of Texas. People joined the Ku Klux Klan and proceeded to murder various blacks, specifically those prominent in the Republican Party. The Klan threatened to kill even more African Americans if they did not quit meeting with party officials. If times became "any worse," King believed soldiers or a police force would be required. If sheriff-elect James Bonner Rogers were permitted to assume office (he was also marshal of the Klan), the Republicans would have a "ruff time." Rogers asserted that he would eliminate any recalcitrant black. King decried that it would "be alas to the darkey in this county."[2]

When the State Police appeared in the area, the *Bryan Appeal* reported on December 1, 1870, that a black member of the organization had killed a white man in Springfield. And, as so many newspapers gratuitously included in their accounts when writing about the police, intoxication played a part. The story, which attempted to discredit the police force, was not that simple. Actually it began when Virginia-born F. P. Wood, District Judge of the 35th Judicial District, ordered Sheriff Peyton Parker to close all drinking establishments during court sessions and to arrest anybody discovered wearing six-shooters. Shortly after this decree went into effect, three drunken men entered town with guns, one of which rode his horse into a store.[3]

Parker, hearing of the disturbance, called upon the State Police to assist him in arresting the offending parties. He requested that the policemen not interfere unless he encountered violent resistance. When the sheriff ordered the men to surrender, they drew their pistols. Two were immediately taken into custody, but one of the individuals fired at State Police Private Merritt Trammell, who was black. The ball passed through his hat, grazing his forehead, and the shock knocked him down. When Trammell got back upon his feet, he raised his shotgun and blasted away, instantly killing the white man. The police had done nothing more than their duty, and Trammell clearly acted in self-defense.[4]

District Judge Wood found Limestone County "public sentiment" unsupportive of law and order. Indeed, the climate of opinion was "unhealthy," worse than any county where he had recently held court. That Trammell was "fully justified" in killing the white man in order to save Parker's life made no difference. A black man had murdered (gunned down even) a white man, which "aroused and developed a latent feeling most unfavorable to the restoration of good government." Wood hoped that by a "strict execution of the law that this feeling may be crushed" and a better attitude developed. Unfortunately, tension continued to mount and would result in Davis's use of his executive power to interfere in county affairs.[5]

Local newspapers used sarcasm to demean the police. The *Kosse Enterprise*, under the heading "equality," claimed a "white" State Policeman ("we mean his cuticle is white") escorted a "negro wench" to Sanger's store. The policeman displayed his gallantry by holding the horse while "Dinah" stepped down. The *Enterprise* referred to this as the "first practical demonstration of social equality in Kosse" and snidely added: "Hurrah for civil rights, all the amendments, reconstruction acts, militia bill and our State Police." Captain George W. Farrow, "who seems to be a perfect gentleman," said the individual would be "discharged." It should be done immediately, screamed the *San Antonio Daily Herald*.[6]

Once the State Police assumed operations, the *Groesbeck Enterprise* took every opportunity to castigate them. Their musings, reprinted in the larger dailies of Texas, gave credence to unsupported charges. The *Enterprise* ignored the carnage committed against blacks but stated that on Tuesday, June 20, 1871, the police had perpetrated yet another "wanton murder" on the person of a Dr. Bradshaw, whose body was "completely riddled with bullets." He reportedly killed one policeman. The *San Antonio Daily Herald* was "not at all sorry" for the latter's death and asked: "How long, O, Lord!" Three months later the *Enterprise* noticed that two black policemen were in jail, allegedly with six murder indictments against them.[7]

Created from Robertson County and organized in 1846, Limestone County divides the ridge between the Trinity and Brazos rivers and is drained by the Navasota. In the "heart of the great agricultural region of Texas," declared the 1871 *Texas Almanac*, much of its land was tillable (about one-third was timber). An eastern and western split defined the topography, a post oak belt versus the blackland prairie. With an average three inches per month rainfall and a sixty-six degree mean temperature, the county seemed an ideal location. The economy depended upon lumbering, farming, and a few pottery works. Cotton emerged as a major crop after the war. Nevertheless, with few slaves, Limestone still became imbued with Old South principles.[8]

Springfield, the county seat, was a small village, but it benefited from the fact that it was on one of the main traveled roads between Houston and North Texas. Locally, it was connected with Fairfield (originally Mt. Pleasant and later the county seat of Freestone) and Palestine, the county seat of Anderson County. Incorporated by the legislature in 1848, the town had 120 residents and attracted gamblers and professional horse racers. By 1860, there were 400 people and several businesses. After the war, when the Houston and Texas Central Railroad sought to build through Springfield, a land price war broke out over the tracks being built three miles from town. Springfield never recovered and was basically abandoned but remained the political center of the county.[9]

In 1870, following the H. & T.C. Railroad decision to establish a town named Groesbeck after one of its directors, Abram Groesbeck, the fate of

Springfield was sealed. In 1871, when the riot occurred, Groesbeck may have had 1,000 residents. The fortunes of the town seemed to rise and fall with the railroad. In 1880, Groesbeck only had 402 citizens (even Kosse had a larger population). Part of the decline stemmed from the railroad's locating its next terminus at Corsicana, in Navarro County, and one in Mexia, which was but fifteen miles from Groesbeck. By 1890 the village had gained more than 260 new residents. Nevertheless, one reason for the clash was the shifting nature of Groesbeck's population and general hostility to the Republican program.[10]

Created from Limestone in 1850 and organized in 1851, Freestone was a slave haven focused upon growing cotton. Both counties were almost equal in physical size and had a similar climate. By 1860 a majority of Freestone's inhabitants (97 percent) had been born in slaveholding states and the slave population had grown from 200 to over 3,000. The bottom lands of the Trinity River (the eastern boundary of the county) and its tributaries, declared one observer, were "equal in every respect to the finest Red River or Mississippi" soil. Fairfield, the county seat, had 472 whites and 177 slaves in 1860, but declined to 358 residents in 1880. (Waco, a major inland town, only had 749 inhabitants in 1860.) The town of Cotton Gin also gained importance.[11]

Although Limestone had been organized earlier, Freestone quickly outstripped the former in population, both white and black. In 1860, Limestone had 4,537 residents, including 1,072 slaves. Freestone comprised 6,881 people, with 3,613 slaves. During the war, both counties experienced an almost twofold increase in their slave population. After the war, white immigration rose considerably. The black denizens increased numerically in Limestone, but their population percentage dwindled in both counties. In 1860, in Limestone, they comprised 24 percent of the citizens; 22 percent in 1870. For Freestone it was 53 percent in 1860 and 41 percent in 1870.[12]

The Freedmen's Bureau agent for this subdistrict, Charles E. Culver, had been gunned down in the streets of Cotton Gin (Freestone), along with an orderly, on November 15, 1867, by William Steward. (He was never prosecuted.) Before his death Culver believed this area to be "as shamelessly a disloyal community as was ever placed upon this earth," which described any town in either county. Individuals openly bragged to Culver that "we ain't whipped and never can be." Blacks were intimidated and "all resemblance of loyalty" was "lain aside and bitter invective" continuously assailed his ears.[13]

Politics also led to resentment and heightened tension. In 1870, in the race for the 19th District House seat to succeed the deceased Robert Crudup, who had died in July, the Republican George W. Patten defeated George Clark. In Limestone County, Patten polled 250 votes to 199 for his opponent. According to Registrar A. G. Moore, only six white men in Springfield voted for Patten, duly noted by the "rebel clerks." Moore, one of the six, told Governor Davis that the Democrats attempted various schemes to discredit the Republicans, but he felt the appointment of Judge Wood, "the rite man in the rite place," would counteract the "rebel democracy," although Davis had few friends among the state representatives. The Republicans faced formidable future opposition.[14]

Although they received little support from the locals, the State Police performed their duties. Two cattle thieves were arrested in Groesbeck by brothers Merritt and Giles Trammell (both black) at the request of the cattle and hide inspector. While transporting the rustlers to the Springfield jail, the two Trammells were attacked by a group of seven men, who aided the prisoners to escape. Two horses were shot in the encounter. But not all those convicted bolted, and the State Police delivered murderers and assorted other criminals for incarceration in Springfield. No matter how successful they proved to be, people desired their removal.[15]

Many in Limestone County despaired of the presence of black State Policemen and later, during the election in October 1871, of Special Policemen temporarily appointed to ensure a fair poll. Whites had previously organized themselves into various units of the Reserve Militia along with W. P. Richardson's Company A of the 5th Regiment of the State Guard. All these military guardians had been established in 1870, almost a year before the Groesbeck "riot." The muster rolls indicate that every individual who joined these companies was white. This was not the pattern that prevailed in other Texas counties where the State Guard tended to attract freedmen, but then Limestone and Freestone counties did not fit the mold.[16]

Merritt Trammell, a black man who headed the State Police in the Limestone/Freestone county area, had a mixed reputation among the local denizens. Nevertheless, Trammell performed his State Police responsibilities with seriousness. On Saturday afternoon September 30, 1871, Trammell was in Groesbeck in Clark's Saloon when J. L. Bolling, a local lawyer, told him that some fellows were "fixing to raise a row." Although Bolling did not identify the potential troublemakers, Trammell informed the on-duty Special Policemen (all black) to be particular about becoming involved in an altercation and "avoid any difficulty these fellows might try to raise." Trammell left for home, three miles outside Groesbeck.[17]

Around 4:30 p.m., after Trammel's departure, gunfire echoed off the walls of Clark's Saloon. A. F. Robbins in Lebermann's Tavern heard the shots and saw flashes of fire. (Groesbeck had a plethora of bars.) The "row" which Bolling had warned about and Trammell had cautioned the policemen to be wary of had come to pass. Dan Gallagher had been drunk and disorderly on the Groesbeck streets on Friday, September 29, and Saturday. He eventually became boisterous in front of Mayor Adolph Zadek's all-purpose establishment. Zadek, a German Jew, requested that he quiet down, but Gallagher ignored him. Mitchell Cotton (black), along with an assistant, arrested Gallagher for disturbing the peace.[18]

As the two policemen escorted Gallagher to jail, they encountered D. C. Applewhite, who told Zadek, "see if you don't see blood and trouble right away. See if he don't snatch one of the niggers pistol's and shoot one of them; I'd like to see one of them arrest me, I am always armed." Applewhite, who was clearly in a surly mood, approached Zadek about posting bond for Gallagher and asserted that "he wanted some damned policeman to try to arrest him." To quiet Applewhite, Zadek accepted him as one of the sureties for Gallagher. Gallagher then exclaimed to the policemen, "God damn your souls." Whether Applewhite and Gallagher knew each other is unknown, but their mutual dislike for the policemen and blacks made them drinking buddies.[19]

Applewhite and Gallagher were determined to provoke a difficulty. Applewhite told the two policemen, who did not respond, "damn them, he would like to see them try to arrest him." After completing the bond requirement with Mayor Zadek, Gallagher and Applewhite, along with John Strasburger and A. G. Hall, entered Clark's Saloon. Four black Special Policemen— Mitchell Cotton, Parson Nathan Jones, Isham Jones, and Festes Johnson ("a yellow man")—followed the white men into Clark's bar. According to one witness (and he was the only one who claimed it), some or all of the policemen may have been intoxicated. Clearly Gallagher was drunk, although Applewhite did not appear to have previously been drinking.[20]

Looking at Gallagher and Applewhite, one of the policemen (probably Cotton) declared, "you are our prisoners." The two white men claimed they had done nothing wrong. Applewhite said that "they can't take me; if they undertake it there will be an insurrection." Provocative words passed between the two white men and the black policemen. Applewhite stepped back, drew his derringer, which Zadek observed, and held it behind him. Cotton raised his "hand and pistol above his shoulder in a striking attitude" while the other policemen remained by the door. Various individuals in the bar hollered "don't shoot," but Cotton, according to lawyer J. S. Thurmond, shot Applewhite. Several other shots followed in quick succession.[21]

In the post office, Joseph F. Pells heard gunfire, as did W. H. McClelland. Foolishly, McClelland "ran into the street." B. Meyer observed a crowd gathered in front of Clark's barroom and saw Hall step out of the saloon and repeatedly holler "don't shoot, be quiet." Meyer noticed that several six-shooters had been raised in the bar and that directly afterwards three or four shots were fired. Applewhite "sprung at the policemen" but passed them and ran across Navasota Street, through French's Auction House and onto Waco Street, pursued by the state officers who continued to shoot at him. On a Saturday afternoon with several town residents either drinking or relaxing, there were many eyewitnesses.[22]

Manager P. H. French was sitting in the doorway of French's Auction House, opposite the saloon playing backgammon with J. L. Bolling, when the firing commenced. French saw two or three shots fired along with gunpowder flashes, but did not know who was responsible. Bolling remarked that it was getting "pretty warm" and they had better get out of range of the gunfire. French eventually returned to the doorway. During the shooting, John T. Dunbar sat on the platform in front of the Groesbeck Donnell House, a boarding establishment. A man informed Dunbar that somebody had been killed. Along with several other citizens, Dunbar went to investigate, as did French. Men were running and shouting: "'Arm and shoot the damned police!'"[23]

Several Groesbeckians saw Applewhite burst from the saloon (their stories were different) and run through French's Auction House followed by four "colored men with six-shooters" (many recognized Cotton), when one of the policemen remarked, "shoot the s.o.b. and take his heart's blood." They chased Applewhite into Waco Street, with several shots (some contended twelve) being fired. Pells observed all this and saw Applewhite fall into the street. Pells jumped in front of the Special Policemen and told them to fire no more as Applewhite was dying. One of them pointed his six-shooter at Pells and asked what he had to say about it. Cotton grabbed his colleague's hand and declared that he would not shoot Pells.[24]

As the policemen stood over Applewhite, George A. Hall heard reports of pistols and saw smoke. Allegedly they made threats that they "would take nothing from nobody." Cotton clutched a revolver in each hand and screamed at McClelland that he had "just killed a white son of a bitch" and if he could load his pistols he "would empty them into" Applewhite again. Pells believed Cotton had been shot in the mouth as blood oozed from it. Cotton told Pells he thought the bullet struck his arm, but he did not know where the ball had entered. Whether the wound was serious or not, Cotton and the other policemen moved toward the mayor's office seeking safety. Pells retreated in the direction of Applewhite's body.[25]

Both Robbins and McClelland approached Applewhite. The latter reached him first and raised the dying man into his arms. He asked Applewhite if he knew him. In the throes of dying, Applewhite nodded his head to signify yes. McClelland, a member of the later inquest and a friend of the auctioneer, clearly saw (as did B. Meyer) that Applewhite had in his hand a one-barrel derringer that had been discharged. (McClelland said that he felt "bad" about Applewhite being killed and was "excited" himself.) They assisted in carrying Applewhite's body into the saloon, but the dead man was later removed to French's Auction House, where he was placed on P. H. French's bed, a fitting place for the auctioneer to lie in repose.[26]

It was later determined that Applewhite had been hit six times, twice in the back. Some citizens contended his body was "literally riddled with balls." R. W. Scott, who stood seventy-five yards away, but in "open and perfect view" of the action, painted a grim death scene. He saw Applewhite clasp his arm around a building post. As the policemen arrived, he fell off the platform and appeared "nearly lifeless." The black men "sprang down, and standing over his body," one of them (probably Cotton) put his pistol against him and fired some three or four times, "each time raising [the body] partly erect while cocking his pistol, and each time when he fired he seemed to stoop and put the pistol against the breast" of auctioneer Applewhite.[27]

Dan Gallagher, the other major white participant, who had been drunk for two days, was observed by S. L. Stevenson standing over the body of Applewhite with a double-barreled shotgun. He was yelling for the white people to arm themselves and "kill the damned nigger state police." Once the body of Applewhite was taken inside, Gallagher ran up Navasota Street with his shotgun. As people rushed outside to determine what was happening, several shots were fired from different streets in Groesbeck. Gallagher continued his tirade and made numerous threats, the purport of which was that the men who had killed Applewhite should not live and that he was hunting the "son of a bitch" who had murdered him.[28]

After taking refuge in the mayor's office, the policemen defied the citizens to arrest or "take them." They prevented anyone from passing the office by presenting their six-shooters and ordering individuals to halt. Suddenly, a shot emanated from the mayor's office. No one was injured. From the time of Applewhite's killing until this incident, the citizens had remained unruly but not totally out of control. Zadek had disappeared. The policemen stood in the doorway hollering, making noise, showing their faces, and dodging back. Some residents agreed to form a committee of twenty-five men to arrest the policemen and promised that they should not be hurt. Ten black men were to be selected to disarm them and aid in transporting them to jail.[29]

Word spread quickly, and the crowd swelled with supporters from the countryside who were armed with shotguns. Inside Zadek's office, the police refused to surrender. Many in the mob wanted them dead or alive. Threats and cries of "kill the damned niggers" were made by those who had come in from outside Groesbeck. The "townies" attempted to quiet the disturbance. Somebody yelled that a "hundred armed negroes" were "coming on horseback, arm yourselves." The crowd dispersed. Several approached French's Auction House (where Applewhite's body remained), demanding guns. French initially refused, but finally relented and dispensed twenty-five shotguns to various individuals. Men began trading guns to prepare themselves for guard duty.[30]

With the rumor circulating that the freedmen numbering a hundred strong were coming to town, whites began to arm "themselves to the teeth." They displayed all kinds of weapons: shotguns, six-shooters, and other implements of destruction. Excitement among the growing assembly was reaching a crescendo; individuals gave incendiary speeches, the gist of which was that the policemen should be killed or, at the very least, "dealt with severely." No one seemed to be in command. Two men addressed the crowd and told them to put away their weapons and that the arrest of the policemen would be effected. Although no agreement existed, the crowd seemed unwilling to let the authorities take the policemen into custody.[31]

The "infuriated crowd" accosted Zadek outside his office and intimidated him into issuing an arrest warrant for the policemen. To further appease the mob, the mayor, according to several accounts, encouraged the citizens to arm. (A resident claimed that up to this time none were "in arms.") By now, with "lawlessness and mobocracy" prevailing, men riding into town armed with double-barreled shotguns, and gunfire erupting from every section of Groesbeck, a full-scale riot seemed a likely possibility. Whites were warned to arm themselves because blacks had weapons and reportedly were marching on Groesbeck. The town was at the "highest pitch" of excitement. Many white Republicans immediately left the town, seeking safety.[32]

Stevenson visited the mayor's office during the excitement and confusion following Applewhite's death. There he saw Cotton, Isham Jones, Parson

Nathan Jones, and various others. He claimed that some of the policemen had been drinking and were partially intoxicated; at least he thought Cotton was drunk. Armed with shotguns and pistols, McClelland, who was also present, advised the Special Policemen to surrender to the civil authorities. They refused to place themselves in the custody of white men and contended they would only capitulate to "colored officers." During this exchange, Cotton stood by the door monitoring the movement and action of the citizens in order to warn the others if they charged Zadek's office.[33]

An hour after the initial shooting, McClelland, Meyer, and Hall saw Trammell ride into town, accompanied by ten to twenty-five armed black policemen. W. A. Patterson, Hall, and Abram Anglin met Trammell. Trammell announced he would arrest the Applewhite killers and stated he could whip twenty-five of the best white men in Groesbeck, but he wanted nothing but what was right. He also said he could command three hundred men. Whites were not afraid of Trammell, claimed Patterson, Hall, and Anglin. Barricaded in the mayor's office, the Special Policemen "defied the authorities and citizens to arrest them, flourishing their six-shooters and firing two or three [warning] shots at parties who were quietly passing on the opposite side of the street."[34]

Trammell and his associates consulted for a considerable time, apparently devising a plan of escape. While Stevenson talked, the Special Policemen rushed out of Zadek's office. Trammell seized the opportunity, and along with Cotton, four or five other State Policemen, and the Springfield contingent, retreated from Groesbeck in the opposite direction of the mob. One witness alleged that the group uttered "threats against the town and white people generally," firing into the air as they left Groesbeck. The policemen and their cohorts, who may have numbered from thirty to fifty, rode about two hundred yards outside of town. They reconnoitered and proceeded to Merritt's home, where the State Police had previously established a local base.[35]

After Trammell had escorted the policemen out of town and away from what would surely have been a lynch mob, the crowd decided that it should go down to the river bottom where the blacks were allegedly congregated, ready for a fight. They still sought revenge on those responsible for Applewhite's death. This citizen conglomeration became even more excited and began to arrange themselves into companies in order to follow the perpetrators. The responsible inhabitants went home, but throughout the night bugle calls and random gunfire continued. Groesbeckians may not have slept much as the situation continued to be disruptive and confusion reigned. A major confrontation seemed to be in the offing.[36]

Merritt (he is also often listed as Merrick) Trammell is one of those elusive figures, black or white, in history that have been described in a variety of ways, but his background has rarely been investigated. When a writer interviewed a nephew of Trammell, Roy (Nig) Trammell, he contended that Merritt was "mean as a snake." But an octogenarian niece of Trammell's, Roberta Williams, claimed "he wasn't an OUTLAW!" According to the 1870 census, he was thirty-eight years of age, a planter, born in Georgia, whose wife, Elizabeth, thirty-three, was a Texas native. With six children (ages fourteen, thirteen, eleven, nine, eight, and six), Trammell was also a preacher and according to local legend propped a shotgun next to the pulpit when he sermonized.[37]

The Trammells had been slaves of Logan A. Stroud, the largest slave owner in Limestone County. Brought to Texas from Georgia, where Stroud had been born, Merritt Trammell was approximately thirty-three years old when freed. During slavery he had been a surreptitious "practicing preacher." One writer mystically and unintelligibly declares that "his African genetic marker, 'amandla,' 'ushujaa,' merged with his environmental factors," produced a "militant ex-slave." Trammell was a bane to the white community. Some described him as a "professional outlaw," but others found his influence and protection necessary. To many, he was the "greatest surprise in Limestone County during Reconstruction."[38]

Shortly after the establishment of the State Police in mid-1870, two of the Trammell brothers (Merritt and Giles) immediately joined the force. While Merritt believed in God as his "spiritual equalizer," he found it necessary to support his belief with a "physical equalizer" (the famous shotgun). Although he may have built the first black church in Limestone County and was referred to as a minister, Trammell led a tempestuous life. After his involvement in the Limestone County martial law affair, he was the leader in dispatching Simp "Dixie" Dixon (a relative of John Wesley Hardin), also a notorious desperado who had murdered a number of African Americans.[39]

Trammell had little economic worth. In 1869, before becoming a State Policeman, he had three horses assessed at seventy-five dollars and assorted property worth ten dollars. By 1870, the value of his horses had increased by twenty-five dollars and his miscellaneous possessions were valued at ninety dollars. After the demise of the State Police, Trammell, the "notorious negro," or "the terror," became an outlaw and desperado. He killed, according to one newspaper account, four men in the Mexia vicinity. When a posse of eight men attempted to capture him three weeks before his death, Trammell killed one of the group named Robert Glendenin. If caught, one newspaper punned, "he will find himself grievously trammeled in all his movements, and, however merrickorious, will hang."[40]

When Trammell, described as a "negro desperado," was dispatched in 1875 by M. D. L. Harcrow, the newspapers evinced a certain schizophrenia about his character and influence. The *Daily Democratic Statesman* declared that Harcrow filled Trammell's body with buckshot, hauled it to Groesbeck, and delivered it to the sheriff with the remark, "here's yer nigger." The *Statesman* opined that the people of the town would "now sleep more quietly of nights" and that Harcrow should receive his reward, which amounted to five hundred dollars. It was reported that "hundreds of persons flocked" to "identify the body, and many a man breathed easier when he saw the black ruffian lying stark in death."[41]

The *San Antonio Daily Express*, a Republican rag, believed Trammell, who had acquired property and a farm, to be a "brave, bold, industrious man, naturally a leader among his people." He became a "rallying point for a number of his people," and thus a "marked man by the local democracy." What Trammell's death illustrated was a "condition of government" that tolerated "barbarism and crime" and placed a "premium upon murder if committed upon the 'nigger.'" It was the "greatest crime of all for a negro to become the owner of a homestead and to be ready to defend himself against a mob." Trammell "may have been a desperate bad man, but he was made so, and his greatest crime was evidently the black skin the Almighty had clothed him with."[42]

One history of Limestone County, written and compiled by blacks, declared that Trammell was "looked on by the white folks as a person who spreaded [sic] dissension among his group and too, he was high tempered and had the reputation of a fighter." The "industrious hard working Trammell brothers," said one writer, "did not aspire to be outlaws." As "freedmen and State Policemen they made gut responses to danger and violence." Referring to him as "Trammel—The Terror," some credited him with the killing of Applewhite, which led Davis to declare martial law. A week after Trammell's death, the black community gathered on the banks of "Jack's Creek and Nigger Creek" to pay their respects and lament his passing.[43]

Due to the heightened emotional state of Groesbeck residents, tragedy could not be averted. Between 10 and 11 p.m. on Saturday night, a few men appeared at the doorway of an "unoffending, innocent" black man named Robert Lee, a liquor store clerk. Lee came out, but was ordered to halt. "Don't you know me?" he replied. Somebody yelled, "pull down on him" and a white man by the name of A. M. Simons (a declared "lunatic") shot Lee. Charged with murder, Simons was arrested and jailed at Springfield. The acting city officials (Charles Eika, D. W. Lewis, and J. D. Robertson) called in medical attendance and conversed with Lee, but he died an hour later.[44]

While the upheaval was occurring in Groesbeck, Limestone County Sheriff Simpson M. Young and his deputy, Captain Newton, headquartered at Springfield, learned of the Applewhite shooting. After they visited the scene, Newton felt lucky to get out alive and Young declared the mob "past all reason," forcing Mayor Zadek to follow their dictates. When Young and Newton returned to Springfield, prominent residents, including W. P. Brown, Dr. M. Kemp, Captain W. H. Richardson, H. M. Roberts, Captain J. W. Stevens, J. L. Farrar, and J. R. Johnson, requested that W. B. Bonner, registrar and district clerk, organize the State Guard. Richardson had called out his company when he heard of the Applewhite killing. Bonner intended to summon the State Police and Special Policemen to restore law and order. The citizens said the "mere sight" of blacks would lead to bloodshed. All African Americans should be kept "out of the way." The committee authorized Captain Richardson's troops (Company A, 5th Regiment, State Guard) to "restrain the mad mob" at Groesbeck, apprehend Applewhite's murderers, and ensure the safety of all Radicals and blacks.[45]

Justice of the Peace Sidney M. Jones and Sheriff Young, accompanied by others, allegedly went to the "boys" (meaning the black policemen), spoke to the men in their hiding place, and promised them that they would be protected and that their colleagues would be safely transported to jail. The accused were persuaded to surrender with the assurance that their lives would be preserved and the Groesbeck mob disarmed. Once they received the promise that the policemen's lives would be safe, the Trammells' followers also insisted they be allowed to accompany their cohorts to jail. It was agreed that twenty blacks and twenty whites would safeguard their passage to Springfield.[46]

After the surrender, the men were escorted to the courthouse in Springfield and placed under a guard of twenty white and twenty black militia. (The wounded man, Cotton, was in no condition to be jailed.) Some citizens proposed charging the courthouse and seizing the prisoners as they desired a "fight with the negroes." As the guards established themselves, a company of armed men from Groesbeck rode into Springfield and allowed Young five minutes to incarcerate the men. Unless this had been done, argued the county officials, a "general massacre of Republicans and negroes would have been the result." Several attempts, all thwarted, were made to fire upon the policemen as they were taken to jail.[47]

Three weeks before turmoil engulfed Groesbeck and all of Limestone County, Texans prepared to go to the polls to elect a congressman and other state and local officials. In this political environment, much hostility had been generated because of the policies of the Davis administration and the fact that the former slaves had been enfranchised. A resurgent Democratic Party planned to oust the Republicans. Voter registration began on September 12 and continued consecutively for the next ten days without interruption. On September 28, the Board of Revision began to discharge their duties to make certain all registrants were qualified. Their deliberations progressed quietly and efficiently.[48]

This special 1871 election would determine the four Texas congressmen who would sit in the national House of Representatives. Scheduled for October 3 through 6, the elections in Limestone and Freestone counties opened amid a tense and potentially volatile situation. As part of the Third Congressional District, county inhabitants had a choice between the Democrat D. C. Giddings and Republican W. C. Clark. Clark was declared the winner, but Giddings contested the outcome and the national House of Representatives supported his claim. Giddings was sworn in, but Limestone and Freestone became the center of controversy because of voting irregularities. The returns were thrown out.[49]

As the county inhabitants voted, a visitor to the area described a frightening scene. "The rebels everywhere are fired up terribly, and they hate the Government and despise and abuse its friends just as they did at the beginning of the war," he wrote. The "Ku-Klux, rebel Democracy," who committed "wholesale butchery" upon black and white loyalists, only understood "power and punishment." Even the law-abiding Democrats did not "comprehend the bitterness and hatred that is rampant in Texas to-day." Being neither bitter nor revengeful themselves, they failed to understand that Texas was "almost in a state of rebellion, and that nothing but immediate and positive action on the part of the government will prevent an outbreak."[50]

The Groesbeck Democratic Party stirred the winds of upheaval, encouraging every member to register "without a moment's unnecessary delay." A Democratic circular, issued on September 15, announced that "undoubted testimony has been received that the Radical element will be required to Register AT ONCE, and that a scheme is on foot to immediately thereafter cause [a] disturbance, so that there shall be grounds to close the books and thereby defeat a full registry of the Democracy." The "hour has come," the party believed, "when peace, order, society and good Government all demand that the intelligence and virtue" of the people be deployed for the "preservation of constitutional liberty."[51]

No matter what white or black observers related, something was askew with the 1871 Limestone County election. For a brief comparison it is worthwhile to see what happened in the election two years previously. In 1869, although the Democrats boycotted the gubernatorial and state contest, the county had 1,152 registered voters divided between 768 whites and 384 blacks, of whom approximately 90 percent of the latter voted Republican. Secretary of State James P. Newcomb reported that in 1871, 1,178 whites cast ballots as compared to only 11 blacks. (The total freedmen registered were 844.) The Democratic candidate for Congress, D. C. Giddings, received a staggering 1,153 votes to the Republican W. C. Clark's measly 28 votes.[52]

Although Applewhite's death and the subsequent upheaval prevented a "fair and free expression of political sentiment," according to the election officials, balloting occurred. The "political bitterness and rancor" led "to the utmost tension of political prejudice." Violence and intimidation prevented a large number of qualified electors from going to the polls. Blacks abandoned the voting booth and white Republicans were intimidated. Democrats became "masters of the field" and vowed vengeance upon their opponents. During the election, the county was wild with excitement, all of which made it impossible to secure "a full, fair and impartial vote." Democrats received almost the entire vote.[53]

Governor Davis was quickly apprised of the Groesbeck and Limestone County troubles—in person, by telegraph, and by horseback courier. With the election still in progress, but almost completed, he selected Mississippi-born District Judge John W. Oliver, of the 33rd Judicial District, who arrived in Texas by 1865, to attempt to sort out the Limestone County mess. And a mess it was. Oliver, not the most even-tempered man, took charge. He swore in a number of citizens as a "special constable force," commanded by C. S. Mitchell. Oliver queried Mitchell as to whether civil law could be enforced and whether writs could be executed. Mitchell claimed there was no obstacle in the way of the civil government exercising its power. Mitchell said that Sheriff Young agreed with his viewpoint.[54]

Davis required that Oliver proceed with firmness in bringing the scoundrels to justice and "not *yield an inch* to the wishes of the mob." Davis had ordered State Police Captain George W. Farrow, "a good officer," to take charge of all police and peace officers in Limestone County. He had also directed Sergeant B. H. Boldridge to report to Farrow with all the available forces in his subdistrict as soon as the election was over. In the meantime, he prepared a State Guard force to send if required. Already contemplating martial law, Davis was thinking that property holders should pay the expenses for five hundred to one thousand troops, as they had composed part of the mob and could have suppressed the upheaval if they had been so disposed.[55]

On October 9, 1871, Governor Davis declared martial law in Limestone and Freestone counties. A variety of sources corroborated the existence of a "combination of lawless men claiming themselves to consist of several thousand persons organized as an insurrectionary force, too strong for the control of the civil authorities." They killed unarmed and "unoffending" citizens in their own homes. Their many other illegal acts included carrying pistols and other weapons, discharging firearms in public places, intimidating the Limestone County civil officials, preventing a fair election, placing pickets upon the public highways, interfering with the United States mail, and cutting telegraph wires.[56]

Davis emphasized that these armed and organized bodies existed contrary to law and were too numerous to be arrested and held by the civil authorities and/or to be tried by the district court. Thus, he felt that the only remedy was to proclaim martial law, suspend the laws, and deny the writ of habeas corpus to anyone until the legislature should take such action as it deemed necessary, or the proclamation was revoked. The governor assessed Limestone County fifty thousand dollars (3 percent on all taxable property), or whatever part of that sum which was necessary, to be levied and collected from all real estate listed on the tax rolls to pay for the occupation. In taking this action, Davis carefully followed the laws enacted by the Twelfth Legislature.[57]

Twenty prominent Groesbeck citizens and other residents sent opposing resolutions to Senator M. H. Bowers and Representatives W. P. McLean and J. W. Robertson (the only assemblyman from both counties) for presentation to the legislature. They blamed the upheaval on four black Special (not State as they claimed) Policemen who murdered a white man and then barricaded themselves in the mayor's office (their number now swollen to twenty) and refused to surrender. The mayor lost control, the police fled, pursued by a posse. When the two races encountered each other, the policemen had been "reinforced by about two hundred colored men, all armed." Eventually, two alleged (not four) murderers were arrested. Quiet returned.[58]

Republican residents had a different perspective. Eight days before the martial law declaration, the sheriff, the registrar/district clerk, and a justice of the peace/judge of the election, S. P. Young, W. B. Bonner, and Sidney M.

Jones respectively, painted a different picture. They exclaimed that "our county is now in a state of riot and insubordination," which demanded Davis's attention. These Republicans disagreed with the outlook of the Groesbeck residents. A policeman had attempted to arrest a man for carrying a concealed weapon, who in turn wounded him. Gunfire was returned, other policemen interfered, and the man carrying the hidden weapon was "dispatched by several shots." A "general uprising" ensued.[59]

The governor acted. He sent Judge Jones a copy of the martial law proclamation for Limestone and Freestone. Davis included the latter county, he informed Judge Oliver, only because he understood that some of the rioters were from there, and that their organization extended into that section. In fact, in terms of the election, Freestone County may have experienced more upheaval than Limestone. Davis told Oliver that Major General A. G. Malloy had left Jefferson with two hundred men and would reach Groesbeck within a week. He would take command of the district. Oliver should remain at Groesbeck and confer with Malloy when the latter arrived.[60]

The next day Davis telegraphed Adjutant General Davidson and ordered him to Groesbeck, if his health permitted. Davidson's object was to organize the enforcement of martial law and arrange for the establishment of a military commission. The governor recommended Malloy as president. Other officers ordered to Groesbeck to compose the military tribunal were Colonel George W. Smith, Colonel Jacob DeGress, Colonel Dickinson, who would serve as the judge advocate, Lieutenant Colonel A. R. Parson, Major Stanley Welch, Colonel Jacob Wagner, Colonel Charles Parker, and Captain Eakin, who was at Sherman. If any of the officers failed to arrive, they had to be replaced by men who could be relied upon to punish according to the proof.[61]

Altogether, Davis estimated that 350 to 400 troops would be present in the county and any calculation of what the costs would entail had to be based upon those numbers. If Davidson discovered that he could perform all the necessary military functions with a smaller force than the governor proposed, the surplus would be ordered home. If men from the Seguin command reached Groesbeck, as Davis had so ordered, they had carbines which could be loaned to those who did not have them. They were to be returned to the state arsenal.[62]

Davis also informed the state House and Senate that he had declared martial law in Limestone and Freestone counties. The House immediately adopted a resolution requiring evidence for the governor's action. Davis submitted copies of letters, and, in addition, provided considerable verbal information from persons who had come from the disturbed district. Some residents and other travelers through the affected counties had made a special trip to inform Davis of the condition of affairs. The informants, Wagner, Joseph F. Pells (the Groesbeck city marshal), and Sidney M. Jones (a justice of the peace and an election judge in Limestone County), spoke of insurrectionists, mail stoppage, the cutting of telegraph wires, and coercion exercised over county officers and citizens.[63]

On October 8, 1871, a day before Davis imposed martial law, the governor telegraphed Major General A. G. Malloy of the State Militia, who was headquartered at Jefferson (Marion County) 188 miles from Groesbeck, ordering him to proceed "at once" to Limestone County "with two hundred picked men fully armed, and with one hundred rounds of ammunition." He was also to hire the necessary transportation, "make all possible despatch," and would receive further instructions when he arrived at his destination. Malloy began immediate preparation and initially raised only 120 men. He did, however, hire five wagons and one ambulance and purchase uniforms, supplies, ammunition, and shotguns, as the arms promised by the state had not yet arrived.[64]

When Malloy sought volunteers for his command, he could only find eight or nine white citizens who "showed a willingness to offer their services. Consequently colored men were selected for the duty." At Jefferson and Marshall, many "hundreds more than were required" volunteered their services. Malloy "necessarily rejected" them. He claimed that his "men behaved admirably during the march." He enforced the strictest discipline, and no man was "permitted to enter the door yard of a citizen, even to obtain water, without orders." That blacks composed the majority of Malloy's troops is not surprising. Blacks supported Davis when he attempted to protect their right to vote, the precise reason for their presence in Limestone County.[65]

When the state troops crossed the Trinity River they discovered a hundred horses saddled and bridled "for miles along the road," and armed men observed their passage. Rumors circulated that the citizens planned to attack them, and "inflammatory harangues were openly made" by the local denizens. One urged that the citizens arm themselves and prevent the passage of the governor's minions. Malloy was persuaded that they were "only deterred from open violence by the belief" that these men were "Regular troops" (probably due to most of them being in a uniform). Malloy's experience was paralleled by the journey of the United States Marshal for the Western District of Texas, Major Thomas F. Purnell, who encountered similar "rebellious spirits."[66]

Those opposed to the governor's action declared that "they had stood this kind of thing long enough and were not going to do so any longer." Through this gauntlet Malloy purchased and paid for forage through the largesse of William Urndenstock, editor of the *Marshall Weekly*, who advanced the necessary funds. When the group reached Groesbeck, they found Colonel G. W. Smith of the State Guards with ninety-two Reserve Militia from Houston, along with members of the State Police. When Malloy ordered the Houston group home, he appropriated eighty-one Winchester rifles. Fortunately, some of the Groesbeck citizens advanced a portion of their "prospective Military tax," which sufficed to pay the men off and to settle their local subsistence bills while in the county.[67]

From the inception of martial law, relations between Captain Farrow and District Judge Oliver quickly deteriorated, due to the latter's perception of his importance. Judge Oliver had assured Farrow that he would make out a list of men's names that he desired arrested and give it to the captain or issue warrants, supplying Farrow with a copy. But he procrastinated in completing this task, which led to missed opportunities. Oliver's tardiness in performing this task proved disastrous. His delay "gave ample time for the escape of nearly all parties who thought themselves in any imminent danger of arrest, and very serious trouble by reason of a strict enforcement of the law," wrote a disgusted Captain Farrow.[68]

Clashes continued over who would direct the martial law forces. Farrow assured Davidson that he would "*command the police force*" and cared nothing for who controlled the militia. As Farrow had been selected as the state's financial agent to collect the military tax, he left Sergeant Boldridge in command and would have no difficulty cooperating with him as the sergeant had served under Farrow for more than three years. To complicate the situation, the head of the militia, George W. Smith, desired to command the State Police because of his militia rank. Farrow believed this "an outrage," and Smith had the temerity to arrest him. The captain acquiesced as he wished no conflict, not because he was guilty of any crime or neglect of duty.[69]

By late October, there were forty-two members of the police force in Groesbeck, twenty-seven regular State Policemen and fifteen Special. Sergeant Boldridge had sent out scouts in search of parties implicated in the riot. They had been unable to capture the ringleaders, and the sergeant feared that the "worst characters" had entirely disappeared.[70]

All was comparatively quiet but "much bitter feeling" and hostility existed against the Guard, the state government, and the police, although presently "somewhat smothered down," wrote the sergeant. Approximately 150 militia, along with State and Special Policemen, were stationed in the two counties. Most of the police were "broke as flat as a flounder" and almost destitute of clothing. If possible, Davidson should send the members one month's pay. They labored under many disadvantages on account of their pecuniary condition. Similar to Farrow, Boldridge had some difficulties with Colonel Smith. Nevertheless, a number of arrests were made despite his interference. The responsible policemen deserved the credit.[71]

On October 24, Farrow, as Special Agent for the State of Texas for Limestone County, issued a circular about the collection of the special military tax. Through orders received from Malloy, he ordered the levying of a total assessment of forty thousand dollars, to be paid by the county citizens to defray expenses of the military commission and State Troops quartered in the area. The tax would be assessed at 3 percent on every one hundred dollars of taxable county property as per the assessment rolls of 1871. All persons owning property in Limestone County were notified to "immediately" appear at his office and pay it. For all who refused or failed to pay within three days, a 10 percent penalty would be added and their property levied upon and sold to satisfy the tax.[72]

Disputes arose about individuals who had already paid their special tax in order to make certain their property would not be seized and sold at auction, but a true account of everything appropriated or collected by representatives of the state was not centrally compiled. The Groesbeck city officers desired part of the tax to pay salaries and the town's indebtedness. Most property seized during the imposition of martial law was redeemed by the owners, but not all. The major controversy arose over the seizing of corn, mules, ponies, and a horse and buggy. Although not of a significant monetary value, these items led to conflicts among the citizens affected and the state administration. Almost all the cases were adjudicated amicably.[73]

Swindling and graft did occur during the period martial law was in force, but the State Police were not implicated. A. G. Malloy contended that Stanley Welch and his son bilked the state out of one-half the property they brought from Springfield. It included some of the French shotguns and other state property. From the merchants who supplied the initial expedition, they extorted 20 percent, claiming they had been paid in full by the state. Teams were hired at $5 per day and the state charged $7.50. Only three-fifths rations were issued to the men. Welch, asserted Malloy, made over $5,000 from these transactions. H. W. Monroe informed the chief that Welch had taken $1,000 in gold and never reported it. The scoundrels should be arrested.[74]

Chief of Police Davidson did not arrive in Groesbeck until October 28. After surveying the scene, the adjutant general directed that Malloy's troops from Jefferson be relieved and return home. He also discharged all the Special

NOTICE!

SPECIAL MILITARY TAX!

Office Special Agent, State of Texas,

Groesbeeck, Limestone Co., Texas,

OCTOBER 24th, 1871.

Pursuant to orders received from

Major General H. G. Maloy, commanding State forces in Limestone County, I am ordered to assess and levy a SPECIAL MILITARY TAX OF FORTY THOUSAND DOLLARS, ($40,000 00,) to be paid by the citizens of Limestone County, to defray the expenses of Military Commission and State Troops now on duty in said County.

I therefore levy a Tax of ~3~ per cent. on the hundred dollars of all taxable property situated in said County, as per Assessment Rolls of 1871.

All persons owning property in Limestone County are notified to appear at my office, in the city of Groesbeeck, *immediately,* and pay the same. All persons refusing or failing to pay said Tax within three [3] days from above date, ten [10] per cent. will be added, and their property levied upon and sold to satisfy said Tax.

GEO. W. FARROW,

Special Agent State of Texas for Limestone County.

This broadside was used to notify the citizens of Limestone County of the levying of a special military tax to help defray the costs of the governor's imposition of martial law in October 1871. *Courtesy of the Texas State Library and Archives Commission.*

Policemen in the two counties. The militia company from Houston had previously been directed to return to the Bayou City. By drastically reducing the numbers of troops stationed in Limestone and Freestone counties, the military tax was proportionally reduced from $40,000, as first assessed, to about $24,000. Davidson believed this sum would cover all expenses incident upon the declaration of martial law.[75]

Captain Farrow, who remained in the area for approximately six weeks and thus had the opportunity to gauge public opinion, believed that the course Davidson pursued while at Groesbeck met with the approval of almost "all good citizens irrespective of party." Judge Wood, who also visited Groesbeck during the imposition of martial law, concurred with Farrow's appraisal. Wood asserted that a majority agreed that Davidson discharged his duties "*fearlessly* and *fairly* and with proper regard" to the inhabitants' "individual rights." The Chief of Police had repeatedly urged the residents to pay the military tax necessary to compensate the troops. This was the only mode of relief from their condition.[76]

Even if the House did not support Davis's policies in Limestone County, militia leaders believed he had acted properly. On their arrival at Groesbeck, Malloy, Smith, Welch, and Griffin "found an intense bitterness of feeling evinced on the part of all who had acted with the mob, and open expression of incendiary sentiments still gave evidence of the fever heat to which the spirit of the insurrectionists had raised." From reliable sources, it was "plain that the riot" was "preconceived and premeditated by a class of men who belonged to regular organized political societies." The "pretext for a precipitation of their intended violence" came from Applewhite's death, but, in fact, "had but little to do with the outbreak."[77]

Klan meetings were held eight miles outside Groesbeck, all of which strongly pointed to the fact that the "insurrection was preplanned and part of an electioneering programme to be carried out." Intimidation of Republicans was commonplace, their property threatened to be burned. Opposition arose to pay the military tax through "tricks and devices," spies abounded, "emissaries from the camps of the violators of the law" roamed about, and the overall animus of the inhabitants was unbelievable. As a result, the collection of the tax proceeded slowly, which only increased the bitterness. If there had been a "laxity of vigilance on the part of the State officers, an attack upon their force would have been made."[78]

Much controversy and confusion surrounds the background and events which led to Governor Davis's declaration of martial law in Limestone and

Freestone counties. Ideology and politics dictated the response of individuals and newspapers to how the administration handled the situation. Even the state House of Representatives censured Davis for placing the two counties under military rule. The testimony of numerous eyewitnesses, observers, and participants in the events was certainly colored by an individual's political affiliation. Mistakes were made by those who supported and implemented the governor's action, but those who steadfastly opposed Republican rule were clearly not blameless. The course they pursued brought harsh consequences.

During and after the brief period of martial law, violence continued to plague the blackland prairie. Outlaws such as Ed Pierce, along with his sidekick Bill McIver of Madison County notoriety, roamed the countryside harassing whites and blacks, mostly the latter. Freedmen complained about violence perpetrated upon them, and Henry Huckaby Senior and Junior were murdered early in 1872. Stories were rampant that former slaves were being eradicated at an alarming rate. One former resident stated that seventeen blacks were killed in Limestone County in one day. Black churches and schools were burned. The body count continued to rise and even included a policeman.[79]

Violence did not abate after the martial law episode in late 1871. By early 1872, the mayor, district clerk, and marshal of Groesbeck reported that "general quietude" prevailed in their region. "Only" four black men had been shot in Limestone County within the past month. The *Daily Herald*, always quick to exploit any situation embarrassing to the Davis administration, stated that as "no citizen is allowed to bear arms, other than the State Police and the pet radicals of the Governor's set, this shooting must have been done by them." The editor inferred that due to the state constabulary's dereliction of duty, the rumor circulated that Davis had "threatened to disband a part of the State Police force."[80]

The *Daily Herald* might belittle Davis and the State Police, but black men and women continued to die in Limestone County. Sheriff S. M. Jones shot a man who had testified about the election irregularities of 1871. Not long before the legislature disbanded the State Police in 1873, forty-two men petitioned the adjutant general requesting a contingent of policemen. "Outlaws have overrun and hold in awe the good people" of the county, they stated. This "intolerable evil" had to be remedied. In addition, unknown assassins had attempted to murder the sheriff, which clearly demonstrated the "sad condition of affairs." At this point, Davis could do little as the police were soon legislated out of existence.[81]

But what happened in Limestone County with the Applewhite murder and its aftermath long remained in the memories of many of the citizens who had opposed the Davis regime. In 1874, after the ascension of a Democratic governor, Richard Coke, an indictment was found against Joseph F. Pells for first-degree murder in the slaying of Applewhite. During that event, Pells had been Groesbeck marshal and deputy postmaster. At the initial trial in Limestone County, Pells was convicted and sentenced to life imprisonment. The judge declared a mistrial and changed the venue to Marlin (Falls County). Additional witnesses were summoned. The jury voted six for acquittal and six for five years' incarceration. A new trial was ordered.[82]

Pells eventually went free because he was never involved in the killing of Applewhite. The vengeance evinced by the citizens and administrations of Texas after the Reconstruction era defies easy conclusions. The events that transpired in Limestone/Freestone counties have long been distorted, and the State Police and Special Police have suffered the contortions of Texas history. The State Police actually performed rather well in this martial law situation, but many have condemned their participation. As this event receded into memory, across Texas State Policemen continued to execute their duties with responsibility. Although their chief possibly performed embezzlement (we are not sure), they made concerted efforts to alleviate the violence and mayhem and rid the Lone Star State of criminals.

The Job Is Relentless

STATE POLICEMEN IN ACTION

Between the establishment of the State Police in July 1870, the declarations of martial law in Hill, Walker, and Limestone/Freestone counties in 1871, and the demise of the organization in 1873, policemen performed a myriad of individual activities. Democratic newspapers constantly assailed them for "killing prisoners while attempting to escape" or murdering innocent victims who opposed the Davis administration, but the State Police executed their assignments rather remarkably. There were members, as is true of any group, who should not have been selected and brought shame and disgrace to the police, but more often than not, they sought to eliminate the criminal element and assist the local constabulary.

Throughout their existence the State Police ranged across much of the eastern portion of Texas and occasionally onto the frontier in performing their duties. From their inception until their disbandment, they experienced all the problems of any large-scale organization. Their creation, with a multi-racial staff, during the turbulent years of Reconstruction was unique among all American states. The responsibilities placed upon them by their creators were enormous. Partially equipped and armed by the state government, along with uniforms and badges, the State Police pursued a quest to reduce violence and apprehend criminals. Their history is one of strange occurrences, and the state legislature ended their tenure on a note of infamy.

Policemen had all the accoutrements of a state sanctioned agency. They wore solid silver badges embossed with the words "State Police," with "a figure denoting the number and the lone star conspicuously raised in the centre." Chief of Police Davidson believed it "imperative that [the] force be uniformed." Their uniforms would be provided at cost (complete and delivered) for eighteen dollars. These perquisites would be deducted from the policemen's pay, but it was important that they present an official image with proper attire. Members also received one Winchester or Joselyn carbine, one sling, one swivel, and one hundred rounds of ammunition. The rifle cost forty dollars and bullets were two dollars for ten rounds.[1]

Governor E. J. Davis, Chiefs of Police James Davidson and Frank L. Britton, and local law enforcement officials kept a close watch on how policemen performed their obligations. The organization continually checked on their own personnel and dismissed those who were found incompetent or who had committed mistakes while in service, and attempted to find able replacements. One problem the constabulary encountered was men claiming to be policemen when they had either never been appointed or had been removed and then continued to act in an official capacity. Although the police force did have difficulties with some of its members, county authorities often requested their assistance in establishing law and order. In short, State Policemen were not the pariahs they have been made out to be.

Policemen were removed for various reasons. The case of John S. Coffey is instructive. Coffey entered the organization as a private shortly after its establishment in mid-1870 and eventually was promoted to lieutenant. But while he performed admirably at times, Coffey also had a penchant for "constant and repeated disobedience of orders," which the chief and Governor Davis found "impossible to tolerate or excuse." They had never ordered him to any duty with confidence that he would go and attend to it or stay where he was ordered to be stationed. "These circumstances," wrote Davis, "have occurred repeatedly within my knowledge." Moreover, citizens had complained about Coffey's conduct and behavior; thus he was dismissed from the force.[2]

Dismissals created difficulties for those sent as replacements. In Navasota, Private Daniel Taylor, a black policeman, had been removed from the force for drunkenness on duty. In fact, some unknown individual had reported the fact to Chief Davidson. When E. T. Randle arrived in the area to assume Taylor's duties, he discovered that Taylor had been led to believe that it was Randle who informed the chief of his inebriation. Moreover, this story was injuring Randle's relations with the black community and the idea was insidiously

Simon Alexander was an African American who served in the State Police from
Austin. In this rare photograph he is seen sporting his State Police badge.
Courtesy of the Austin History Center, Austin Public Library.

circulated by local Democrats, further damaging his status. Randle trusted
that Davidson would inform Taylor of the facts and that he was innocent of
any wrongdoing.[3]

Even when State Policemen were discharged for mistakes in performing
their obligations, they still received citizen support. John Ramshay of Centerville (Leon County) wrote the chief that David Price had been suspended
for an error in arresting a person in Houston. But in Leon County, Price, according to Ramshay, had "done his duty fully and squarely." He and a local
judge had signed Price's bond and both men continued to have confidence
in his abilities. The Democrats highly rejoiced at Price's "discomfiture," and
Ramshay hoped that he would be reinstated. Whatever the nature of Price's
Houston problem, Davidson refused to be persuaded by Ramshay's plea and
upheld Price's removal from the force.[4]

From Cherokee County, Sheriff Richard B. Reagan wrote Chief of Police
Davidson that a number of Jacksonville citizens inquired about the status of

Irving Moore and Frank Passons, who claimed to be State Policemen. For several weeks they had boarded at a "regular public bawd house," carousing night and day with prostitutes and gallivanting with the women publicly. Moore provoked a difficulty with a citizen and in the ensuing fight "got bruised up some." He and Passons left town but threatened to return and seek revenge. In sum, they conducted "themselves in a disgraceful manner." Reagan had been informed that Moore was not a policeman and had been indicted in Brown County for murder.[5]

The sheriff described Moore as a "desperado and very bad man." Moore had previously been a member of the State Police, but Davidson had dismissed him for his conduct and for causing trouble at Linn Flat in Nacogdoches County. Reagan obviously did not know that Moore had been discharged and inquired as to what was precisely his status so he could deal with him. The county officer did not believe that Moore had any authority as a policeman. If he was an officer, "his conduct is certainly a disgrace to the service and I deem it my duty to inform you of it." Passons was technically still a policeman, but after Reagan's comments, Davidson quickly removed him from the organization.[6]

One of the problems State Policemen encountered was individuals passing themselves off as members of the organization, when, in fact, they did not belong. Private S. E. McFarland, a twenty-nine-year-old policeman from Austin, noticed that R. N. Baker carried a revolver in violation of state law. He accosted Baker, asking why he had it in his possession. Baker responded that he was also a member of the State Police. McFarland requested his papers and badge, but the bogus policeman claimed he had left them at home. McFarland "couldn't see it" and incarcerated Baker. When the would-be "knight of the club," as the *Daily State Journal* labeled the imposter, failed to prove his story in court, Baker was fined twenty-five dollars.[7]

The State Police constantly investigated their own. An example is the case of J. M. Redmon from Gainesville (Cooke County), who entered the force as a private and finished as a lieutenant. One of the more efficient members of the State Police, and often called upon to perform hazardous duties, he also examined other officers. In one case, Redmon had to explore the activities of Lieutenant J. H. Adams of Hempstead, who had been commissioned in 1872 as a sergeant, and, because of his performance, became lieutenant in 1873. (This was not surprising because, as we have seen, Davidson, and later Britton, decided to promote individuals within the State Police to positions of command, rather than search outside.)[8]

The Adams case is somewhat inconsequential, but it demonstrates how the State Police made certain members properly perform their assignments. Chief of Police Britton directed Adams to arrest a man charged with an Austin murder before the train left Hempstead for Houston, but Adams missed its departure allegedly because he was engaged in a card game at Nooners saloon. Redmon interviewed the individuals involved, including a twelve-year-old boy. The lieutenant, a private, and a deputy sheriff appeared too late at the depot. Adams, mad at himself because he had lost a thousand dollars through his failure to apprehend the fugitive, made immediate arrangements to board a freight to Houston, but the murderer was subsequently captured at Hockley.

Adams admitted he was under the impression that the train would arrive later than it did and regretted his mistake. He did everything he could to pursue the killer after he realized that the train had departed. Others, including the telegraph operator, Private William K. Locke, another State Policeman, and Joseph Nooner, the owner of the saloon, confirmed the account that Adams gave Redmon. Nooner asserted that Adams, who did not drink, was indeed playing cards but did not tarry once he received the telegram from Chief of Police Britton. He simply did not know the time the train left. In this instance, a policeman made a mental mistake but clearly did not neglect his duty. In any event, the wanted man was arrested.[9]

Redmon also surveyed policemen in a specific area to determine their work attitude, their personal habits, and their financial status. For example, in Corsicana (Navarro County), he found the small contingent well armed, mounted, and willing to do their duty anyplace that they might be assigned. Some were in debt, although the charges would be paid when they received their pay. As to gambling, drinking, and visiting houses of ill fame, Private C. D. Blood informed Redmon that the group was innocent of such charges, which citizens corroborated. On the whole, they did "very good service" and had recently made seven arrests. Only Private E. M. Hutch spoke of resigning, but not because he was unwilling to do duty elsewhere.[10]

Policemen did not always receive their pay on time, which had nothing to do with Davidson's later alleged defalcation. After the initial passage of the State Police law, subsequent sessions of the Twelfth Legislature, and indeed the Thirteenth, saw the agency as a drain on the state budget. In 1871, Davis could write to one of his police lieutenants that the long delay in paying the police was a deficiency in the treasury. The recent "long" session of the legislators had consumed all the money, but Davis was making arrangements to pay all debts to the policemen, and would immediately dispense back pay. Within two or three months, Davis informed Sergeant Wentworth Manning, all obligations would be quickly honored.[11]

Although policemen desired to remain in a familiar environment, that is, close to home, since it was a mobile group, Davidson emphasized they had to be willing to serve wherever stationed. Lieutenant/Captain Thomas Williams may have been the most persistent State Policeman about staying, or being assigned, near his residence (Lockhart, Caldwell County). He was not alone in wishing this. Serving in Rusk County, on the Sabine-Angelina divide, in eastern Texas, far away from his Fort Bend County family, Lieutenant Thomas Sheriff, a twenty-six-year-old white, was an able and efficient officer. Chief of Police Davidson's response was firm, but demonstrated confidence in Sheriff: "It is important that you should remain where you are, an election is soon to be held there, and it is necessary that the disturbances charged as taking place at the last election should be provided against."[12]

What kinds of duties and responsibilities State Policemen performed in their posted stations has never been explained or even examined. They have been so denigrated that no one has bothered to investigate whether the derogatory newspaper reports were actually close to the mark. Take the brief career of James Ryan, a Navasota (Grimes County) resident, who posted his five-hundred-dollar bond (even though the county court clerk misspelled his name) and was commissioned as a private in the State Police in July 1872. He qualified on the same day. Assigned to his locality, Ryan was immediately engaged by city authorities to keep the peace at public meetings, although he had submitted his bond to the state and never received a badge.[13]

Ryan reported a "difficulty" between whites and blacks that occurred at a country store, resulting in the death of one individual, Sam Moody, and the wounding of three others in what he described as a "drunken fight," all the parties "being considerably intoxicated." The justice of the peace investigated the altercation, and all but one of the individuals (who were incarcerated) were placed under bond. During the trial, assisted by Private James B. Porter, the two policemen guarded the prisoners. All these facts had been duly relayed to their superior, Lieutenant J. H. Adams, who was headquartered in Hempstead. Ryan declared that he was doing all he could "in the way of having the laws executed."[14]

Ryan arrested white and black men for assault and battery on their wives; jailed individuals for fighting, carrying concealed weapons, murder, breaking and entering, and disorderly conduct; and searched for horse thieves, once spending "two days scouring thickets." On March 12, 1873, Ryan attempted to arrest the individuals who had stolen three bales of cotton. Fired upon by a white man and a black man, Ryan's horse was instantly killed. He knew the men whom he pursued and believed they remained in the neighborhood. More importantly, would the state pay for his horse, which was worth seventy-five dollars? What procedure, he queried, was required for reimbursement? Ryan remarked that "this county will soon be in a bad fix should the police be discontinued."[15]

Private Ryan exemplified the rank and file of the State Police who regularly filed official reports. A committed policeman, Ryan intended to resign from the force on January 10, 1873. "The condition of my family is such to require my general attendance," he wrote Chief of Police Britton, and trusted there would be no difficulty in replacing him with an "efficient man." Ryan did not leave the service in spite of receiving little pay. Informed that funds were exhausted, Ryan had been in the "service so long and having drawn my pay regularly as long as it lasts I do not now propose to quit the Police force because there is not at this time money to pay us, and if it be satisfactory," he desired "to remain on the Police force—so long as I do my duty."[16]

Similar to James Ryan, A. L. Roy of Giddings (Lee County) was a private in the State Police, but, unlike Ryan, he serviced several counties, although they tended to adjoin one another. Joining the organization about the same time as Ryan, July 1872, Roy remained until almost the demise of the state constabulary. Serving under both Captains McNelly and Williams, in Lee, Waller, and Fayette counties, and in northeastern Texas in Wood County, Roy was an active policeman who traveled extensively. He chased horse "theaves," made sure telegraph wires were not cut, and arrested two men, one for "cutting" his wife and the other for drawing a derringer and shooting his neighbor. They "had been disturbing the peace a great deal."[17]

Roy, like many other policemen who often moved about, complained about not receiving his pay, or when he did, that his wages had been discounted by 30 percent. Moreover, he had difficulties with his bond and had never received his police commission or a copy of his official duties. Since he traveled much of the time, which entailed considerable expense, it was essential that he be furnished with the proper papers and a regular salary. In mid-1872, Roy served in the Rio Grande expedition under the command of Captain McNelly. This group of State Policemen went to the Nueces Strip, specifically Dimmit County, to end cattle raids by Indians and Mexicans. Very little seems to have been accomplished on this venture.[18]

Roy occasionally accompanied Captain McNelly, but his later efforts were concentrated in Fayette, Gonzales, and Bastrop counties, where he made sure festivities involving a circus remained peaceful as some parties had threatened to kill him and terrorize the performers and the town. He chased individuals charged with assault with intent to kill and captured one in Fayette County. Roy arrested men for playing cards (Davidson was keen on eradicating gambling) and for horse theft. He even arrested a former State Policeman, F. B. Lancaster, for illegally carrying a weapon. Lancaster had earned the enmity of Winchester (Fayette County) citizens, a "very rough place" with a great deal of rowdiness, for posing as a captain in the state organization.[19]

Roy encountered trouble with the new chief of police, Frank L. Britton, for not reporting, but the private had been in contact with Captain McNelly. He actively pursued his assignments, arresting violators for "packing a pistol," charging men with assault to murder, and chasing fugitives. He sought out horse thieves, murderers, robbers, disturbers of the peace, and escaped prisoners, who became a common problem in postwar Texas. In this case, the men had broken out of the Brenham jail and had secreted themselves in the woods. Observed by several individuals, the fugitives were well armed and intended to fight if an attempt were made to capture them. Citizens were afraid their horses would be stolen, but none disappeared.[20]

In every jurisdiction, policemen had to contend with the murder of African Americans. On April 10, 1873, Daimon Walters, a freedman, who was hunting for oxen, was murdered near Colonel Caesar Moore's farm in Fayette County. On the way home Walters visited with Moore, where he traded his pistol for a shotgun. About two hundred yards from the house, Walters was hit by a shotgun blast, with nineteen pellets entering his body and sixteen in his left arm. Previous to this, Walters had been quarreling with a neighbor, Bing Abner, and they had been "packing arms for one another," but had recently made amends. The citizens told Roy they were in danger, afraid to venture out after dark, as a group of rowdies, who carried pistols publicly, created such a ruckus.[21]

Much hostility existed against the State Police, but many residents across the state appreciated their services and requested that policemen serve in their vicinity. For example, sixty-six residents of McDade (Bastrop County) wrote Chief of Police Davidson pleading that Private M. L. Woolley, a twenty-eight-year-old white man, be permanently stationed in the county. He had performed many services in the community, had become acquainted with the people generally, and thus was "esteemed by all for his many commendable traits of character." The citizens believed his influence would do more

Police Notice.

To the Citizens of Red River City
and Vicinity :
Having been appointed by Gen.
Jas. Davidson, Chief of Police of
Texas, a member of the State Police,
I take this method of informing the
public of the fact, and I would res-
pectfully ask all good citizens to as-
sist me in sustaining and enforcing
good order in this community.
J. Q. A. CARTER.
Sept. 29, 1872.

When J. Q. A. Carter was appointed to the State Police in 1872, he took the opportunity
to post flyers announcing his appointment and making an appeal to the citizens
of his community for support in his efforts to enforce law and order.
Courtesy of the Texas State Library and Archives Commission.

than "anyone else could possibly do in carrying out the duties of his office and keeping order and quiet." Davidson complied.[22]

From almost the beginning of the Davis administration and the formation of the State Police, the force had to deal with the Ku Klux Klan in its many forms. Although there was a fine line between the Klan and gangs of desperadoes (often both groups masked themselves), they nonetheless created upheaval and social chaos in the communities where they operated. For example, six men in "red flannel masks" brutally murdered two men in Jackson County in 1871 and burned the house. They spared a freedwoman and a boy. In Cherokee County, where a Klan-style raid occurred, a schoolteacher was slain along with a young boy, and another man wounded. The State Police captured the perpetrators, who were eventually tried and one sentenced to death.[23]

In Bell County, where the Klan declared their intention to clean up the "Nigger-police" and intimidate black voters, the State Police had difficulties in extinguishing their presence as many were sympathetic to their designs. Lieutenant A. C. Hill, who had been ordered by Governor Davis to collect names and descriptions of Klan personnel of those of the "Golden Star order," arrived in Tarrant County with a police reinforcement in time to prevent a courtroom riot by Klan sympathizers. Much to the "chagrin of the mobocrats," crowed the *Daily State Journal*, Hill's deft action prevented an imminent armed conflict. And in 1872 and 1873, the State Police entered Erath, Comanche, and Rusk counties to end Klan terrorism.[24]

Of course, the state's Democratic press accused the police of chasing shadows at the urging of the freedpeople. The *State Gazette* complained that policemen never earned "their salt" and never pursued "real offenders." They devoted their "precious time and talents" searching for "imaginary Ku Klux Klans and traveling post haste from place to place at the instance of superstitious, credulous negroes." The newspaper went on to say that when an individual requested police assistance to capture horse thieves it was refused. But, in fact, Private J. C. Martin, aided by citizens, arrested those responsible. *Flake's Daily Bulletin* followed a similar tack, writing that the police stationed in Bremond were alarmed when a number of goats came into town "bleating and roaring." Thinking they were Klan members, they went for them in "military style, shooting revolvers, and running them down, until the mistake was discovered."[25]

Throughout their thirty-six-month existence the State Police ranged across the state, suppressing disturbances in numerous counties. In addition to attempting to suppress the Ku Klux Klan, the organization hunted down desperadoes, murderers, horse and cattle thieves, and numerous other miscreants who committed assorted crimes; quelled clashes between whites and blacks; and responded to county officials whenever they requested assistance. The police have received so much criticism that it is often forgotten that in many instances before they were disbanded, local authorities pleaded with the governor and the Chief of Police to send in a force to restore law and order to their section if there were none stationed in their area.

When Falls County officials required assistance to levy some executions, they called upon the State Police. Lieutenant W. T. Pritchett, with a small contingent, arrested between ten and fifteen blacks and whites for assorted offenses. As an election approached, Washington County authorities requested fifteen State Policemen and fifteen Winchesters. When William A. Posey, a notorious outlaw, remained at large in McLennan County, S. H. Renick, a local official, thought a reward for his capture would be beneficial and that the State Police should pursue Posey, "since the sheriff and his subordinates here are well and personally known throughout the county and every movement of theirs is soon given publicity." Atascosa County petitioned Davis to appoint a policeman for their county to end lawlessness and cattle rustling.[26]

At a time when the Democrats actively sought to dismantle the "governor's hounds," thirty Red River County citizens wrote Davis asking for the presence of the State Police in their area. "All over the State the people are demanding the continuance of this force," asserted the *Daily State Journal*, "while their representatives (the Democratic portion of them) are doing their utmost to abolish it. Adjutant General Britton has furnished the police requested." And the presence of policemen in western parts of the state, such as in Menard, McCulloch, and Mason counties, led to a reduction in cattle rustling and to the people "getting very peaceable," although there was some concern among Mason Countians, who were "peaceable and orderly," that Davis might proclaim martial law.[27]

Close to the Oklahoma border in Wise County, Private D. P. Baker felt surrounded by "Rebels," since it was not far from Fort Worth, which he considered the "Rebel stronghold for northern Texas." In the same area, Montague County was "rebel in every sense of the word" and Jack County was the "fastest place in Texas." Gambling and escaped prisoners were problems, although Wise County was peaceable compared to its neighbors. A few more State Policemen would reduce the problems, but Baker had sent Sergeant J. R. Payne, with two men, to Denton. He would still like to "give this country a thorough cleaning out." Apparently, policemen also dealt with the Indians if they threatened the settlements and often had to serve as escorts.[28]

Local law enforcement officials too often confronted armed mobs, who defied civil authority and made it impossible to execute the law. When these situations occurred as, for example, in Bosque County, then county officers turned to the state for aid, requesting that the State Police quell the rowdy element and bring the lawbreakers to justice. A similar pattern prevailed in Medina County, where a freedman was killed, another individual mutilated, and assaults, nightly disturbances, and cattle theft occurred with impunity. At least two policemen were required as the county was a central point on the most traveled road to Mexico and the route of many fugitives. The men would be assisted by the inhabitants who were loyal and law abiding.[29]

Politics also compelled county officials to request the presence of the State Police. Because of the "demoralized condition" of the opposition in Brazoria County, the Unionists, who were "devoted to the maintenance of the equal rights of all men and have dared to assert and maintain their principles," required protection. The initial hullabaloo began when Davis appointed a black man as inspector of hides and animals. A justice of the peace, J. S. Rogers, along with his wife, was assaulted on the streets of Columbia because he upheld the selection. Davis supporters were so unpopular and unsafe they felt constrained to call upon him for protection but wanted only "sober steady men [to] be sent." On three different occasions police privates had been assigned to the area and "in every instance they have been intemperate men." Two had to be arrested.[30]

To be sure, Davis did have State Police personnel report on the political climate in various sections. After traveling over Cherokee County and interviewing every black man he met, Lieutenant Thomas Sheriff declared that the "freedmen here in a mass seem terror stricken from the manner in which the election was conducted outside and around the polls." And the white Republicans seemed to be "awe stricken not from their defeat but from the way in which they were insulted and abused." During the polling, the United States flag was "torn down," trampled, and spat upon. Sheriff concluded that there was a "kind of awe or dread overshadowing the county." Panola County evinced much the same characteristics.[31]

After numerous accounts of violence and criminality surfaced in Davis County, where sheriff's deputies refused to summon black men for jury duty, and Sandy Williams, a black man, was shot down in his cabin by "masked and blackened men," cries for a State Police presence emerged. In addition, a woman was beaten nearly to death with hickory poles and a black man was robbed and his niece raped. "Peace in Texas can only be preserved by the exercise of an unceasing and unremitting vigilance," wrote the *Daily State Journal*, "ever prompt to meet and foil the first movements of anarchy, and resolutely bent on the enforcement of law." But the police also prevented disturbances between whites and blacks, as they did in Houston County, when race relations deteriorated to their lowest level.[32]

The State Police continued to be active while they existed. They arrested men who shot each other, assassins, fugitives from other states, and even black men for assorted crimes. On one occasion they arrested several men who had disrupted a town in Robertson County. Although they received much criticism from the press, largely due to exaggerated reports that Lieutenant Emil Kellner supposedly arrested an invalid three times, the *San Antonio Daily Herald* exclaimed that "such an outrage has never before come to our knowledge and should damn the perpetrators to everlasting infamy." They did receive praise from black Texans for their attempts to reduce violence perpetrated against the freedpeople. Ranging across the state in pursuit of several gangs, horse thieves, cattle rustlers, desperadoes, and murderers, for the most part, the policemen acquitted themselves quite well.[33]

A troublesome area during the entire tenure of Governor Davis was Bastrop County. This section experienced constant turbulence from desperadoes, the Ku Klux Klan, and assorted criminals. Schoolhouses were burned, teachers kidnapped and whipped; armed men terrorized the community of Serbin and committed other depredations. To end the lawlessness, Davis called upon one of his most trusted and reliable State Police officers, Lieutenant Thomas Williams. He was ordered to the county with a police detachment to take "prompt and effective measures" to end the disturbances and arrest those responsible for the violent acts. "No measures," Davis informed Williams, would be "left unemployed" by him to "free the county from the presence of these desperadoes and bring peace and order in that locality."[34]

Although Williams was to confer with the sheriff and other law enforcement officials to gather information about the criminals, the grand jury did not cooperate. They failed to indict anybody for the flagrant violence which had pervaded the county for the past ten months—including seven murders, three whippings by the Klan, and one school and one church burned. Incensed at the inaction, Davis exclaimed that after he had provided the citizens an opportunity to rectify the situation, they remained blind to the violence and allowed it to continue. The governor would have to "find another way to reach the scoundrels who commit the outrages." Talk of law and order was "mere nonsense" as long as the violators went unpunished. He requested the district judge to "give them the usual warning."[35]

J. B. McFarland, judge of the 29th Judicial District, wondered what was meant by the "usual warning." In such cases, Davis said, he preferred to "send a notice to the people and authorities of counties where outrages repeatedly happen and no one is punished, that martial law will be the consequence of further failure to administer the law." The grand jury, after examining two hundred witnesses, found no evidence of the existence "of any persons calling themselves Ku-Klux." Davis had information that left "not a shadow of doubt" that such combinations existed. Davis was incredulous that the grand jury did not examine those who "*had seen* Ku-Klux," or if they did, they ignored the testimony. Davis refused to see this "whipping, and burning, and shooting go on indefinitely."[36]

The conservative press, *Flake's Daily Bulletin*, not only criticized the State Police but refused to believe that events in Bastrop County were as bad as depicted. Allegedly, Private Nathaniel Moore, a forty-year-old white, became drunk and violent, and Judge McFarland had to interfere. In retaliation, the police rode through town "crying to the citizens, 'Rats, to your holes!'" Of course, the newspaper believed such reports, but they knew full well that accounts in the "Radical press" about lawlessness and crime in the area were "exaggerations and misrepresentations." The county presented as "peaceable a condition as before the war," and statements to the contrary notwithstanding, there simply was not a problem.[37]

Regardless of what newspapers wrote, upheaval characterized Bastrop. On August 11, 1871, Private August Werner of the State Police was slain by Ben "Bird" Yoast while discharging his duties; two others were wounded. Davis offered an eight hundred dollar reward for "his *body*." Yoast later surrendered, was released on five thousand dollars' bail, and claimed "justifiable homicide." This killing provided the *Daily State Journal* with an opportunity to lambast the Democrats. The German citizens of Bastrop had become more "resolute and united than ever in their uncompromising resistance to Democracy." They well remembered, the paper editorialized, the "tragic persecutions of Union Germans in 1862, and they realized that Democratic success at the polls would cause a repetition of those scenes of tyranny and bloodshed." Shortly after this murder, a freedman was cold-bloodedly killed.[38]

Into 1872 and 1873, Bastrop County continued to experience problems with the Klan and desperadoes. When indictments were handed down, the grand jury and witnesses were threatened with death. In fact, a key testifier, Patrick Wormley, was murdered. Once again Lieutenant Thomas Williams entered the area and, along with Marshal Thomas F. Purnell and his son, executed writs. Rewards were offered and they managed to arrest John Gorman, who had been indicted by a grand jury for "Ku-Kluxism," charged with killing a black man near Hog Eye as well as a Bastrop white man. In addition, a gang of fourteen outlaws rode around with double-barreled shotguns, threatening to exterminate all State Policemen and firing into the homes of "respectable citizens."[39]

The outrages ceased, but quietude did not reign in Bastrop County. By early 1873, the inhabitants complained of having to abandon their homes, as several desperadoes, who constantly defied the law, attempted to murder individuals and their families. The concerned residents pleaded with Davis to immediately send some policemen as they had no confidence in the county officers, as they were unable to make any arrests. In fact, they requested Lieutenant Williams be sent as he was acquainted with the country and knew the residents. Unfortunately, Williams was slated to go to Lampasas. These "good, law abiding citizens" were responsible members of society and they hoped the governor would "take immediate steps."[40]

Gaming establishments and gambling houses also became a concern of the State Police. Both Captains George W. Farrow and L. H. McNelly concentrated upon these wagering dens in Calvert (Robertson County), Kosse (Limestone County), Galveston, Houston, and along the Houston and Texas Central Railroad. Although policemen occasionally arrested some of the "light-fingered gentry" and closed some gambling shops, they quickly re-opened after the departure of the force. No matter what steps the police took in combating the widespread prevalence of wagering on dice and cards, too often information was disseminated about their arrival and they discovered a closed casino. Only a "high public moral sentiment," according to one news-paper, could squash this evil.[41]

One of the stranger events in which the State Police participated was the quarantine in Brazos Santiago (Cameron County) in April 1871. The legis-lature had enacted a law in mid-1870 to establish a quarantine station. The next year Davis declared such a necessity prevailed on the coast. The officials were to employ a *competent and good physician* as health officer to check landing vessels and conduct a rigid examination to make certain the health of the crews was satisfactory. Davis ordered that the municipal authorities at the mouth of the Rio Grande and various incorporated cities appoint an official to enforce quarantine regulations. Applications were received, and Albert Wood was appointed by the Brownsville officials on April 10.[42]

The 1871 quarantine imbroglio in Brownsville and Brazos Santiago did not do justice to Governor Davis or the State Police. Albert Wood, who was "not a lawful health officer," and in fact had no medical credentials, was appointed to be the health officer to determine the condition of ships. The Brownsville city council disagreed and a major political confrontation occurred. Unwise-ly, Davis sent the State Police to enforce his order. Lieutenant William Burke and his force were arrested, in a rather informal manner, by Brownsville of-ficials, but their attempts to enforce the quarantine law were dismissed. Davis made every effort to exert his power as governor, but in this case it was mis-placed and the State Police received another "black eye."[43]

The State Police also became involved in what was known as the Rio Grande Expedition. An influential Dimmit County rancher, Levi English, probably exerted some influence on the administration to have a force sent to South Texas to end or, at least, reduce cattle rustling. The special group, led by Captain McNelly, comprised approximately thirty men. Before leaving for the Rio Grande frontier, Governor Davis addressed the policemen in Austin, where he praised McNelly and cautioned the force to respect the rights of the good citizens in the area which they operated. The expedition lasted only a few weeks and did not participate in any significant action, although some newspapers seemed to think Davis desired a war with Mexico.[44]

Along with the early embarrassment caused by the action of Jack Helm, and the problems encountered in the declarations of martial law, the assassination of two men brought more disrepute upon the State Police. At 1 p.m. on Thursday, December 14, 1871, in Linn Flat, located fourteen miles northwest of Nacogdoches, State Policeman Columbus Y. "Bud" Hazlett and Special Policeman William J. Grayson murdered David W. Harvell. At midnight on December 19, they assassinated the town constable, John Birdwell. The killings "struck terror to the hearts of the people," declared a local writer. The "citizens felt as though they were left without any protection from the law."[45] Although the State Police had existed for a year and a half, the Linn Flat affair brought increased criticism to the already beleaguered Republican-sponsored agency.

One of the oldest counties in the state, Nacogdoches was officially organized in 1837. Located deep in the East Texas timberlands, Nacogdoches County is approximately 140 miles northeast of Houston. Drained by the Angelina River and the Attoyac Bayou, the county's primary industry was lumber. Peopled by immigrants from the Old South and the border states, the area was isolated because it lacked transportation facilities. Although the economy depended on subsistence farming, in 1860 slaves comprised 28 percent of the population and their numbers increased by almost one thousand during the Civil War.[46]

Linn Flat was settled in the late 1830s. Named for a group of linden trees that surrounded the small prairie where the town was established, it was insular and remote. Animosities from the war years lingered and festered. They would openly erupt in 1867 with the reestablishment of military rule. By 1871, when the community became involved with the State Police, it was a thriving and well-populated area. The census of 1870 listed 327 households which comprised 1,785 people: 1,378 whites, 378 blacks, and 29 Native Americans. Whites accounted for 77 percent, blacks 21 percent, and Indians but 2 percent of the Linn Flat population.[47]

Nacogdoches County was Democratic before the war. In 1860, Southern Democrat John C. Breckinridge received almost 70 percent of the vote. The vote on secession was 317 for and 94 opposed. The county supported the Confederacy and sent two thousand men to defend its honor. A small Unionist element existed but did not emerge until after the war. Linn Flat became a hotbed of Unionism and Republicanism.[48]

By 1870, the portion of African Americans in the total population of Nacogdoches County had risen to 34 percent. While blacks comprised only one-third of the county population, they had been persecuted ever since freedom arrived in mid-1865. The Bureau of Refugees, Freedmen, and Abandoned

Lands (Freedmen's Bureau) established an agency in the county in 1867. The observations and reports of the agents suggest that blacks received harsh treatment. Direly hated, these government officials assisted the black community, but their efforts were largely in vain. In this arc along Texas's eastern border outrages against blacks "rose to a height of horror."[49]

Sheriff Richard D. Orton seemed helpless to prevent violence perpetrated upon the former slaves. When bureau agents informed him of such acts, he could muster no support. A white man shot a black man in the head for reporting him to the bureau. As the black man lay prostrate, he was also shot in each arm and the shoulder. When another black man was shot in the back of the head, the civil authorities labeled it "*suicide.*" The Ku Klux Klan rode nightly, and freedpeople began sleeping in the woods to avoid them.[50]

Politics brought new dimensions to the murder of blacks. By late 1868, violence aimed at white and black members of the Union League, the political organization for the Republican Party, reached serious proportions. There "ought be something done for the protection of the freedpeople and Union men residing in this District," wrote Bureau agent Alex Ferguson. Two black members of the League had been killed, one a seventy-year-old preacher. William J. Grayson, a Special Policeman and also head of the League; James M. Hazlett (Bud's father), a registrar; and various other prominent individuals had been targeted for extermination. Even Ferguson's father-in-law had disappeared and he was afraid to go into the country to search for him.[51]

On December 14, 1871, Justice of the Peace Gibson Dawson, a Tennessee-born farmer, was holding his regular court in Linn Flat. At the same time, the two policemen, Grayson and Hazlett, were riding "around over the land seeking disloyal troublemakers." They chose Linn Flat for their "field of operations because there was quite a sprinkle of republicans thereabouts, from whom they expected moral support." While lawyer John R. Clute, an "old gentleman" of Douglass, addressed the court, Grayson and Hazlett became loud and vociferous, continually interrupting the proceedings, "putting the barrels of their guns through the window and running the justice from the room." An exasperated Dawson issued arrest warrants and charged them with contempt of court.[52]

The State Policeman Columbus Y. "Bud" Hazlett had a fascinating background. He was born in Alabama in 1848. His father, James Marion Hazlett, served in the Third Brigade, Texas State Troops, in Captain C. C. Grayson's Company, but apparently deserted. He allegedly gathered a large number of men and went north, where he became a guerrilla and, according to folklore, befriended Jesse and Frank James. At age fourteen Bud was caught by a group of men who wanted to know where his father had gone. They tortured him through repeated hangings to reveal the whereabouts of his father, but he knew nothing. He crawled to a neighbor's house where he recuperated. His father became a doctor after the war, but bitter feelings existed toward him in the community.[53]

After the war, so the story goes, Bud became a "justifiable" murderer. His two sisters, Mary E. and Harriett M., became ill and needed medicine. Bud was sent to get it. After purchasing the medicine and placing it in his saddle bags, Bud saw a man walking away from his horse. He rode home, where Dr. Hazlett administered the proper dosage to the girls, one of whom died before he realized that it contained poison. The other daughter was given an antidote. When told that the medicine had been poisoned, Bud rode into town, where he found the man who had been next to his horse and killed him.[54]

Bud skedaddled. Captured in Rusk, Texas, he escaped jail but later was arrested in San Antonio on another charge. He settled briefly in Alpine before returning to Nacogdoches. He fell in love with a woman named Polly whose uncle disliked Bud. Bud's father warned the man not to antagonize Bud or his son would kill him, but if he left him alone he had nothing to fear. Polly warned Bud that her uncle intended to bushwhack him, but Bud turned the tables and killed him. He stood trial and was released. He married Polly and they had two children. Bud joined the State Police in 1871 after living in Texas for twenty-two years.[55]

William J. Grayson, the special policeman who directly participated in the Linn Flat raid, was a forty-one-year-old Alabama-born farmer. When the murders occurred in 1871, Grayson had been a state resident for thirty-six years. During the Civil War, he served in the 12th Texas Infantry (Young's Regiment) as a private. During Reconstruction he led the local Union League and was appointed to the roster of the Nacogdoches County Special Police in September 1871. These men fell into a unique category as they could be called out by the governor to quell a crisis, but they were only paid for the time they actually served.[56]

Little is known about the men who joined Hazlett and Grayson. We do know that James Marion Hazlett, Bud's father, was involved. In 1863, although stories circulated that he supported the Union Army, he joined the Third Brigade, Texas State Troops, from Nacogdoches County. After the war, in 1871, he was an election judge and a registrar as well as a Special Policeman. Grayson's brother, twenty-nine-year-old James M. Grayson, was

Texas-born and a neighbor of Justice Dawson. The group also contained the twenty-six-year-old E. F. Deshazo. The one black man of the group, a Special Policeman named John J. "Jordan" King, seems to have lived in the state since the close of the war. None of these men were ever convicted.[57]

The warrants for the courtroom behavior of Grayson and Hazlett were served by Linn Flat Constable John Birdwell, a fifty-nine-year-old Tennessee-born farmer. He summoned David W. Harvell, a forty-nine-year-old Kentucky-born agriculturist to assist in the apprehension of the two men. Birdwell told Hazlett that he had a warrant for his arrest. Hazlett immediately surrendered. The constable inquired about Grayson's whereabouts. At the shop, replied Hazlett. Birdwell ordered Hazlett to call Grayson. When Grayson approached, Hazlett said, "I am a prisoner," and Grayson exclaimed, "The hell you are. Die before you surrender." Harvell informed Hazlett he had to give up his gun.[58]

Hazlett wondered if Birdwell really demanded his weapon and remarked, "here are the contents of it," as he fired a bullet into Harvell's chest. Mortally wounded, Harvell retreated to S. D. Carver's store, picked up a double-barreled shotgun, and sprayed Hazlett with a load of birdshot. Harvell fired again, wounding Grayson in the head. Grayson responded. Full of lead, Harvell staggered back into the store and died within a few minutes. The two men retreated to Grayson's home, about three miles north of Linn Flat. After killing Harvell, they supposedly collected thirty or forty African Americans and "openly defied the law of the land."[59]

The Harvell murder created outrage in Linn Flat and throughout Nacogdoches County, and a large number of citizens joined posses to hunt down Grayson, Hazlett, and others who associated with them. The *Clarksville Standard* asserted that "all persons implicated, as well as those killed, were whites, and all of them Republicans." A reward of five hundred dollars was offered for the capture of the "dastardly scoundrels," which would be paid by the sheriff.[60]

Information about the murder of Harvell was relayed to Sheriff Orton, who formed a posse of ten or fifteen men. On December 16 they rode to Linn Flat, where they discovered an "awful state of affairs." The people, described as "despondent and panic-stricken," believed the "foot of the tyrant was upon their necks." Acting cautiously, Sheriff Orton obtained murder warrants for the arrest of Hazlett and Grayson from Justice of the Peace Gibson Dawson, who lived a mile and a half west of Linn Flat. After securing the warrants, Orton and his group proceeded to Grayson's home. On the way they encountered twenty-five or thirty "well-armed" blacks.[61]

Compelled to surrender, the freedmen were disarmed and sent under guard to Nacogdoches. The sheriff's party proceeded to Grayson's house, but neither of the men could be located. They searched the area as far as Cherokee and Rusk counties but found no trace of them. After returning to Nacogdoches, Orton opposed the release of those blacks who had been sent to town because he believed that with Grayson and Hazlett still at large they might join with them. Nevertheless, Orton finally relented and freed them.[62]

Sheriff Orton, claimed one writer, was "equal to the emergency." He wanted to avoid more bloodshed, maintain the supremacy of the law, and punish the criminals. The Orton family originated in Tennessee, but Richard, elected sheriff of Nacogdoches County in 1866, 1869, and 1880, was native born in 1841. During the war he served with Captain J. R. Arnold in the Fourth Brigade of the Texas Militia. First elected sheriff in 1866, he was disqualified when the military ousted Governor James W. Throckmorton and many other Democrats. The Republicans assumed control of the state in 1870, but Orton won reelection. He later established the *Nacogdoches Chronicle*, a weekly newspaper.[63]

About midnight on December 19, 1871, five days after the murder of Harvell, Constable John Birdwell of Linn Flat was called to his door and "shot down, like a dog, upon his own threshold," or as one newspaper related, "while his faithful wife was clinging to his arm." When Sheriff Orton arrived, Birdwell's body had still not been prepared for burial. Birdwell, a "respected and law abiding citizen," had numerous friends but they were "afraid to act or venture beyond their homes lest they should be blasted down," wrote a local chronicler long after the event. Orton summoned Justice of the Peace Dawson to hold an inquest. A jury ruled that Birdwell had died from a gunshot wound at the hands of unknown parties, although Dawson issued warrants for the arrest of Hazlett, W. J. and J. M. Grayson, John Jordan King, and E. F. Deshazo. One hundred men joined Orton in hunting for these five men as Birdwell was being buried on December 22.[64]

While Sheriff Orton searched the county and surrounding area, Grayson and Hazlett fled to Austin, seeking sanctuary under the wing of Chief of Police Davidson. Fueled by rumors that the two men had secreted themselves somewhere in Nacogdoches County, and from this base instigated the freedpeople to "deeds of violence," white fear of a black insurrection became so great that Sheriff Orton authorized his men to confiscate any weapons blacks might have. He did this, wrote a nineteenth-century historian, "as much for the protection of the negroes themselves as for any other purpose."[65]

Richard D. Orton served as sheriff of Nacogdoches County during the Linn Flat affair, in which a State Policeman and a Special Policeman murdered several persons, creating a tense and volatile situation that further tarnished the reputation of the State Police. *Courtesy of Bryan H. Davis.*

Whether Orton's action "alloyed" white excitement over what were clearly rumors, he disbanded the posse and then traveled to Rusk, the Cherokee County seat, to secure the intervention of District Judge Mijamin Priest of the 4th Judicial District, and a Governor E. J. Davis appointee, to influence the two men to surrender. Orton also seems to have attempted to obtain a personal interview with Hazlett. Once it became known that Hazlett and Grayson were in the state capital, Governor Davis investigated what had occurred.[66]

State Senator William H. Swift of Nacogdoches County also traveled to Austin to confer with the governor. Swift, according to reports, took with him the "verdict of the coroner's juries, and the evidence of officers in the cases." He wanted to convince Davis "to protect peaceable citizens against the desperadoes who disgrace the uniform of [the] State Police." It was feared that Hazlett and Grayson would defy the civil authorities unless prosecuted under order of the governor. Davis promised to have the murderers apprehended and brought to justice.[67]

Late in December, Davidson related to Judge Priest that Governor Davis wanted him to go to Nacogdoches, accompanied by Swift, and investigate the troubles between the men "said to be policemen and the citizens." Numerous newspaper accounts existed about what had happened at Linn Flat, but all were plagued with contradictions. Davis required someone on the scene whom he could trust. Almost simultaneously, Davidson took steps to have one of the most respected and responsible of State Policemen, Thomas Williams, assume control of Hazlett and Grayson, return them to Linn Flat, and transfer them to the civil authorities.[68]

Hazlett and Grayson, accompanied by J. M. Hazlett, King, and Deshazo, arrived in Austin the day after Swift had informed Davis and Davidson of events. The others remained hidden while the State and Special policemen made their presence known to the chief of police. Davidson ordered their arrest and placed them in the custody of Williams to be taken to Nacogdoches County.[69]

On Monday, January 15, 1872, Williams and other policemen escorted the prisoners into Linn Flat and found the citizens armed and so excited that they considered it "unsafe to go to trial." The lieutenant informed Sheriff Orton that if the locals disbanded he would furnish four policemen and the sheriff would be allowed four assistants to protect Hazlett and Grayson so that a trial could commence. The sheriff rejected this proposal and demanded that Grayson and Hazlett be turned over to them immediately, which Williams refused to do. Because of the tension in Nacogdoches County, Williams and his entourage returned to the relative safety of Rusk County.[70]

Negotiations between Sheriff Orton and Lieutenant Williams resumed on Thursday, January 18. They reached a tentative agreement by which Williams would escort the prisoners to Linn Flat for trial. Williams changed his mind, and the next day the police left Nacogdoches County for Henderson. It was believed they intended to take the prisoners back to Austin by railroad or that they would return to Linn Flat with a heavy guard of blacks and scalawags, overawe the court, and secure an acquittal. About 5 a.m., fifty to seventy-five men in search of Hazlett and Grayson "dashed" into Henderson, armed with double-barreled shotguns, surrounded various houses, and created a general disturbance.[71]

Meanwhile, Judge Priest, accompanied by Judge Sam A. Wilson, District Attorney Jefferson Shook, and W. L. David, arrived at the "seat of war" to investigate the murders at Linn Flat. Judge Priest went at the request of Sheriff Orton, as it was thought his presence would do more to control the Hazlett/Grayson mob than any other. Cloaked with judicial authority, it would be Priest's job to prevent a confrontation between Nacogdoches County citizens and the State Police, who had been reinforced by a number of sympathetic inhabitants.[72]

Judge Priest returned from Linn Flat with news that the Grayson/Hazlett crowd, estimated at sixty to five hundred, was entrenched near the Rusk County line. He ordered out the militia and issued arrest writs. James McRoberts, a Rusk County Special Policeman, was captured and marched off "with all the pomp and circumstances of glorious war," claimed one newspaper, but another believed they would be "shielded and protected by the Radical authorities." The *Daily State Journal*, a Davis supporter, concluded that the mob, who did "their devilment under the cloak of authority," controlled "one old Ku Klux Justice of the Peace" who issued warrants "by the day" and served every Union man within ten miles.[73]

On Monday, January 29, Williams declared that he would deliver the prisoners to Sheriff Orton in two days. Orton and Williams agreed the former would provide a guard of eight men to take charge of Hazlett and Grayson. Judge Priest and District Attorney Shook agreed to assist at the trial. Although court opened on February 1, Williams refused to deliver the prisoners and declared he "would spill the last drop of blood in their defence." Priest assured Williams that the prisoners would be protected from violence if they stood trial, but Williams remained steadfast. Justice Dawson issued warrants

for King and J. M. Hazlett and gave them to Williams, who continued to refuse to execute them.[74]

Madison G. Whitaker, a fifty-nine-year-old farmer, was deputized to
execute the warrants issued by Priest for the arrest of King, J. M. and Bud
Hazlett, and Grayson. Whitaker demanded Williams turn over the men but
was refused. While Whitaker attempted to negotiate with Williams, a party
of citizens rode into Rusk County seeking information about the State Police and the followers of Hazlett and Grayson. They were allegedly told that
Hazlett, Grayson, and James Wallace were riding about the area summoning
blacks to meet at the house of the Rusk County sheriff to aid in resisting arrest. From many sources Orton ascertained that a considerable force had assembled near the county line to protect the murderers. On Friday, February
2, a posse from Nacogdoches moved into Rusk County and learned that the
resisters had gone toward Henderson that morning. Having the proper arrest
warrants, this hastily formed contingent followed them.[75]

According to the *Texas State Gazette*, Grayson and Hazlett, about whom
"such an excitement" had been raging in Nacogdoches, were brought back to
Austin by Williams and the other policemen who had them in charge. They
contended that it was necessary because the two men could neither receive a
fair trial nor be protected from the "mob that were determined to take their
lives." Chief of Police Davidson turned them over to the Travis County sheriff for safekeeping. He planned in a few days to proceed with them to Nacogdoches, with the "view of ascertaining the exact facts in this important case."
The state government desired that the men be tried "under the laws of the
land, and not by the bloody code of lynch."[76]

In the second week in February 1872, Chief of Police Davidson ordered
Lieutenant Williams, then in Lockhart, to report to Austin with his force.
Governor Davis directed that Davidson assume custody of Hazlett and Gray-
son and transport them to Nacogdoches County, or to wherever Judge Priest
could be found so they could undergo an examination on murder charges.
"Great excitement" and "considerable feeling" existed against them, wrote
Davidson. Governor Davis felt that Judge Priest should be apprised that
Davis believed the personal safety of Hazlett and Grayson while waiting trial,
and during the proceedings themselves, "would be better secured" if they
were confined in "some county remote from the local prejudice."[77]

Williams and his assistant had been indicted because they brought Grayson and Hazlett out of Nacogdoches County. The governor did not think
they could, "or should, be held to appear to answer any such charges as they
undoubtedly thought they were doing their duty and that the course they

adopted was essential to the safety of the prisoners." Davis admitted that the two men could have been in error, but from what Judge Priest reported, the governor believed their fears had solid foundation. Davidson, when he arrived in Nacogdoches, would call the matter to the judge's attention so that such action might be taken that would not prevent the two men from "attending to their duties as required by law."[78]

On February 27, Williams and Sergeant William H. Baker, who had been ordered back to Nacogdoches, arrived. To their amazement, they discovered Chief of Police Davidson and Sergeant Thomas G. Martin already present. Davidson desired to see the situation for himself. Sergeant Baker was not favorably impressed. He wrote that the people imagined they still "lived in a miniature confederacy—they have no idea that the South has ever lost any of the prestige of its former glory, and any man differing with them in politics is in danger; of all the lawless counties in the State this leads; the sheriff with a mob thinks nothing of taking all the freedmen's arms and destroying them." Of all the "God forsaken counties in the State this beats all—disregard for law, for feelings of Republicans, for brutality towards the colored people, and violence generally."[79]

Even though Sergeant Baker may have depicted the residents of Nacogdoches County in an unfavorable light, they did perform the necessary judicial functions when they accused and tried Hazlett, Grayson, and their cohorts. The grand jury, which met in February 1872, charged the two Hazletts, the two Graysons, King, Grimes, and Deshazo with murder, but the evidence suggests that only William J. Grayson and Columbus Y. "Bud" Hazlett were ever convicted. Apparently the other men were able to prove that they did not participate in the killing of Harvell and Birdwell but did accompany the State and Special policemen from time to time. All these individuals may have been politically linked through the Union League and their Republican Party affiliation.[80]

Nevertheless, Grayson and Hazlett were tried at the June 1872 term of the district court and found guilty of the murder of Birdwell. (They were not simultaneously tried for the Harvell killing.) Sentenced to life imprisonment, Hazlett escaped, but Grayson served fourteen years in the state penitentiary at Huntsville. He received a pardon from Governor John Ireland at the insistence of a number of Rusk and Nacogdoches County citizens, along with the local state senator, and because of his unusually "good conduct since his imprisonment." Moreover, it had never been alleged he was the murderer. Hazlett, on the other hand, was killed, perhaps evading apprehension, near Woldron (Scott County), Arkansas, in 1877.[81]

The State Police of Republican Governor Davis received a host of bad publicity related to this incident. To be sure, Hazlett was a member of the state organization, but of course his killing of Harvell and Birdwell had neither been ordered nor justified. Precisely why Harvell and Birdwell were killed may never be known. There is simply no evidence in all the materials, either primary or secondary, that would account for these assassinations. Perhaps it was prewar animosities, Civil War entanglements, or family feuds with relatives that desired a settlement to a squabble. Whatever the case may have been, Hazlett supplied the "trigger finger" in murdering the two men, Grayson's pardon suggesting his innocence.

Although the leaders of the State Police from its very inception attempted to screen applicants (earlier sources all claim this was not done), Hazlett had long been a resident of Texas, and if his background was somewhat dubious, he certainly qualified as an individual suitable for the new organization that Governor Davis wanted to create to reduce the amount of violence then prevalent in the Lone Star State. Overall, the State Police did not evince these characteristics of wanton murder and midnight assassination, but many newspapers claimed otherwise. The Linn Flat affair is a sad commentary upon what the State Police attempted to do, but in protecting the right to a jury trial Williams gave them legitimacy and ably performed his duty.

One of the unfortunate ironies in the history of the State Police was the tenure of Chief of Police James Davidson. The Scotsman was selected by Governor Davis for his administrative and disciplinary skills. In these two areas, Davidson did not disappoint the chief executive. Although at times he may have been too rigid in his standards and too quickly dismissed individuals from the organization for minor infractions, Davidson traveled around the state checking on the force and viewing them in action. Davidson was also attentive to citizen complaints about policemen and, in general, immediately removed those who brought shame and disgrace to the organization. It was his financial shenanigans that destroyed his reputation.

That James Davidson embezzled $37,434.67 from the state treasury while serving as adjutant general/chief of State Police has long been accepted in the canons of Texas history. Even though Davidson left the state, interestingly enough on a mission to New York City at the bequest of Governor Davis, he had previously been investigated by the legislature for his accounting procedures in the Hill and Walker County martial law affairs. No anomalies had been discovered. Moreover, Davidson had previously resigned from the state government in November 1872 and mounted a campaign to win a seat in the state legislature. He broke with Davis and supported land grants for prospective railroads, which Davis vehemently opposed.[82]

Once the shortage of funds was discovered, Davis sent Captain L. H. McNelly to New York City in pursuit of Davidson. He checked the register of the St. Nicholas Hotel and found that Davidson had left on November 26, 1872. The former chief probably went to Canada, where McNelly followed the trail but failed to find him. The state offered a $3,000 reward for his delivery to Austin, but Davidson managed to elude everyone. It was alleged that he eventually fled to Belgium, but there is no doubt that he finally settled in New Plymouth, New Zealand, where he married Jane Ryan in October 1874.[83]

Davidson served as mayor, coroner, and member of the Armed Constabulary Force in New Plymouth for a number of years. It is clear that the residents knew nothing of any previous charges of suspected embezzlement back in Texas. In 1885, while employed as a clerk and bookkeeper in a butchering establishment, a discrepancy in the business's financial ledgers was uncovered. Highly respected in the community, Davidson was demonstrably distraught over the prospect of having to face public censure for irregularities in his bookkeeping. Although the butcher accounts were "not quite correct," according to W. Bayly, the proprietor, he did not dismiss Davidson from his position. When Davidson left work in the afternoon, various residents described him as looking "strange" and "quite troubled in mind," verging on "insanity." He decided to end his life. Amidst a cluster of pines and blue gum trees in the back of his home, Davidson committed suicide on April 7, 1885, and was buried on April 9.[84]

Davidson's replacement as chief of the State Police, Francis (Frank) L. Britton, was a cousin to Governor Davis's wife, Anne Elizabeth. His father, Thomas P. Britton, was born in Virginia, and his mother, Eveliner Bayless, in Kentucky. Frank Britton was born in Indiana about 1847. Forbes Britton, father of Davis's wife, was a brother of Thomas P. Britton. Too young to participate in the Civil War, Frank joined the Tenth Cavalry, 125th Regiment, on March 30, 1865, two weeks before Appomattox, and was mustered out in Vicksburg, Mississippi. He served as chief of police/adjutant general until Davis left office in 1874. In 1877 Britton married Rose Marie LeClere of Galveston. There he practiced law until 1880 when he removed to Silver Cliff, Colorado, where he died of tuberculosis on October 26, 1880.[85]

Britton became head of the State Police at a critical time in Davis's governorship. The 1872 elections had produced a resounding Democratic victory. One of the first orders of business was to dismantle the militia and police,

Frank L. Britton was appointed adjutant general of Texas in 1872 when James Davidson
resigned this position. Britton was a cousin of Anne Elizabeth Britton Davis,
wife of Governor Davis. *Courtesy of David and Harriett Condon.*

the cornerstones of the governor's law and order agenda. Before all this happened, but while the legislature was debating disbandment of Davis's program, a major problem emerged in Lampasas County: a clash was brewing between a local family, the Horrells, and law enforcement officials. In many respects what happened in Lampasas County presaged the course of the legislators. The demise of the State Police, although technically a legal decision, actually occurred amidst a hail of bullets in a local Lampasas saloon.

Lampasas

THE DEATH OF THE STATE POLICE

In the 1872 Texas election the Democrats solidified control of the Thirteenth Legislature and anticipated the termination of the State Police. The Democratic victory stimulated the belief that the state authorities were to be deprived of enforcing the laws and preserving the peace. The "desperate element has broken loose," decried *Norton's Union Intelligencer*. The law was "trampled under foot" and lawmen "shot down." The *Daily State Journal* echoed this sentiment when it declared that the prospective removal of the State Police had "encouraged the lawless to break out all over the State." Desperadoes were "too strong for the civil officers of the county." This "malicious spirit" needed to be crushed.[1]

A few papers gave some grudging praise for the organization and even performed an occasional about-face in support of police efforts, but in general the "governor's hounds" were detested and often vilified, as was Governor E. J. "Despot" Davis. James B. Gillett, who became a Texas Ranger, painted the force as a political entity when he stated that "naturally they were rank Republicans, and many of them were termed carpetbaggers. This body was never popular in Texas, especially as many of the force were negroes."[2] Publicly, the State Police were condemned at every turn and generally described as misfits and law breakers. The denouement began in early 1873. Just before the final disbandment of the organization, four policemen died in a hail of bullets inside a Lampasas, Texas, saloon.

An 1872 immigrant circular described Lampasas County, which had been created in 1856 from parts of Travis and Bell counties, as a section where the "scenery was everywhere wild, romantic and beautifully picturesque." The topography included "high and rolling" hills with valley land covered by cedar, post, and scrub oak. The area contained excellent timber, a prairie endowed with a variety of grasses where mesquite predominated, streams that abounded with fish, and forests that teemed with game. The Brazos and Colorado rivers split the region and provided water for stock-raising and grain crops. Droughts occurred (the one in 1871 was the worst in history), but the farmers persevered and raised a full wheat crop and one-half of a normal corn yield.[3]

Located on the Sulphur Fork of the Lampasas River, the town of Lampasas (sixty-five miles northwest of Austin) had 1,200 inhabitants in 1870. Widely touted for the curative power of its two "celebrated" sulphur springs and portrayed as "one of the handsomest, liveliest and most flourishing towns in South Western Texas," the citizens were depicted as "peaceable, hospitable, intelligent and law abiding." But Lampasas also gained a reputation for disturbances and general rowdiness. By the early 1870s, the population of Lampasas County was 2,400, "with the exception of 15 or 20," all "entirely of the white race!," according to Thomas Pratt in the Texas Almanac. It was, crowed Pratt, "emphatically a white man's county."[4]

Between 1871 and 1873 the State Police were in, around, and through Lampasas for a variety of reasons. As the county seat, the town was prone to trouble whenever courts were in session. To prevent difficulties, Adjutant General James Davidson ordered Sergeant L. C. Locke, along with ten men, to be available whenever a judge requisitioned a detachment during court days. Davidson expected that Locke would be able to rid the section of desperadoes and criminals, but also use his force to operate against the Indians. Locke and his contingent arrived in late February 1871. Some internal trouble did surface among the policemen, but they attempted to ensure that the citizens lived peacefully.[5]

Shooting and hollering at night by outcasts disturbed Lampasas residents. The culprits could not be brought to justice, complained a law officer, because "they shoot and run off," and no one would identify them. The White and Gibson office on Main Street was a prime "specimen of this character, having some twenty or thirty bullets fired through it by these parties." All windows in the Lampasas Dispatch office had been broken out because the paper criticized some of the "atrocious acts of 'the bunch.'" Other instances of a similar nature were simply too numerous to mention. Cattle rustlers also appeared, and the county continued its efforts to field a stable militia to combat the un-ruliness from both within and without.[6]

Chief of Police James Davidson did not believe that Lampasas Sheriff Shadrack T. "Shade" Denson (1833–1892), who served in that office between 1870 and 1873, performed his duties very effectively and suggested more than once to Governor Davis that Denson be removed and someone more suitable named to replace him. What galled Davidson was the frequent escape of prisoners from the Lampasas jail after they had been transferred to Denson for safekeeping. To Davidson, this pattern of criminals being released from custody after being placed in Denson's hands evinced a "negligence very reprehensible in an officer." Unless the Lampasas sheriff could satisfactorily explain why these jailbreaks could not be prevented, Davidson asserted that steps would be taken looking to Denson's "removal from office."[7]

Davidson's relations with Sheriff Denson remained strained throughout his tenure as adjutant general. During 1871 and 1872 Davidson monitored Lampasas affairs and occasionally reminded Denson of what should be done to protect the citizens in their person and property. Extralegal activities needed to be prevented, Davidson emphasized, and individuals should use the courts and not the rope to redress their grievances. Denson had to make it abundantly clear to Lampasas County residents that lawlessness could not and would not be tolerated. Disturbances continued, however, not only in Lampasas but in the surrounding counties. Repeated outrages, disruption of elections, and criminal reprisals plagued the section.[8]

The major component in the final State Police drama was the Horrell brothers. Considerable ink has been expended upon the Horrells. Their ca-pers led directly to the killing of the State Policemen, and they undoubtedly organized the ambush. Although it is quite difficult to pinpoint family activi-ties during these turbulent years, much of what transpired in the way of may-hem and murder can be traced to the escapades of the Horrells. According to a local history publication, they were a "respected and well-liked" family. The brothers were "known for their skill with firearms and considered dangerous to fool with" and "many of their friends and followers were just as tough." These types of individuals were not welcomed neighbors.[9]

The original defender and mythmaker of the Horrell family was John Duff Green. Born in Lampasas County in 1874 (he died in 1960), Green empha-sized that the Horrells were "fine men, born of a splendid lineage, brave and courageous to a fault, but a little wild, possibly extraordinarily wild, when it came to drinking and shooting up the town at night for fun or sport." They fired their guns in the air, shooting at no one, but their "actions almost scared the life out of the tamer elements" among Lampasas inhabitants. The Horrells, in Green's words, simply exemplified the spirit of frontier life. Local officers, unable to cope with the situation and to curb the nocturnal activities, turned to the state for assistance. A "legal gun force" (the State Police) was dispatched from Austin to quell the disturbances. In a "bungled attempt" to arrest the Horrells, four policemen were killed.[10]

Former Texas Ranger Gillett's characterization adds some twists, but like most other authors, after first explaining how respectable the Horrells were and establishing their credentials, they eventually end up as murderers, outcasts, and dead. Gillett declared that as "native Texans" and "raised on the frontier," the family "stood well in the community, but were considered dangerous when aroused." Not surprisingly, the brothers were "expert riders, and, having grown up with firearms in their hands, were as quick as chained lightning with either Winchester or pistol." But later, after all their difficulties, the Texas Rangers "accomplished the impossible in rounding up the most desperate band of men that ever lived."[11] Who were the Horrells?

The Horrell clan originated in Virginia and later moved to Kentucky, Arkansas, and finally Texas. Samuel was born about 1820 in Kentucky, traveled with his father to Arkansas where he met his wife Elizabeth (Wells), and married her on July 15, 1838. Farming and buying land in Montgomery County, Arkansas, Samuel prospered and eventually acquired 160 acres, two horses, and six cows. For whatever reason, the family uprooted themselves again and moved to Lampasas, settling on Lucy Creek, ten miles northeast of town in 1857 or 1858 on a farm they bought from Mose Jackson. During the war Samuel sold this place and bought a tract on the site of the old Townsend mill. Although Samuel was by all accounts a good citizen, his sons experienced numerous difficulties after his death.[12]

Samuel's father, Benedict, a Virginia native, may also have migrated about the same time as his son. Samuel and Elizabeth were parents of eight children (seven boys and one girl); Nichols says seven. Five of the eight offspring were born in Arkansas. Little seems to be known about Samuel, or the early history of the Horrells for that matter, but they are often discussed in glowing terms. In 1868, Samuel sold the farm and intended to move to California but only made it as far as Las Cruces, New Mexico. Here the second oldest son, John, was waylaid and killed by Earl[y] Hubbard in a dispute over pay. After John's demise, Samuel was slain by Apaches. The remainder of the family returned to Lampasas in March 1869.[13]

Samuel's wife, Elizabeth, is listed in the 1870 agricultural census as a 45-year-old farmer who owned one-half section of land, with 40 acres improved and 280 acres unimproved, valued at four hundred dollars cash. The land was worth a little over one dollar an acre. She had four cows worth forty dollars and she produced farm goods worth two hundred dollars. Her daughter Sarah A. lived with her, and the census-taker had a higher estimate of Elizabeth's worth than did the agricultural assessor. The former assessed Elizabeth's worth at twelve hundred dollars in land and three hundred dollars of personal property. (Also in the household was a twenty-six-year-old woman housekeeper.) What happened to the farm is unknown, but this enterprising woman moved into Lampasas to reside at 508 South Western.[14]

As noted earlier, Samuel and Elizabeth had eight children, all boys but one. William C. joined the Confederate Army but died from sickness. Where and when is unknown. John W. died in New Mexico before 1870. Samuel M., along with his sister Sarah, avoided troubles with the law and lived relatively peaceful lives. James Martin (Mart), Thomas L., Benjamin F., and Merritt attracted the attention of local law enforcement officials and finally the State Police. The four Horrell brothers involved in murdering the four members of the state constabulary had neither deep roots nor much economic stake in Lampasas. In fact, later descriptions of the Horrells as significant members of the community are obviously wide-of-the-mark.[15]

What do we know about the sons of Elizabeth? Contemporary descriptions are apt. Mildly prosperous was Benjamin F., listed as married (both had been born in Arkansas), seventeen years of age in 1870, a farm laborer with a one-month-old son appropriately named Thomas. Benjamin had personal property valued at $475. In the agricultural census he is listed as having no land, three horses, one mule, five cattle, all enumerated at $250, with farm production assessed at $25. Thomas (not listed in the agricultural but in the population census) was two years older, also born in Arkansas, and also a farm laborer, but his wife was a native Texan. He had $300 of appraised property. (Bill [William] Sneed, a future cohort, lived with them.)[16]

James M. "Mart" was a twenty-four-year-old farmer, who along with his wife (Artemissa), had been born in Arkansas, although their year-old daughter was a native Texan. Mart was listed as a farmer, with $400 of real estate and $800 of personal property. (He is not listed in the agricultural census, which probably means he did not own the land he farmed or else he managed the acreage.) Actually, Mart was head of an extended household that included a twenty-two-year-old woman, Arkansas born, and a young man, age twenty, who was a hired hand on the farm. Most important of the extra dwellers was Merritt, sixteen years old in 1870. Why Merritt lived with his brother, as opposed to his mother's accommodations, is not at all clear.[17]

The following Horrell men are important for the State Police killing: James M. (Mart), Thomas L., Benjamin F., and Merritt. They participated in the ambush of the four policemen and later died violent deaths themselves. The manner of their demise might raise the question of whether "they could have made good people," according to Nichols, "but it seems that it was not in them." Their later involvement in the feud with the Higgins family, commonly known as the Horrell-Higgins Feud, and their activities in the Lincoln County war in New Mexico, are reasons for reevaluation. Benjamin F. was shot to death in Lincoln County in December 1873. Merritt was killed in Lampasas in January 1877. Mart and Thomas L. were murdered in the Meridian jail in December 1878.[18]

Adjutant General F. L. Britton did not have the same opinion of the Horrells as their hangers-on. Britton stated that the Horrells and their comrades numbered about twelve or fifteen men, "whose occupation was the branding, killing and skinning of other people's cattle." Headquartered at the Lampasas Saloon, they drank, gambled, and stored their ammunition in the barroom. They shot into citizens' houses and made a general nuisance of themselves. After the Indian "menace" subsided, many of the locals who drifted in and out of jobs and towns had nothing to occupy their time. Attaching themselves to the Horrells, whose reputation had quickly become unsavory, these characters helped cause Lampasas to become the scene of considerable strife.[19]

On January 14, 1873 (two months before the State Police incident), as the district court adjourned for dinner, Sheriff Denson heard hollering coming from town and observed a crowd of men near A. J. Northington's store. Denson immediately approached the group and inquired about the origins of the ruckus. Informed that it emanated from George Washington "Wash" Short in Scott's saloon, Denson entered, told Wash he was under arrest for disturbing the peace, and grabbed him. Wash resisted, and Marcus "Mark," his brother, drew his six-shooter while informing the sheriff he would not arrest Wash. Mark then split the two men apart by running between them. (The Shorts were friends of the Horrells.)[20]

When Mark broke Denson's grip on Wash, Wash instantly drew his pistol, "swearing vengeance all the while." Denson several times called for assistance in arresting Wash, but his plea was resolutely ignored. Meanwhile, the three men continued to scuffle. As Denson fended off their pistols, the two Shorts and Denson ended up in the street. Because no one had appeared to aid the sheriff, Denson thought his only "show was to fight my way out alone." He drew his revolver, but Mark still held on to him. Mark caught the sheriff's pistol, which prevented Denson from shooting Wash and, in turn, Wash shot him. Denson was wounded seriously enough that he blacked out for a time after being shot.[21]

Patrick H. Guinaty, a Horrell supporter, stood guard with a Winchester rifle and also brought Wash a horse. The Horrells informed the posse that they had provisions for the Shorts and planned to feed and protect them. Thomas Sparks, a fifteen-year resident of Lampasas County, foreman of the grand jury at the district court session of January 14, and Denson's brother-in-law, contended that there were "at least a dozen men, well armed, manifesting a determination to violently resist any attempt that might be made to arrest the Shorts." He saw at least five guns, which had been stolen from a "minute company" in the "hands of these desperadoes." After the Short and Horrell brothers had left, Sparks and his group gathered more men and pursued Wash and Mark. They searched in vain and returned to Lampasas.[22]

Although the precise circumstances are vague, another serious problem confronted local officials when Company M of the Lampasas County Minute Men became involved in the disruption of the district court session. First, Adjutant General Britton demanded a full report of the minutemen's role and the nature of the engagement. Second, he concluded that as a result of "conduct subversive of law and order," the company was disbanded. Lieutenant A. P. Lee, who had served as a sergeant in the defunct company, was ordered to "collect all arms" and ammunition in possession of the company members. Lee also had to hold an election for the selection of a new commander. Britton wanted only "good and law abiding men" accepted into the new unit. The reorganized company, minus any Horrells or supporters, became official on February 22.[23]

Ten days after the district court disturbance, Adjutant General Britton sent William Woods, a special state agent for the frontier forces, to Lampasas to supervise the minute company reorganization. He would ascertain which militia men were implicated in the fracas and report all particulars. Woods was also to determine the status of the new company in relation to mounts, arms, and general deportment. While all this was taking place at the state capitol, in Lampasas the members of the county court, although humiliated, felt it their duty to report certain facts to Governor Davis and "ask such assistance" as he, in his wisdom, thought "proper to give us." In a condition of upheaval, Lampasas needed the State Police.[24]

The justices confirmed Denson's version of the Short encounter. He suffered from a gunshot wound "in hand to hand combat with two of the offenders and ruffians, while ten or twelve others stood ready" with weapons to prevent the "good citizens from assisting the sheriff." Because they were unable to execute the laws, the county court members requested that Davis provide them with a "police force sufficient to enable" the local law officers to enforce law and order. The court officers also recommended four men to serve as members of the State Police and suggested that a reward of $500 be offered by the governor for the apprehension of Wash and Mark Short, or $250 for either, as both had been involved in the Denson shooting.[25]

Chief of Police Britton and Governor Davis worked closely with the members of the Lampasas County court and transmitted six blank Special Police commissions with oaths. The adjutant general requested that the "requisite number of reliable and law abiding men be selected for this service by your body and commissions issued to them." Special Policemen were those appointed to temporarily assist persons engaged in the late disturbance in which Sheriff Denson had been wounded as well as any other individual in the section who might be evading the law.[26]

On February 10, 1873, to alleviate the increasing tension in Lampasas, Governor Davis revoked that part of his April 13, 1871, proclamation that exempted Lampasas County residents from the "keeping and bearing of deadly weapons." As a frontier county, Lampasas had been excluded from the law's provisions, but now, according to Davis, a "large majority of the citizens" requested that the exception be withdrawn. All state and municipal officers were charged with enforcing the act, and the sheriff would post a copy of the proclamation at a "conspicuous place at the Court House" and one in each judicial precinct. On the same day, Adjutant General Britton ordered Sergeant J. M. Redmon to investigate the turbulent state of affairs in Lampasas.[27]

By the time Redmon was sent to Lampasas to ascertain the condition of the town, he had extensive experience in the State Police and encounters with numerous bad men. No stranger to violence and outlaws, Redmon was born in 1839, lived in Cooke County, and served as a sergeant in the Civil War in McCord's Frontier Regiment, Texas Cavalry. He joined the State Police in 1871 and was particularly active in North Texas, notably in Montague, Comanche, Grayson, Denton, and Cooke counties, basically his home region.

Redmon's actions suggest that he was fearless in pursuit of lawbreakers (he killed at least two men) and had been responsible for the capture of the notorious desperado Loss Kimble.

Although Redmon, at one point in his State Police career, had been charged by a fellow officer, Private John A. Truelove, with betraying a confidence, drunkenness on the streets of Gainesville, and violation of state law by arresting individuals in the Chickasaw Nation, he successfully refuted the allegations and proved that he had "always been sober, industrious, discreet and active in the discharge of his official duties." Later, Redmon would attempt unsuccessfully to capture the famous gunfighter John Wesley Hardin and his gang. Before and after his sojourn in Lampasas, Redmon demonstrated a deep commitment to his responsibilities in the State Police. He died in Gainesville in 1877 after being married but six months.[28]

Sergeant Redmon arrived in Lampasas on the evening of February 12, 1873, where he was to consult with the county court and the minuteman commander A. P. Lee. Adjutant General Britton ordered privates E. H. Happe, Samuel Wicks, William Waltz, and John Salmon to proceed to Lampasas and report to Redmon. Redmon found the "state of affairs to have been as bad if not worse than represented" at headquarters. The exception to this situation had been the "last few nights," owing, Redmon wrote, "to the expected arrival of a Police force." The anticipation of their presence held the disreputable element in check. With the appearance of Redmon in Lampasas, the process of implementing the governor's declaration about six-guns could begin.[29]

On February 17, Redmon cautiously posted the governor's decree, thinking "it best to give" the citizens a "day or so in order that the news may spread fully all over the County" before he commenced to enforce the law, but most of the townsmen had already "laid off their arms." If they offered resistance, Redmon admitted that he could do little as he had but four other State Policemen (John Salmon, A. L. Roy, W. H. Evans, and E. H. Hosse) in his contingent. Redmon realized that his force was insufficient to meet the demands of the situation and informed the adjutant general that there should be "at least twenty five good men (all white)" to "patrole the streets of a night, and then should that fail give them a little Martial Law."[30]

Redmon had no doubt that as soon as "all the police leaves" Lampasas, the troublemakers would commence "carrying their pistols again, at least that is the opinion of most of the law abiding men of the County." Some of the concerned citizens desired that a force be permanently present, and said so, telling the governor that they fervently wished the "police force [be] stationed" in Lampasas "all the time." Expecting more manpower, the nine policemen sent as reinforcement (privates H. R. Street, M. L. Wooley, J. W. M. Harris, John Downey, C. M. Jennings, E. S. Gantt, G. A. Hall, J. M. Brown, and C. L. Bell) had not as yet reported. T. D. Hayworth had accepted a "special commission" as a policeman but would only serve in Lampasas County.[31]

Redmon also wrote about the condition of Lampasas affairs as "they now stand." His first object was to see Justice Thomas Pratt. He inquired if there had been any warrants issued for the arrest of those parties who had been shooting upon the streets of Lampasas. Pratt said no. Redmon probed further, wondering if Pratt "could not get some one who had seen them violating the law" in order to swear out arrest warrants. The justice of the peace informed Redmon that the people were afraid "to make complaints against them." Beyond Pratt, Redmon queried "many" of the "good citizens" of Lampasas. The only information he could glean was "that there has been shooting done in the town but by who[m] they don't know," and no warrants had been issued.[32]

The disruption of Lampasas town life occurred frequently in the early 1870s. Those residents who desired law and order, but were afraid to make a formal complaint, retarded the efforts of the local authorities and prevented state assistance. Sheriff Denson obviously knew that he could not maintain peace himself and that the opposition simply had too many guns. Redmon suggested that surely someone had observed these nightly charades who would swear to viewing them. He soon learned that everyone was "afraid to make complaint against them." Redmon himself often watched the "streets of night," sometimes until 3:30 a.m., "but detected none of them in their shooting though, some of them did shoot a few times" when his "men were absent."[33]

Redmon also interviewed the new minuteman commander, Lee, but learned nothing significant from him. As we have previously seen, a "minute men" company had been organized on February 22, and Lee stated to Redmon that "they was [sic] all good men." Redmon concurred and informed Adjutant General Britton that he had "seen nothing to the contrary." All "state arms" had been turned over to George E. Haynie, a previous commander, except one that had been lost (the adjutant general had Turner's affidavit to that effect) and one in the possession of Ben Horrell, which if not returned the Horrells indicated they would reimburse the state for its cost. There was little chance the state would ever see the weapon or the money.[34]

Redmon expected reinforcements, but so far the only additional policeman to report was Henry Biddy. Biddy's traveling companion, a black policeman (unidentified), had been delayed because on the trip to Lampasas he could not stay in the same lodgings as his white counterpart. Biddy left on February 17 and Redmon ordered William Williams, Samuel Norwood, and William Waltz back to Austin. They had no money, could be of "no service" to him, and were in "danger" of losing their lives most "any night." Through "policy," Redmon thought it best to send them away. Redmon observed that "there is much to be done in this section" and he would like "very much to remain and do it," but a court obligation forced him to leave.[35]

Redmon sent privates Happe, Roy, and Evans "out west" (two miles from Camp Colorado at Sam Gholson's ranch) to investigate Richard Dublin and Ace Lankford Jr. for murdering George W. Hughes and Robert T. Payne and to locate the killers of a black man named Price. Price had been "most brutely [sic] murdered" for his money in Brown County at Baker's Ranch. The suspects included "Wild" Bill Longley, John Jones, Joe J. Albert, Hammond, and two unknowns. Longley and his gang were fifteen miles above Camp Colorado on Hordes Creek. They were "all together at times and go well armed having a Winchester or other guns equaly [sic] as good, and two six shooting revolvers each." Hosse took a deposition from a freedman who had been an eyewitness.[36]

In Lampasas County, privates Hosse, Roy, and Evans arrested A. Wilkenson and Bill Hoffman for killing cattle for their hides, the former being fined, including costs, sixty-two dollars, and the latter "twenty some odd" dollars. Although sporadic shooting had begun again in the town at night, Redmon had not been able to identify the parties as the gunfire occurred "after night when most people were in bed." Clearly the sergeant was frustrated by not being able to apprehend the culprits even though his men had been active outside the town. He fully understood that he needed more men to patrol the streets at night and, as we earlier saw, Redmon was not above using the ultimate power of the governor to end these disturbances: martial law.[37]

Redmon learned nothing about the Short brothers, but he believed that they were "out west with the rest of the murder[er]s." On February 26, as Redmon and his subordinates prepared to leave Lampasas, Sheriff Denson wrote to Adjutant General Britton. In "all probability" they would "return no more," Denson lamented, but while the policemen were "in our midst," they "conducted themselves as gentlemen" and had "done good service since" their arrival. He believed that the "good of the country" depended "very much on their return to our midst again." The sheriff also requested that "four or five good men" be stationed permanently in the town "until scoundrels can be brought to justice or driven from our midst."[38]

The local citizens believed that something had to be done to quell these disturbances and insisted on receiving State Police reinforcements. Finally, on March 10, 1873, Adjutant General Britton ordered Captain Thomas Williams to proceed without delay to the town and arrest all violators of the law which forbade the wearing of weapons inside the town limits. He was to be accompanied by a detachment of seven policemen. Williams's group was to be equipped with five Winchester carbines and fifty rounds of ammunition for each weapon. Carbines were standard fare for the police, but it might be argued that the amount of bullets allotted each man indicated that they were expecting major problems.[39]

Williams's mission: "to aid the local authorities in quelling a band of desperadoes who are committing outrages, and riding over the community" and attempting to murder Sheriff Denson. The State Police troop was also to end the "shooting into the citizen's houses" and prevent other illegal acts. The Horrell group numbered between twelve and fifteen men. None possessed a sterling reputation, although some did seem to have a surface respectability. The desperadoes included: Thomas, Mart, Merritt, and Ben Horrell, Ben Turner, Joe Bolden, Allen Whitecraft, James G. Grizzell, Jerry Scott, Bill Bowen, Billy Gray, G. W. "Wash" and Mark Short, Jim Jenkins, and Sam and Billy Sneed.[40]

Who were the Horrell associates? No background information could be discovered about Turner, Bolden, Whitecraft, Bowen, or Scott. If it was the same Grizzell listed in the 1870 census, then James D. was a 28-year-old farm laborer, with a wife and two children. Alabama born (his sister had married John Horrell), he owned $550 worth of real estate and had personal property valued at $790. Billy (William) Gray was a 24-year-old Missouri-born son of a farm laborer. (Apparently farm life did not suit him.) Jenkins was a 38-year-old teamster, North Carolina born, worth $1,700 in total property, whose household comprised two other families. Billy (William) Sneed was a 24-year-old native Texan who lived with Thomas Horrell.[41]

The man who led the State Police into Lampasas, Thomas Williams, was born in Stone County, Missouri, on November 23, 1844. His parents, Enoch and Emaline, had moved in the late 1840s to Caldwell County, Texas, where Thomas's father earned a living as a farmer and a millwright. (Thomas's parents, who were strong Union supporters, moved to Newton County, Missouri, in 1867.) During the antebellum years, Thomas was a stock raiser. What he did in the early part of the war is unknown (obviously he supported the Union), but on December 28, 1863, Williams enlisted in Company B of the

1st Texas Cavalry U.S. Volunteers at Brownsville and eventually attained the rank of second lieutenant. Once hostilities ceased, he married and dabbled in politics.[42]

Although not born in Lockhart (thirty miles south of Austin), Caldwell County, Williams had been a resident there since about 1848. Williams married Mattie G. Elgin in 1868, fathered two children, served as county clerk and as an assistant assessor of internal revenue in the 2nd Division in the 3rd District of Texas. He was a committed Republican. His first wife died in late 1870. A year later he wed Elizabeth "Lizzie" Baker. Tennessee born, more importantly she was the daughter of Thomas H. and Margaret Baker. Baker had carved out a small political career for himself, serving as county judge, as agent of the Freedmen's Bureau, and as a State Senator in the 12th and 13th Legislatures.[43]

What Williams had done before the Republicans took power in 1870 and authorized a state constabulary is not always clear. Yet, he must have attracted some notice as Governor Davis and the newly designated Chief of Police James Davidson immediately commissioned him a lieutenant in the State Police. Although the administrative powers sought to move Williams away from his home region of Lockhart, he successfully resisted most of these efforts. By late 1870, as the State Police became more completely organized, Williams assumed control of five counties in the 1st Police District. More critical sections needed attention, and Williams was ordered to Goliad, but circumstances forced him to resign his commission in the first month of 1871.

What Williams did in his six-month hiatus from the State Police is unknown, but by mid-1871 he had been reinstated in the organization at his former rank. Williams served in Mount Enterprise (Rusk County) and various other sections, but by April 1872 he had applied once again to be stationed at Lockhart. His request was rejected by Governor Davis. He resigned and briefly entered politics. In this instance, he was pitted against some longtime stalwarts who had even more influence than his father-in-law, Baker. He declared for one of three state representative seats from the 27th District (which comprised Caldwell, Gonzales, and Guadalupe counties). Williams exhausted his bank account and finished a distant fifth out of six contestants.[44]

Williams had cast his political lot at the wrong time as a Republican backlash occurred across the state in 1872. Thus, because of his dire monetary need, Williams turned to the occupation he apparently knew best and requested that he once again be appointed to the State Police. In November 1872, Williams, "having lost greatly both in time and money in the past campaign," was commissioned a captain by Chief of Police F. L. Britton, who had recently assumed the position of adjutant general. Williams investigated lawlessness in McDade, Ledbetter, and Giddings, among other towns. When the Lampasas trouble began, Williams was ordered there to enforce the governor's prohibition on carrying guns.[45]

On the morning before Williams and his squad entered Lampasas, the *Daily State Journal* later reported, the Horrells and their followers ("bloodthirsty wretches" and "monsters") took up their usual residence at the saloon "with murder in their hearts." They attempted to bring about an altercation with Lieutenant Lee of the minutemen company on the same morning Williams was assassinated. "But for the coolness of Lee the work of blood would have begun earlier in the day," the *Journal* suggested. The fugitives remained in town and had "consolidated with the Short band, another organization of outlaws, for mutual protection and to facilitate their objects of plunder and murder."[46]

As Williams and his detail began their trek to Lampasas to meet their deadly fate, all seemed to be placid on the surface. In fact, the local newspaper described an almost idyllic setting where peace reigned and a town seemingly undisturbed by rowdiness or undesirable characters. The *Dispatch* wrote: "weather pleasant; health good; business flush; money getting plenty; times easy; town improving; country setting up; fishing parties common; boat riding frequent; school teachers busy; lawyers lazy; doctors idle; merchants pleasing; hotel keepers smiling; blacksmiths hammering; carpenters nailing; butchers flourishing; farmers plowing; old folks gardening and young folks courting."[47]

Williams and his seven-man escort arrived in Lampasas at about one o'clock on March 14. What transpired immediately after that is not precisely clear, although there are various versions. When Williams rode into town he allegedly saw Bill Bowen (a Horrell brother-in-law) wearing a pistol and entering Scott's saloon. Adjutant General Britton reported that Williams arrested Bowen for carrying a six-shooter. This is confirmed by various newspaper accounts. "With breathtaking foolhardiness," according to Frederick Nolan, the Horrells' biographer, "Williams decided to take on the clan on their own turf." Accompanied by J. M. Daniels, Wesley Cherry, and Andrew Melville, they walked into the bar. Britton said they were lured into the establishment "under some pretense."[48]

One of the major sources of information that has often been used to chronicle the Lampasas troubles, the Horrells, and the death of the four policemen is John Nichols, who served as a county judge from 1897 to 1900 and as a justice of the peace, but was not present in Lampasas when the altercation between the Horrells and the State Police occurred. Nichols, born in Missouri in 1841, arrived in Lampasas in the late 1850s. During the war he served with Samuel Horrell, senior and junior, in the Frontier Regiment of Mounted Volunteers, Captain J. J. Callan's company. Eighty-six years old when interviewed about his recollection of these happenings, Nichols had been living in New Mexico when the events occurred in Lampasas. Nichols died in 1929.[49]

In 1927, John Nichols recalled that the police went into the saloon and the "Horrells happened to be there." Williams did not know them but they knew the uniforms. They left "a Nigger out to watch their horses." (Nichols believed there were "eight or ten" State Police.) They were taking a drink when Williams, by Nichols's recollection, said they had come after the Horrells. One of the Horrells replied that "they were there and they could take them if they wanted to, and began shooting." Mart was said to have shot Williams and Tom got one "as he ran off." The "Negro [Robert Jones] who had been left to hold their horses passed Dr. Andy Fields' residence, seventeen miles out on the road towards Austin and they said that he had never taken up his rope."[50]

Although we will never know what happened in the State Police "massacre," as the *Daily State Journal* referred to the killings, or what words were exchanged, much of the evidence points to the fact that it was an ambush. Williams, Cherry, Daniels, and Melville never had a chance. Newspapers reported that when the men arrived, the captain "heard of the presence" of a "number of men who were armed, and one man armed with a pistol displayed himself" and then went into the barroom. Williams sent "three of his men to different points" and along with the three privates entered the saloon to arrest Bill Bowen. Williams ordered his men not to draw their weapons "or make any demonstrations, as he preferred to make a peaceable arrest."[51]

Williams stepped into the room, spotted Bowen, and "demanded his surrender." Bowen refused and Williams "attempted to wrest his pistol from him, the rest of the men simply looking on, with their backs turned to the bar." At this juncture "a volley was fired into the police from behind, by at least eight or ten men." Williams was hit by three bullets. The first went in the back of his head and "entirely through the face." When he turned the second and third slugs struck him in the chest. His assassins were near him when they fired. Daniels died instantly, receiving several shots in the head and body, one of which passed "from one ear to the other." Cherry suffered a fatal chest wound as did Melville, but the latter lingered for almost a month before dying.[52]

With "twenty or more shots" fired from "Winchester carbines," it is not surprising that the State Policemen went down. Adjutant General Britton declared that the "manner in which the assassins were stationed and the accuracy of their fire, gave the policemen no chance to defend themselves against the cowardly attack." What many previous writers dismissed were newspaper reports on the Lampasas incident. The stories were based upon statements made by Melville before he succumbed to his fatal wound. It must be remembered that Melville was wounded on March 14 but did not die until April 10. (He was twenty-five.) Melville had been a member of the State Police for only three weeks when he met the Horrells.[53]

According to Adjutant General Britton, Thomas, Mart, and Merritt Horrell, along with Ben Turner, Joe Bolden, Allen Whitecraft, James Grizzell, Jerry Scott, Bill Bowen, and Bill Gray were in the saloon and many "secreted themselves behind screens and doors." After the killing the desperadoes came out and attacked the three remaining policemen. In an exchange of gunfire, Mart and Thomas Horrell were wounded, Mart "in the back of the neck" by Private Henry Eddie (Eddy). At the inquest held on March 20, with Thomas Pratt, the acting coroner presiding, the verdict was that the policemen's deaths were caused by Thomas and Merritt Horrell, Turner, Bolden, Whitecraft, Grizzell, Scott, Bowen, and Gray.[54]

The desperadoes Whitecraft, Grizzell, Scott, and Mart Horrell were arrested. Mart, wounded in the head in the shootout, had been carried to his mother's house (some two hundred yards from the saloon) by Tom and Merritt, and thus was in no condition to evade search parties. He was subsequently captured. After this, Tom (who had apparently been shot just "below the shoulder blade") and Merritt rode out of town and escaped the numerous groups which had banded together to capture the killers. Although an intensive search was made for the remaining Horrells and their cohorts, they were never found. The Horrells did not "leave the Lampasas country until September as they stayed out scouting around the mountains."[55]

The civil authorities were dismayed by the killings although they probably did not fear the imposition of martial law as the legislature was moving toward eliminating the State Police. They did quickly make funeral arrangements for the three dead State Policemen to take place the following day. On Saturday, March 15, 1873, "with honor and respect by the people of Lampasas," Williams, Cherry, and Daniels were buried in the local cemetery. Although the state never particularly pursued the killers of these three men and largely ignored the fact that they had been shot down in cold blood, a few of the assemblymen retained some dignity. On March 26 the Texas Senate appropriated five hundred dollars to have the men reinterred in the State Cemetery in Austin.[56]

While Lampasas citizens paid their final respects to Williams, Cherry, and Daniels, Andrew Melville lingered near death at the Huling Hotel. Although "being kindly attended" to by Sergeant W. A. Johnson, his condition worsened and all "proved unavailing." Melville died on April 10 and was also buried in Lampasas. Britton informed Melville's sister in Providence, Rhode Island, that her brother was a "brave and an efficient officer" killed by desperadoes. Any assistance Britton could render either in removing his remains or adjusting his accounts would be "proffered readily." If Melville's sister wanted the body removed, he suggested the "propriety of deferring the same until next fall" when the warm weather had subsided.[57]

Upon verbal instructions received from Governor Davis on March 15, Chief of Police Britton left for Lampasas on March 16 at 11 a.m. Accompanied by twelve State Policemen, they were to investigate the State Police killings. They camped that evening twenty-five miles from Lampasas as the horses were tired and some of the men had "straggled behind," their horses not able to keep pace "owing to the rapidity of the march." They were met by Lieutenant Lee, commander of Company M, Minute Men, who, along with one of his men, was on his way to Austin to seek police reinforcements. Lee said his men were "barricaded in a rock house," expecting an attack from the "outlaws and their friends," whom they estimated at forty or fifty individuals.[58]

Britton had his men mount and proceeded to Lampasas, where they arrived at 5 a.m. on March 17. According to Britton, the "worst state of affairs possible existed in the town and county. The citizens were panic stricken, had closed their stores," and the policemen discovered that "all business had stopped in anticipation of an attack from the mob party." The adjutant general quickly and wisely dispatched a courier to Burnet County, ordering Lieutenant John Alexander to report to him with his company as soon as possible. Along with Sheriff Denson, Britton began to investigate the reasons for the disturbance and why the town had now become an armed camp. A search party was formed and the citizens promised their cooperation.[59]

The number of men comprising the various forces is uncertain (one newspaper claimed 150), but it included the Lampasas County Minute Men under Lee's direction, a detachment of Burnet County Minute Men commanded by Sergeant W. H. Shelburne, the State Police under Britton's control, and a posse of "many good citizens" under Sheriff Denson's supervision. For five days they scoured the countryside in the Lampasas region as thoroughly as possible and visited Burnet, Llano, Coryell, and Williamson counties, searching for the murderers. Along with evidence from other sources, Britton became convinced they had "fled to the frontier." Lieutenant Madison Wear and ten State Policemen, as the citizens requested, were stationed in Lampasas.[60]

From March 16 until March 20, Britton and the various groups pursued the police killers, but some members of the local establishment refused to cooperate with the state in capturing the remaining members of the Horrell gang. The Chief of Police excoriated the Williamson County Sheriff, John L. Peay, for allowing the murderers to stop and stay about Georgetown "unmolested" by Peay, his deputies, or any other county officers, "notwithstanding their presence, and the crimes they had committed were generally known to the community." In addition, Britton called upon the assistance of John Alexander, the commander of Company O of Minute Men from Burnet, who refused to obey or even respond to his call for help.[61]

The four prisoners under arrest—Jerry Scott, Mart Horrell, Allen Whitecraft, and James Grizzell—who had been indicted by a grand jury, were committed to the Travis County jail "for safe keeping" until the meeting of the next term of the district court. Britton believed that if he had left them in the Lampasas County jail, "their friends would rescue them." He also recommended that a reward of five hundred dollars be offered for each one of the individuals implicated by the verdict of the jury of inquest. "These men are of the very worst reputation," Britton maintained, "and are so feared by the citizens of the county in which they live that one yell from them to 'hide out' is sufficient to close all doors within hearing."[62]

Davis followed Britton's recommendation for a monetary incentive and on March 25 offered a three thousand dollar reward, five hundred dollars apiece, for the apprehension (arrest and conviction) of Thomas and Merritt Horrell, Ben Turner, Joe Bolden, Bill Bowen, and Billy Gray, known to have been involved in the killing of the State Policemen and still at large and fugitives from justice. They were "lawless men" engaged in murder and "various other outrages upon the peaceable citizens" of Lampasas County and had been charged with "many felonies." They had managed to elude the various groups that had attempted to discover their whereabouts after the murders at the saloon. If captured, they were to be delivered to the sheriff.[63]

On March 21, Lampasas County citizens assembled in a mass meeting to express their sentiments about the recent spate of events. Adjutant General Britton addressed the throng, as did other prominent residents of the town and county. In his quite diplomatic speech, Britton emphasized the "valuable assistance rendered" by Sheriff Denson, Lieutenant Lee, and the Lampasas Minute Men, along with many good citizens of the area. The county authorities had graciously paid for the board of the men and horses of the State Policemen and agreed to do the same for the minute companies. Britton was clearly satisfied with the response of the inhabitants in their effort to track down the Horrells. Unfortunately, their search came to naught.[64]

The citizens drafted four resolutions to demonstrate their appreciation for the state's response and to suggest what action they planned for the future to end the reign of such men as the Horrells and their followers. First, the people thanked the State Police "for their gentlemanly deportment" and "for their unceasing efforts to restore order and the dominion of law." Second, they pledged their "unqualified support" in bringing criminals to justice and to "resist any injury to the person or property of any" other. Third, they would provide information and "personal aid" to the sheriff. Finally, they requested that a sufficient number of State Police remain to maintain order until local authorities could "check the lawless."[65]

"Much excitement" followed the return of Adjutant General Britton's group in Austin on March 22 with four prisoners: Scott (of saloon fame), Mart Horrell (who had received a neck wound in the Williams altercation), Whitecraft, and Grizzell (one of whom the *Daily State Journal* emphasized was the "murderer" of Williams), in "carriages filled with police." The four men had originally been arrested by Denson and Lampasas citizens and closely guarded. The *Democratic Statesman* said that the "whole affair shows that all the good citizens of the community were outraged by the course of these outlaws." The *Journal* opined that "all of the parties killed are well known and good citizens, and have families to mourn their untimely taking off."[66]

A meeting of the late officers and soldiers of United States volunteers, directed by Governor Davis and George W. Paschal, occurred on the day Britton returned to Austin with some of the killers. The object of the meeting was to accord Williams a proper burial. With "feelings of horror and indignation" they learned of the "brutal and dastardly murder" by "assassins and desperadoes" and desired that his remains be removed from Lampasas to the State Cemetery in Austin. It was decided a memorial should be presented to the legislature to encourage the offer of a reward for those who committed the recent murder. They also sent their "heartfelt sympathy" to the family "in this hour of their affliction, bereavement and sorrow."[67]

Williams's body did not arrive in Austin from Lampasas until April 9, 1873, almost a month after his death. An "eloquent" public funeral was held on April 11 at the United States district courtroom. Among those in attendance were Governor Davis, Adjutant General Britton, the state treasurer, the superintendent of education, the black state senator George T. Ruby, and various other members of the legislature. The body was transported by wagon (the hearse was too small to receive his casket) to the State Cemetery, where the Odd Fellows read resolutions. The *Daily State Journal* left a fitting epitaph for Williams: he fell in the "path of duty" and "died in the defense of law and order, and his name deserves to be enrolled among the heroic dead."[68]

The *Daily State Journal* also extolled Williams's virtues and asserted that he exemplified members of the State Police. The paper stated that the Williams murder would "cause a shock to our State, and sorrow to the entire community where he has lived most of his life." Known for "his bravery and excellent bearing," the newspaper wrote that the "disturbed condition" of Texas "would not permit a man of such activity to remain idle." He had proved through his efficiency the extent of his valuable talents. Williams had brought dedication to the organization and "fallen in the path of duty, while enforcing the law, and protecting life and property." The *Journal* waxed ecstatic when it exclaimed that he was "so gallant, young, brave, [and] generous."[69]

After the killing of the State Policemen, Lampasas affairs remained unsettled. The *Dispatch* thought the Thirteenth Legislature a "fraud upon the people," which was the "universal opinion without regard to party." The citizens were in the process of selecting a mayor and it was feared that they might have to look beyond the county in their search. Even though the temperance movement made inroads into Lampasas, there were still "many bar-rooms." As for cattle rustling, it continued to be a problem as the recent investigation of a herd near Lampasas demonstrated. The cattle belonged to various persons in the vicinity who had "never sold or authorized them to be sold." This was "cattle stealing by wholesale."[70]

Within two weeks after being taken to Austin, Horrell and Scott were transferred to the Georgetown jail on a writ of habeas corpus. Mrs. Horrell was permitted to stay at the jail and nurse her husband. Britton could not leave them in Lampasas as the town had no jail to speak of and he was certain that the friends of the two men would make a determined effort to effect their release. Britton probably believed that since he had the citizens and the militia mobilized, along with outside support, the Horrell gang would not be so brazen as to attempt a rescue of their comrades from the State Police detachment headed by the adjutant general. In fact, the Horrells were regrouping and waiting for a more advantageous moment.[71]

On Friday night about 11 p.m., May 2, 1873, a body of approximately thirty-five men (another source claimed "forty or upwards") armed with Spencer rifles and six-shooters rode north through Georgetown in Williamson County. They shortly returned (the citizens were now really alarmed) and surrounded the jail and the adjacent guardhouse. The deputy sheriff and four guards were barricaded inside the buildings. The citizens could provide no relief because of the "siege and fire of the marauders." The engagement continued for over an hour, with perhaps 250 to 1,000 shots exchanged. The guards finally exhausted their supply of ammunition. With superior numbers, the gang of men who intended to release those incarcerated made their move.[72]

The assailants succeeded in ascending the stairs, and "[Bill] Bowen broke in the door with a sledge hammer." Two other prisoners indicted for horse stealing, Barry and Whittington, were also freed. A. S. Fisher, a Georgetown lawyer who worked as a guard, was seriously injured, shot in the side and the leg. It was thought that a "number of the ruffians were wounded," as evidenced by the large quantity of blood on the saddle of a captured horse. The attackers were readily recognized, including the leader, a brother of Horrell, who warned the citizens to "stand back, he did not want to injure them, but he was determined at any sacrifice to release the prisoners." They succeeded in making their escape.[73]

The startling news of the liberation of the "Lampasas murderers" was "well calculated to give the most serious alarm to the good citizens," who would "now be made the prey of these ruffians," exclaimed one newspaper. Another envisioned the possible inauguration of a "reign of terror" of the "most frightful character—citizens murdered, or driven from their homes to eat the bitter bread of exile." Would "anarchy and bloodshed" finally "triumph over law and public morality?" Had society at last come to the point where each man was "to buckle on his six-shooter and, in defiance of all human authority, look to his own right arm for defence?" It feared that the days of vigilante committees were "soon to be revived."[74]

In April 1873, the assemblymen enacted legislation which officially incorporated the city of Lampasas to be governed by a mayor and eight aldermen. In May the citizens conducted a "peaceable" election in a "quiet manner." But that may have been the only calm aspect of life in the town. Indian resistance intensified with the elimination of the State Police, and desperadoes "in different portions of the State have banded together and bid open defiance to the law and the officers of the law," wrote the *Journal.* The Georgetown jail escapade had been "passed over almost unnoticed." Murderers and outlaws went back "to their old neighborhood" and "bid defiance to the sheriff and peace officers" of Lampasas County.[75]

By early July, Lampasas society again became disordered. The Horrells and others had made several visits to Lampasas and "in the face of the Authorities," the city attorney, Charles H. Porter, wrote Governor Davis, "play billiards in our saloons and our officers dare not arrest them." An ordinance prohibiting the carrying of deadly weapons within the corporate limits had

Porter wondering whether the members of a minute company, when not on duty, had a right to carry arms. They were "not doing a particle of good," and some members were "in the habit of coming to town and getting drunk." There were few Republicans in Lampasas, and Porter had "already made enemies of a few (bad ones)" for prosecuting them before the mayor's court.[76]

The same men who had previously originated much of the trouble again appeared on the streets. An anonymous letter writer told the editor of the *Daily State Journal* that after interviewing the Horrells he had concluded they were "still in the notion to murder and rob," stealing every horse and cow in the county, and when the livestock was claimed by the rightful owners, the Horrells rubbed the "muzzles of their guns and pistols" in their faces and dared them "to resent it." Comprising about twenty well-armed men, they defied everybody and were "supported by several" of the "oldest citizens." They had been "raising hell," and when a man caught them with his horse "or sees them come and drive him away he is afraid to mention it to his best friend."[77]

At the end of July, another Lampasas writer, almost illiterate, requested that Davis "take some steps to bring thease out lawd harrels [Horrells] to justice." Preparing to leave soon with their stolen cattle, the Horrells were "going to drive a great many peoples stock and they cant help themselves." If the frontier forts were notified, the soldiers could either catch or kill them and return the animals. If they could be brought to justice "it would doe more good than any thing that could be done to stop crime in this country than anything that could be imagined." Equally disturbing was the fact that the minute men were on good terms with the Horrells, traded with the group, and assisted them and simultaneously drew pay from the state.[78]

As fall approached and the Horrells/State Police confrontation lapsed into memory, life in Lampasas settled into a familiar pattern, punctuated by a destructive natural disaster which almost obliterated the town. Company M Minute Men, under the command of E. W. Greenwood, was mustered into service. When Deputy Sheriff Albertus Sweet and a posse attempted to arrest Bill Dixon for horse theft, an altercation ensued which left Philip Sutton (Dixon's father-in-law) and Dixon dead. Justifiable homicide, said the jury. The Indians conducted raids, stealing a hundred horses on one venture, but settlers had to be cautious about guarding their property from not only the Indians but also "from the hands of the many thieves now infesting the frontier."[79]

As detrimental to Lampasas life as the outcasts was nature. First, the army worm, "or something similar," was "seriously injuring the Hungarian grass" in the section, stripping the grass of its blades and "leaving nothing but the stalk and heads," which made it useless as feed. Heavy rains began in late September and continued into early October, inundating Lampasas with fourteen inches or more of water and doing inestimable damage. Stores were swept away along with houses, and three adults and three children drowned in the flood. After the water subsided, only one store in town remained, the grinding mills either gone or badly crippled, and people "entirely destitute of clothing, houses and money."[80]

Three and one-half years after they killed the four State Policemen, the Horrells encountered a courtroom. The trial of Mart, Thomas, and Merritt took place at the October 1876 term of the district court and resulted in the "acquittal of all the parties, without the necessity of the jury leaving their seats." The *Houston Daily Telegram*, hostile to the Davis administration, stated that "it was proven by the several witnesses that one of the policemen fired the first shot [which contradicts every bit of available documentary evidence] as he entered the saloon," while Captain Williams was having "an animated controversy with Bill Bowen, whom he had arrested for carrying a six-shooter, and was endeavoring to take away from the saloon."[81]

George Washington "Wash" Short, who might be credited with originating the Lampasas scenario because of his drunkenness and wounding the sheriff in the initial confrontation which led to the appearance of the State Police, was arrested in November 1879 in Montague County. He was placed under bond to appear at district court to answer charges of assault with intent to murder Sheriff Denson on January 14, 1873, plus three other indictments against him for cattle theft. (His brother, Mart Short, had been killed in 1876 by Denson's son, Sam.) What exactly happened in these cases is unknown, and the final fate of Wash is similarly unknown. Nevertheless, he fit into the Horrell mold and his characteristics mirrored those of his associates. None of the group had enviable reputations.[82]

The Horrells continued to find trouble. (This should have suggested something about the family to previous writers.) Once again, the charges suggested cattle stealing. Facing a formidable family of the area, the Higgins, led by John Pinckney Calhoun "Pink" Higgins, a rancher, and perhaps "Lampasas' most noted gun fighter," a feud began. It reached serious proportions in January 1877, when Pink murdered Merritt in cold blood in Scott's saloon. After intermittent clashes between the opposing forces, on June 7, 1877, the two sides (seven Horrells and four Higginses) confronted each other in town and began shooting. For all the gunfire, which lasted until early afternoon, only two people were fatally or seriously wounded.[83]

The Horrells disappeared. After rumors circulated of another impending confrontation between the two families, the Texas Rangers interceded, negotiated a peace with the Horrells (they had been led to the hiding place by a Higgins cohort), and took them into custody. The Higginses were also arrested. The total included twelve prisoners (five Horrells, three Higginses, and four others). Major John B. Jones of the Frontier Battalion served as a mediator between the warring factions and managed to have all parties sign an agreement to end the feud. It succeeded, at least openly. Privately, there may have been more violence. In December 1878, Mart and Tom were killed in the Meridian jail, their bodies riddled "with bullets."[84]

Thus ended the saga of the Horrell clan. That they were a "respected and well-liked family," or "old settlers," or members of the "cattle gentry" is to be seriously doubted. They were rarely any of these. They were not "common thieves," but they did perform lawless acts that made outlaws of them. They were not native Texans, although they probably did grow into adulthood on the frontier. Moreover, as now seems obligatory in the promotion of local legends, the brothers were as quick as "chained lightning" with either a pistol or a Winchester. (Interestingly enough, they always seemed to use their weapons from ambush positions.) In fact, there is nothing in the literature to suggest that the Horrells were either well liked or respected.

Ignoring the land which Elizabeth owned and the little stock, there is no indication that the Horrell brothers farmed it after she moved into town. The only successful brother, Samuel, did not participate in his brothers' activities. Collectively, the four brothers involved in the killing had little land or stock. Benjamin F., Thomas, Mart, and Merritt were basically farm laborers who owned almost no cattle but some personal property. To be sure, all but Merritt were married, but if we consider the sources that tell us something about their economic status, they were a far cry from being members of any kind of gentry, cattle or otherwise. Most of the stories that surround the Horrell brothers are simply that; they were rustlers.

As the evidence attests, throughout their lives, the Horrells spelled trouble, and those who associated with them increased the likelihood of a deathly encounter. They invited suspicion through their cattle-rustling, murdering state officials, and harassing local innocents. They posed as farmers or stock raisers, but the preponderance of the source material leads to the conclusion that this family had an unpleasant streak about it and wished to abide by their own rules no matter where they lived. In every locale where the Horrells resided, problems arose, involving murder and other unpleasant consequences.

Regardless of how past writers have described them, the Horrells clearly were undesirable elements within the community.

Although the Horrells have received the "glory" from the 1873 State Police killing, maybe it should be the four men that died in attempting to bring some peace and justice to the frontier and local communities that should be reconsidered. These men and the majority of other State Policemen who appeared in various Texas locales during the force's existence performed their duties rather well. In the entire Lampasas scenario, there is little information to suggest that the State Police did anything other than acquit themselves respectfully, whether individually or as a group. These men were neither "fiends from hell," as they have so often been portrayed, nor the violators of civil and personal rights.

Four State Policemen died as a result of the Horrell ambush in Lampasas. Indeed, the State Police, as individuals or as an organization, never acted so properly in approaching a town as did Williams and his men in March 1873. Numerous prominent legal and civil officials had requested the adjutant general to send a force, and Williams was an excellent choice to lead the contingent, with considerable previous police experience. His job, along with that of his subordinates, was to enforce the law regarding the wearing of weapons in town and reduce the numerous disturbances that had disrupted the area. Although their action ended in the cold-blooded murder of four men, they certainly did not perform in a way that denigrated the organization to which they belonged.

While the Lampasas crisis was in the making, Governor Davis and Chief of Police Britton were at war with the Thirteenth Legislature in a final valiant effort to save the State Police. From its very inception, the Democrats had opposed the organization. Newspapers across the Lone Star State, a majority of the Democratic persuasion, had ceaselessly hammered at the foibles, mistakes, and so-called oppressiveness of the state gendarmes. No mistakes of the force, no matter how small or large, went unnoticed, and, indeed, many times they were magnified out of proportion to the incident or event. The assassination of four State Policemen in Lampasas fazed the legislature not at all. They dispensed entirely with the "governor's hounds."

Epilogue

Addressing the opening of the Democratically controlled Thirteenth Legislature two months before the Lampasas massacre, Governor E. J. Davis knew his militia system and the State Police were about to be eliminated. One of his two major goals during his tenure had been to "restrain that lawlessness which always unfavorably distinguished our people, but had become shockingly intensified by the habits taught our young men in military camps." Reviewing his measures to "suppress lawlessness," Davis had established the militia for "preservation of the peace," which gave him the authority to "suspend the laws within disturbed districts." Compelled to do so on three occasions, the knowledge that the governor had this power prevented additional upheaval.[1]

Moreover, the State Police had "relieved the State of multitudes of bad characters," but Davis did not think their services could, as yet, be dispensed with. During their thirty-month existence, they had cost the state a total of $408,274.12, or an annual cost of $163,309.64. In this same time span they had arrested 581 individuals charged with murder, another 760 for attempting to kill, 1,748 with various felonies, and several thousand who had committed lesser offenses. They had also recovered and returned considerable amounts of property to owners, of which no accounting had been kept. While performing their duties, eleven policemen had been slain and a large number wounded. Their overall efficiency had been impaired because of the depreciation of state warrants by which they were paid. This amounted to about half their regular pay.[2]

Davis admitted that after the resignation of Chief of Police James Davidson on November 4, 1872, it was discovered his accounts were incorrect. An examination revealed a shortage of close to forty thousand dollars. This had been a rather recent development in Davidson's character because an earlier accounting by the legislature suggested his budget was in order. The comptroller had disregarded Davis's instructions of March 18, 1872, which forbade the "drawing of money from the Treasury without vouchers filed, showing lawful disbursement." Ignoring this admonition, Davidson was furnished "facilities for running up the greater part of this amount" and embezzled the money that should have been paid to claimants. Davis hoped the sum would soon be made up.[3]

When the Thirteenth Legislature convened in January 1873, the major agenda focused upon eliminating the militia system and the State Police, which Davis had created in 1870. Personal animosities and legal confrontations compounded the solons' decision. Although both the Senate and the House desired to abolish the militia completely, Davis vetoed the bill. The intended law, the governor correctly observed, was "beyond the power of the Legislature," as it violated both the state and the United States constitutions. In fact, if the politicians had not provided for such an organization it would be imperative that they immediately do so. But since they had already done so the repeal was "null and void."[4]

Davis provided the legislators with an alternative to complete elimination by suggesting that they simply excise three sections of the original law. Those provisions had initially dealt with the State Guard, the power to declare martial law, and the trials of offenders who were initially responsible for the suspension of the laws in the first place. Although the *Daily State Journal* cautioned the members to "go slow in the tearing down business," as it was "easy to tear down, but hard to build up," the legislators were on a mission. They responded to Davis's suggestion and repealed the three obnoxious portions of the 1870 legislation, amended two other sections, and abolished the Special Police.[5]

The day after Davis sent his message to the legislature defending his militia system and, significantly, the State Police, the House took the initiative in moving to eliminate the police completely and was quickly joined by the Senate. The conservative press added its support for police disbandment, declaring that in "rare instances" it might have "rendered service to the cause of law and order, yet upon the whole, we are convinced that the existence of the police force, has been an exciting cause of crime." Using the specious argument that desperadoes took advantage of the "popular prejudice against" the force, the press insisted that these desperadoes would "resist arrest to the death, when they would yield at once to the sheriff or constable."[6]

In his veto of the House bill to abolish the State Police, Davis reiterated the fact that he did not think the organization should be purged. He understood that a majority of the House members disagreed with him on this subject, and that an unqualified repeal was pending. Davis, therefore, directed the adjutant general to poll county sheriffs for the number of homicides, or attempts at murder, which occurred in their counties since January 1, 1873. From official reports (twenty-nine) and unofficial ones (twenty-five), seventy-eight people had been slain and there were seventy-two attempted killings in the fifty-four counties reporting. These statistics were "probably short of the full number of crimes of that nature," and other offenses were not noted.[7]

Extrapolating from the figures, Davis suggested that if the proportion of murders, or attempts, averaged the same in the remaining 135 inhabited counties of the state as they did in the 54 reported, the results would be ominous. More than likely, the results would be higher rather than lower, the governor argued, which would mean 195 violent deaths in three months. If extended to the entire year, this would translate into 780 murders. Whether this estimate was valid or not, the fact remained that seventy-eight people had been dispatched in the first three months of 1873 in only a third of the state's counties. But even as bad as the situation remained, Davis felt conditions had improved, as suggested by a comparison with the 1869 crime report compiled by the United States Army. Thus, to further civilize the state and bring "lawbreakers to justice," Davis believed it more "advisable to strengthen and amplify" the State Police.[8]

To illustrate the unfortunate lawless condition of Texas, and the "extraordinary insecurity of life," Davis compared Texas to New York. Although cities perhaps had a larger criminal element than rural districts, New York with a population of 3,880,735 in 1860 had a total of only thirty-seven murders. Texas, with 818,579 inhabitants in 1870, had a far higher homicide rate. But homicide was not the only problem. In fact, in fourteen counties citizen delegations or county officers had called upon the state government for "assistance to overcome lawless combinations too strong for the local authorities." Davis candidly admitted this was a "bad record," and one which the state might try to "hide from people of the outside world whom we are inviting to come" to Texas.[9]

This approach, however, would be "neither manly nor Statesman like to shrink, *ourselves*, from its contemplation." It was in the best interest of Texas that this phenomenon be fully understood and the citizens be "ready to face and suppress this evil." Unquestionably, decent citizens deplored the circumstances and desired a remedy, only differing as to means. Some suggested giving sheriffs more power, and others said large rewards "should be offered for all offenders indiscriminately." Additional plans had also been proposed. Davis declared all these devices would cost as much, if not more, than the present system. They could not be "effective because they all fail in the essential of having a paid and efficient body of men, *under one head*, ready at a moment to move in any direction either to assist the local authorities or to follow and arrest fugitives from justice."[10]

For months, asserted Davis, the State Police had been less efficient than might be expected had they received the compensation nominally allowed them by the state. Notwithstanding this problem, they had arrested thousands of offenders for a variety of offenses. To be sure, in three or four instances, policemen had criminally murdered citizens. These examples, Davis admitted, "furnish an unfailing supply of texts for arguments against the system." Whether the police were to blame, or the character of the individuals killed was the compelling reason for their deaths, had never been adjudicated by any tribunal. Davis refused to discuss the issue of guilt or innocence. But even if some had wrongly acted, was this a "reasonable argument to use against the whole system?"[11]

Sheriffs, deputies, constables, and city police had also committed despicable acts, but it would be manifestly unfair to argue that these officials should be eliminated. Beyond this, those who condemned the State Police for a host of wrongs never considered the many "gallant men" of the force who had "died or risked life in the enforcement of the laws." Davis contended that several had been killed outright and many more wounded. Considering these reasons, Davis requested the House reconsider their appeal. The impression that it would pass had already "emboldened law breakers and bad men," along with a "swelling of the tide of lawlessness." If the police acts were defective, and if bad men through such defects had been appointed to the organization, or if they could be advantageously modified, Davis's solution was to dismiss them and amend the law. The governor was willing to cooperate with the legislature to increase the efficiency of the State Police.[12]

The *Daily Democratic Statesman* expressed the dominant thinking of the legislature, and probably Texans in general, when it stated that "any law that gives the criminal classes a pretext for the commission of crime, or elevates them into popular heroes and martyrs, is eminently demoralizing, and ought to be removed from the statute book." Because of the extreme unpopularity of the State Police, any party who shot one of its members was "looked upon as a popular hero, rather than as a murderer." The Democratic legislature did not need any urging from their supporters in the press to remove the hated organization. It took three months of wrangling, but the House overrode Davis's veto, 58 to 7, and the Senate similarly did so 18 to 7.[13]

Although not in direct response to the Democratic newspapers' notions about the removal of the police, earlier the *Houston Union* had provided a compelling counterargument to hostile police thinking. "After all the furor the Democrats have raised about the use" by Davis of the police, "what peaceable, law-abiding man is hurt by it?" asked the administrative organ. It did not bear hard "upon the mass of the peaceable citizenship." If the force oppressed people in general, it would affect members of both political parties. Nobody was hurt by Davis's "rigid programme" except the "desperadoes, lawbreakers, murderers and assassins, and their friends." The clamor raised against the governor for "swooping down like a thunderbolt" upon criminals was unjustified. Thus, the Democrats had "stained themselves with blood, and placed themselves in opposition to the enforcement of the laws."[14]

Although much negative information has been written about the State Police, no one has ever analyzed the roster (see appendix) of who served in the organization. Altogether, 1,090 men are listed, only 950 of them actually performed service. Of those who joined the constabulary about whom we have definite background information, 574 were white, 126 black, 15 Mexican, and a considerable 235 unknowns. This means that whites comprised 60 percent of the membership, blacks 13 percent, and Mexicans but 1.5 percent. The problem, of course, is the vast number of unknowns, which are almost one-quarter of the total. These preliminary numbers do strongly suggest that African Americans comprised a significantly smaller percentage of the force than has previously been stated, but in some ways are misleading.

The length of duty for all members averaged six months. During the existence of the police, after they had reached a reasonably full complement, there were about 175, with fluctuations, of course, in the field in a typical month. This is the minimum length for every individual, and indeed there are several cases that far exceed this mean. This included not only officers, but all the lower ranks as well. An interesting factor is the age of the participants. For those who began their career in the police, whites averaged almost thirty years of age, blacks twenty-nine, and Mexicans thirty-three. The unknowns came in at twenty-eight. Those who joined were quite clearly in the prime of their lives and neither impaired nor demonstrably disabled.

DAILY HERALD
EXTRA

The Sceptre of the Tyrant Broken!

THE CHAINS SHATTERED!

The People Free!

The People of the State of Texas are to-day delivered of as infernal an engine of oppression as ever crushed any people beneath God's sunlight. The damnable Police Bill is ground beneath the heel of an indignant Legislature. The following dispatch from Hon. John Henry Brown sounds with the ring of a bugle the glad tidings:

AUSTIN, Texas, April 22, 1873.

Special Dispatch to the Daily Herald:
The Police Law is abolished over the Governor's veto. " Glory to God in the highest, and on earth Peace, good will towards men."
(Signed)   JOHN HENRY BROWN.

When the State Police Law was repealed in 1873, there was much rejoicing by a large segment of the population. This leaflet was inserted in all the issues of the *Dallas Daily Herald* of April 22, 1873. *Courtesy of the Dolph Briscoe Center for American History, Austin.*

An unsettling problem occurs, however, with the percentage of blacks in the State Police. If we assume an equal distribution of races among the unknown group, then blacks would have comprised almost 18 percent of the organization. But further analysis indicates that the breakdown of the unknowns is not equal. If we look at rank by race, it tends to show that blacks are underreported, and further investigation proves this is the case. Again, assuming an equitable race distribution among the unknowns, the percentage of privates in this group would be approximately 72 percent, which is quite close to the actual number of 73 percent, but these figures are somewhat deceiving. In order to achieve the actual reporting of privates among the unknowns, the percentage of blacks would have to be about 29, thus raising the percentage of black members in the agency to over 20 percent.

Although there are not enough data samples among the higher ranks to ascertain any meaningful results, the limited material does suggest an even higher black composition among active policemen. And when status changes are considered (promotion or end of service), even more dramatic results are produced. Based on dismissal results, blacks should make up about 66 percent of the unknowns. For resignations, they constituted about 60 percent, and for discharges, blacks form almost the entire population of unknowns. If we average these results to about 75 percent of those not listed by any race, blacks will account for about 32 percent of all who served for any length of time in the State Police, even though the analysis confirms that African Americans had by far the shortest average tours of duty among those reported. (The unknowns have an even shorter length.)

What all this conjecture seems to indicate is that there was a high percentage of blacks listed among the unknowns. But this is difficult to quantify, since it is not an intermediate result (one would expect the term length of the unknowns to be between that of the whites and blacks). Nevertheless, it is yet another data point suggesting the black percentage in the unknown racial group is probably substantially higher than in the general population. In fact, they may account for a majority of the unknown group. Moreover, geographical categorization points to a significant number of blacks among the unknowns. This correlation is not as obvious as those previously discussed because of the small number of samples and given the large number of counties involved.

Although a more rigorous statistical analysis might be performed to estimate the number of actual black policemen who served, based upon the simple results described above, it is safe to say that African Americans comprised far more than the reported percentile. A reasonable estimate would probably be in the 30 percent range, which is still smaller than what the majority of contemporary observers complained about in relation to the number of black policemen in the field. A reading, for example, of Democratic newspapers for the years 1870–1873, when the State Police patrolled Texas, would lead one to believe that black policemen were everywhere and everyplace. Such was not the case, but the constant reiteration of these themes made believers out of the populace.

Even though the State Police may have been the first major state organization in United States history to employ both African Americans and Mexicans, it was clearly not an equal-opportunity promotion employer. Republicans may have emphasized equality before the law for all people, but this did not mean that nonwhites could advance in state office as whites did. We know that no African American served in the upper echelons of the state government during the rule of Governor Davis. (There were two black state senators.) This pattern also held true for the State Police, and the disparity in promotions by race bears out this discriminatory pattern. There were no black captains, only one lieutenant, and one sergeant; all others were privates. The results for Mexicans are almost identical, although none of these individuals were ever promoted to sergeant, lieutenant, or captain.

The State Police were not evenly distributed geographically or racially throughout Texas. Almost all policemen served either in east or south Texas, or in the far western portion in the El Paso district. As we have seen, they were involved in apprehending criminals of all stripes and all races. In the major confrontations where Governor Davis declared martial law, only one of the counties, Walker, had a black majority. Although troubles did occur in other counties that had 5,000 or more black inhabitants (Austin, Bastrop, Brazoria, Fayette, Fort Bend, Grimes, Harris, Harrison, Rusk, Smith, and Washington), nothing of the magnitude similar to where Davis intervened took place. To be sure, there was an important altercation in Smith County where two black policemen killed two white men, but these seem to have been rare instances.

The perception that African Americans formed a significant component of State Police members was fostered by contemporary newspapers and Democratic politicians. (They may have confused them with Special Policemen.) Part of this hostility stemmed from the fact that those who opposed the Republican program believed that blacks should play a subsidiary and subservient role in society, even if they had been emancipated and endowed with civil liberties comparable to those of whites. By mounting a major propaganda campaign against anything that smacked of Republican ideals, especially black State Policemen, newspapers convinced many Texans that these individuals were everywhere and that they continually violated the rights of citizens. Although it certainly occasionally happened, this was not a general pattern of blacks who became full-time members of the organization.[15]

During the existence of the State Police, eleven of their men (eight whites and three blacks) were slain in assorted encounters with criminals and desperadoes. The first was Jim Smalley, a black private, murdered by John Wesley Hardin in January 1871. Hardin claimed the organization was "composed of carpet-baggers, scalawags from the North, with ignorant Negroes frequently on the force" and that other members belonged to "some secret vigilant band." Policemen were also killed in other altercations while performing their duties, as was Werner in Bastrop. In addition, they became targets for assassination by lawless types throughout the state, the most glaring example being the four killed in the Lampasas saloon. It is impossible to determine the precise number who were injured in the line of duty.[16]

Policemen killed individuals, mostly in self-defense. For example, a man named John Moike was charged with embezzlement. A trial date was set, but before it could occur, he appropriated a horse for his own use that belonged to the government. Two State Policemen tracked him to a ranch twelve miles from San Antonio, where he was arrested. His hands were tied and they were returning him to jail. Moike managed to get loose, seized the pistol of one of the policemen, and was about to fire when the other policeman shot him through the neck, killing him instantly. He was referred to as a "dangerous desperado, who bore a conspicuous part in the Maximilian war." The horse was also recovered.[17]

Depending upon the political bent of the newspaper, when State Policemen had to dispatch somebody, they were either condemned or praised. A man named Jack Mitchell, in an unnamed county, allegedly "surrounded by his wife and children, at his home," was slain "without having an opportunity to surrender." Sergeant William E. Evans informed the chief that Mitchell refused to submit, attempted to shoot the police, so they "riddled him with bullets." The same reaction occurred when policemen murdered a Lamar County man. In this instance, Chief Britton ordered a local justice of the peace to investigate the affair. In El Paso, Lieutenant A. H. French slew B. F. Williams, who had wounded State Senator A. H. Fountain and murdered a judge.[18]

One of the myths surrounding the State Police is that they fostered an image where they shot first and asked questions later. After the 1871 elections in Smith County, two prominent whites were killed when an altercation occurred with the police. After the arrest by policemen (mostly black) in Wood County for violations of the Ku Klux Klan Act, the prisoners were transported to Tyler. They selected Reuben E. House as their attorney, and a former mayor of Tyler, F. A. Godley, also consulted with the defendants. In a saloon encounter, two black State Policemen, Randall Johnson and W. J. Ingram, scuffled with the defendants. House and Godley died, and Johnson and Ingram fled. Both Godley and House became part of the honor roll of those slain by the police.[19]

To counter the "roll of honor" of State Policemen who had fallen in the line of duty, the Democrats responded with their own "roll of horror" of eighteen citizens murdered by the police. D. M. Prendergast, who compiled the list, hated the police and had criticized the organization and asserted they had been a "constant source of irritation wherever they have been." To say "nothing of the many minor offenses of which they have been guilty," he contended, they had "brutally murdered quite a number of the quiet and peaceable citizens of the State." Prominently mentioned were Godley and House in Smith County, the Kellys in DeWitt County, Applewhite in Limestone County, and Birdwell in Nacogdoches County.[20]

Like any such organization, the State Police had individuals who violated the law, although not an inordinate number as many past writings have claimed. Indeed, the State Police were by no means flawless and made their share of mistakes, but not on the level suggested by hostile authors. Perhaps the most notorious, whom we have already met, was Jack Helm. But the Madison County and Linn Flat affairs further damaged the reputation of its members. Policemen encountered legal difficulties, including forgery, blackmail, accepting bribes, assault and battery, rape, murder, and resisting arrest. Others were summarily dismissed for disobedience of orders. But newspapers also reported false stories about policemen being jailed.[21]

One of the incredible allegations about the State Police is that they only focused their attention upon white transgressions and ignored those of African Americans. Such is not the case. The State Police force was an equal-opportunity arrester, and when blacks violated the legal rules of the state, officers had no compunction about taking them into custody. And, it did not matter whether they violated the mores of the white or black communities in which they lived. The State Police saw their duty as arresting violators of the law. Indeed, conflicts pervaded the Texas black community, but compared with what whites were perpetrating upon the freedpeople, along with their superior numbers in percentage of the population, it was natural that more whites were arrested.

Three years after the demise of the State Police, an editorial in a newspaper far afield from the Lone Star State defended the organization. "The condition of society in Texas must be far from satisfactory to the best class of its citizens," editorialized the *St. Louis Republican*. The "alarming prevalence of crime, and the apparent inability of the local authorities to suppress the criminals, has stimulated discussions as to the best means of affording security to life and property." Davis had created a mobile force which was "undoubtedly salutary in holding the lawless class in check." Some gravely objected to the system, and undoubtedly "wrongs were committed for which the people had but a slim show for redress."[22]

The people demanded its disbandment and the Democrats complied. But a three-year experience without the police had "effected almost a complete revolution of public sentiment in regard to the matter." Citizens demanded better protection than local law officials could afford. Thus, the idea was generated for a "state detective force" similarly modeled after the State Police and under the governor's command. The difference was that the head of the state would make the initial selection of its members, but they would have to be approved by the State Senate. Their powers would be co-equal with those of a sheriff, who if called upon for assistance had to comply, but they could arrest offenders in any county.[23] This, of course, was precisely what the State Police did.

Abbreviations

AG	Adjutant General
AGC	Adjutant General's Correspondence
AGO	Adjutant General's Office
AGR	Adjutant General's Records
AHC	Austin History Center
ARIS/TSLAC	Archives & Information Services Division/Texas State Library and Archives Commission
BRFAL	Bureau of Refugees, Freedmen, and Abandoned Lands
DBCFAH	Dolph Briscoe Center for American History
DSJ	*Daily State Journal*
DT	Department of Texas
EJD	Edmund J. Davis
EMP	Elisha M. Pease
5MD	Fifth Military District
FLB	Frank L. Britton
GP	Governor's Papers
JD	James Davidson
JRC	*Journal of the Reconstruction Convention*
JWT	James W. Throckmorton
LPB	Letter Press Book
LR	Letters Received
NA	National Archives
NHT	*New Handbook of Texas*
OCA	Office of Civil Affairs
OR	Operations Reports
RG	Record Group
SP	State Police
SPC	State Police Correspondence
SWHQ	*Southwestern Historical Quarterly*
UTA	University of Texas, Austin

Notes

INTRODUCTION

1. S. O. Young, *True Stories of Old Houston and Houstonians: Historical and Personal Sketches* (Galveston: Oscar Springer, 1913), pp. 12–14.

2. General W. H. King, "The Texas Ranger Service and History of the Rangers, with Observations on Their Value as a Police Protection," in *A Comprehensive History of Texas, 1685 to 1897*, ed. Dudley G. Wooten (Dallas: William G. Scarff, 1898), p. 329; Charles William Ramsdell, *Reconstruction in Texas* (New York: Columbia University Press, 1910), p. 302; Young, *True Stories of Old Houston and Houstonians*, pp. 12–14; Seth Shepard McKay, "Texas Under the Regime of E. J. Davis" (M. A. thesis, University of Texas, Austin, 1919), pp. 109–113; Walter Prescott Webb, *The Texas Rangers: A Century of Frontier Defense* (Boston: Houghton Mifflin Company, 1935), p. 221; Marion Humphreys Farrow, *The Texas Democrats: Early Democratic History in Texas* (San Antonio: The Naylor Company, 1959), pp. 16–26; William Curtis Nunn, "A Study of the State Police During the E. J. Davis Administration" (M. A. thesis, University of Texas, Austin, 1931), p. 192; Nunn, *Texas Under the Carpetbaggers* (Austin: University of Texas Press, 1962), pp. 43–92; Frederick Wilkins, *The Law Comes to Texas: The Texas Rangers, 1870–1901* (Austin: State House Press, 1999), pp. 17–22; C. F. Eckhardt, *Tales of Badmen, Bad Women, and Bad Places: Four Centuries of Texas Outlawry* (Lubbock: Texas Tech University Press, 1999), p. 83; Allen G. Hatley, *Texas Constables: A Frontier Heritage* (Lubbock: Texas Tech University Press, 1999), pp. 50–52. Many of the same ideas expressed by the above authors were originally presented during the Reconstruction era in Charles B. Pearre, *A Review of the Laws of the Twelfth Legislature of the State of Texas, Enacted in the Year 1870 and 1871, and the Oppressions of Governor E. J. Davis' Administration Exposed* (Baltimore: J. D. Lipscomb & Co., Printers, 1872). Pearre was a Waco lawyer.

3. Ann Patton Baenziger, "The Texas State Police During Reconstruction: A Reexamination," *Southwestern Historical Quarterly* [henceforth referred to as SWHQ] 72 (April 1969), pp. 470–491; Otis Singletary, *Negro Militia and Reconstruction* (Austin: University of Texas Press, 1957) has a brief account of the police. Newer perspectives are provided in Chuck Parsons, "Texas State Policeman Redmon in Lampasas," *The Brand Book* 23 (Winter 1984), pp. 11–16; Barry A. Crouch and Donaly E. Brice, "'Dastardly Scoundrels': The State Police and

the Linn Flat Affair," *East Texas Historical Journal* 37 (Spring 1999), pp. 29–38. Several more recent entries involving the State Police are Chuck Parsons and Marianne E. Hall Little, *Captain L. H. McNelly, Texas Ranger: The Life and Times of a Fighting Man* (Austin: State House Press, 2001); Crouch, "Captain Thomas Williams: The Path of Duty," in *The Human Tradition in Texas*, ed. Ty Cashion and Jesus F. de la Teja (Wilmington, DE Scholarly Resources Inc., 2001), pp. 71–86; Allen G. Hatley, *Bringing the Law to Texas: Crime and Violence in Nineteenth Century Texas* (La Grange, TX: Centex Press, 2002), pp. 55–66; Reginald G. Jayne, "Martial Law in Reconstruction Texas" (M. A. thesis, San Houston State University, Huntsville, TX, 2005).

4. George C. Rable, *But There Was No Peace: The Role of Violence in the Politics of Reconstruction* (Athens: University of Georgia Press, 1984), p. 105; W. Marvin Dulaney, *Black Police in America* (Bloomington: Indiana University Press, 1996), p. 14; Merline Pitre, "A Note on the Historiography of Blacks in the Reconstruction of Texas," *Journal of Negro History* 66 (Winter 1981–1982), p. 343; *Senate Journal of the Twelfth Legislature, Called Session* (Austin: Tracy, Siemering & Co., 1870), p. 85; Carl H. Moneyhon, *Republicanism in Reconstruction Texas* (Austin: University of Texas Press, 1980), p. 139. On the weapons question see Stephen P. Halbrook, *Freedmen, the Fourteenth Amendment, and the Right to Bear Arms, 1866–1876* (Westport, CT: Praeger, 1998).

5. Frederick Nolan, *Bad Blood: The Life and Times of the Horrell Brothers* (Stillwater: Barbed Wire Press, 1994), p. 20; Rable, *But There Was No Peace*, p. 105; Dennis C. Rousey, "Yellow Fever and Black Policemen in Memphis: A Post-Reconstruction Anomaly," *Journal of Southern History* 51 (August 1985), pp. 357–374; "Black Policemen in New Orleans During Reconstruction," *Historian* 49 (February 1987), pp. 223–243; *Policing the Southern City: New Orleans, 1805–1889* (Baton Rouge: Louisiana State University Press, 1996); Howard N. Rabinowitz, "The Conflict Between Blacks and the Police in the Urban South, 1865–1900," *Historian* 39 (November 1976), pp. 62–76; *Race Relations in the Urban South, 1865–1900* (New York: Oxford University Press, 1978), pp. 41–43.

6. Dulaney, *Black Police in America*, pp. 14–15. Levi Neal, a black deputy marshal in Bryan, was shot and killed on February 24, 1900; *Austin American-Statesman*, August 10, 2000, p. 8B.

7. Rable, *But There Was No Peace*, pp. 105–106; Pitre, "A Note on the Historiography of Blacks in the Reconstruction of Texas," p. 343.

8. Nolan, *Bad Blood*, p. 24; Pauline Buck Hohes, *A Centennial History of Anderson County, Texas* (San Antonio: The Naylor Company, 1936), p. 52. For a later period see Harry Krenek, *The Power Vested: The Use of Martial Law and the National Guard in Texas Domestic Crisis, 1919–1932* (San Antonio: Presidial Press, 1980).

9. Until recently there had never been a balanced scholarly account of the Texas Rangers. However, two books published in the past decade appear to have filled this void. They are *The Men Who Wear the Star: The Story of the Texas Rangers*,

by Charles M. Robinson III, published by Random House in 2000, and Robert M. Utley's *Lone Star Justice: The First Century of the Texas Rangers*, published in 2002 by Oxford University Press.

10. David W. Blight, *Race and Reunion: The Civil War in American Memory* (Cambridge: Harvard University Press, 2001); Gary W. Gallagher and Alan T. Nolan (eds.), *The Myth of the Lost Cause and Civil War History* (Bloomington: Indiana University Press, 2001); James M. McPherson, "Southern Comfort," *New York Review of Books*, April 12, 2001, pp. 28, 30–31.

CHAPTER ONE

1. W. Eugene Hollon, *Frontier Violence: Another Look* (New York: Oxford University Press, 1976), p. 36; C. L. Sonnichsen, *I'll Die Before I'll Run: The Story of the Great Feuds of Texas* (New York: Harper & Brothers Publishers, 1951), xvi; Stephen Powers, *Afoot and Alone: A Walk From Sea to Sea by the Southern Route: Adventures and Observations in Southern California, New Mexico, Arizona, Texas, Etc.* (Hartford: Columbian Book Company, 1886), pp. 117, 119 (italics ours); Bill O'Neal, "Violence in Texas History," *Texas: A Sesquicentennial Celebration*, ed. Donald W. Whisenhunt (Austin: Eakin Press, 1984), pp. 353–369. For background, see David J. Weber, *The Spanish Frontier in North America* (New Haven: Yale University Press, 1992), pp. 147–203; Donald E. Chipman, *Spanish Texas, 1519–1821* (Austin: University of Texas Press, 1992); Richard Maxwell Brown, *Strain of Violence: Historical Studies of American Violence and Vigilantism* (New York: Oxford University Press, 1975), p. 236; Henry P. Lundsgaarde, *Murder in Space City: A Cultural Analysis of Houston Homicide Patterns* (New York: Oxford University Press, 1977), pp. 173–192. In general, see David T. Courtwright, "Violence in America," *American Heritage* 47 (September 1996), pp. 37–51. For the Texas/Western/Southern connection see Patrick George Williams, "Redeemer Democrats and the Roots of Modern Texas, 1872–1884" (Ph.D. diss., Columbia University, 1996), pp. 1–18; Walter L. Buenger, "Texas and the South," *SWHQ* 103 (January 2000), pp. 309–324.

2. Kenneth S. Greenberg, *Honor and Slavery: Lies, Duels, Noses, Masks, Dressing As a Woman, Gifts, Strangers, Humanitarianism, Death, Slave Rebellions, the Proslavery Argument, Baseball, Hunting, and Gambling in the Old South* (Princeton, NJ: Princeton University Press, 1996). There is a reasoned discussion of the concept in Orlando Patterson, *Slavery and Social Death: A Comparative Study* (Cambridge, MA: Harvard University Press, 1982), pp. 77–101; Bertram Wyatt-Brown, *Southern Honor: Ethics and Behavior in the Old South* (New York: Oxford University Press, 1982); ibid., *The Shaping of Southern Culture: Honor, Grace, and War, 1760s–1880s* (Chapel Hill: University of North Carolina Press, 2001); Edward L. Ayers, *Vengeance and Justice: Crime and Punishment in the 19th-Century American South* (New York: Oxford University Press, 1984), pp. 9–33; John Hope Franklin, *The Militant South, 1800–1861* (Cambridge: Belknap Press

of Harvard University Press, 1956); Dickson D. Bruce Jr., *Violence and Culture in the Antebellum South* (Austin: University of Texas Press, 1979); Darden Asbury Pyron, "Lawlessness and Culture in the American South," *Virginia Quarterly Review* 61 (Autumn 1985), pp. 741–751.

3. Powers, *Afoot and Alone*, pp. 117, 119. Almost every nineteenth-century visitor to Texas, of whatever class or race, commented upon the regional "gun culture" and the high number of murders. This contrasts sharply with the thesis in Michael A. Bellesiles, "The Origins of Gun Culture in the United States, 1760–1865," *Journal of American History* 83 (September 1996), pp. 425–455; *Arming America: The Origins of a National Gun Culture* (New York: Alfred A. Knopf, 2000). See also, Donald Curtis Brown, "The Great Gun-Toting Controversy, 1865–1910: The Old West Gun Culture and Public Shootings" (Ph.D. diss., Tulane University, 1983).

4. Richard Maxwell Brown, *No Duty to Retreat: Violence and Values in American History and Society* (New York: Oxford University Press, 1991); "Violence," in *The Oxford History of the American West*, ed. Clyde A. Milner II, Carol A. O'Connor, and Martha A. Sandweiss (New York: Oxford University Press, 1994), pp. 393–425; "Historiography of Violence in the American West," in *Historians of the American West*, ed. Michael P. Malone (Lincoln: University of Nebraska Press, 1983), pp. 234–269; Paul D. Lack, *The Texas Revolutionary Experience: A Political and Social History, 1835–1836* (College Station: Texas A&M University Press, 1992); Gary L. Roberts, "Violence and the Frontier Tradition," in *Kansas and the West: Bicentennial Essays in Honor of Nyle H. Miller*, ed. Forrest R. Blackburn, Edgar Langsdorf, Robert W. Richmond, Joseph W. Snell, and Homer E. Socolofsky (Topeka: Kansas State Historical Society, 1976), pp. 96–111. We are not subscribing to the Celtic heritage thesis proposed by Forrest McDonald and Grady McWhiney, "The Antebellum Southern Herdsman: A Reinterpretation," *Journal of Southern History* 41 (May 1975), pp. 147–166; "The South from Self-Sufficiency to Peonage: An Interpretation," *American Historical Review* 85 (December 1980), pp. 1095–1118; and McDonald and Ellen Shapiro McDonald, "The Ethnic Origins of the American People, 1790," *William and Mary Quarterly*, 3rd Ser., 37 (April 1980), pp. 179–199.

5. Andres Tijerina, *Tejanos and Texas Under the Mexican Flag, 1821–1836* (College Station: Texas A&M University Press, 1994), pp. 79–82.

6. John H. Jenkins, ed., "Regulations for the National Militia of the State of Coahuila y Texas, 1828," *Texas Military History* 7 (Autumn 1968), pp. 195–220; Henry W. Barton, "The Anglo-American Colonists Under Mexican Militia Laws," *SWHQ* 65 (July 1961), pp. 61–71; Gregg Cantrell, *Stephen F. Austin: Empresario of Texas* (New Haven: Yale University Press, 1999), pp. 202–66; Thomas Ewing Cotner, *The Military and Political Career of Jose Joaquín de Herrera, 1792–1854* (Austin: University of Texas Press, 1949), p. 47; Eugene C. Barker, "The Government of Austin's Colony, 1821–1831," *SWHQ* 21 (January 1918), pp. 232–233; Allan Robert

Purcell, "The History of the Texas Militia, 1835–1903" (Ph.D. diss., University of Texas, Austin, 1981), pp. 52–66, 68, 71–100; Tijerina, *Tejanos and Texas Under the Mexican Flag*, pp. 86–90.

7. Tijerina, *Tejanos and Texas Under the Mexican Flag*, pp. 86, 92.

8. Barton, "The United States Cavalry and the Texas Rangers," *SWHQ* 63 (April 1960), pp. 495–510; Purcell, "The History of the Texas Militia," pp. 68, 71–100; Harold J. Weiss, Jr., "Flying Forces: The Origins of the Texas Rangers," paper presented at the Texas State Historical Association Convention, Austin, March 1997. The material on the Texas Rangers is massive and of varying quality. See Webb, *The Texas Rangers*; and, most recently, Charles M. Robinson III, *The Men Who Wear the Star: The Story of the Texas Rangers* (New York: Random House, 2000); and Robert M. Utley, *Lone Star Justice: The First Century of the Texas Rangers* (New York: Oxford University Press, 2002); Llerena B. Friend, "W. P. Webb's Texas Rangers," *SWHQ* 74 (January 1971), pp. 293–323. Another entry is Frederick Wilkins, *The Legend Begins: The Texas Rangers, 1823–1845* (Austin: State House Press, 1996); *The Law Comes to Texas: The Texas Rangers, 1870–1901* (Austin: State House Press, 1999); Mark E. Nackman, "The Making of the Texan Citizen Soldier, 1835–1860," *SWHQ* 78 (January 1975), pp. 237, 244. See also his controversial *A Nation Within a Nation: The Rise of Texas Nationalism* (Port Washington, NY: Kennikat Press, 1975). Nackman, in "The Making of the Texan Citizen Soldier," states that the Rangers "might be regarded as a quasi-institution of antebellum Texas in the sense that they constituted an ever-present feature of the country, but it must be emphasized that they never acquired official status as an organization proper" (p. 249). Weiss combines these ideas and declares that the years from 1823 to 1874 were the "heyday of the Rangers as citizen soldiers. Within this time frame ranging companies and other volunteer units engaged in a military struggle with Indian tribes and Mexicans for control of the land." "The Texas Rangers Revisited: Old Themes and New Viewpoints," *SWHQ* 97 (April 1994), p. 622. Cf. Julian Samora, Joe Bernal, and Albert Pena, *Gunpowder Justice: A Reassessment of the Texas Rangers* (Notre Dame, IN: University of Notre Dame Press, 1979); Alfredo Mirande, *Gringo Justice* (Notre Dame, IN: University of Notre Dame Press, 1987).

9. Harry F. Lupold, ed., "A Union Medical Officer Views the 'Texians,'" *SWHQ* 77 (April 1974), pp. 481–486. From the other side see John Q. Anderson, *A Texas Surgeon in the C.S.A.*, No. 6, "Confederate Centennial Studies" (Tuscaloosa, AL: Confederate Publishing Company, 1957), who chronicles the career of Dr. Edward W. Cade, Yankee born, who settled near Brenham and was, according to family tradition, killed by a carpetbagger, pp. 112–113; and Thomas W. Cutrer, ed., "'An Experience in a Soldier's Life': Civil War Letters of Volney Ellis, Adjutant Twelfth Texas Infantry Walker's Texas Division, C.S.A.," *Military History of the Southwest* 22 (Fall 1992), pp. 109–172; *Ben McCulloch and the Frontier Military Tradition* (Chapel Hill: University of North Carolina Press, 1993), pp.

117–187. Also see Ludwell H. Johnson, *Red River Campaign: Politics and Cotton in the Civil War* (Baltimore: Johns Hopkins University Press, 1958).

10. Richard B. McCaslin, *Tainted Breeze: The Great Hanging at Gainesville, Texas, 1862* (Baton Rouge: Louisiana State University Press, 1994); "Dark Corner of the Confederacy: James G. Bourland and the Border Regiment," *Military History of the West* 24 (Spring 1994), pp. 57–70; David Paul Smith, *Frontier Defense in the Civil War: Texas' Rangers and Rebels* (College Station: Texas A&M University Press, 1992); Grady W. Box, "The Civil War in North Central Texas: Its Impact on Frontier Families, 1860–1874" (M.S. thesis, Texas Women's University, 1991), pp. 21–65; Robert L. Kerby, *Kirby Smith's Confederacy: The Trans-Mississippi South, 1863–1865* (New York: Columbia University Press, 1972); Daniel O'Flaherty, *General Jo Shelby: Undefeated Rebel* (Chapel Hill: University of North Carolina Press, 1954), pp. 207–225; John C. Walker, "Reconstruction in Texas," *Southern Historical Society Papers* 24 (1896), pp. 41–57; Joseph Howard Parks, *General Edmund Kirby Smith, C.S.A.* (Baton Rouge: Louisiana State University Press, 1954), pp. 456–480; Purcell, "The History of the Texas Militia," p. 195; Albert D. Richardson, *Beyond the Mississippi: From the Great River to the Great Ocean; Life and Adventure on the Prairies, Mountains, and Pacific Coast, 1857–1867* (New York: Bliss & Company, 1867), p. 226; Frederick Law Olmsted, *Journey Through Texas: A Saddle-Trip on the Southwestern Frontier*, ed. James Howard (Austin: Von Boeckmann-Jones Press, 1962 [1856]), p. 24; Thomas North, *Five Years in Texas, or, What You Did Not Hear During the War From January 1861 to January 1866: A Narrative of His Travels, Experiences, and Observations, in Texas and Mexico* (Cincinnati: Elm Street Printing Co., 1866), pp. 102–103, 106.

11. John Q. Anderson, ed., *Brokenburn: The Journal of Kate Stone, 1861–1868* (Baton Rouge: Louisiana State University Press, 1955), pp. 227, 250.

12. Purcell, "The History of the Texas Militia," pp. 195–96; William L. Richter, *The Army in Texas During Reconstruction, 1865–1870*" (College Station: Texas A&M University Press, 1987), pp. 11–46; Robert W. Shook, "Federal Occupation and Administration of Texas, 1865–1870" (Ph.D. diss., North Texas State University, 1970), pp. 1–335; James E. Sefton, *The United States Army and Reconstruction, 1865–1877* (Baton Rouge: Louisiana State University Press, 1967); B. W. Aston, "Federal Military Reoccupation of the Texas Southwestern Frontier, 1865–1871," *Texas Military History* 8 (1970), pp. 123–134; Thomas T. Smith, *The U.S. Army and the Texas Frontier Economy, 1845–1900* (College Station: Texas A&M University Press, 1999); *The Old Army in Texas: A Research Guide to the U.S. Army in Nineteenth-Century Texas* (Austin: Texas State Historical Association, 2000).

13. Purcell, "History of the Texas Militia," p. 195.

14. North, *Five Years in Texas*, pp. 102–103.

15. Hiram Clark (Agent, Clinton) to J. P. Richardson, March 3, 1868, C-49, OR (first quote); DeWitt C. Brown (Agent, Paris) to Richardson, March 31, 1868, B-106,

OR (second quote), both in BRFAL, Texas, RG 105 (NA). See also Richter, "'The Revolver Rules the Day!': Colonel DeWitt C. Brown and the Freedmen's Bureau in Paris, Texas, 1867–1868," *SWHQ* 93 (January 1990), pp. 303–332.

16. A. J. Hamilton to Andrew Johnson, July 24, 1865, Andrew Johnson Papers (Manuscript Division, Library of Congress); Dan T. Carter, *When the War Was Over: The Failure of Self-Reconstruction in the South* (Baton Rouge: Louisiana State University Press, 1985), pp. 25–27, 32, 255–256. Hamilton's response to the violence is downplayed in John L. Waller, *Colossal Hamilton of Texas: A Biography of Andrew Jackson Hamilton; Militant Unionist and Reconstruction Governor* (El Paso: Texas Western Press, 1968), pp. 59–94. Into 1866 and thereafter, Texas planters still discussed a gradual emancipation of three to five years; Thomas P. Collins (Crockett) to Thaddeus Stevens, February 19, 1866, Cont. 6, Thaddeus Stevens Papers (Manuscript Division, Library of Congress).

17. Hamilton to E. M. Gregory (AC, Texas), September 27, 1865, Unregistered Letters, 1865–1866, Texas, M821, Reel 17, BRFAL, RG 105, NA.

18. Hamilton to Johnson, August 30, 1865, Johnson Papers; George C. Rable, *But There Was No Peace,* p. 13; Joel Gray Taylor, *Louisiana Reconstructed, 1863–1877* (Baton Rouge: Louisiana State University Press, 1974), pp. 63–64; Alan Coleman Ashcraft, "Texas: 1860–1866: The Lone Star State in the Civil War" (Ph.D. diss., Columbia University, 1960); "Texas in Defeat: The Early Phase of A. J. Hamilton's Provisional Governorship of Texas, June 17, 1865 to February 7, 1866," *Texas Military History* 8 (1970), pp. 199–219; Nora Estelle Owens, "Presidential Reconstruction in Texas: A Case Study" (Ph.D. diss., Auburn University, 1983), pp. 1–155; Walter Tribble Chapin, "Presidential Reconstruction in Texas, 1865–1867" (M.A. thesis, North Texas State University, 1979).

19. *Report of the Joint Committee on Reconstruction* (Washington, DC: GPO, 1866), pp. 36–37; Richard Lowe, "The Joint Committee on Reconstruction: Some Clarifications," *Southern Studies* 3 [New Series] (Spring 1992), pp. 55–65; John G. Clark, "Historians and the Joint Committee of Reconstruction," *Historian* 23 (May 1961), pp. 348–361; "Radicals and Moderates on the Joint Committee on Reconstruction," *Mid-America* 45 (April 1963), pp. 79–98. Major General David S. Stanley concurred with Strong's perception. Without the presence of the military, blacks would be held in a "bondage more galling than they were ever held before" and in a detestable manner (*Report,* p. 40). For general military reaction see Shook, "Federal Occupation and Administration of Texas"; and Richter, *The Army in Texas During Reconstruction;* Leon F. Litwack, *Been in the Storm So Long: The Aftermath of Slavery* (New York: Alfred A. Knopf, 1979), pp. 276–277; Charles V. Keener, "Racial Turmoil in Texas, 1865–1874" (M.A. thesis, North Texas State University, 1971); James M. Smallwood, *Time of Hope, Time of Despair: Black Texans During Reconstruction* (Port Washington, NY: Kennikat Press, 1981); James Marten, "'What is to Become of the Negro?': White Reaction to Emancipation in Texas," *Mid-America* 73 (April–July 1991), pp. 115–133.

20. Benjamin C. Truman, "Affairs in Texas," *New York Times*, February 19, 1866, p. 1; *Advice After Appomattox: Letters to Andrew Johnson, 1865–1866*, "Special Volume No. 1 of the Papers of Andrew Johnson," ed. Brooks D. Simpson, LeRoy P. Graf, and John Muldowny (Knoxville: University of Tennessee Press, 1987), pp. 175–183.

21. *New York Times*, February 19, 1866, p. 1.

22. Rable, *But There Was No Peace*, pp. 13, 71; C. C. Rister, "Outlaws and Vigilantes of the Southern Plains, 1865–1885," *Mississippi Valley Historical Review* 19 (March 1933), pp. 537–554.

23. Edward King, *The Great South*, ed. W. Magruder Drake and Robert R. Jones (Baton Rouge: Louisiana State University Press, 1972 [1875]), pp. 138–139.

24. P. H. Sheridan (Commander, Department of the Gulf) to J. W. Throckmorton, January 18, 1867, Texas Adjutant General's Office, 1839–1879, Papers, DBC-FAH, UTA; Richter, "'Tyrant and Reformer: General Charles Griffin Reconstructs Texas, 1866–1867," *Prologue* 10 (Winter 1978), pp. 225–241; John Conger McGraw, "The Texas Constitution of 1866" (Ph.D. diss., Texas Technological College, 1959); Purcell, "The History of the Texas Militia," pp. 198–199; Claude Elliott, *Leathercoat: The Life History of a Texas Patriot* (San Antonio: Standard Printing Co., 1938), pp. 119–178; Kenneth Wayne Howell, *Texas Confederate, Reconstruction Governor James Webb Throckmorton* (College Station: Texas A&M University Press, 2008), pp. 119–125. For the various laws see John Sayles, (ann.), *The Constitutions of the State of Texas, with the Reconstruction Acts of Congress, the Constitution of the Confederate States, and of the United States*, 3rd ed. (St. Louis: Gilbert Book Company, 1888).

25. Sheridan to Throckmorton, October 19, 1866, Records of James W. Throckmorton, Texas Office of the Governor. ARIS/TSLAC, hereafter cited as GP (JWT), ARIS/TSLAC; Edwin M. Stanton to JWT, October 11, 1866, in *Dallas Weekly Herald*, October 20, 1866, p. 2; Purcell, "History of the Texas Militia," pp. 201–203; Howell, *Texas Confederate*, pp. 122–125.

26. Sinclair to Kirkman, July 2, 1867, AC, LR, S-272, BRFAL, Texas, RG 105, NA; Richter, "Who Was the Real Head of the Texas Freedmen's Bureau?: The Role of Brevet Colonel William H. Sinclair as Acting Assistant Inspector General," *Military History of the Southwest* 20 (Fall 1990), pp. 121–156.

27. Purcell, "History of the Texas Militia," pp. 203–204; Crouch, "'All the Vile Passions': The Texas Black Code of 1866," *SWHQ* 97 (July 1993), pp. 21–23; Crouch, "'To Enslave the Rising Generation': The Freedmen's Bureau and the Texas Black Code," in Randall M. Miller and Paul A. Cimbala, ed., *The Freedmen's Bureau and Reconstruction: Reconsideration* (Bronx, NY: Fordham University Press, 1999), pp. 261–287.

28. Robert Joseph Franzetti, "Elisha Marshall Pease and Reconstruction" (M.A. thesis, Southwest Texas State University, 1970), pp. 25–26; Purcell, "History of the Texas Militia," pp. 211–212; Richter, "General Phil Sheridan, the Historians, and Reconstruction," *Civil War History* 33 (June 1987), pp. 131–154.

29. Purcell, "History of the Texas Militia," pp. 209–210.

30. O. D. Barrett (New Orleans) to B. F. Wade, July 7, 1867, Benjamin F. Wade Papers (Manuscript Division, Library of Congress); John M. Carroll, "The Doubleday Myth and Texas Baseball," *SWHQ* 92 (April 1989), pp. 597–612; Rable, *But There Was No Peace*, p. 87; Eric Foner, *Reconstruction: America's Unfinished Revolution, 1863–1877* (New York: Harper & Row, 1988), pp. 204–205.

31. Mrs. L. E. Potts (Paris, TX), to Mr. President, June ?, 1866, Sheridan Papers, Cont. 4, Manuscript Division, Library of Congress.

32. Ronald N. Gray, "Edmund J. Davis: Radical Republican and Reconstruction Governor of Texas" (Ph.D. diss., Texas Tech University, 1976), p. 124.

33. Moneyhon, *Republicanism in Reconstruction Texas*, pp. 92–93.

34. *Journal of the Reconstruction Convention, Which Met at Austin, Texas, June 1, A.D., 1868* (Austin: Tracy, Siemering & Co., 1870), pp. 131, 956 (hereafter *JRC*); Donald Campbell (Jefferson) to Pease, December 31, 1867; C. C. Caldwell (Marshall) to A. W. Longley, January 2, 1868; J. Schutze (Bastrop) to Pease, March 28, 1868; all in records of the third term of Elisha Marshall Pease, Texas Office of the Governor, ARIS/TSLAC. Hereafter cited as GP (EMP), ARIS/TSLAC; Betty Jeffus Sandlin, "The Texas Reconstruction Constitutional Convention of 1868–1869" (Ph.D. diss., Texas Tech University, 1970), pp. 33–35; John Pressley Carrier, "A Political History of Texas During the Reconstruction, 1865–1874" (Ph.D. diss., Vanderbilt University, 1971), pp. 198–248; James A. Baggett, "The Rise and Fall of the Texas Radicals, 1867–1883" (Ph.D. diss., North Texas State University, 1972), pp. 71–95.

35. *JRC*, pp. 30, 34, 43; Sandlin, "The Texas Reconstruction Constitutional Convention," pp. 71, 252.

36. *JRC*, p. 34; Sandlin, "The Texas Reconstruction Constitutional Convention," appendix.

37. *JRC*, pp. 110–111; Sandlin, "The Texas Reconstruction Constitutional Convention," appendix.

38. *Report of Special Committee on Lawlessness and Violence in Texas* (Austin: Printed at the Office of the *Daily Republican*, 1868), p. 11.

39. John Pressley Carrier, "Constitutional Change in Texas" (M.A. thesis, North Texas State University, 1967), pp. 98–99; *San Antonio Daily Express*, July 2, 1868, p. 2.

40. J. Warren Bell to My dear Sir, September 14, 1868, *The Papers of Andrew Johnson, September 1868–April 1869*, ed. Paul H. Bergeron (Knoxville: University of Tennessee Press, 1999), XV, pp. 56–58.

41. *JRC*, pp. 503–505, 698; Sandlin, "The Texas Reconstruction Constitutional Convention," pp. 77–78. The convention resolved on July 20, by a vote of 56 to 21, to request General J. J. Reynolds to arrest Gillespie, arraign him before a military commission, and suppress the newspaper.

42. Ibid., *passim*; Crouch, "Reconstructing Brazos County: Race Relations and the Freedmen's Bureau, 1865–1868," in *The Freedmen's Bureau and Black Texans*

(Austin: University of Texas Press, 1992), pp. 102–127; Crouch and Donaly E. Brice, *Cullen Montgomery Baker: Reconstruction Desperado* (Baton Rouge: Louisiana State University Press, 1997); James M. Smallwood, Barry A. Crouch, and Larry Peacock, *Murder and Mayhem: The War of Reconstruction in Texas* (College Station: Texas A&M University Press, 2003), p. 77.

43. *JRC*, p. 195.

44. *Report of Special Committee*, pp. 4–5; Sandlin, "The Texas Reconstruction Constitutional Convention," p. 74.

45. *JRC*, pp. 195, 200.

46. Ibid., pp. 200–203. The two commanders were Major General Winfield Scott Hancock and Brevet Major General Robert C. Buchanan, both of whom the Republicans believed were overly sympathetic to the Conservatives/Democrats.

47. Ibid., pp. 500–502.

48. *Report of Special Committee*, pp. 6, 9. On Baker, see Crouch and Brice, *Cullen Montgomery Baker*; Rick Miller, *Bloody Bill Longley* (Wolfe City, TX: Henington Publishing Company, 1996).

49. Crouch, "A Spirit of Lawlessness," pp. 218–219; *Report of the Joint Committee on Reconstruction*, pp. 48, 75; George Custer to Zachariah Chandler, January 8, 14, 1866, vol. 3, Zachariah Chandler Papers (Manuscript Division, Library of Congress). The Bureau's reaction to the violence can be followed in Crouch, *Freedmen's Bureau and Black Texans*; William L. Richter, *Overreached on All Sides: The Freedmen's Bureau Administration in Texas, 1865–1868* (College Station: Texas A&M University Press, 1991). See also, Cantrell, "Racial Violence and Reconstruction Politics in Texas, 1867–1868," *SWHQ* 93 (January 1990), pp. 333–355. The most thorough violence study is Rebecca A. Kosary, "Regression to Barbarism in Reconstruction Texas: An analysis of White Violence Against African-Americans from the Texas Freedmen's Bureau Records, 1865–1868" (M.A. thesis, Southwest Texas State University, 1999); C. Vann Woodward, "Birth of a Nation," *New York Review of Books*, November 20, 1980, p. 49; *Origins of the New South, 1877–1913* (Baton Rouge: Louisiana State University Press, 1951), p. 159; *DSJ*, August 31, 1871, p. 1; Baenziger, "Bold Beginnings: The Radical Program in Texas, 1870–1873" (M.A. thesis, Southwest Texas State University, 1970), p. 14; DeWitt C. Brown to Richardson, December 31, 1867, AC, OR, B-71; Charles Schmidt (Agent, Sumpter) to Richardson, April 30, 1868, AC, S-199, OR; Edward C. Henshaw (Agent, Marshall) to Vernou, December 31, 1868, AC, H-11, OR, all in BRFAL, Texas, RG 105, NA; Richter, "'This Blood-Thirsty Hole': The Freedmen's Bureau Agency at Clarksville, Texas, 1867–1868," *Civil War History* 38 (March 1992), pp. 51–77.

50. Barbara Leah Clayton, "The Lone Star Conspiracy: Racial Violence and Ku Klux Klan Terror in Post–Civil War Texas, 1865–1877" (M.A. thesis, Oklahoma State University, 1986), pp. 14–16; Allen W. Trelease, *White Terror: The Ku Klux Klan Conspiracy and Southern Reconstruction* (New York: Harper and Row,

1971), pp. 137–148; James Smallwood, "When the Klan Rode: White Terror in Reconstruction Texas," *Journal of the West* 25 (October 1986), pp. 4–13.

51. Ibid.

52. *JRC*, 2nd Sess., pp. 110–111 (Reynolds Report). See also Joseph G. Dawson III and James A. Baggett, "Joseph Jones Reynolds," *NHT*, V, pp. 556–557; Zenobia Self, "Court-Martial of J. J. Reynolds," *Military Affairs* 37 (April 1973), pp. 52–56. Reynolds served as commander of the Fifth Military District on three different occasions; see Richter, *The Army in Texas*, p. 52.

53. *JRC*, 2nd Sess., p. 111 (Reynolds Report). He listed Van Zandt, Smith, and Marion counties as examples.

54. Ibid.; *Report of the Secretary of War*, November 20, 1869, *House Exec. Docs.*, 41st Cong., 2nd Sess., No. 1, Pt. II [Serial 1412] (Washington, DC: GPO, 1869), p. 705; Benjamin P. Thomas and Harold M. Hyman, *Stanton: The Life and Times of Lincoln's Secretary of War* (New York: Alfred A. Knopf, 1962), p. 512.

55. *JRC*, 2nd Sess., pp. 111–112 (Reynolds Report).

56. Ibid.

57. Ibid., pp. 107–109; Robert Standfield to E. M. Pease, January 4, 1869, GP (EMP), ARIS/TSLAC; Robert I. Johnson, "Elisha Marshall Pease: Unionist and Reconstruction Governor" (M.A. thesis, Midwestern University, 1972), pp. 109–110; Roger Allen Griffin, "Connecticut Yankee in Texas: A Biography of Elisha Marshall Pease" (Ph.D. diss., University of Texas, Austin, 1973), pp. 220–221; Benjamin Hillon Miller, "Elisha Marshall Pease: A Biography" (M.A. thesis, University of Texas, Austin, 1927), pp. 149–153.

58. Carrier, "A Political History of Texas," pp. 294–336; Moneyhon, *Republicanism in Reconstruction Texas*, pp. 82–110; ibid., *Edmund J. Davis of Texas: Civil War General, Republican Leader, Reconstruction Governor* (Fort Worth: Texas Christian University Press, 2010), pp. 133–153; Sandlin, "The Texas Reconstruction Constitutional Convention," pp. 195–198; Randolph B. Campbell, *Grass-Roots Reconstruction in Texas, 1865–1880* (Baton Rouge: Louisiana State University Press, 1997), p. 18; Gray, "Edmund J. Davis," pp. 150–158.

59. F. P. Wood (Brenham) to Pease, July 1, 1869; Philip Howard (Meridian) to Hamilton, August 12, 1869; George Quinay (Wharton) to Pease, August 14, 15, 1869; A. G. Walker (Fort Worth) to Pease, September 16, 1869; William C. Syput and Eight Others (Cameron) to Pease, all in GP (EMP), ARIS/TSLAC; Carrier, "The Political History of Texas," pp. 327–340; Brooks D. Simpson, "'Let Us Have Peace,'" in *The Reconstruction Presidents* (Lawrence: University Press of Kansas, 1998), pp. 133–162; Joseph J. Reynolds to Ulysses S. Grant, September 4, 1869, in *New York Times*, October 5, 1869, p. 5 (the letter also appeared in *Flake's Bulletin*, October 5, 1869, p. 1); Moneyhon, *Republicanism in Reconstruction Texas*, pp. 115–116; ibid., *Edmund J. Davis of Texas*, pp. 142–143.

60. Dale Baum, "Chicanery and Intimidation in the 1869 Texas Gubernatorial Race," *SWHQ* 97 (July 1993), pp. 37–54; ibid., *The Shattering of Texas Unionism:*

Politics in the Lone Star State During the Civil War Era (Baton Rouge: Louisiana State University Press, 1998), pp. 180–228; Moneyhon, *Republicanism in Reconstruction Texas,* pp. 104–128; ibid., *Edmund J. Davis of Texas,* pp. 149–153; Carrier, "A Political History of Texas," pp. 389–404; Campbell, *Grass-Roots Reconstruction,* p. 19, claims the radicals had "working majorities in both houses of the new state legislature" (12th Legislature).

61. Carrier, "A Political History of Texas," pp. 407–408; Richter, *The Army in Texas,* pp. 172–186; Smith, *The Old Army in Texas,* pp. 110–111; Shook, "The Federal Military in Texas, 1865–1870," *Texas Military History* 6 (Spring 1967), pp. 45–53; ibid., "Federal Occupation and Administration of Texas," pp. 486–489; Robert Wooster, "The Army and the Politics of Expansion: Texas and the Southwestern Borderlands, 1870–1886," *SWHQ* 93 (October 1989), pp. 151–167.

CHAPTER TWO

1. EJD to U.S. Grant, February 24, 1870, pp. 40–41, Executive Record Book, Secretary of State, ARIS/TSLAC; Christian G. Nelson, "Rebirth, Growth, and Expansion of the Texas Militia, 1868–1898," *Texas Military History* 2 (February 1962), p. 2; James A. Baggett, "Beginnings of Radical Rule in Texas: The Special Legislative Session of 1870," *Southwestern Journal of Social Education* 2 (Spring–Summer 1972), p. 28; Moneyhon, *Republicanism in Reconstruction Texas,* pp. 129–151; Gray, "Edmund J. Davis: Radical Republican and Reconstruction Governor of Texas," pp. 186–191; Carrier, "A Political History of Texas," pp. 424–426; Carl J. Moneyhon, *Texas After the Civil War: The Struggle of Reconstruction* (College Station: Texas A&M University Press, 2004), pp. 117–118.

2. EJD to Reynolds, May 7, 1870 (two letters), pp. 118–119, both in Executive Record Book, Secretary of State, ARIS/TSLAC.

3. *Senate Journal, Twelfth Legislature, First Session* (Austin: Tracy, Siemering & Co., State Journal Office, 1870), pp. 10–12.

4. Ibid., pp. 10–14.

5. Ibid., p. 15.

6. Ibid.

7. *General Laws of the Twelfth Legislature, Called Session, 1870* (Austin: J. G. Tracy, State Printer, 1870), pp. 11–16; ibid., *First Session, 1871* (Austin: J. G. Tracy, State Printer, 1871), pp. 181, 23–24; Otis A. Singletary, "The Texas Militia During Reconstruction," *SWHQ,* 60 (July 1956), pp. 26–28; Purcell, "The History of the Texas Militia, 1835–1903," pp. 221–227. It is interesting to note that the law organizing the State Guard/Reserve Militia also mentioned the State Police as part of the military forces of Texas, but the police had yet to be established, although they did come into being a week later.

8. *Senate Journal, First Session,* pp. 85–86; *House Journal of the Twelfth Legislature, First Session* (Austin: Tracy, Siemering & Co., State Journal Office, 1870), pp. 104–105, 154. For editorial comment see *San Antonio Daily Herald,* June 5, 1870,

p. 2; *DSJ*, May 19, 1870, p. 1. For the political maneuvering see A. M. Gibson, *The Life and Death of Colonel Albert Jennings Fountain* (Norman: University of Oklahoma Press, 1965), pp. 65–71; John M. Brockman, "Railroads, Radicals, and the Militia Bill: A New Interpretation of the Quorum-Breaking Incident of 1870," *SWHQ* 83 (October 1979), pp. 105–122; "Railroads, Radicals, and Democrats: A Study of Texas Politics, 1865–1900" (Ph.D. diss., University of Texas, Austin, 1975), pp. 82–112. Democratic opposition is chronicled in Farrow, *The Texas Democrats*.

9. Ann Patton Malone, "Matt Gaines: Reconstruction Politician," in *Black Leaders for Their Times*, ed. Alwyn Barr and Robert A. Calvert (Austin: Texas State Historical Association, 1981), pp. 59–60, 73; Carl H. Moneyhon, "George T. Ruby and the Politics of Expediency in Texas," in *Southern Black Leaders of the Reconstruction Era*, ed. Howard N. Rabinowitz (Urbana: University of Illinois Press, 1982), p. 381; Alwyn Barr, "Black Legislators of Reconstruction Texas," *Civil War History* 32 (December 1986), p. 347; Eric Foner, *Freedom's Lawmakers: A Directory of Black Officeholders During Reconstruction* (New York: Oxford University Press, 1993), pp. 80–81, 187; Barry A. Crouch, "Hesitant Recognition: Texas Black Politicians, 1865–1900," *East Texas Historical Journal* 31 (Spring 1993), pp. 41–58.

10. *General Laws of the Twelfth Legislature, Called Session* (Austin: J. G. Tracy, State Printer, 1870), Ch. XIII, p. 19. If no adjutant general existed, the governor could appoint, with the Senate's approval, a chief who would receive an annual salary of $2,500.

11. Ibid.

12. The mileage and compensation paid for conveying prisoners would be deducted from appropriations for "costs due sheriffs' from the State," *General Laws of the Twelfth Legislature of the State of Texas, First Session-1871*, p. 973.

13. Ibid., pp. 973–974; *Message of Gov. Edmund J. Davis* (Austin: J. G. Tracy, State Printer, 1871), p. 13. The governor, or the chief of police, with the former's authority, could authorize conductors and baggage masters on all railroads or other public conveyances to act as special policemen when it was deemed necessary. The designated conductors and baggage masters would receive no compensation from the state for services rendered under this act. Conductors would have all the power and authority of peace officers under state law. The act would take effect on May 2, 1871.

14. EJD to Senators and Representatives from Texas (Washington, DC), May 5, 1870, Executive Record Book, p. 116, Secretary of State, ARIS/TSLAC.

15. FLB to Chief of Police, San Francisco, January 20, 1873, pp. 241–243, AG Letterpress Book, ARIS/TSLAC; JD, Compiled Service Records of Union Volunteer Soldiers, Records of the AGO Office, RG 94, NA. The latter has JD born in Kelso, England, instead of Kelso, Roxburgh, Scotland.

16. Ibid.; Carl Moneyhon, "James Davidson," *NHT*, II, p. 522.

17. *DSJ*, June 26, 1870, p. 2; August 21, 1870, p. 2; *Houston Daily Union*, February 16, 1871, p. 2; Nunn, "A Study of the State Police," pp. 25–27. On Loughery see Randolph B. Campbell, *A Southern Community in Crisis: Harrison County, Texas, 1850–1880* (Austin: Texas State Historical Association, 1983), *passim*; Max S. Lale, "Robert W. Loughery: Rebel Editor," *East Texas Historical Journal* 21 (1983), pp. 3–15. For other comments on Loughery, with his own letters and editorials, see C. G. Garland (Jefferson) to E. M. Pease, March 9, 1869, 5MD, LR, Box 6, RG 393, NA. Loughery believed the military despotic, but Garland thought that Texas "north of the 32d parallel, needs a fresh reconstruction."

18. For all the sheriffs' reports which cover Anderson to Zapata counties, see Reports of Crimes, Arrests, and Fugitives, 1870–1873 and State Police Correspondence, State Police Records, Reconstruction Records, Adjutant General's Department, ARIS/TSLAC; *Report of the Adjutant-General of the State of Texas, From June 24, 1870, to December 31, 1870* (Austin: Printed by Tracy, Siemering & Co., 1870), p. 11 (hereafter, *AG Report*, with year); *DSJ*, August 21, 1870, p. 2. Nunn, "A Study of the State Police," p. 28, seemingly doubts Davidson's statistics. For a wonderful description of the adjutant general's office see the *Houston Union*, September 29, 1871, p. 2.

19. G. D. Kelley (Sheriff, Anderson County) to JD, July 12, 1870, SPC, ARIS/TSLAC; Sammy Tise, *Texas County Sheriffs* (Albuquerque: Oakwood Printing, 1969), p. 1.

20. Kelley to JD, July 12, 1870, SPC, ARIS/TSLAC.

21. James E. Brady (Mayor, Bastrop) to JD, August 4, 1870, SPC, ARIS/TSLAC; Crouch, "Hesitant Recognition," p. 54; Foner, *Freedom's Lawmakers*, 93–94.

22. *AG Report*, 1870, p. 9. For early removals see *DSJ*, September 18, 1870, p. 2; September 23, 1870, p. 1. The *Journal* exclaimed that the police contained "no berth for sluggards, knaves or fools."

23. *AG Report*, 1870, pp. 10–11.

24. The First Police District included the counties of Taylor, Callahan, Eastland, Erath, Hood, Johnson, Hill, Bosque, Comanche, Brown, Coleman, Runnels, Concho, Bell, McCulloch, San Saba, Hamilton, Milam, Lampasas, Coryell, McLennan, Falls, Burnet, Llano, Mason, Menard, Kimble, Gillespie, Blanco, Travis, Williamson, Burleson, Bastrop, Caldwell, Hays, Comal, Kendall, Kerr, Edwards, Bandera, Bexar, Guadalupe, Medina, Uvalde, and Kinney; General Orders No. 1, Office of the Chief of Police, July 4, 1870, SPC, ARIS/TSLAC.

25. The Second Police District comprised the counties of Jones, Shackelford, Stephens, Palo Pinto, Parker, Tarrant, Ellis, Navarro, Henderson, Smith, Rusk, Panola, Hardeman, Wilbarger, Wichita, Knox, Baylor, Archer, Clay, Montague, Cooke, Grayson, Fannin, Lamar, Red River, Bowie, Haskell, Throckmorton, Young, Jack, Wise, Denton, Collin, Hunt, Hopkins, Titus, Davis (Cass), Dallas, Kaufman, Wood, Upshur, Marion, Harrison, and Van Zandt; SPC, ARIS/TSLAC.

26. The Third Police District encompassed the counties of Limestone, Freestone, Anderson, Cherokee, Nacogdoches, Shelby, Robertson, Leon, Houston, Angelina, San Augustine, Sabine, Madison, Trinity, Newton, Jasper, Tyler, Polk, Walker, Brazos, Grimes, Montgomery, Liberty, Hardin, Orange, Harris, Chambers, Jefferson, Fort Bend, Brazoria, and Galveston; SPC, ARIS/TSLAC.

27. The Fourth Police District embraced the counties of Washington, Fayette, Austin, Gonzales, Colorado, Lavaca, Wharton, Wilson, DeWitt, Jackson, Matagorda, Victoria, Karnes, Atascosa, Frio, Zavala, Maverick, Dimmit, La Salle, McMullen, Live Oak, Bee, Goliad, Refugio, Webb, Calhoun, San Patricio, Encinal (later part of Webb), Duval, Nueces, Zapata, Starr, Hidalgo, and Cameron; SPC, ARIS/TSLAC.

28. Ibid.

29. Roster of the State Police, 1870–1873, State Police Military Rolls, Military Rolls, Texas Adjutant General's Department, ARIS/TSLAC (hereafter cited State Police Roster, ARIS/TSLAC).

30. 1850 United States Population Census, Red River County, Texas, p. 197; 1860, p. 60; 1870, p. 95; 1880, p. 170; 1900, p. 31; *Red River Co. Cemeteries* (Clarksville: Published by Bertha L. Gable, 1986), IV, p. 11; Virgil D. White (transc.), *Index to Indian War Pension Files, 1892–1926* (Waynesboro, TN: The National Historical Publishing Company, 1987), I, p. 18; JD to E. M. Alexander, July 7, 1870, p. 7, Letterpress Book, State Police Correspondence, AGR, ARIS/TSLAC (hereafter cited as SPLPB, ARIS/TSLAC).

31. Much of the background information on Helm was supplied by the Cooper High School History Group in Cooper, Texas (Delta County). They did a superb job in searching the census and local sources for information. The most balanced appraisal of Helm (not Helms) is David Pickering and July Falls, *Brush Men and Vigilantes: Civil War Dissent in Texas* (College Station: Texas A&M University Press, 2001), pp. 41–42, 46–50, 52, 56–59, 63–66. The 1870 United States Population Census, DeWitt County, p. 239, gives Helm's age as thirty, which would mean he was born in 1840; J. Helm, *Cotton Worm Destroyers*, Patented May 20, 1873, Box TXC 142, Roy Sylvan Dunn Papers, DBCFAH, UTA. C. L. Sonnichsen has continued the Helm bashing in *NHT*, III, pp. 547–548; VI, pp. 162–163 (Sutton-Taylor Feud).

32. Cooper High School History Group; *Dallas Herald*, September 16, 1865, p. 2; *Biographical Souvenir of the State of Texas* (Chicago: F. A. Battey & Company, 1889), pp. 385–386.

33. Ibid.; Chris Emmett, *Shanghai Pierce: A Fair Likeness* (Norman: University of Oklahoma Press, 1953), p. 66; Helm to E. M. Pease, June 30, 1868; Helm to Pease, January 26, 1869, both in GP (EMP), ARIS/TSLAC; *Galveston Daily News*, July 24, 1869, p. 2; August 24, 1869, p. 2; *DSJ*, August 6, 1870, p. 5.

34. Much has been written about the feud. Sonnichsen's account, "Sutton-Taylor Feud," *NHT*, VI, pp. 162–163, is confusing. He implicates the State Police in the

quarrel, but the feud had begun long before the police were formed and only briefly involved the organization through Helm. Perhaps the best introduction to the sordid story is Parsons, "The DeWitt County Feud," in *The History of DeWitt County, Texas*, by the DeWitt County Historical Commission (Dallas: Curtis Media Corporation, 1991), pp. 30–45. A comprehensive history of the Sutton-Taylor Feud can be found in Chuck Parsons, *The Sutton-Taylor Feud: The Deadliest Blood Feud in Texas* (Denton: University of North Texas Press, 2009). A new interpretation of the Sutton-Taylor Feud can be found in James M. Smallwood, *The Feud That Wasn't: The Taylor Ring, Bill Sutton, John Wesley Hardin, and Violence in Texas* (College Station: Texas A&M University Press, 2008).

35. C. S. Bell (Special Officer) to Lieutenant W. A. Thompson, June 8, 1869, Box 27; Bell to C. E. Morse (Secretary of Civil Affairs), December 22, 23, 29, 1869, January 14, 1870, all in Box 23; Bell to Morse, May 11, 1870, Box 24; Helm to Thompson, July 7, 1869; Helm to Reynolds, July 8, 1869, September 2, 1869; Helm to A. K. Foster (County Judge, Lavaca County), September 2, 1869, Foster to Helm, September 12, 1869; Foster to Major Charles A. Wikoff (Columbus), September 12, 1869, all in Box 7; W. L. Jacobs (Clinton) to Wikoff, March 14, 1870, Box 24, M. P. Hunnicutt to Reynolds, August 6, 1869; Hunnicutt to Morse, August 30, 1869, both in Box 7; Bell to Morse, August 8, 1869, Box 7; Captain T. M. K. Smith to Lieutenant C. L. Davis, August 8, 1869, Box 7; Helm to Reynolds, May 30, 1870, Box 25, all in 5MD, OCA, LR, RG 393, NA. On Bell, see his obituary in the *New York Times*, February 24, 1879, p. 3 (courtesy of Chuck Parsons).

36. Helm, "Oath of Office," April 27, 1870, Bonds and Oaths, Secretary of State, ARIS/TSLAC; Wesley Ogden (District Judge, 10th Judicial District) and Other Citizens to Pease, [1869], GP (EMP); Helm to Davis, June 14, 1870, and June 26, 1870, both in Records of Edmund J. Davis, Texas Office of the Governor, ARIS/TSLAC (hereafter cited as GP [EJD], ARIS/TSLAC); *San Antonio Daily Herald*, June 24, 1870, p. 2, which reported that Bell claimed he and Helm had killed thirty-one men. The article appeared in response to criticism of the two men by the prominent Republican politician J. L. Haynes.

37. *Gonzales Inquirer* quoted in the *Daily Herald* (San Antonio), July 27, 1870, p. 2. See also the Helm notes of July 19, 1870, SPC, ARIS/TSLAC.

38. Thomas W. Cutrer, "Leander H. McNelly, *NHT*, IV, p. 445; James P. Major (Major General, C. S. A., Houston) to LHM, May 28, 1865, Leander H. McNelly Papers (DBCFAH, UTA); N. A. Jennings, *A Texas Ranger* (Dallas: Turner Company, 1930), pp. 57–70; George Durham, *Taming the Nueces Strip: The Story of McNelly's Rangers* (Austin: University of Texas Press, 1962); Webb, *The Texas Rangers*. A totally unreliable biography is Bob Scott, *Leander McNelly: Texas Ranger: He Just Kept On Keepin' On* (Austin: Eakin Press, 1998). A superb account is Parsons and Hall, *Captain L. H. McNelly, Texas Ranger*.

39. Roster of the State Police, ARIS/TSLAC; T. R. Fehrenbach, *Lone Star: A History of Texas and the Texans* (New York: The Macmillan Company, 1968), p. 575.

Fehrenbach also claimed that "McNelly was a great captain. He was the epitome of the Texan in action, and he set a record of courage, cunning, and audacity that was never to be surpassed."; *DSJ*, March 17, 1871, p. 2. See also the Walter Prescott Webb Papers (DBCFAH, UTA).

40. 1880 United States Population Census, McLennan County, Texas, 3rd Ward, Waco, p. 26; "Registered Deaths of the City Health Physician, Waco," *Heart of Texas Records*, 24 (Spring 1981), p. 32; Janet B. Hewett (ed.), *The Roster of Union Soldiers, 1861–1865, Ohio* (Wilmington: Broadfoot Publishing Company, 1999), II, p. 247; *McLennan County, Texas Cemetery Records* (Waco: Central Texas Genealogical Society, 1965), I, p. 88; *Early Waco Obituaries and Various Related Items, 1874–1908* (Waco: Central Texas Genealogical Society, Inc., 1980), p. 5; *Memorial and Biographical History of McLennan, Falls, Bell and Coryell Counties, Texas* (Chicago: The Lewis Publishing Company, 1893), pp. 113–114; Tony E. Duty, "The Home Front: McLennan County in the Civil War," *Texana* 12 (1974), pp. 222–223; *Galveston Daily News*, July 23, 1870, p. 3. See also C. E. Morse to Colonel John B. Johnson, December 2, 1869 (telegram), with clipping; Hunnicutt to Johnson, December 2, 1869, all in Box 22, 5MD, OCA, LR, RG 393, NA.

41. JD to W. Rogers (La Grange), September 5, 1870, p. 206; JD to William M. Speights, December 10, 1870, p. 641, both in SPLPB, ARIS/TSLAC; State Police Roster, ARIS/TSLAC. Speights's son, J. H. H. "Sonny" Speights was also a State Policeman and was wounded in an encounter with John Wesley Hardin; see Parsons, "Gunfire in Hemphill," *True West* 46 (December 1999), pp. 13–17.

42. *DSJ*, September 17, 1870, p. 1.

43. *Democratic Statesman* (Austin), September 26, 1871, p. 2; Farrow, *The Texas Democrats*, p. 21.

44. *San Antonio Daily Herald*, September 16, 1871, p. 2; *Austin Democratic Statesman*, September 14, 1871, p. 2.

45. *Houston Daily Union*, September 29, 1871, p. 1. The observer may have been W. H. Quayle or Quail but probably not the Quayle mentioned in *NHT*, V, p. 383, who was a Confederate officer who moved to Mexico after the war. For confirmation of these insights see the Henry Orsay Papers, DBCFAH, UTA.

46. *AG Report*, 1870, p. 9; *DSJ*, November 12, 1870, p. 2.

47. Crouch, "A Spirit of Lawlessness: White Violence; Texas Blacks, 1865–1868," *Journal of Social History* 18 (Winter 1984), pp. 217–232; Greg Cantrell, "Racial Violence and Reconstruction Politics in Texas, 1867–1868," *SWHQ* 93 (January 1990), pp. 333–355; Keener, "Racial Turmoil in Texas"; Moneyhon, *Republicanism in Reconstruction Texas*, pp. 92–96; Clayton, "The Lone Star Conspiracy"; Bill O'Neal, "Violence in Texas History," in *Texas: A Sesquicentennial Celebration*, ed. Donald W. Whisenhunt (Austin: Eakin Press, 1984), pp. 353–369; C. C. Rister, "Outlaws and Vigilantes of the Southern Plains, 1865–1885," *Mississippi Valley Historical Review* 19 (March 1933), pp. 537–554; Kosary, "Regression to Barbarism in Reconstruction Texas." Louisiana rivaled Texas for bloodshed; see Gilles Vandal, "'Bloody Caddo': White Violence Against Blacks in a Louisiana

Parish, 1865–1876," *Journal of Social History* 25 (Winter 1991), pp. 373–388; "Black Violence in Post-Civil War Louisiana," *Journal of Interdisciplinary History* 25 (Summer 1994), pp. 45–64. Vandal, in *Rethinking Southern Violence: Homicides in Post-Civil War Louisiana, 1866–1884* (Columbus: Ohio State University Press, 2000), p. 13, states that during this era 4,986 killings occurred in Louisiana. He further asserts that after the war Louisiana emerged "as the most violent Southern state, with the sole exception of Texas" (p. 4).

48. Luke Gournay, *Texas Boundaries: Evolution of the State's Counties* (College Station: Texas A&M University Press, 1995), pp. 64–65; *Texas Almanac for 1871* (Galveston: Richardson, Belo & Co., 1871), p. 134; Mavis P. Kelsey Sr. and Donald H. Dyal, *The Courthouses of Texas* (College Station: Texas A&M University Press, 1993), p. 187; Ann E. Hodges, "Madison County," *NHT*, IV, pp. 454–456; Randolph B. Campbell, *An Empire for Slavery: The Peculiar Institution in Texas, 1821–1865* (Baton Rouge: Louisiana State University Press, 1989), p. 265; Ricky Floyd Dobbs, "'A Slow Civil War': Resistance to the Davis Administration in Hill and Walker Counties, 1871" (M.A. thesis, Baylor University, 1989), pp. 47–48. In 1860, the county had a population of 2,238 and by the end of 1870, 4,062 residents, with 105 individuals dying during the year; *Navasota Ranger* quoted in *Flake's Daily Bulletin*, December 7, 1870, p. 2.

49. Captain Thomas H. Horton (11th Infantry) to Morse, May 22, 1869, DT, LR, Box 17, RG 393, NA; "Citizen" (Madisonville) to E. J. Davis, August 9, 1870, in *DSJ*, August 20, 1870, p. 2. The article, really a letter written by J. D. McMahon, was entitled "Lawlessness in Madison County." The same letter, but addressed to Chief of Police Davidson, is in SPC, Register of Letters Received, August 1870–January 1871, p. 47, AGR, ARIS/TSLAC. McMahon was a significant player in Madison County politics, serving as a member of the Board of Appeals and district clerk in the fall of 1870, Election Registers, Madison County, 1870, pp. 428–429, Secretary of State Records, SPC, ARIS/TSLAC. Horton originally set bail at $5,000 but it was later rejected by the district judge.

50. John W. Clarkson (Madisonville) to EJD, August 27, 1870, GP (EJD); JD to George W. Farrow (Bryan City), July 29, 1870, pp. 82–83, SPLPB, both in ARIS/TSLAC.

51. Citizens (28 signed; led by C. G. Scott, Presiding Justice of Madison County, Madisonville) to EJD, September 27, 1870, GP (EJD), ARIS/TSLAC.

52. 1870 United States Population Census, Madison County, Texas, p. 29; State Police Roster, ARIS/TSLAC; Muster and Pay Roll of Captain John H. Patrick, 8th Regiment, Company G, State Guard, September 20, 1870, Military Rolls, ARIS/TSLAC. Madison County citizens also organized companies A, B, and C, of the 32nd Texas Reserve Militia in October 1870, Military Rolls, AGR, SPC, ARIS/TSLAC. These three units had a total of only four black members. The law that created the State Guard and the Reserve Militia is in H. P. N. Gammel (comp. and arr.), *The Laws of Texas, 1822–1897* (10 vols.; Austin: The Gammel Book Company, 1898), VI, pp. 185–190.

53. Patrick to C. D. Harn (State Representative), September 5, 1870, GP (EJD), ARIS/TSLAC.

54. JD (by Henry Orsay, Chief Clerk) to Patrick, October 29, 1870, p. 451; JD (by Orsay) to Farrow, October 28, 1870, p. 452; JD to Patrick, October 30, 1870, p. 454 1/4; JD to Harn and Patrick, November 2, 1870, p. 473, all in SPLPB; JD to Patrick (Groesbeck), December 9, 1871, p. 364, AGLPB No. 5, all in ARIS/TSLAC. For the problem that another State Policeman caused Davis and Davidson, see Crouch and Donaly E. Brice, "'Dastardly Scoundrels': The State Police and the Linn Flat Affair," *East Texas Historical Journal* 37 (Spring 1999), pp. 29–38.

55. Clipping, December 6, 1870, GP (EJD), ARIS/TSLAC.

56. Ibid.; *Brazos Eagle* quoted in *Flake's Daily Bulletin*, November 19, 1890, p. 1; Cecil N. Neely, "An Early History of Madison County, Texas" (M.A. thesis, Sam Houston State University, 1971), pp. 63–64; Nunn, *Texas Under the Carpetbaggers*, pp. 53–54; Dobbs, "'A Slow Civil War,'" pp. 50–52. The *Eagle* stated that nine shots were fired at Copeland. The remaining four blacks escaped by another door. The *Galveston News* mistakenly reported that Tinsley, a lieutenant in the State Police, along with two other policemen, had been killed in the confrontation; *News* quoted in the *Houston Daily Union*, December 17, 1870, p. 2. Many Democratic newspapers published wild rumors and incredible falsehoods about the State Police.

57. Harn (Navasota) to JD, November 6, 1870, p. 167 (telegram); November 7, 1870, p. 167; EJD to JD, November 7, 1870, p. 167 (telegram); Harn and John Gibbs (Navasota), November 8, 1870, p. 167 (telegram); Harn (Bryan City) to JD, November 9, 1870, p. 167 (telegram); Harn to JD, November 15, 1870, p. 167 (telegram); November 14, 1870, p. 168 (telegram); Sarah H. Patrick to JD, [November 8, 1870], p. 168; H. M. Reid (Madisonville) to JD, November 16, 1870, p. 168; Neighbors (Madisonville) to JD, November 16, 1870, p. 169; Drew Wyche and Others (Bryan) to JD, November 8, 1870, p. 168, all in Register of Letters Received, August 1870–January 1871, State Police Correspondence, State Police Records, Reconstruction Records, Texas Adjutant General's Department, ARIS/TSLAC (hereafter cited as SP Register of Letters Received, Aug. 1870–Jan. 1871, ARIS/TSLAC). That McIver had a band of one hundred men is surely an exaggeration.

58. J. R. Burnett (Madisonville) to EJD, November 7, 1870, GP (EJD), ARIS/TSLAC; *A Legislative Manual for the State of Texas . . ., 1879–1880* (Austin: E. W. Swindells, 1879), p. 244; Campbell, "Scalawag District Judges: The E. J. Davis Appointees, 1870–1873," *Houston Review* 14 (1992), pp. 75–88; Armistead Albert Aldrich, *The History of Houston County Texas* (San Antonio: The Naylor Company, 1943), pp. 135–136.

59. Burnett to EJD, November 7, 1870, GP (EJD), ARIS/TSLAC; *Daily Houston Telegraph*, November 26, 1870, p. 4. Burnett told Patrick that he violated the law in taking away the arms of citizens. Patrick's response was that he had orders "to do as he did." Clearly, he did not receive these instructions from headquarters.

60. *DSJ*, November 11, 1870, p. 2; Clipping, December 6, 1870, GP (EJD), ARIS/ TSLAC; *Daily Houston Telegraph*, November 26, 1870, p. 4. Interestingly enough, just before the Madison County troubles occurred, Davis and his family visited Corpus Christi (his hometown) "for needful rest and change." Davidson was also absent from the capitol, traveling to the "mountains near Fredericksburg, for his health," *DSJ*, November 5, 1870, p. 1. The *Houston Daily Union* reported that when Davis was inaugurated he left considerable legal business unfinished. His partner, John Bernard Murphy, a conservative Democrat, disposed of most of the backlog, but specific cases required the governor's attention. He appeared in person to avoid any legal suffering by his clients. Although the *Telegraph* disparaged the Davis trip, the *Union* felt that "all fair minded people will say it was an act highly creditable" and "applaud" the governor for his "fidelity to his clients," November 24, 1870, p. 2. On Murphy, see Frank Wagner, "John Bernard Murphy," *NHT*, IV, p. 894.

61. *Houston Daily Union*, November 26, 1870, p. 1. *Flake's Daily Bulletin* wrote that when Davidson passed through Galveston on his way to Madison County to investigate the "riot," he conversed with a reporter, who claimed that from Davidson's evidence the situation was "greatly exaggerated." It seemed that only one person named Copeland had been slain, November 19, 1870, p. 1. A seven-line summary of Davidson's speech appeared in the *Daily Houston Telegraph*, November 26, 1870, p. 4.

62. *Houston Daily Union*, November 26, 1870, p. 1. In addition, Davidson contended that $25,000 worth of stolen horses, mules, and cattle had been returned to the rightful owners.

63. Ibid.

64. Ibid.

65. Ibid.

66. Thomas Sheriff (Lieutenant, State Police, Madisonville) to Editors *Union*, November 23, 1870, in *Houston Daily Union*, November 28, 1878, p. 2. The *Union*, along with the *DSJ* and *San Antonio Express*, was admittedly supportive of the administration.

67. *Daily Herald* (San Antonio), December 20, 1870, p. 2.

68. Harn to JD, September 30, 1870, p. 87; Patrick (Navasota) to JD, November 24, 1870, p. 168 (telegram); J. M. Gibbs (Navasota) to JD, November 26, 1870, p. 173 (telegram); ibid., November 27, 1870, p. 173 (telegram); Harn (Navasota) to JD, November 27, 1870, p. 173 (telegram); December 2, 1870, p. 176 (telegram); L. H. McNelly to JD, [November 1870], p. 173; November 30, 1870, p. 176; Patrick to JD, December 1, 1870, p. 176 (telegram); McMahon to JD, December 5, 1870, p. 195; Benjamin F. Huffman (Madisonville) to JD, December 16, 1870, p. 208; Tom Keesee (Madisonville) to JD, December 30, 1870, p. 233, all in Register of Letters Received (August 1870–January 1871), ARIS/TSLAC; Orsay to Farrow, October 28, 1870, p. 452; JD to Vernon, December 6, 1870, p. 617, both in SPLPB;

State Police Roster, all in ARIS/TSLAC. One hostile newspaper wrote that "fifty of the reserve forces were ordered" from Galveston County to Madison to put down "lawlessness and crime." After their return, they claimed "quietude" reigned, their mission being "worse than useless—they were taken from their business to restore law and order, where all was peace, and its citizens generally law-abiding," *Navasota Ranger* quoted in *Flake's Daily Bulletin*, December 7, 1870, p. 2; Sloan to EJD, December 3, 1870, GP (EJD); JD to Patrick (Navasota) care of Harn, December 28, 1870, SPLPB, p. 795; Patrick (Austin) to EJD, February 3, 1871, GP (EJD), all in ARIS/TSLAC; *Daily Houston Telegraph*, November 26, 1870, p. 4. The Patrick letter was written on House of Representatives stationery. Indeed, Patrick did not disappear from the Texas scene. In 1871 he was president of the Limestone County Union League. The next year he became the Groesbeck City Marshal, received complaints about his performance from the mayor, resigned, and was appointed to the board of aldermen; Political Documents, 1871–80, James P. Newcomb Papers, DBCFAH, UTA; J. S. Thurmond (Mayor, Groesbeck) to AG, March 30, 1872, T-28, p. 857; Patrick to AG, April 16, 1872, Endorsement, Newcomb (Secretary of State), April 25, 1872, P-46, pp. 698–699, all in Register of Letters Received (September 1871 to September 1872), ARIS/TSLAC.

69. Richard Sloan (Navasota) to EJD, December 3, 1870, GP (EJD), ARIS/TSLAC.

70. Ibid.

71. Petition from Citizens of Madison County [January 1873], GP (EJD); Memorials and Petitions, both in ARIS/TSLAC. Apparently Madison County did employ some Special Policemen during the election; see Roster of Special Policemen, Madison County, p. 208, State Police Military Rolls, Military Rolls, Texas Adjutant General's Department, ARIS/TSLAC (hereafter cited as Roster of Special Policemen, ARIS/TSLAC). M. W. Burney was the sheriff from November 8, 1872, to February 15, 1876; Tise, *Texas County Sheriffs*, p. 350.

72. Petition from Citizens of Madison County [January 1873], Memorials and Petitions; F. L. Britton (AG and Chief of Police) to Lieutenant H. H. Adams (Hempstead), January 24, 1873, p. 289; Britton to Burnett, January 25, 1873, p. 296, both in AGLPB, all in ARIS/TSLAC; *Journal of the Senate of Texas: Being the Session of the Thirteenth Legislature* (Austin: John Cardwell, State Printer, 1873), January 31, 1873, p. 109.

73. Ibid. (all sources).

74. *DSJ*, November 12, 1870, p. 2.

75. JD to Helm, August 12, 1870, p. 117; August 15, 1870, p. 130; August 30, 1870, p. 180, SPLPB, ARIS/TSLAC; *DSL*, August 14, 1870, p. 1.

76. JD to Helm, August 31, 1870, p. 190; September 6, 1870, p. 216, SPLPB, ARIS/TSLAC.

77. JD to Helm, August 31, 1870, p. 190, SPLPB, ARIS/TSLAC; *DSJ*, September 2, 1870, p. 1.

78. *Weekly Austin Republican*, September 14, 1870, p. 2; November 2, 1870, pp. 2–3; *DSJ*, October 19, 1870, p. 2; Victor Rose, *The Texas Vendetta; or, The Sutton-Taylor Feud* (New York: J. J. Little & Co., 1880), pp. 40–48.

79. State Police Roster, ARIS/TSLAC; *Daily Herald* (San Antonio), September 16, 1870, p. 2; *DSJ*, October 13, 1870, p. 2; *Weekly Austin Republican*, October 12, 1870, p. 2; W. W. Boyce and John R. Baylor to the Editor, November 11, 19, 1870, in *Daily Herald*, November 22, 1870, p. 1; [John Gus Patton], "Judge Patton Reminisces," in *The History & Heritage of Goliad County*, ed. Jakie L. Pruett and Everett B. Cole (Austin: Eakin Publications, Inc., 1983), pp. 305–306.

80. B. J. Pridgen to JD, September 27, 1870, Executive Record Book, pp. 443–445, Secretary of State, ARIS/TSLAC; Seabury Phillips (DeWitt County) to Major S. H. Lathrop, August 28, 1867, DT, LR, Box 2, RG 393, NA; Rose, *The Texas Vendetta*, pp. 38–40. On Pridgen see Craig H. Roell, "Bolivar Jackson Pridgen," *NHT*, V, p. 337.

81. JD to W. Longworth, September 27, 1870, p. 315; Henry Orsay to Private C. C. Simmons, October 8, 1870, p. 387; JD to Henry Maney (Judge, 22nd Judicial District), October 31, 1870, p. 455; JD to Pridgen, October 31, 1870, p. 456, all in SPLPB, ARIS/TSLAC; *DSJ*, October 13, p. 2; October 19, p. 2; October 22, p. 1; October 23, 1870, p. 1; *Daily Herald* (San Antonio), November 22, 1870, p. 1, stated that as a result of the grand jury allowing two of the men involved in killing the Kellys to testify, the body was "thus constituted into a court, hearing testimony *pro* and *con* and admitting the evidence of criminals in regard to their criminality." See also Tise, *Texas County Sheriffs*, p. 157.

82. For a brief summary of Helm's State Police career and death, see Pickering and Falls, *Brush Men and Vigilantes*, pp. 108–114, 118–125, 127, 129–38; *DSJ*, December 4, 1870, p. 1; *DSJ*, December 8, 1870, p. 1; *Weekly Austin Republican*, December 7, 1870, p. 2; December 14, 1870, p. 4; *Daily Herald* (San Antonio), December 9, 1870, p. 2; December 20, 1870, p. 2; April 21, 1871, p. 2; General Order, JD, December 7, 1870, p. 620; JD to Captain Robert F. Haskins (Helena), December 5, 1870, p. 602, both in SPLPB, ARIS/TSLAC; Helm to EJD, December 7, 1870, GP (EJD), SPC, ARIS/TSLAC; C. L. Patterson to Roy Sylvan Dunn, January 15, 1950; Statement of Hans O. Pattillo, September 1, 1950, both in Dunn Papers, DBCFAH, UTA; Leon Metz, *John Wesley Hardin: Dark Angel of Texas* (El Paso: Mangan Books, 1996), pp. 109–112; *Fayette County New Era* (La Grange), August 8, 1873, p. 4; "The Killing of Jack Helm," John W. Hunter Literary Effort, Manuscript Collection, ARIS/TSLAC; Parsons, "The DeWitt County Feud," pp. 36–37; Parsons, *The Sutton-Taylor Feud*, pp. 127–132.

83. *Message of Gov. Edmund J. Davis*, pp. 10, 12–13. Davis also recommended that no more than "twenty special policemen for each county be authorized to deal with 'ordinary emergency' to assist the local authorities." They would be paid only when in actual service. As earlier noted, this idea was implemented later in 1871.

84. Ibid., pp. 11–12.

85. Ibid. "Many of the arrests made by the Police," Davis declared, had been "of this class of persons, and many of the offenders" had fled the state, "ridding" Texas "of a reckless and vicious class." Between July and December 1870, the *DSJ* commented almost daily upon State Police arrests.

86. Ibid., pp. 12–13.

CHAPTER THREE

1. EJD to B. F. Yerby (Foreman, Grand Jury, Hill County) and Others, March 3, 1871, p. 226, LPB, GP (EJD); also on pp. 238–240, Executive Record Book (October 10, 1870–May 30, 1871), Vol. II, both in ARIS/TSLAC. Dobbs, "'A Slow Civil War,'" contains valuable material on Hill County and the sequence of events that led to the declaration of martial law; especially Chapter 4, "A Broken Trust: The Hill County Rebellion, January, 1871," pp. 56–79. Dobbs, however, did not include some of the significant original source material and extensively relied upon the published account of the Hill County conflict.

2. Hardin describes the scene in detail (some 1,000 words) in his autobiography, and an indictment was issued in 1872; see [John Wesley Hardin], *The Life of John Wesley Hardin, from the Original Manuscript, as Written by Himself* (Seguin, TX: Smith & Moore, 1896), pp. 17–22; Richard C. Marohn, *The Last Gunfighter: John Wesley Hardin* (College Station: Creative Publishing Company, 1995), pp. 23–25, which has a garbled account and relies upon Hardin. The best explanation is Chuck Persons, "'Tell Wes to be a good man . . .': Examining an Early Hardin Killing," *NOLA* 6 (April 1981), pp. 3–8 (also in *East Texas Historical Journal* 20, no. 2 (1982), pp. 46–56); Metz, *John Wesley Hardin: Dark Angel of Texas*, pp. 19–21, 209, 213; James Verdo Reese, "A History of Hill County, Texas to 1873: (M.A. thesis, University of Texas, Austin, 1961), pp. 143–149, which also mentions Hardin, asserts that "numerous horse and cattle thieves operated in the area, making raids from the Cross Timbers which provided excellent cover for their camps. The local authorities were powerless to control the situation, and the entrance of the State Police into the county to assist them was a signal for the whole citizenry to turn to obstructionism," p. 144. The question is why would the inhabitants become obstructionist when they obviously needed assistance and requested it?

3. *A Memorial and Biographical History of Johnson and Hill Counties, Texas* (Chicago: Lewis Publishing Company, 1892), pp. 207–209, 212; Weldon B. Hartsfield, "A History of Hill County, Texas" (M.A. thesis, Austin College, 1938); Colonel Harold B. Simpson, *Hill County (Texas) Trilogy* (Hillsboro: Hill College Press, 1986), p. 35; *Texas Almanac for 1871*, p. 119; *NHT*, III, pp. 619–621. On Hill's background see *NHT*, III, pp. 611–612; T. C. Richardson, *East Texas: Its History and Its Makers*, ed. Dabney White (4 vols.; New York: Lewis Historical Publishing Company, 1940), III, p. 1011; Gournay, *Texas Boundaries*, pp. 63–64.

4. *A Memorial and Biographical History*, pp. 216–217, 219. Lexington, founded about 1851, was halfway between Peoria and Hillsboro. Later named Union Bluff, it

was the only polling place in 1853; Claude Dooley, Betty Dooley, and the Texas Historical Commission, *Why Stop?: A Guide to Texas Historical Roadside Markers* (Houston: Gulf Publishing Company, 1985), p. 234; Hill County Historical Commission, *A History of Hill County, Texas, 1853–1980* (Waco: Texian Press, 1980), pp. 146, 306, 309, 399, 405; *Texas Almanac for 1871*, p. 119. On Hillsboro (originally spelled Hillsborough), see *NHT*, III, p. 623; Peoria, *NHT*, V, p. 147.

5. Campbell, *An Empire for Slavery*, p. 265; Simpson, *Hill County (Texas) Trilogy*, p. 36. For a detailed examination of slavery in this area see William Dean Carrigan, "Between South and West: Race, Violence, and Power in Central Texas, 1836–1916" (Ph.D. diss., Emory University, 1999); "Slavery on the Frontier: The Peculiar Institution in Central Texas," *Slavery and Abolition* 20 (August 1999), pp. 63–96.

6. *A Memorial and Biographical History*, p. 246; *Rand McNally's Pioneer Atlas of the American West* (Chicago: Rand McNally & Company, 1956 [1876]), p. 67. In 1871, for example, the *Texas Almanac* could exclaim, "there are but few blacks in the county," p. 119.

7. Return of Crimes Committed, Hill County, Beauchamp, Sheriff [July 1870], Reports of Crimes, Arrests, and Fugitives, State Police Records, Reconstruction Records, Texas Adjutant General's Department, ARIS/TSLAC. Dobbs, in "'A Slow Civil War,'" asserted that throughout the first six months of 1870, Hill County experienced eleven murders, a rate of nearly 1.75 per 1,000 persons, p. 58. This is incorrect and includes those from the previous two years. For earlier violence see Barry A. Crouch, "A Spirit of Lawlessness: White Violence, Texas Blacks, 1865–1868," *Journal of Social History* 18 (Winter 1984), pp. 217–232; Greg Cantrell, "Racial Violence and Reconstruction Politics in Texas, 1867–1868," *SWHQ* 93 (January 1990), pp. 333–355.

8. Background on West is courtesy of Dave Johnson. See also F. M. Cross, *A Short Sketch—History from Personal Reminiscences* [sic] *of Early Days in Central Texas* (Brownwood, TX: Greenwood Printing Company, 1910), pp. 114–116. For a completely unreliable account see Kirkpatrick, *The Early Settlers Life in Texas and the Organization of Hill County*, pp. 79–82, and Bailey, *A History of Hill County*, pp. 119–120, who views West as some kind of "hero"; *State of Texas v. Kynch West*, Bill of Indictment, October 18, 1889, no. 2638, Extradition Papers, Secretary of State, ARIS/TSLAC; Tise, *Texas County Sheriffs*, p. 258.

9. William Chambers (Waco) to EJD, June 20, 1870, GP (EJD), ARIS/TSLAC. For background on Chambers see *NHT*, II, pp. 31–32. The Democrats later impeached Chambers but failed to convict him. See *The State of Texas Against William Chambers, Judge First Judicial District. Before the Senate of the Fourteenth Legislature, Sitting as a High Court of Impeachment. Proceedings and Evidence* (Austin: Cardwell & Walker, Printers, 1874).

10. Chambers to EJD, June 20, 1870, GP (EJD), ARIS/TSLAC. Chambers served as District Judge for the First Judicial District, headquartered in Beaumont; see

Randolph B. Campbell, "Scalawag District Judges: The E. J. Davis Appointees, 1870–1873," *Houston Review* 14 (1992), pp. 75–88.

11. *DSJ*, August 4, 1870, p. 7, which printed the governor's proclamation verbatim.

12. 1870 United States Population Census, Hill County, Texas, p. 407; 1867 Voter Registration, Hill County, #271; Register of Elected and Appointed State and County Officials, 1870–1873, pp. 322–323, Election Registers; Evin Beauchamp, Bonds and Oaths, Secretary of State, all in ARIS/TSLAC; Reese, "A History of Hill County," pp. 134, 174.

13. *DSJ*, July 29, 1870, p. 6.

14. For a totally distorted account of West, along with the doings of his acquaintances, in a chapter entitled "The Re-Construction: Rule of Carpet Baggers and Negro Police," characterized as an era of "mob law," see A. Y. Kirkpatrick, *The Early Settlers Life in Texas and the Organization of Hill County* (Hillsboro, TX: Privately printed, 1909), pp. 79–82. Kirkpatrick portrays the desperadoes as reliable community citizens when all the evidence suggests otherwise. Kirkpatrick's story line is recounted with embellishment, most of it wrong and distorted, including names and dates along with truly outrageous charges and exaggerations in Ellis Bailey, *A History of Hill County, Texas, 1838–1865* (Waco: Texian Press, 1966), pp. 114–122. On Martin, see Simpson, *Hill County (Texas) Trilogy*, p. 52.

15. 1870 United States Population Census, Hill County, Texas, p. 379; Statement of H. W. Young to EJD, November 6, 1870, GP (EJD), ARIS/TSLAC; Bailey, *A History of Hill County*, p. 120, for a fanciful story and background on Atchison.

16. Statement of John J. Gage and H. Harvick to EJD, November 6, 1870, GP (EJD); also in Executive Record Book (October 10, 1870–May 30, 1871), Vol. II, pp. 82–83, both in ARIS/TSLAC. Bailey, in *A History of Hill County*, p. 120, claims that Atchison and Beauchamp drank together in Bateman's saloon in Hillsboro where the State Police arrested him. While en route to Waco, Atchison managed to escape. Beauchamp, according to Bailey, carried papers for Atchison's arrest, but did not bother him because the sheriff was "afraid of lead poison," p. 120. Atchison's case for the murder of the freedman Alex Shaw was tried in early 1871. He pled self-defense and claimed Shaw did not die from the wound as "from exposure in sleeping out of doors on a certain night." One of his lawyers was future governor Richard Coke. J. W. Oliver, the presiding judge, was "distinguished for perspicuity and a clear laying down of the law." The jury found Atchison not guilty, and one newspaper contended that he "stands high among his neighbors, and when in his right mind is said to be a quiet good citizen." *Waco Register* quoted in *Houston Daily News*, January 11, 1871, p. 1.

17. 1870 United States Population Census, Hill County, Texas, Precinct #1, pp. 386, 396. There was also twenty-one-year-old Augustus A. Cox, with a wife and infant, but he was Texas born and had $700 assessed real and personal property, p. 382. The other Cox was a Texas-born farmer named John P. who had real estate worth $3,000 and personal property at $2,000, with an Alabama-born wife and

four children (three girls and a boy), along with a fifty-eight-year-old woman living in the household. (She may have been his or his wife's mother), p. 393. Neither of these latter two were likely brothers, nor does their description lead one to believe they participated in the nefarious activities of Kinch West.

18. M. P. Hunnicutt (Captain, SP) to EJD, September 3, 1870, Executive Record Book (January 18, 1870–October 27, 1870), Vol. I, pp. 377–380, ARIS/TSLAC. For problems in Waco, see *DSJ*, August 9, 1870, p. 5. A riot occurred there on August 6, with one man killed and three wounded. Seriously injured was black State Police Private William Summers.

19. Ibid.; JD to Hunnicutt, July 7, 1870, p. 9; July 11, 1870, pp. 38–39; July 26, 1870, pp. 74–75; July 28, 1870, p. 80; July 29, 1870, p. 81, all in SPLPB, ARIS/TSLAC; *Galveston Daily News*, July 23, 1870, p. 3. Hunnicutt stated that it was his aim "to allow no necessity for calling out the militia in any instance, in this District." This was also the governor's goal.

20. JD to Hunnicutt, July 28, 1870, p. 80; July 29, 1870, p. 81; August 12, 1870, p. 114; September 1, 1870, p. 195; October 19, 1870, p. 417, all in SPLPB; and the correspondence in Executive Record Book (January 18, 1870–October 27, 1870), Vol. I, pp. 377–384, all in ARIS/TSLAC. Davidson dismissed Hunnicutt, to which Davis assented, for neglect of duty, leaving his post without authority or just cause, and failing to defend one of the men in his command. Actually, the charges were false. Hunnicutt earlier traveled to Houston, Galveston, and Beaumont on police business and left an affidavit with the proper judicial and legal officials defending the policeman in his command charged with murder. Political factionalism among the Republicans also contributed to Hunnicutt's difficulties. Hunnicutt's letters suggest that he was more interested in protecting his integrity than in maintaining his captaincy. This episode can be followed in EJD to Hunnicutt, August 23, 1870, p. 156; JD to Hunnicutt, September 1, 170, p. 195, both in SPLPB, ARIS/TSLAC; Hunnicutt to EJD, September 3, 1870; September 5, 1870; September 28, 1870; I. L. L. McCall (Waco) to EJD, September 5, 1870; N. W. Battle (Waco) to Whom It May Concern, September 5, 1870, all in GP (EJD), ARIS/TSLAC. Later, the *San Antonio Daily Herald*, January 28, 1871, p. 2, declared that Hunnicutt, a former Captain in the State Police at Waco "and of course very 'loil,'" [loyal] had recently been "arrested on a very serious charge," but no particulars were given. *Flake's Daily Bulletin* (Galveston), January 24, 1871, p. 4, ran a similar story.

21. EJD to Don Campbell (President, State Senate), February 8, 1871, pp. 108–111, LPB, GP (EJD); also in Executive Record Book (October 10, 1870–May 30, 1871), Vol. II, pp. 195–196, both in ARIS/TSLAC; also published in *Message of Gov. Edmund J. Davis, with Documents in Relation to Lawlessness and Crime in Hill and Walker Counties* (Austin: J. G. Tracy, State Printer, 1871), pp. 3–4, 12–13 (hereafter cited *Message and Documents*). The same printed material on Hill County may be found in the *Senate Journal of the Twelfth Legislature* (Austin: J. G. Tracy, State

Printer, 1871), pp. 189–203. Pritchett wrote that he did not send the men as he "thought it useless to do so after" the sheriff "refused them, and from the orders received" from Davidson.

22. JD to L. J. Hoffman (Waco), September 20, 1870, p. 273, SPLPB, ARIS/TSLAC; *DSJ*, September 23, 1870, p. 1; Hoffman to JD, September 2, 1870, in *Message and Documents*, p. 10. Nagle, born in New York City, was a private (later sergeant) for three years in the 3rd US Cavalry and honorably discharged in 1866. B. Rush Plumly, a prominent Galveston politician, wrote that Nagle was "worthy and capable." He was commissioned on July 11, 1870; Pierce Nagle to EJD, July 9, 1870, SPC, ARIS/TSLAC. For more on Hoffman, see John B. Johnson (Captain, 6th U. S. Cavalry) to C. E. Morse (Secretary of Civil Affairs, 5MD), May 12, 1869; Endorsement, J. J. Reynolds (Commander, 5MD), May 29, 1869, Endorsement, E. M. Pease (Governor), May 31, 1869; Statement of James Campbell, June 21, 1869; Johnson to Morse, June 23, 1869; Hunnicutt (Special Officer) to Johnson, June 23, 1869, all in 5MD, OCA, LR, Box 33, RG 393, NA.

23. JD, Order, September 21, 1870, p. 281; JD to Hoffman, September 20, 1870, p. 277; JD to Sergeant George E. Haynie, September 21, 1870, p. 288, all in SPLPB, ARIS/TSLAC. Hoffman had earlier accepted a position as marshal of Waco and Davidson terminated him because, by the laws of Texas, "you cannot hold two offices at one and the same time," JD to Hoffman, September 22, 1870, p. 296, SPLPB, ARIS/TSLAC. Hunnicutt had initially recommended Hoffman for the State Police. Hoffman had served in the US Army. A "man of property," he "suffered persecution on account of his political opinions." Moreover, Hoffman knew all the country above Waco and had the "facilities for finding the rendezvous of a number of desperate characters." Hunnicutt needed his assistance in capturing three white men who had murdered a black man in Hill County, Hunnicutt to JD, July 11, 1870; Hoffman to JD [July 1870], both in SPC, ARIS/TSLAC.

24. JD to Beauchamp (Sheriff, Hill Co.), September 20, 1870, p. 274, SPLPB, ARIS/TSLAC.

25. Beauchamp to JD, September 16, 1870, in *Message and Documents*, p. 9; JD to Beauchamp, September 20, 1870, p. 274, SPLPB, ARIS/TSLAC.

26. JD to Thomas Williams (Lt., SP), September 23, 1870, p. 304; November 1, 1870, p. 465, SPLPB, ARIS/TSLAC. On Williams, see Crouch, "Captain Thomas Williams," pp. 71–86.

27. Williams to JD, November 4, 1870, *Messages and Documents*, pp. 15–16. Williams was an excellent officer but often neglected his paperwork. As late as November 1, Davidson ordered Williams to furnish a report of his Hill County activities "giving all particulars," JD to Williams, November 1, 1870, p. 465, SPLPB, ARIS/TSLAC.

28. Ibid.; Waco *Register* quoted in *DSJ*, October 7, 1870, p. 4.

29. *Weekly Austin Republican*, October 5, 1870, p. 2; *Waco Register* quoted in *DSJ*, October 7, 1870, p. 4.

30. EJD to Beauchamp, October 3, 1870, pp. 364–365, SPLPB, ARIS/TSLAC; also in *Message and Documents*, p. 12.

31. EJD to Campbell, February 8, 1871, pp. 108–111, LPB, GP (EJD); EJD to Beauchamp, October 3, 1870, pp. 364–365, SPLPB, both letters in ARIS/TSLAC; both are reprinted in *Message and Documents*, pp. 3–4, 12–13.

32. Citizens of Hill County (86 Petitioners) to EJD, October 22, 1870, pp. 14–17, Executive Record Book (October 10, 1870–May 30, 1871), Vol. II, Secretary of State, ARIS/TSLAC.

33. Ibid.

34. Ibid. (all sources).

35. Ibid. (all sources).

36. JD to Lt. W. T. Pritchett (Waco), October 11, 1870, p. 397; October 25, 1870, pp. 425–427 (2 letters); October 25, 1870, p. 427; October 30, 1870, pp. 366–367; JD to Pvt. William Gibson (Austin), October 19, 1870, p. 416; JD to Mrs. J. C. Martin (Fort Graham, Hill Co.), October 19, 1870, p. 419; JD to John A. Burnett (District Clerk, Hill Co.), October 22, 1870, p. 421; JD to Hoffman, November 1, 1870, p. 464, all in SPLPB, ARIS/TSLAC. Problems with personnel plagued the Waco detachment. One State Policeman was charged with disobeying orders, failing to obtain a leave of absence, and neglect of duty. Another was reported as unfit and a third as "worthless." Sergeant Haynie, one of the more competent men, resigned.

37. William E. Evans (Hillsboro) to JD, November 9, 1870, *Message and Documents*, pp. 16–17.

38. Ibid.

39. JD to Pritchett, October 11, 1870, p. 397; October 30, 1870, pp. 366–367; November 12, 1870, p. 525; November 15, 1870, pp. 545–546; JD to Hoffman, November 26, 1870, p. 566; JD, Special Order, November 5, 1870, p. 505, all in SPLPB; Wood to EJD, November 6, 1870, GP (EJD), along with affidavits from various Hill County residents; also in Executive Record Book (October 10, 1870–May 30, 1871), Vol. II, pp. 82–83, all in ARIS/TSLAC.

40. Ibid.

41. Wood to EJD, November 9, 1870, p. 81, Executive Record Book (October 10, 1870–May 30, 1871), Vol. II, p. 81; Wood to EJD, November 10, 1870, GP (EJD), both in ARIS/TSLAC.

42. Wood to EJD, November 10, 1870, GP (EJD), ARIS/TSLAC. On Abbott, see Richardson, *East Texas: Its History and Its Makers*, III, pp. 226–227. Abbott served in the Twelfth Legislature and was chairman of the Hill County Democratic Executive Committee for a number of years.

43. Election Returns, Hill County, Texas, 1870, Secretary of State, ARIS/TSLAC.

44. EJD to Yerby and Others, March 3, 1871, pp. 222–227, LPB, GP (EJD); also in Executive Record Book (October 10, 1870–May 30, 1871), Vol. II, pp. 238–240; EJD to Don Campbell (President, State Senate), February 8, 1871, p. 195, Executive

Record Book, all in ARIS/TSLAC; JD to EJD, February 1, 1871, *Message and Documents*, p. 5; *Tri-Weekly Houston Union*, January 20, 1871, p. 1.

45. *Houston Daily Union*, January 5, 1871, p. 2.

46. *A Memorial and Biographical History*, pp. 457–458, 464; Hill County Scrapbook, DBCFAH, UTA; Bailey, *A History of Hill County*, pp. 40–42; David Minor, "James J. Gathings," *NHT*, III, pp. 116–17. The names of the thirteen children were Jennie, James, Lottie, William C., Benjamin C., Mattie, Carrie, George W., David A., Cornelia, Ervin W., Emma, and Susan. Minor says that Gathings was born in Anson County, North Carolina.

47. Ad Valorem Tax Roll, Hill County, Texas, 1854, ARIS/TSLAC; 1870 United States Population Census, Hill County, Texas, p. 113.

48. Ad Valorem Tax Rolls, Hill County, Texas, 1860 & 1870, for J. J. Gathings, ARIS/TSLAC.

49. EJD to Yerby and Others, March 3, 1871, pp. 222–227, LPB, GP (EJD); also in Executive Record Book (October 10, 1870–May 30, 1871), Vol. II, pp. 238–240, both in ARIS/TSLAC; JD to EJD, February 1, 1871, *Message and Documents*, pp. 5–6; *A Memorial and Biographical History*, pp. 224–225; *Houston Daily Union*, January 5, 1871, p. 2.

50. Ibid. (all sources).

51. JD to EJD, February 1, 1871, *Message and Documents*, p. 6. According to one writer who garbled the story and the facts: "The officers and the negroes then started toward Covington. Gathings had them arrested before night, for searching his house without legal authority. They gave bonds for their appearance at court, but sent word that they were going to mob Gathings, and the citizens stood guard at his house for eight nights. The mob, however, did not appear. Nor did they appear at court, although Gathings and his friends were on hand," *A Memorial and Biographical History*, pp. 224–225; *Houston Daily Union*, January 5, 1871, p. 2. For another account that is a mishmash, see Captain Henry W. Strong, *My Frontier Days & Indian Fights on the Plains of Texas* (Dallas: n. p., [1925]), pp. 6–7; a copy is in ARIS/TSLAC.

52. JD to EJD, February 1, 1871, *Message and Documents*, p. 6.

53. Ibid. The *Waco Examiner* opined that Lieutenant Pritchett was "to blame" for the arrest of the State Policemen while they attempted to apprehend the "murders [*sic*] of the Willinghams." This "same game" had been played "in the Colorado and Cherokee outrages," cited in the *Tri-Weekly Houston Union*, January 20, 1871, p. 1. A different perspective is provided in the *Houston Daily Union*, January 5, 1871, p. 2, which asserted that the "police are officers of the law and were engaged in the discharge of their legitimate duties. We do not think that the law requires that the police should suspend pursuit in such a case in order to take out a warrant of search. And all concerned in Hill will probably find in the end that it is easier and better to yield compliance with the law and the means used to enforce it than to resist the same." See also the *Daily Union*, January 12, 1871, p. 2, for

additional savage editorial comment against those who asked to be forgiven for their participation in the war and sought clemency.

54. Ibid., pp. 6–7. Unfortunately, the Hill County courthouse burned in 1874 and thus there is no official account of these proceedings.

55. JD to EJD, February 1, 1871, *Message and Documents*, pp. 6–7. The *San Antonio Daily Herald*, January 5, 1871, p. 2, citing the "sensational dispatch" of the *Houston Union*, stated that Pritchett, Sergeant Evans, and five State Policemen were "ambushed and captured by twenty-five outlaws," carried to Hillsboro, where they escaped on December 29, and made their way to Waco. The *Houston Daily Union*, January 9, 1871, p. 2, editorialized that "if the murderers of Christ were Democrats," then the newspapers who supported the party "would attempt to shield them."

56. EJD, Proclamation, January 10, 1871, *Message and Documents*, p. 18.

57. EJD, Special Orders, No. 3, January 11, 1871; EJD to JD, January 11, 1871, both in *Message and Documents*, pp. 18–19. With a small force, the Chief of Police started on his way to Hill County on January 12, 1871. He was, however, detained en route by a "very severe norther," accompanied by a terrible snow and hail storm. He did not arrive in Hillsboro until Sunday, January 15.

58. JD to EJD, February 1, 1871, *Message and Documents*, p. 7.

59. Ibid.; State Guard Muster and Pay Roll, Company H, Sixth Regiment, January 10–24, 1871 (Georgetown), Military Rolls, ARIS/TSLAC.

60. JD to EJD, February 1, 1871, *Message and Documents*, pp. 7–8. According to one history, "during reconstruction, Colonel Gathings incurred the displeasure of the carpetbag authorities, and was mulcted of $3,000, which he paid rather than have the county placed under martial law, as the officer threatened to do." The writer believed the "state police and military officers with negro troops were particularly obnoxious in their behavior" in Hill County; Richardson, *East Texas: Its History and Its Makers*, III, pp. 639, 1007. One local aficionado declared that "in the meantime Governor Davis issued writs for the arrest of Gathings and his friends, to be served by Sheriff [John P.] Grace; but when the matter again came up the authorities said they wanted only an amicable adjustment and proposed to release Gathings if he would pay the cost of the proceedings thus far, which amounted to nearly $3,000, and which was readily raised by Gathings and his friends. Afterward, when Coke was elected Governor, the State reimbursed Gathings. James T. Ratcliff, of Hillsboro, was his attorney," *A Memorial and Biographical History*, p. 225. Also see the recollection of Strong, *My Frontier Days & Indian Fights*, p. 7.

61. JD to EJD, February 1, 1871, *Message and Documents*, p. 8.

62. EJD to Campbell, February 8, 1871, pp. 108–111, LPB, GP (EJD); also in Executive Record Book (October 10, 1870–May 30, 1871), Vol. II, pp. 195–196, both in ARIS/TSLAC; also in *Message and Documents*, p. 3.

63. JD to Grace, January 24, 1871, pp. 165–166, SPLPB, ARIS/TSLAC. In later correspondence, Grace inquired about the money paid by Gathings, which Davidson

referred to the governor. The Chief of Police reiterated that he wanted Grace to attend to the *Examiner* matter and also begin enrolling militia and the problem with the comptroller would be rectified; JD to Grace, February 11, 1871, pp. 287–288, SPLPB, id. There are no extant copies of the *Examiner* for this period.

64. Ibid.

65. Grand Jury, Hill County to EJD, February 24, 1871, GP (EJD), ARIS/TSLAC. The letter is printed verbatim in the *Galveston Daily News*, March 12, 1871, p. 1. The following signed the letter: B. F. Yerby (Foreman); Robert K. Lee; Thomas Bell Jr.; James Y. Blocker; E. Pierce; R. M. Graham; E. Robert; J. F. Herod; R. A. Gee; A. Robert; William Powell; J. B. Doat; P. Webb; David Johnson; James Oliver; G. R. Williams. Of the sixteen who signed the letter, ten are not listed in the 1870 census.

66. EJD to Yerby and Others, March 3, 1871, p. 223, LPB, GP (EJD); also in Executive Record Book (October 10, 1870–May 30, 1871), Vol. II, pp. 238–240, both in ARIS/TSLAC. Davis's response was also printed in the *Galveston Daily News*, March 12, 1871, p. 1.

67. Ibid. The Senate Committee on Militia, composed of George T. Ruby, J. S. Mills, Phidello W. Hall, and Henry Rawson, examined the Hill County records in regard to the enforcement of martial law and the fines assessed upon various individuals. They discovered "no excess has been committed by the Governor in this respect" and that the militia act of 1870 defined the duties and powers of Davis and his military subordinates, "and in the opinion of the committee, they have duly complied with the same," *Senate Journal of the Twelfth Legislature of the State of Texas*, pp. 270–271; *Members of the Texas Legislature, 1846–1992*, Vol. 1. The *Cleburne Chronicle* mistakenly stated that Davis "refused to send a committee, or recommend to the Legislature to send a committee to investigate the outrages committed by his police" in Hill County. "He thinks it all right; besides, he cares to hear only one side of the matter, and that is his and his captain's side," cited in *Flake's Daily Bulletin* (Galveston), March 31, 1871, p. 2.

68. EJD to Yerby and Others, March 3, 1871, pp. 224–225, LPB, GP (EJD), ARIS/TSLAC.

69. Ibid., pp. 225–226.

70. Ibid., p. 226. For pro and con editorial comment see *Galveston Daily News*, March 12, 1871, p. 2; *Houston Daily Union*, January 28, 1871, p. 2, quoting *DSJ*.

71. A. M. Douglass to Editor of the *Examiner*, June 24, 1871, in *San Antonio Daily Herald*, July 20, 1871, p. 2. These letters originally appeared in the *Waco Examiner*. Both newspapers were virulently anti-Republican. Douglass was Tennessee born and migrated to Texas in 1866, served in the fourteenth, fifteenth, and sixteenth Texas legislatures, and was chairman of the Hill County Democratic Executive Committee. *A Memorial and Biographical History*, p. 639.

72. A. M. Lawrence to Douglass, April 25, 1871; R. R. Booth to Douglass, May 13, 1871; Grace to Douglass, May 13, 1871, all in *San Antonio Daily Herald*, July 20, 1871, p. 2. In an editorial, the *Herald* referred to Davis as an "unscrupulous

villain" who had robbed the treasury of millions for his "personal aggrandizement" and subjected and overpowered a "proud and gallant people" to "craven and ignorant" carpetbaggers.

73. Purnell to AG, December 22, 1871, H-228, p. 354; July 13, 1872, H-219, p. 399, Register of Letters Received (September 1871–September 1872), Departmental Correspondence, Texas Adjutant General's Department, ARIS/TSLAC (hereafter cited as AG LR, ARIS/TSLAC); *Daily Herald* (San Antonio), December 29, 1871, p. 3. The *Herald* reported on September 16, 1871, p. 2, that Davis had sent Major George W. Smith into Hill County with "twenty-five picked State Policemen, for the avowed purpose of preserving order, but with private instructions, we have no doubt, to get up a row if possible."

74. *Daily Herald* (San Antonio), January 6, 1872, p. 2. In the state senate race the tabulation gave C. M. Winkler (Navarro), 671; J. W. Kemble (Ellis), 643; L. E. Gillett (Hill), 456; J. J. Gathings (Hill), 359; R. R. Booth (Hill), 161; W. W. Knight, 58; and I. N. Davis, 51. On the proposal to move the state capitol from Austin, Hill County cast their votes for Waco, 890; Austin, 59; and Houston, 10. In the justice of the peace contest in precinct no. 2, Philip Gathings received 437; F. M. Weathered, 312; J. M. Mullen, 121; and Watson, 12; Election Returns, Hill County, Texas, 1872, Secretary of State, ARIS/TSLAC.

75. *DSJ*, April 5, 1873, p. 2.

76. JD to Hart and Booth, April 7, 1871, p. 81, SPLPB, ARIS/TSLAC.

77. Resolutions of the House (W. C. Walsh, Chief Clerk), January 18, 1873, SPC, ARIS/TSLAC; FLB to M. D. H. Taylor (Speaker of the House), January 21, 1873, p. 234, AG LPB, ARIS/TSLAC. On the Democrats see Williams, "Redeemer Democrats and the Roots of Modern Texas, 1872–1884."

78. *Special Laws of the State of Texas: Passed at the Session of the Fourteenth Legislature, January 13, 1874* (Houston: A. C. Gray, State Printer, 1874), p. 33.

79. Mrs. V. A. Hoffman (Hillsboro), September 17, 1871, H-44, pp. 326–327; John C. Chapman (Brigadier General, Reserve Militia, Lancaster), October 1, 1871, C-50, pp. 116–117; Chapman, October 20, 1871, C-80, p. 121; R. G. Kees (Hill County), November 24, 1871, K-60, p. 448; George A. O'Brien (Waco), January 20, 1872, O-3, p. 654; Joel A. Lufkin (Sergeant, State Police) [September 1872], L-2, p. 481, all letters to AG, AG LR (synopsis), ARIS/TSLAC. The Hoffman story is peculiar. A Waco lawyer, John T. Flint, informed Davis in late 1870, when Hoffman was Waco marshal, that there were indictments against him and that Hoffman "could not reflect credit" on Davis's administration. One indictment was from Ellis County and two were pending in Hill County on which *nolle prosequi* was entered because of a change of district attorneys and no preparation made for trial. All Waco desired was a "good, efficient and honest man" and the Republicans were "entitled to the office." Davis responded: "So long as no charge is substantiated against" Hoffman in connection with him being marshal, the governor "could not consider charges of the nature disclosed by the indictment sent"—at least unless Hoffman was "convicted under it." Davis

wrote that "it would not do to assume the truth of these charges before trial, or investigation"; John T. Flint to EJD, December 25, 1870, GP (EJD); EJD to Flint, December 28, 1870, p. 96, LPB, GP (EJD), both in ARIS/TSLAC.

80. *DSJ*, March 2, 1871, p. 4.

81. Resolutions of the House (W. H. Sinclair, Speaker), September 22, 1871; Henry Orsay (Chief Clerk, AG) to Sinclair, October 3, 1871; A. Bledsoe (Comptroller) to Sinclair, October 17, 1871; State of Texas in Account Current with Alfred D. Evans, Paymaster, March 15, 1871, all in Correspondence, Texas Adjutant General's Department, ARIS/TSLAC (hereafter cited as AGC, ARIS/TSLAC).

CHAPTER FOUR

1. EJD to Don Campbell (President, State Senate), February 8, 1871, *Message and Documents*, pp. 4–5. The same material was also published in the 1871 *Senate Journal* and partially in the *Houston Daily Union*, February 16, 1871, p. 2. An adequate summary of the Walker County difficulty is Ricky Floyd Dobbs, "Defying Davis: The Walker County Rebellion, 1871," *East Texas Historical Journal* 32 (Fall 1993), pp. 34–47; "Walker County Rebellion," *NHT*, VI, pp. 801–802. Dobbs covered the same ground in "'A Slow Civil War.'" There is also an account of the Walker County problem in Parsons and Little, *Captain L. H. McNelly*, pp. 69–81.

2. Dobbs, "'A Slow Civil War,'" p. 85. In petitioning the legislature to change the name of Walker to Hood County in 1863, the citizens manifested "their detestation" of Robert J. Walker, formerly of Mississippi, "but now of Yankeedom," who owed his "nurture as a man of political distinction to the South against which he has turned traitor, and which he has aided in trying to enslave to the vilest despotism on earth," Petition of Walker County citizens (55 signatures), November 31, [1863], Memorials and Petitions, Records of the Legislature, ARIS/TSLAC; *House Journal of the Tenth Legislature, Regular Session of the State of Texas, November 3, 1863–December 16, 1863*, comp. James M. Day (Austin: Texas State Library, 1965), pp. 199, 215; Gammel, *The Laws of Texas*, V, p. 753. The joint resolution declared that the county was now named for Captain Samuel H. Walker, the distinguished Texas Ranger, who fell in Mexico, "while gallantly fighting for the rights and honor" of the state; John Leffler, "Walker County," *NHT*, VI, pp. 799–800; Gournay, *Texas Boundaries*, p. 53.

3. Leffler, "Walker County," *NHT*, VI, p. 800, states that the county had 8,633 slaves in 1864. The number should be 5,275. The higher number is for Washington County; Campbell, *An Empire for Slavery*, p. 266; John W. Baldwin, "An Early History of Walker County, Texas" (M.A. thesis, Sam Houston State Teachers College, 1957); Dobbs, "'A Slow Civil War,'" p. 85; Joe T. Timmons, "The Referendum in Texas on the Ordinance of Secession, February 23, 1861: The Vote," *East Texas Historical Journal* 11 (Fall 1973), p. 16. Thirty-six percent of the county farmers owned fifty acres or more of land, and 2 percent had over five hundred acres.

4. George P. Rawick, ed., *The American Slave: A Composite Biography, Supplement Series 2* (10 vols.; Westport, CT: Greenwood Press, 1979), V, Pt. 4, p. 2453. McAdams stated that after about an hour had passed, a "covered wagon came by with two men with rags over their faces got out and picked her up and put her in that wagon and that was the last I'se ever heard of the negro woman or the white people either, and ever last one of us negroes that were left we went home and went in a hurry, cause we did not know how many more of us would be done just like that negro woman"; *Texas Almanac For 1871* (Galveston: Strickland & Clark, 1871), pp. 155–156, 226 (hereafter *TA*, with the year); Campbell, *An Empire for Slavery*, p. 266; Dobbs, "'A Slow Civil War,'" p. 84; Campbell, "Defying Davis," pp. 36–37; Richter, *Overreached on All Sides*, p. 183; Paul J. Sugg, "Freedmen's Bureau in Walker County, 1866–1868" (unpublished ms., Sam Houston State University, Huntsville). For Walker County blacks see *TA, 1873* (Galveston: Strickland & Clark, 1873), p. 53; C. W. Wilson, "The Negro in Walker County" (M.A. thesis, Sam Houston State Teachers College, 1934); Bettie Hayman, "A Short History of the Negro of Walker County, 1860–1942" (M.A. thesis, Sam Houston State Teachers College, 1942).

5. Muster Roll of Company A, 21st Regiment, Reserve Militia, October 1, 1870; Muster Roll of Company B, 21st Regiment, Reserve Militia, October 29, 1870, both in Reserve Militia Military Rolls, Military Rolls, Texas Adjutant General's Department, ARIS/TSLAC; Muster Roll of Company B, 1st Regiment, State Guards, October 15, 1870, State Guard Military Rolls, Military Rolls, Texas Adjutant General's Department, ARIS/TSLAC.

6. *1870 Walker County Census*, comp. Anthony Vincent Banes and Dennis Michael Lawlis (Huntsville: Walker County Texas Genealogical Society, 1993), p. 17; *DSJ*, January 27, 1871, p. 2; *Houston Daily Union*, February 1, 1871, p. 2; Charles Taylor Rather, "Around the Square in 1862 with a Barefoot Boy," in *Huntsville and Walker County, Texas: A Bicentennial History*, comp. and ed. D'Anne McAdams Crews (Huntsville: Sam Houston State University Press, 1976), p. 139; J. R. Burnett to EJD, January 12, 1871, p. 22; W. E. Horne to EJD, January 26, 1871, p. 21, both in *Message and Documents*.

7. *DSJ*, January 27, 1871, p. 2; *Houston Daily Union*, January 16, 1871, p. 2; January 24, 1871, p. 2.

8. *1870 Walker County Census*, pp. 18, 74, 153; 1870 United States Population Census, Walker County, Texas, p. 316. Harding was a retired farmer and merchant.

9. Ibid.; *State of Texas v. Nat Outlaw, et al.*, Opinion Delivered by Judge [J. R.] Burnett, January 11, 1871, in *Houston Daily Union*, February 9, 1871, p. 2; *DSJ*, January 27, 1871, p. 2; *Galveston Daily News*, January 25, 1871, p. 2; J. M. Maxey to Editors *News*, February 14, 1871, in *Galveston Daily News*, March 9, 1871, p. 1.

10. *Houston Daily Union*, January 18, 1871, p. 2; *Galveston Daily News*, January 25, 1871, p. 2; *The State of Texas Against Hon. James R. Burnett, Judge Thirtieth Judicial District; Evidence Taken Before the Joint Committee of the Fourteenth Legislature*

Appointed to Investigate Charges Preferred by an Address for Removal from Office (Austin: J. D. Elliott, State Printer, 1874), p. 14; Horne to EJD, January 26, 1871, *Message and Documents*, p. 21.

11. EJD to Burnett, December 12, 1870, LPB (Dec. 6, 1870–Jan. 2, 1871), p. 34, GP (EJD), ARIS/TSLAC.

12. Burnett to EJD, December 19, 1870, GP (EJD), ARIS/TSLAC; Richter, *Overreached on All Sides*, p. 246.

13. Testimony of J. H. Whitehead; Testimony of Burnett; Testimony of Colonel Murray, February 24, 1871, all in Court Martial Proceedings v. Cyrus Hess, 1871, Court Martial Proceedings, State Guard and Reserve Militia Records, Reconstruction Records, Texas Adjutant General's Department, ARIS/TSLAC (hereafter cited as Hess Court Martial Proceedings, ARIS/TSLAC); Burnett to EJD, December 19, 1870, December 30, 1870; Goddin and Green to Williams, July 23, 1870, all in GP (EJD); 1867 Voter Registration, #1323, Walker County; Election Registers, Walker County, all in ARIS/TSLAC; Campbell, "Scalawag District Judges: The E. J. Davis Appointees, 1870–1873," *Houston Review* 14 (1992), pp. 78, 81; Richter, *Overreached on All Sides*, p. 246; Tise, *Texas County Sheriffs*, p. 518. Burnett was Georgia born; his Thirtieth Judicial District comprised Grimes, Walker, Madison, and Polk counties.

14. Testimony of Burnett, February 24, 1871, Hess Court Martial Proceedings, ARIS/TSLAC; Maxey to Editors *News*, February 14, 1871, in *Galveston Daily News*, March 9, 1871, p. 1; *Houston Daily Union*, January 14, 1871, p. 2; January 16, 1871, p. 2; January 24, 1871, p. 2; February 1, 1871, p. 2; *DSJ*, January 27, 1871, p. 2; *Walker County, Texas: A History* (Dallas: Curtis Media Corporation, 1986), p. 451; Crews, comp. and ed., *Huntsville and Walker County, Texas*, p. 110; Walker County Scrapbook, DBCFAH, UTA. On Baker see J. H. Freeman, "James Addison Baker," *NHT*, I, pp. 347–348; for Hightower see Kevin Ladd, "Lewis Buckner Hightower, Sr.," *NHT*, III, p. 607. Hightower, a Democrat, was born in 1838 in Alabama, moved to Texas in the 1850s, supported secession, became judge of the Ninth Judicial District in 1888, and died in 1918. Maxey said he never saw the Jones affidavit. H. W. Graber wrote that three men were arrested by McNelly "for whipping a few insolent negroes who had insulted some young ladies on the street returning home from a shopping tour," *The Life Record of H. W. Graber: A Terry Texas Ranger, 1861–1865; Sixty-two Years in Texas* (n.p.: privately printed, 1916), pp. 333–334. Parsons and Little, *Captain L. H. McNelly*, place Jenkins among the insulters, p. 73, but there is no evidence at all for this and Graber never mentioned any names.

15. *Houston Daily Union*, January 24, 1871, p. 2. The *Union Republican*, Mortimer H. Goddin's paper, also denounced the attempt to destroy liberties "for without law there can be no liberty." The newspaper trusted that "reflecting people would come out "boldly and give assurances that the good people and county of Walker shall never again be so grossly and wickedly outraged."

16. Testimony of Burnett, February 24, 1871, Hess Court Martial Proceedings, ARIS/TSLAC. The next day Maxey and Baker called at Burnett's office claiming they regretted the occurrence.

17. Testimony of William McElroy; Testimony of Burnett; Testimony of Colonel Murray, February 24, 1871, all in Hess Court Martial Proceedings, ARIS/TSLAC.

18. *State of Texas v. Nat Outlaw et al.*, in *Houston Daily Union*, February 9, 1871, p. 2; Testimony of Burnett, February 24, 1871, Hess Court Martial Proceedings, ARIS/TSLAC.

19. Ibid. (all sources).

20. Ibid. (all sources).

21. "The Huntsville Difficulty," *Galveston Daily News*, January 25, 1871, p. 2. Maxey elaborated in detail the alibis of the four men. He suggested they were nowhere near where the killing of Jenkins occurred. His conclusion: "so much for making judges out of politicians." The admission of authorship is in Maxey to Burnett, February 3, 1871, *Houston Daily Union*, February 9, 1871, p. 2. Maxey disingenuously stated that his partner, Baker, had nothing to do with the matter, and although the article was not intended for publication, "they show the *controlling, leading facts in proof of the alibi* claimed by my clients" and he had "no apology to make for their publication." The *Union* supported Burnett's decision and wrote that he was "not to be intimidated by the Ku Klux in the discharge of his duty."

22. Burnett to Editors *Union*, February 3, 1871, in *Houston Daily Union*, February 9, 1871, p. 2. Burnett also stated: "Do me the justice to believe that an officer, who has sworn to discharge his duties faithfully and impartially, would be at least as apt to act conscientiously and do right as paid advocates and other interested parties." Horne to EJD, January 26, 1871, in *Message and Documents*, p. 21.

23. W. E. Horne to EJD, January 26, 1871, in *Message and Documents*, pp. 19–20, 22–23; *Houston Daily Union*, January 16, 1871, p. 2; January 24, 1871, p. 2; *DSJ*, January 27, 1871, p. 2; Testimony of Burnett, February 24, 1871, Hess Court Martial Proceedings, ARIS/TSLAC. For an idea of how newspapers could distort events, the *Crockett Herald*, as quoted in the *Dallas Herald* of March 11, 1871, p. 1, stated that one of the State Policemen fired at Baker, "who was standing quietly in the courthouse yard at the time of the melee there!" As Baker was employed by the friends of the prisoners, that is the supposed reason "for the murderous assault." He was known to be "one of the most amiable and gentlemanly men" in the state. In all the testimony, and other newspaper accounts, there is no indication Baker was a target of anyone. Burnett later said that he thought if an attack came, it would be outside the courthouse.

24. Horne to EJD, January 26, 1871, pp. 19–20; Burnett to EJD, January 12, 1871, p. 22, both in *Message and Documents*; *Houston Daily Union*, January 16, 1871, p. 2; January 24, 1871, p. 2; *DSJ*, January 27, 1871, p. 2; Testimony of William McElroy; Testimony of J. H. Whitehead; Testimony of Burnett, February 24, 1871, all in

Hess Court Martial Proceedings, ARIS/TSLAC. Outlaw had secured a pistol from a black desk occupied by the defense counsel.

25. Horne to EJD, January 26, 1871, pp. 19–20, in *Message and Documents*; *Houston Daily Union*, January 24, 1871, p. 2; *DSJ*, January 27, 1871, p. 2; *Flake's Daily Bulletin* (Evening Edition), Monday, January 23, 1871, p. 1.

26. *DSJ*, January 27, 1871, p. 2. The *Houston Daily Union*, January 16, 1871, p. 2, stated three citizens had been wounded in the altercation. Rather, in "Around the Square in 1862," said horses were "saddled and bridled and conveniently placed for the boys to make their getaway," p. 139.

27. Testimony of Burnett, February 24, 1871, Hess Court Martial Proceedings, ARIS/TSLAC; L. H. McNelly (Captain, State Police) to JD, January 13, 1871, AGC, ARIS/TSLAC. McNelly closed his brief report by stating: "I am on my back and write badly"; Horne to EJD, January 26, 1871, in *Message and Documents*, pp. 20–21.

28. *DSJ*, January 27, 1871, p. 2.

29. Burnett to EJD, January 12, 1871, in *Message and Documents*, p. 24.

30. EJD to Burnett, January 20, 1871, LPB (Jan. 3, 1871–Mar. 16, 1871), p. 58, GP (EJD) (also in *Message and Documents*, p. 25); Proclamation Declaring Martial Law in Walker County, January 20, 1871, AGC, all in ARIS/TSLAC; *Flake's Daily Bulletin*, March 4, 1871, p. 5.

31. Special Orders, No. 18 (EJD), February 15, 1871; EJD to JD, February 15, 1871, both in Court Martial Proceedings, General (1870–1871), Court Martial Proceedings, State Guard and Reserve Militia Records, Reconstruction Records, Texas Adjutant General's Department, ARIS/TSLAC (hereafter cited as General Court Martial Proceedings, ARIS/TSLAC).

32. EJD to JD, February 15, 1871; General Court Martial Proceedings, both in ARIS/TSLAC.

33. EJD to Burnett, January 11, 1871, p. 20; January 30, 1871, p. 83, LPB, GP (EJD); Burnett (Anderson) to EJD, February 6, 1871, GP (EJD) (also in *Message and Documents*, pp. 25–26), all in ARIS/TSLAC.

34. Burnett to EJD, February 6, 1871, GP (EJD), ARIS/TSLAC.

35. *Senate Journal of the Twelfth Legislature*, pp. 158, 187–210, 270–71. G. R. Shannon dissented from the majority. He argued that because the legislature was in session the governor had no warranty to declare martial law according to how the law was written. Moreover, the law did not authorize him to delegate authority to do these things to the adjutant general (February 23, 1871), pp. 282–284.

36. *Senate Journal*, pp. 249, 279, 326; *Journal of the House of Representatives of the Twelfth Legislature*, Part First (Austin: J. G. Tracy, State Printer, 1871), p. 369.

37. Citizens of Huntsville (66 of them) to JD, February 23, 1871, AGC, ARIS/TSLAC.

38. JD to McNelly, February 13, 1871, p. 296; JD to Farrow, Pritchett, Slade, and Browning, February 13, 1871, p. 297, both in SPLPB, No. 2 (January 3, 1871–April

26, 1871), ARIS/TSLAC; JD to EJD, February 23, 27 (telegram), 1871; JD to Mc-
Nelly, February 24, 1871 (telegram); JD to Raymond and Whitis, February 27,
1871, all in AGC, ARIS/TSLAC.

39. JD, Special Order, February 22, 1871, *Court Martial Proceedings v. Thomas Walker*, 1871, Court Martial Proceedings, State Guard and Reserve Militia Records,
Reconstruction Records, Texas Adjutant General's Department, ARIS/TSLAC
(hereafter cited as Walker Court Martial Proceedings, ARIS/TSLAC).

40. *Court Martial Proceedings v. George W. Rather*, 1871, Court Martial Proceedings,
State Guard and Reserve Militia Records, Reconstruction Records, Texas Ad-
jutant General's Department, ARIS/TSLAC (hereafter cited as Rather Court
Martial Proceedings, ARIS/TSLAC).

41. In general see the "Court Martial Proceedings," February–March, 1871; *State
of Texas v. George Rather*; Court Martial Order No. 1, February 25, 1871; EJD,
Proclamation, March 22, 1871, ARIS/TSLAC; *San Antonio Daily Herald*, March
1, 1871, p. 2.

42. Hess Court Martial Proceedings, ARIS/TSLAC; *San Antonio Daily Herald*, October 26, 1871, p. 2, stated that in a report from Davidson's office, Hess's fine was
listed as $100 but documents demonstrated he paid the full $250. Hess promptly
paid the fine to Davidson, who, the former sheriff claimed, promised to refund
the fine but failed to do so. Writing over a year later, Hess claimed he had heard
that the governor believed the money should be remitted. Since he was poor and
in need of funds, he prayed Davis would consider returning the fine, Hess to
EJD, May 22, 1872, SPC, ARIS/TSLAC.

43. *Court Martial Proceedings v. Nathaniel Outlaw*, 1871, Court Martial Proceedings,
State Guard and Reserve Militia Records, Reconstruction Records, Texas Ad-
jutant General's Department, ARIS/TSLAC (hereafter cited as Outlaw Court
Martial Proceedings, ARIS/TSLAC).

44. Ibid.; Special Order No. 3, March 2, 1871,; General Orders, March 6, 1871; Special
Orders, March 6, 1871, ARIS/TSLAC.

45. Pardon of Nat Outlaw, March 11, 1871, Executive Record Book (E. J. Davis–Richard Coke, January 8, 1870 to February 9, 1874), p. 424, Secretary of State Records, ARIS/TSLAC.

46. George W. Farrow to JD, March 3, 1871, SPC, ARIS/TSLAC; JD to EJD, February 23, 1871 (telegram); JD to Farrow, March 6, 1871 (telegram), both in AGC,
ARIS/TSLAC. In an interesting sidelight, two days before Farrow's resignation,
Sergeant Benjamin F. Huffman accused Farrow of allowing gambling in Kosse
in December 1870. Farrow allegedly told Huffman that if they stopped wagering
it would kill the town; Statement of Huffman, March 1, 1871, ARIS/TSLAC.

47. JD to Farrow, March 29, 1871, pp. 714, 722; JD to Goddin, March 29, 1871, p.
721; JD to James Bennett, March 31, 1871, p. 746, SPLPB, No. 2, ARIS/TSLAC.
Davidson also informed Farrow that he could not determine what reasoning
the captain used in concluding that "all parties fines are entitled to executive
clemency unless you desire to place yourself prominently in opposition" to the

operations of Walker County martial law. He disapproved of Farrow's action and if it continued he would be dismissed.

48. JD to Farrow, March 29, 1871, p. 722; April 8, 1871, pp. 838–839; April 21, 1871, p. 953; JD to McNelly, April 13, 1871, p. 878; Special Police Order, April 13, 1871, p. 881, all in SPLPB, No. 2, ARIS/TSLAC.

49. JD to Sergeant B. F. Boldridge, December 12, 1870, p. 651, SPLPB, No. 1 (July 1 to December 31, 1870); Report of Boldridge, n.d. [February 1871], SPC; Receipt to W. H. Webb, March 7, 1871, AGC, all in ARIS/TSLAC.

50. JD to EJD, March 2, 4, 5, 6, 1871 (telegram); JD to C. W. Gardiner (Austin), March 2, 1871 (telegram); JD to J. P. Butler, March 2, 1871 (telegram); JD to Donnan, March 6, 1871 (telegram), all in AGC; JD to Private James Houston, March 18, 1871, p. 602; JD to Private William Gerhardt, March 18, 1871, p. 603; JD to T. A. Greasky, March 23, 1871, p. 659, all in SPLPB, No. 2 (January 3 to April 26, 1871), all in ARIS/TSLAC.

51. Special Orders, March 6, 1871, Correspondence, State Guard and Reserve Militia Records, Reconstruction Records, Texas Adjutant General's Department, ARIS/TSLAC; Receipt of C. D. Harn, August 25, 1871, AGC, ARIS/TSLAC; *Union Republican* (Huntsville), April 5, 1871, p. 2. The *Galveston News*, March 7, 1871, p. 2, was appalled that Goddin was designated to collect the military tax and referred to Davidson as a "mercenary" for appointing him commander.

52. *Galveston Daily News*, March 8, 1871, p. 2; also in *DSJ*, March 17, 1871, p. 2, and Walter Prescott Webb Papers, Box 2M278, DBCFAH, UTA.

53. Ibid. (all sources).

54. Ibid.; *San Antonio Daily Herald*, March 11, 1871, p. 2.

55. *DSJ*, March 17, 1871, p. 2.

56. Ibid.; *Galveston Daily News*, March 8, 1871, p. 2. Joe Franz wrote that while McNelly convalesced, he stated his "distaste" for Davis and law enforcement officials, "none of whom were sufficiently forthright for him." Davis established the State Police to "re-establish order and to assure the perpetuation of Republican control," and Walter Prescott Webb, with his Confederate and Democratic biases, also detested them. They were hated by the "substantial element of ex-Confederates." McNelly, a "leading segment of the so-called 'Texas Traitors,'" joined the police because he was a "man of action." Franz ignores all his duties and service before and after the Huntsville incident, where he wrongly says McNelly received a wound similar to the injury inflicted upon him at the Battle of Mansfield; Joe B. Franz, "Leander H. McNelly," in *Rangers of Texas* (Waco: Texian Press, 1969), pp. 136–137. Unfortunately, this publication has no bibliography or notes, but apparently Franz took much of his material from George Durham. Franz also asserted that McNelly "must be branded as brutal. He observed a code that few men—and he was one of the few—could live up to" and "to a superstitious enemy was often believed to be incorporeal," p. 144.

57. Maxey to Editors *News*, February 14, 1871, in *Galveston Daily News*, March 9, 1871, p. 1.

58. *Galveston Daily News*, March 17, 1871, p. 2.
59. *Flake's Daily Bulletin*, March 1, 1871, p. 4; March 18, 1871, p. 4; *San Antonio Daily Herald*, March 1, 1871, p. 2; March 6, 1871, p. 2; March 10, 1871, p. 2; March 22, 1871, p. 2; July 29, 1871, p. 1; *Dallas Herald*, March 11, 1871, p. 1; *Huntsville Item* quoted in *Daily Herald*, October 26, 1871, p. 2.
60. Resolution, House, September 22, 1871, A. Bledsoe (Comptroller) to William H. Sinclair (Speaker, House) October 17, 1871, both in AGC, ARIS/TSLAC.
61. Edward T. Randle to JD, September 23, 1872, SPC, ARIS/TSLAC.
62. *Proceedings of the Tax-Payers' Convention, of the State of Texas, Held at the City of Austin, Sept. 22d, 23d and 25th, 1871* (Galveston: Printed at the News Steam Book and Job Office, 1871), p. 16; Otis A. Singletary, "The Texas Militia During Reconstruction," *SWHQ* 60 (July 1956), pp. 29–30.

CHAPTER FIVE

1. *General Laws of the Twelfth Legislature of the State of Texas, First Session—1871* (Austin: J. G. Tracy, State Printer, 1871), pp. 973–974.
2. James King (County Clerk, Fairfield) to EJD, April 10, 1870, GP (EJD), ARIS/TSLAC. King had also served as county commissioner and registrar; see Elected and Appointed Officials, Freestone County, Secretary of State Records, pp. 252–253, 304–307, ARIS/TSLAC.
3. *Bryan Appeal* quoted in the *Houston Daily Union*, December 9, 1870, p. 4; Campbell, "Scalawag District Judges: The E. J. Davis Appointees, 1870–1873," *Houston Review* 14 (1992), p. 81.
4. *Bryan Appeal* quoted in the *Houston Daily Union*, December 9, 1870, p. 4.
5. F. P. Wood (Springfield) to EJD, December 6, 1870, GP (EJD), ARIS/TSLAC.
6. *Kosse Enterprise* quoted in *San Antonio Daily Herald*, December 20, 1870, p. 2. See also Leon Joseph Rosenberg, *Sangers': Pioneer Texas Merchants* (Austin: Texas State Historical Association, 1978), pp. 13–26.
7. *San Antonio Daily Herald*, June 23, 1871, p. 1, June 28, 1871, p. 2; *Houston Daily Telegraph*, September 12, 1871, p. 4, both reprinted stories from the *Groesbeck Enterprise*. District Judge Wood desired to establish a Republican newspaper in this section, but it came to naught; see Wood (Corsicana) to EJD, September 21, 1870, GP (EJD), ARIS/TSLAC. We found no evidence that a Dr. Bradshaw was murdered by the State Police or that two policemen had been indicted for six killings.
8. Ellen Maschino, "Limestone County," *NHT*, IV, pp. 198–200; Hampton Steele, *A History of Limestone County, Texas* (Mexia, TX: News Publishing Company, n.d.), pp. 1–37; *Texas Almanac For 1871*, pp. 130–131, 226; Bella French Swisher, ed., *The American Sketch Book: An Historical and Home Magazine* (Austin: Sketch Book Publishing House, 1881), pp. 85–93, which has a garbled account of the martial law episode; C. S. Bradley, "A Sketch of Limestone County," in *Groesbeck Journal*, May 15, 1936, p. 1; Gournay, *Texas Boundaries*, p. 51; David N.

Strickland, *Household: 1870 Surname Census* [Limestone County] (Mexia, TX: Limestone Genealogy Association, 1988).

9. Ray A. Walter, *A History of Limestone County* (Austin: Von Boeckmann-Jones, 1959), pp. 24–37; Vivian Elizabeth Smyrl, "Springfield, Texas," *NHT*, VI, pp. 45–46; Denny Parker Cralle, "Glamorous Early Day History Entwined Around Old Springfield—Limestone's First Capitol," in *Groesbeck Journal*, May 15, 1936, pp. 1, 4. Walter has a good account of the death of Springfield, pp. 37–38. One newspaper, the *Groesbeck Journal*, later contended that along with the conflict over the railroad's buying land for the right-of-way or the inhabitants' donating it, the "negro problem" also helped doom Springfield, May 15, 1936, p. 4.

10. Stephanie Panus, "Groesbeck, Texas," *NHT*, III, pp. 349–350; *Memorial and Biographical History*, pp. 366–367, 376–377 (for Kosse); *Texas Almanac For 1871*, pp. 130–131, 226.

11. John Leffler, "Freestone County," *NHT*, II, pp. 1171–1173; *Memorial and Biographical History*, p. 419; [Freestone County Historical Commission], *History of Freestone County* (Fairfield: n.p., 1978), pp. 7–12, 93–94; *Texas Almanac For 1871*, pp. 130–131; Gournay, *Texas Boundaries*, p. 60.

12. Francis A. Walker, comp., *The Statistics of the Population of the United States* (3 vols., Washington, DC: GPO, 1872), I, pp. 64–67; Campbell, *An Empire for Slavery*, p. 265. Campbell's figures based upon the county tax rolls are always lower than the census numbers. *Texas Almanac For 1873*, p. 51; [Freestone County Historical Commission], *History of Freestone County Texas* (1978), pp. 7–11.

13. J. H. Bradford (Captain, 26th Infantry, Post Commander, Centerville) to AAG (DT), November 16, 1867, DT, LR, Box 1, RG 393, NA; James Smallwood, "Charles E. Culver, a Reconstruction Agent in Texas: The Work of Local Freedmen's Bureau Agents and the Black Community," *Civil War History* 27 (December 1981), pp. 350–361. For a different perception of Culver's murder see Walter, *A History of Limestone County*, pp. 55–56.

14. Election Returns, 1870, Freestone County, Secretary of State Records; A. G. Moore to EJD, December 20, 1870, GP (EJD), both in ARIS/TSLAC.

15. *Flake's Daily Bulletin* (Galveston), May 16, 1871, p. 5; Receipt for Prisoner, Sheriff Peyton Parker (Limestone County), August 19, 1871, AGC, ARIS/TSLAC. Another Trammel brother, Wood, was a Special Policeman, Roster of Limestone County Special Policemen, pp. 196–197, Roster of Special Policemen, AGC, ARIS/TSLAC. The jail was again besieged in September by a group of desperadoes who intended to free a murderer, but the sheriff managed to thwart the escape attempt. The citizens provided almost no assistance and were "backward" in responding to his summons; *DSJ*, September 15, 1871, p. 4.

16. Muster Rolls of Companies A, B, C, D, and E, 1871, Reserve Militia, Limestone County, AG Military Rolls, ARIS/TSLAC. The units contained 100, 100, 100, 100, and 103 men respectively.

17. Statement of Merritt Trammell, October 14, 1871, AGC, ARIS/TSLAC.

18. Statement of S. L. Stevenson, October 28, 1871; Statement of B. Meyer, October 27, 1871; Statement of N. H. Williams, October 25, 1871, all in AGC; Statement of Zadek, October 5, 1871, Election Returns, Limestone County (contested), 1871, Secretary of State Records, all in ARIS/TSLAC.

19. A. Zadek Jr. to Lt. Col. J. W. Dickenson (Judge Advocate), October 23, 1871; Statement of S. L. Stevenson, October 28, 1871; Statement of B. Meyer, October 27, 1871; Statement of N. H. Williams, October 25, 1871, all in AGC, ARIS/TSLAC; Zadek, p. 194; Statement of Registrar, pp. 203–204, who referred to the men as "special police" whom Zadek used to "preserve the peace"; Scott, p. 233, all in *Journal of the House of Representatives of the Twelfth Legislature, Adjourned Session—1871* (Austin: J. G. Tracy, State Printer, 1871) (hereafter cited as *HJ*).

20. Statement of Stevenson, October 28, 1871; Statement of Meyer, October 27, 1871; Statement of Williams, October 25, 1871, all in AGC; Roster of Limestone County Special Policemen, pp. 196–197, Roster of Special Policemen, all in ARIS/TSLAC; Zadek, p. 194; Thurmond, p. 195; Robertson, p. 234; Hall, p. 235; Strasburger, p. 237; Seth B. Anglin, p. 234; J. D. Parish, p. 223, all in *HJ*; *Dallas Herald*, October 7, 1871, p. 2; *Austin Democratic Statesman*, October 5, 1871, p. 2. Anglin testified before the legislature that Cotton and one of his cohorts were in a "state of intoxication" and they had also been "in the same condition" the previous night at a circus performance, where Cotton and two or three others "created so much disturbance that they came near breaking up" the festivities.

21. Ibid. (all sources); Dr. R. A. Watkins, pp. 237–238; Memorial of Citizens, pp. 218–219; Statement of Registrar, pp. 203–204, all in *HJ*; Statement of Thurmond, October 5, 1871, Election Returns, Limestone County (contested), 1871, Secretary of State, ARIS/TSLAC. Hall testified that he neither saw Applewhite with a gun nor did he observe him make any attempt to secure one. Robertson asserted that one of the policemen (unidentified) walked up to Applewhite, who was "making no resistance," placed his pistol against his body, and fired. Cotton also shot Applewhite, who had drawn no pistol, nor was he attempting to draw any. In his affidavit, Robertson contended he was standing "within arms length" of Applewhite (Robertson, p. 234). It is clear that Applewhite had a weapon or Cotton would not have been wounded as he was not shot by one of his fellow policemen.

22. Statement of Joseph F. Pells, October 27, 1871; Statement of McClelland, October 27, 1871; Statement of Meyer, October 27, 1871, all in AGC, ARIS/TSLAC; Zadek, pp. 194–195; Thurmond, pp. 195–196; Hall, pp. 235–236; Watkins, pp. 237–238; Memorial of Citizens, pp. 218–219; Statement of Registrar, pp. 203–204, all in *HJ*.

23. Statement of P. H. French, n.d., AGC; Statement of Bolling, October 5, 1871; Statement of John T. Dunbar, [October 1871]; Huston to Oliver, October 5, 1871, all in Election Returns, Limestone County (contested), 1871, Secretary of State, ARIS/TSLAC; Statement of Dunbar, pp. 193–194; Huston, p. 199, both in *HJ*.

Dunbar wrote that "Groesbeck in hands of mob. Five hundred men under arms. Too hot for me, had to leave"; Dunbar to R. R. Cobb, October 2, 1871, Election Returns, Limestone County (contested), 1871, Secretary of State, ARIS/TSLAC.

24. Statement of French, n.d.; Statement of Pells, October 27, 1871; Statement of Robbins, October 28, 1871; Statement of Meyer, October 27, 1871; Statement of Hall, October 26, 1871; Statement of Stevenson, October 28, 1871; Statement of McClelland, October 27, 1871, all in AGC, ARIS/TSLAC.

25. Ibid. (all sources).

26. Statement of Pells, October 27, 1871; Statement of Robbins, October 28, 1871; Statement of French, n.d.; Statement of McClelland, October 27, 1871; Statement of Meyer, October 27, 1871, all in AGC, ARIS/TSLAC.

27. Parish, p. 223; Robertson, p. 234; Thurmond, p. 196, Scott, p. 232; Watkins, pp. 237–238; Zadek, pp. 194–195, all in *HJ*; Statement of Stevenson, October 28, 1871; Statement of McClelland, October 27, 1871, all in AGC, ARIS/TSLAC. Zadek believed that Applewhite received the mortal wound in the saloon when the gunfire began; 1870 United State Population Census, Robertson County, Precinct #5, p. 241; James L. Hailey, "Bremond, Texas," *NHT*, I, p. 721. Mrs. Applewhite, who was forty-eight years old, died in Kosse on March 27, 1893, and was buried in Bremond. Her husband, said one newspaper, who was "well and favorably known throughout the state," was killed by Davis's "negro state guard"; *Galveston Daily News*, March 29, 1893, p. 2; Michael Kelsey, *The Southern Argus: Obituaries, Death Notices, and Implied Deaths, June 1860 Through June 1874* (Bowie, MD: Heritage Books, 1996), p. 269. The idea that Applewhite was "well and favorably known" in Texas is grossly overblown.

28. Statement of Williams, October 25, 1871; Statement of Meyer, October 27, 1871, both in AGC, ARIS/TSLAC.

29. Statement of French, n.d.; Statement of Robbins, October 28, 1871; Statement of Pells, October 27, 1871; Statement of McClelland, October 27, 1871; Statement of Hall, October 26, 1871, all in AGC, ARIS/TSLAC.

30. Statement of French, n.d.; Statement of Meyer, October 27, 1871, Statement of Hall, October 26, 1871, all in AGC, ARIS/TSLAC.

31. Statement of French, n.d.; Statement of Pells, October 27, 1871; Statement of Robbins, October 28, 1871; Statement of Hall, October 26, 1871; Statement of McClelland, October 27, 1871, all in AGC, ARIS/TSLAC.

32. Thurmond, pp. 196–197; Zadek, p. 195; Patterson, p. 238; Blakey, p. 229, all in *HJ*.

33. Statement of Stevenson, October 28, 1871; Statement of Meyer, October 27, 1871, both in AGC, ARIS/TSLAC.

34. Statement of McClelland, October 27, 1871; Statement of Meyer, October 27, 1871, both in AGC, ARIS/TSLAC; Anglin, pp. 239–240; Hall, pp. 236–237; Strasburger, p. 237; Scott, pp. 232–233; Statement of Registrar, p. 204; Patterson, p. 238; Memorial of Citizens, p. 219, all in *HJ*.

35. Memorial of Citizens, p. 219; Scott, pp. 232–233; Anglin, pp. 239–240; Statement of Registrar, p. 204, all in *HJ*.

36. Statement of Hall, October 28, 1871; Statement of Meyer, October 27, 1871, both in AGC, ARIS/TSLAC.

37. Doris Hollis Pemberton, *Juneteenth at Comanche Crossing* (Austin: Eakin Press, 1983), p. 62.

38. Pemberton, *Juneteenth*, pp. 50–52. Stroud and his wife owned one hundred slaves, and he was an estate agent for another seventy bondspeople; Campbell, *An Empire for Slavery*, pp. 275–276; Alwyn Barr, *Black Texans: A History of Negroes in Texas, 1528–1971* (Austin: Jenkins Publishing Company; Pemberton Press, 1973), p. 60.

39. Pemberton, *Juneteenth*, pp. 64–65; JD (Huntsville) to Donnan (AG Office), March 2, 1871 (telegram), AGC, ARIS/TSLAC.

40. Ad Valorum Tax Rolls, 1869, 1870, Limestone County, ARIS/TSLAC; *Galveston Daily News*, May 23, 1875, p. 1; May 28, 1875, p. 1; *Daily Democratic Statesman* (Austin), May 25, 1875, p. 1; June 1, 1875, p. 1; *Groesbeck Journal*, May 15, 1936, p. 4.

41. M. D. L. Harcrow received five hundred dollars for the body of Merrick [*sic*] Trammell, paid July 9, 1875, pp. 926–927, General Warrant Register (Volume 5), January 1874–August 1875, Warrant Registers, Records, Texas Comptroller's Office, ARIS/TSLAC. Harcrow was clearly a despicable character. He attempted to bill the state for posting notices on the homes of black Corsicana residents, ordering them to vacate the premises, FLB to M. D. L. Harcrow (Corsicana), December 31, 1872, AG LPB, No. 10, p. 452. ARIS/TSLAC.

42. *San Antonio Daily Express*, June 19, 1875, p. 2.

43. Walter Cotton, comp., *History of Negroes in Limestone County* (n.p.: n.p., n.d.), p. 12; Pemberton, *Juneteenth*, p. 83.

44. Thurmond, p. 197; Hall, pp. 236–237; Simons, pp. 238–239; Statement of Registrar, pp. 203–204; Memorial, p. 221, all in *HJ*; Statement of N. H. Williams, October 25, 1871; Statement of W. H. McClelland, October 27, 1871, both in AGC, ARIS/TSLAC; J. B. Simons, a brother of the shooter, said he suffered "violent spasms" from 1856 until 1867, and then became rheumatic. The Anderson County district court had "condemned" him as a lunatic when a Dr. J. D. Rankin in Springfield took charge of him. His treatment failed. Simons was now continually given morphine as without it he "don't seem to know what he is doing."

45. Huston, pp. 198–201; Scott, p. 233; Statement of Registrar, p. 204; Rankin, p. 225, all in *HJ*; Statement of S. M. Jones, November 2, 1871, AGC, ARIS/TSLAC; Huston, p. 199; Bonner, p. 204, both in *HJ*; W. H. Richardson (Captain, Company A, 5th Regiment, State Guards) to AG, October ?, 1871, R-39, p. 745, AG LR (synopsis); Muster Roll of Company A, 5th Regiment, State Guard, Annual Returns of Militia, Military Rolls, ARIS/TSLAC; Statement of W. H. McClelland, October 27, 1871, AGC, ARIS/TSLAC. Prendergast (1816–1910) was Tennessee born, moved to Texas in 1841, and practiced law in Limestone County. A wealthy slaveholder and Democrat, he represented the county in the Secession

Convention. He served briefly in the war, was elected a representative to the Tenth Legislature, and during Reconstruction avoided politics except for the Tax-Payers' Convention in 1871. Elected to the house in the Thirteenth Legislature in 1873, the next year he was appointed by Governor Richard Coke judge of the Thirty-third Judicial District. He later became a prohibitionist. Campbell, "Davis M'Gee Prendergast," *NHT*, V, p. 326.

46. Huston, pp. 199–200, *HJ*.
47. Statement of Registrar, p. 205, *HJ*. Rankin, in *HJ*, p. 226, said that Merritt Trammell came to Springfield with the prisoners with an armed force estimated at two hundred. He "drew off" after the prisoners were jailed.
48. Statement of S. J. Weaver and M. A. Tucker, *HJ*, p. 206.
49. Carl H. Moneyhon, *Texas After the Civil War: The Struggle of Reconstruction* (College Station: Texas A&M University Press, 2004), pp. 176–183; Ramsdell, *Reconstruction in Texas*, pp. 306–311; Nunn, *Texas under the Carpetbaggers*, pp. 90, 97–102; Carrier, "A Political History of Texas," pp. 490–497.
50. *DSJ*, September 14, 1871, p. 2. The writer of the letter was "E. H. Q.," who remains unidentified.
51. Walter, *History of Limestone County*, p. 58.
52. W. B. Bonner (Registrar), S. M. Jones, John H. Welch, Alfred Bryan (All Election Judges), and S. J. Weaver and M. A. Tucker to EJD and James P. Newcomb (Secretary of State), n.d., pp. 207–208, all in *HJ*; *Texas Almanac For 1871*, pp. 130–131, 226. Of the 1,188 who voted, the board had objected to 79, and 200 more had improperly registered after only a two-month county residence when the law required six months. An additional 150 men were induced by the prevailing bitterness of partisan feeling to vote against their inclinations. Of the total number of blacks registered (844), fully two-thirds would have supported the Republicans. By eliminating the rejected voters and those registered from the number actually polled and subtracting those who would have cast their ballot with the Republicans, it left a balance of 734 Democrats and 737 votes which would have been given to Republicans if a fair election had been held. They were of the opinion that all the county returns be thrown out on account of an unfair election, but they left the decision to Davis.
53. Statement of S. J. Weaver and M. A. Tucker, p. 207; W. B. Bonner (Registrar), S. M. Jones, John H. Welch, Alfred Bryan (all Election Judges) to EJD and James P. Newcomb (Secretary of State), n.d., p. 207, both in *HJ*.
54. Memorial of Citizens, p. 221; Affidavit of C. S. Mitchell, pp. 230–231, both in *HJ*; "Roll of Special Constable Force," November 4, 1871, AGC, ARIS/TSLAC; Campbell, "Scalawag District Judges," pp. 81, 86.
55. EJD to Oliver, October 5, 1871, LPB, pp. 369–370, GP (EJD), ARIS/TSLAC. Davis offered a reward of six hundred dollars for the body of anyone shown to be connected directly with the murder of Lee and the promise of a free pardon to anyone associated with the killing who would turn state's evidence. Oliver was to let this fact be generally known.

56. Proclamation of Martial Law in Freestone and Limestone Counties, October 9, 1871, AGC, ARIS/TSLAC. The proclamation was reprinted in the *San Antonio Daily Herald*, October 17, 1871, p. 2. Campbell, *Grass-Roots Reconstruction in Texas*, asserts that Judge John W. Oliver convinced Davis "to declare martial law in Limestone County on the grounds that Republicans there were not safe." Other county officials persuaded Davis to act, not Oliver. For similar reasoning see Tony E. Duty, "The Home Front—McLennan County in the Civil War," *Texana* 12 (1974), pp. 224–225. Duty's essay is based upon limited documentation.

57. Proclamation of Martial Law in Freestone and Limestone Counties, October 9, 1871, AGC, ARIS/TSLAC.

58. *Austin Democratic Statesman*, October 12, 1871, p. 1; *San Antonio Daily Herald*, October 17, 1871, p. 2. Bowers, whose home county was Travis (Austin), and McLean, from Titus County in northeast Texas, seemed to have no connection with the Limestone/Freestone imbroglio. Robertson (who succeeded S. J. Adams) did represent Freestone. The Senator for Limestone was S. W. Ford, who replaced A. J. Evans, a black, both from Waco, and for Freestone, P. W. Hall of Calvert (Robertson County). The representatives, in addition to McLean, were D. R. Burley, also from Calvert, and Silas Cotton, black, another Calvert resident; and for Limestone, David Medlock from Springfield, another black man, Shep Mullens, also black, from Waco (who had died on August 6, 1871), and George W. Patten (who succeeded the deceased Robert Crudup). Apparently these individuals were not "safe" enough to trust with resolutions opposing the governor's policy.

59. S. M. Jones, W. B. Bonner, and S. P. Young (Springfield) to EJD, October 1, 1871, HJ, p. 192; Election Returns, Limestone County (contested), 1871, Secretary of State, ARIS/TSLAC. Jones was Georgia born in 1832, moved to Texas in 1857, and served in Company K, Bass's Twenty-ninth Cavalry during the Civil War. Later, he was Justice of the Peace of Precinct No. 5 for a decade, Deputy United States Marshal for four years, and finally Kosse postmaster; *Memorial and Biographical History of Navarro, Henderson, Anderson, Limestone, Freestone and Leon Counties* (Chicago: Lewis Publishing Company, 1893), pp. 758–759.

60. EJD to Oliver, October 9, 1871, LPB, p. 380, GP (EJD), ARIS/TSLAC. Reynolds did not respond until November 2 about ammunition for the battery of artillery in possession of the state. The question of immediate necessity for its issue no longer existed. If another occasion arose when ammunition might be needed, Reynolds said the ordnance department should be contacted with a view of procuring the assent of the proper officials to issue a suitable amount of ammunition, should an emergency require it; EJD to Reynolds, November 2, 1871, LPB, p. 444, GP (EJD), ARIS/TSLAC.

61. EJD to JD, October 10, 1871, LPB, pp. 381–382, GP (EJD), ARIS/TSLAC; *Austin Democratic Statesman*, October 12, 1871, p. 2.

62. EJD to JD, October 10, 1871, LPB, pp. 381–382, GP (EJD), ARIS/TSLAC.

63. EJD to the Hon. Senate and House of Representatives of the State of Texas, October 10, 1871, p. 385; EJD to William H. Sinclair (Speaker, House), October 12, 1871, pp. 390–391, both in LPB, GP (EJD), ARIS/TSLAC.

64. A. G. Malloy (Major General Commanding, Headquarters State Troops, Springfield) Report, October 22, 1871; Louis H. Schubert (Lieutenant, SP) to JD, October 24, 1871, both in AGC, ARIS/TSLAC.

65. Malloy Report, October 22, 1871, AGC, ARIS/TSLAC.

66. Ibid.

67. Ibid.; *Austin Democratic Statesman*, October 17, 1871, p. 1; *San Antonio Daily Herald*, October 26, 1871, p. 2. The officers present in Malloy's command included Assistant Adjutant General J. H. Roberts, First Lieutenant C. H. Welch, and Captain Leonidas Greenleaf.

68. Farrow to JD, October 15, 1871, AGC, ARIS/TSLAC.

69. Ibid.; Farrow to JD, October 20, 1871, both in AGC, ARIS/TSLAC.

70. Ibid.

71. B. F. Boldridge (Sergeant, SP, Commanding) to JD, October 21, 1871, AGC, ARIS/TSLAC.

72. Circular, "NOTICE!, SPECIAL MILITARY TAX!, Office Special Agent, State of Texas, October 24, 1871, Broadsides Collection, Broadside #179; Farrow to JD, October 24, 1871, AGC, all in ARIS/TSLAC. Actually, the collecting process had begun on October 19, "Collections 19th Oct. 1871," AGC, ARIS/TSLAC. Simultaneously with the imposition of the military assessment, Limestone County residents also had to pay their regular state and county taxes for 1871; Special Order No. ?, November 6, 1871, AGC, ARIS/TSLAC; *Dallas Herald*, November 4, 1871, p. 2; December 9, 1871, p. 1.

73. John R. Henry to JD, December 22, 1871; George W. Smith (Colonel, 5th Regiment, State Guards) to JD, November 29, 1871; Stanley Welch (Major, 5th Regiment, State Guards) to JD, November 29, 1871; John R. Shafter (Major, Reserve Militia) to JD, November 28, 1871; John R. Henry (Springfield) to JD, December 4, 1871; Farrow to JD, November 10, 1871; M. H. Williams (Mayor, Groesbeck) to JD, November 3, 1871; Smith to JD, January 9, 1872, AGC, all in ARIS/TSLAC; J. H. Roberts to JD, January 23, 1872, SPC, ARIS/TSLAC; Affidavit of Richardson, December 4, 1871; Statement of Smith [1871], both in Election Returns, Limestone County (contested), 1871, Secretary of State, ARIS/TSLAC; Farrow to "Gents", January 10, 1872, in *DSJ*, January 12, 1872, p. 2; Farrow to JD, December 4, 1871 (telegram); John W. Irwin to JD, December 4, 1871; Stanley Welch (Major, 5th Regiment, State Guard) to JD, December 5, 1871; James F. Pells to JD, December 10, 1871; December 13, 1871; Farrow (late Special Agent, State of Texas) to JD, December 19, 1871, all in AGC, ARIS/TSLAC; L. H. Schubert (Lieutenant, SP) to JD, January 23, 1872; Farrow to JD, December 4, 1871, both in SPC, ARIS/TSLAC; Statement of William C. Hodges, December 2, 1871, Election Returns, Limestone County (contested), 1871, Secretary of State, ARIS/TSLAC.

74. Malloy (Jefferson) to JD, January 20, 1872 [1871]; H. W. Monroe (Gonzales) to JD, December 3, 1871; H. W. Morgan (Deputy US Marshal, Groesbeck) to JD, December 13, 1871, AGC, ARIS/TSLAC. Monroe also said that Welch and Judge Thornton collected $2,700 in gold in one day and kept it. Morgan stated that he paid $32.75 coin for clothing and $2.50 for whiskey for Welch, but was never reimbursed. Davidson righted these matters; Malloy to JD, January 23, 1872, AGC, ARIS/TSLAC.

75. JD to EJD, November 10, 1871, AGC, ARIS/TSLAC.

76. JD to Farrow, December 20, 1871; JD to Wood, December 21, 1871; Wood to JD, December 21, 1871, all in AGC, ARIS/TSLAC.

77. George W. Smith, Stanley Welch, William H. Griffin, John N. Shafter, L. W. Collins, and Alfred D. Evans to EJD, November 17, 1871, in *DSJ*, November 23, 1871, p. 4; Malloy to EJD, November 18, 1871 (telegram), November 18, 1871, Election Returns, Limestone County (contested), 1871, Secretary of State, ARIS/TSLAC.

78. Ibid.

79. J. W. Parker (M. D., Waller Prairie, Limestone County), November 6, 1871, P-63, p. 688; Bonner to AG, January 28, 1872, B-294, p. 609, all in AG LR; EJD to The Sheriff, or any State Police of Freestone County, Texas, November 24, 1871, LPB, p. 67; EJD to T. D. Prowell (Cotton Gin), December 14, 1871, p. 143; EJD to S. M. Jones (Sheriff, Limestone County), December 27, 1871, p. 221, all in LPB (November 15, 1871–May 20, 1872), GP (EJD); Special Orders, No. 12, October 27, 1871, AGC, all in ARIS/TSLAC; Waller County Scrapbook, Box 3L473, DB-CFAH, UTA.

80. *DSJ*, January 4, 1872, p. 3; *San Antonio Daily Herald*, January 6, 1872, p. 2.

81. *DSJ*, January 27, 1872, p. 2; February 8, 2873, p. 2; March 3, 1873, p. 2; *San Antonio Daily Herald*, July 14, 1872, p. 2.

82. *Galveston Daily News*, September 20, 1874, p. 2.

CHAPTER SIX

1. JD to E. M. Alexander, September 6, 1870, SPLPB, No. 1, pp. 212–213; General Order, No. 2, September 20, 1870, p. 314, both in SPLPB, ARIS/TSLAC; *Waco Register* quoted in the *Daily Houston Telegraph*, January 18, 1871, p. 4. A newspaper later reported that a large number of Sharp's carbines, with an abundant supply of ammunition, were received by Adjutant General Frank L. Britton as part of the quota due Texas from the national government. They were issued to the frontier forces as the state legislature was about to eliminate the State Police, *Neosho* (Missouri) *Times*, March 20, 1873, p. 1.

2. EJD to A. S. Shuford (Quitman), October 14, 1872, p. 619 and EJD to R. F. Campbell (Bastrop), April 10, 1872, p. 515, LPB, GP (EJD), ARIS/TSLAC.

3. Ed T. Randle (Navasota) to JD, September 7, 1872, SPC, ARIS/TSLAC.

4. John Ramshay (Centerville) to JD, May 20, 1872, SPC, ARIS/TSLAC.

5. R. B. Reagan (Sheriff, Cherokee County) to JD, June 3, 1872, SPC, ARIS/
   TSLAC; Tise, *Texas County Sheriffs*, p. 97.
6. Ibid.
7. *DSJ*, January 23, 1873, p. 4.
8. J. M. Redmon (Hempstead) to FLB, March 7, 1873, SPC, ARIS/TSLAC.
9. All statements in SPC; J. H. Adams (Hempstead) to FLB, March 14, 1873, SPC,
   ARIS/TSLAC.
10. Sergeant J. M. Redmon (SP, Corsicana) to JD, June 13, 1872, SPC, ARIS/TSLAC.
11. EJD to Sergeant Wentworth Manning (SP, Canton), July 13, 1871, p. 21, LPB, GP
    (EJD), ARIS/TSLAC.
12. EJD to Thomas Sheriff (Rusk), July 18, 1871, p. 66, LPB, GP (EJD), ARIS/
    TSLAC.
13. James Ryan (Pvt. SP, Navasota) to JD, August 22, 1872; Bond for $500, August
    8, 1872, both in SPC, ARIS/TSLAC. In a similar vein, another policeman who
    performed many of the same functions as Ryan was Private/Sergeant Thomas H.
    Doran, a twenty-seven-year-old white from Austin, who was described as an "ef-
    ficient and energetic officer." He served the State Police for much of its existence;
    DSJ, April 11, 1872, p. 3; April 12, 1872, p. 3; June 10, 1872, p. 3; October 14, 1872, p. 3.
14. Ryan to FLB, March 31, 1873, SPC, ARIS/TSLAC.
15. Ryan to FLB, March 6, 1873; March 13, 1873; March 31, 1873; April 3, 1873; April
    7, 1873 and April 26, 1873, all in SPC, ARIS/TSLAC.
16. Ryan to FLB, December 30, 1872; March 8, 1873, both in SPC, ARIS/TSLAC.
17. A. L. Roy (Private, SP, Giddings) to JD, September 4, 1872; September 29, 1872;
    December 6, 1872; and January 16, 1873, all in SPC, ARIS/TSLAC.
18. Roy to JD, September 9, 1872; December 6, 1872; December 12, 1872; January
    16, 1873; January 24, 1873, all in SPC, ARIS/TSLAC; Parsons and Little, *Captain
    L. H. McNelly*, pp. 107–113. Roy was forced to provide a new bond as his former
    sureties had withdrawn.
19. Roy to JD, December 12, 1872. Endorsement, FLB, "Tell him he must give a new
    bond as his former sureties have withdrawn."; Roy to FLB, January 16, 1873; Jan-
    uary 24, 1873; April 3, 1873, all in SPC, ARIS/TSLAC.
20. Roy to FLB, April 3, 1873; April 5, 1873; April 12, 1873; Receipt for Prisoners, A. F.
    Dornwell, Justice of the Peace (Winchester), April 12, 1873; Roy to FLB, April 22,
    1873, all in SPC, ARIS/TSLAC.
21. Roy (Winchester, Fayette County) to FLB, April 14, 1873, SPC, ARIS/TSLAC;
    Walters's shotgun was not loaded.
22. W. D. Rutherford and 65 Residents (McDade) to JD, November 15, 1872, SPC,
    ARIS/TSLAC.
23. *DSJ*, May 9, 1871, p. 4; August 4, 1871, p. 2
24. A. R. Parsons (Belton) to EJD, September 27, 1871, GP (EJD); EJD to Lieutenant
    A. C. Hill, December 16, 1871, p. 158; EJD to S. W. March (Mount Enterprise),
    July 30, 1872, p. 287; EJD to FLB, November 21, 1872, p. 41; EJD to H. L. Ray

(Dallas), November 15, 1872, p. 19; EJD to E. W. Whitten (Dublin), November 22, 1872, p. 50; February 10, 1873, p. 483, all in LPB, GP (EJD), ARIS/TSLAC; *DSJ*, June 21, 1872, p. 2; January 2, 1873, p. 2; January 23, 1873, p. 2.

25. *State Gazette* quoted in *DSJ*, August 2, 1871, p. 2; *Flake's Daily Bulletin*, August 8, 1871, p. 4.

26. *Flake's Daily Bulletin*, December 28, 1870, p. 2; J. J. Stockbridge and Committee of Four (Brenham) to EJD, September 26, 1871, AGC; S. H. Renick (Waco) to EJD, July 11, 1872, SPC; 12 Atascosa County Citizens (Somerset) to EJD, July 30, 1872, SPC, all in ARIS/TSLAC.

27. *DSJ*, February 6, 1873, p. 2; Private T. A. Burns (SP, McCulloch Co.) to JD, January 20, 1871, SPC, ARIS/TSLAC; 43 Mason County Citizens to EJD, January 31, 1871, GP (EJD), ARIS/TSLAC.

28. D. P. Baker (Thompsonville, Wise County) to JD, March 10, 1871; Captain H. J. Richarz (4th Company, Frontier Forces, Fort Inge) to JD, January 16, 1871, AGC, ARIS/TSLAC.

29. G. W. Paul (Deputy Sheriff, Bosque County) to FLB, January 23, 1873, in *DSJ*, January 23, 1873, p. 2; Richarz to JD, March 16, 1871, AGC, ARIS/TSLAC.

30. J. S. Rogers (Justice of the Peace, Columbia) to EJD, August 13, 1872, SPC, ARIS/TSLAC.

31. Lieutenant Thomas Sheriff to EJD, January 21, 1871, GP (EJD), ARIS/TSLAC; EJD to J. J. Fain (Carthage), September 7, 1871, p. 228; EJD to M. Priest, August 12, 1871, p. 199; EJD to James C. Anderson, August 14, 1871, p. 210, LPB, GP (EJD), ARIS/TSLAC; *DSJ*, June 8, 1871, p. 2; November 8, 1871, p. 2; December 9, 1871, p. 2.

32. *DSJ*, May 13, 1871, p. 4; *Flake's Daily Bulletin*, March 30, 1871, p. 2; EJD to S. H. Canfield, James Randall, J. Anthony and Others (Cold.), December 10, 1870, p. 32, LPB, GP (EJD), ARIS/TSLAC.

33. *Flake's Daily Bulletin*, September 22, 1870, p. 5; February 15, 1871, p. 3; March 28, 1871, p. 5; April 11, 1871, p. 4; April 12, 1871, p. 5; April 14, 1871, p. 4; April 16, 1871, p. 5; *Houston Daily Union*, November 21, 1870, p. 2; February 3, 1871, p. 1; *DSJ*, September 13, 1870, p. 2; September 17, 1870, p. 1; April 25, 1871, p. 4; June 7, 1871, p. 1; August 12, 1871, p. 2; August 26, 1871, p. 2; September 7, 1871, p. 3; October 27, 1871, p. 1; October 28, 1871, p. 5; November 9, 1871, p. 4; April 11, 1872, p. 3; April 12, 1872, p. 2; April 23, 1872, p. 3; April 30, 1872, p. 2; May 14, 1872, p. 3; *Norton's Intelligencer* in *DSJ*, July 20, 1872, p. 1; *San Antonio Daily Herald*, August 16, 1870, p. 3; James Russell (Bryan) to EJD, August 3, 1870, GP (EJD); EJD to J. Douglas Brown (Trinity Station), March 21, 1873, p. 660, LPB, GP (EJD), ARIS/TSLAC.

34. *DSJ*, June 6, 1871, p. 2; July 8, 1871, p. 2; EJD to Lieutenant Thomas Williams, July 19, 1871, pp. 69–71, LPB, GP (EJD), ARIS/TSLAC. The presence of Williams and his men led to a dispute over $5.75 allegedly owed by Private H. R. Rush to a boardinghouse keeper named J. B. Rein. Rush disputed the bill. See J. B. Rein (Serbin) to JD, February 19, 1872; H. R. Rush (New Anhalt, Burleson County) to JD, March 3, 1872, both in SPC, ARIS/TSLAC.

35. Ibid.; EJD to J. B. McFarland (Judge, 29th Judicial District), July 31, 1871, pp. 136–137, LPB, GP (EJD), ARIS/TSLAC.

36. EJD to McFarland, August 4, 1871, pp. 162–164; EJD to Colonel B. Trigg (District Attorney), August 5, 1871, p. 166, LPB, GP (EJD), ARIS/TSLAC. Davis stated that if possible, he wished to avoid declaring martial law, but he would if it became impossible to "procure the trial and conviction" of the offenders.

37. *Flake's Daily Bulletin*, August 4, 1871, p. 3; August 10, 1871, p. 3. For a different perspective see *DSJ*, August 10, 1871, p. 2. They observed that "when tribunals sworn to indict crimes cover them over with the name of 'harmless sports,' an appeal justly lies to a higher power, and the appeal will not be made in vain."

38. EJD to J. E. Cope (Justice of the Peace, Bastrop), September 6, 1871, p. 225, LPB, GP (EJD), ARIS/TSLAC; *DSJ*, August 17, 1871, p. 2; August 29, 1871, p. 2; August 30, 1871, p. 2; September 3, 1871, p. 2; November 7, 1871, p. 3; November 14, 1871, p. 1; *San Antonio Daily Express*, November 9, 1871, p. 2; *Flake's Daily Bulletin*, August 30, 1871, p. 3, claimed the slain black man was a thief; Parsons and Little, *Captain L. H. McNelly*, pp. 94–95.

39. *DSJ*, July 18, 1872, p. 2; August 20, 1872, p. 2; August 24, 1872, p. 3; November 20, 1872, p. 2.

40. August Emil Voigt, Hermann Louis Pester, Constantin Voigt, Aug. Voigt, Ferd. Voigt (Bastrop) to EJD, and R. F. Campbell to EJD, February 10, 1873, in *DSJ*, February 12, 1873, p. 2.

41. *Houston Daily Union*, December 9, 1870, p. 1; *Flake's Daily Bulletin*, December 15, 1870, pp. 1, 4; December 23, 1870, p. 4. The police, on occasion, attempted to eradicate prostitution. *Flake's Daily Bulletin*, April 16, 1871, p. 5.

42. All the documents surrounding this event are in William H. Russell, *A Full Statement of the Facts and Records Connected with the Enforcement and Quarantine at Brazos Santiago, Texas* (Brownsville: Ranchero Print, 1871), which can be found at DBCFAH, UTA. There are also extensive letters covering the controversy in Davis's Letterpress Book for 1871, in ARIS/TSLAC.

43. Ibid.

44. *DSJ*, July 10, 1872, p. 3; July 11, 1872, p. 3; July 12, 1872, p. 2; July 23, 1872, p. 2; July 26, 1872, p. 2. There is an extended discussion of this group in Parsons and Little, *Captain L. H. McNelly*, pp. 107–113.

45. Richard W. Haltom, *History and Description of Nacogdoches County, Texas* (Nacogdoches, 1880), p. 39. Haltom's essay on Linn Flat is also reprinted in Nugent E. Brown, *The Book of Nacogdoches County, July 1, 1927* (Houston: n.p., 1927), pp. 35–46.

46. Christopher Long, "Nacogdoches County," *NHT*, IV, pp. 925–929; Campbell, *An Empire for Slavery*, p. 266.

47. Long, "Linn Flat, Texas," *NHT*, IV, pp. 208–209. The numbers are our own count and are based upon the information in Carolyn Reeves Ericson, *The People of Nacogdoches County in 1870: An Edited Census* (Lufkin, TX, 1977), pp. 163–199;

Bertha M. Parmelly, "Linn Flat Raid Spread Death, Fear Despair," *Daily Sentinel* (Nacogdoches), July 18, 1960, Part 1, p. 4.

48. Long, "Nacogdoches County," *NHT*, IV, p. 927; Joe T. Timmons, "The Referendum in Texas on the Ordinance of Secession, February 23, 1861: The Vote," *East Texas Historical Journal* 11 (Fall 1973), pp. 16, 18.

49. Francis A. Walker, comp., *The Statistics of the Population of the United States, Ninth Census, 1870* (3 vols.; Washington, DC, 1872), I, pp. 64–66; Richter, *Overreached on All Sides*, p. 274; Crouch, *The Freedmen's Bureau and Black Texans.*

50. Alex Ferguson (Agent, Nacogdoches) to Charles A. Vernou (Acting Assistant Adjutant General [AAAG]), December 5, 1868, Assistant Commissioner (AC), Letters Received (LR), F-62; Ferguson to J. P. Richardson (AAAG), April 15, 1868, AC, LR, F-31; T. M. K. Smith (Agent, Nacogdoches) to Richardson, November 5, 1867, S-65, Operations Reports (OR), both in AC, Texas, BRFAL, RG 105, NA; Richter, *Overreached on All Sides*, pp. 274–275; Crouch, "A Spirit of Lawlessness: White Violence; Black Texans, 1865–1868," Journal of Social History 18 (Winter 1984), pp. 217–232.

51. Ferguson to Vernou, December 1, 1868, AC, LR, F-60, Texas, BRFAL, RG 105, NA.

52. *Clarksville Standard*, January 13, 1872, p. 2; Haltom, *History and Description*, p. 39; Parmelly, "Linn Flat Raid," Part 1.

53. Lee Lance Albright, "Columbus Y. 'Bud' Heaslet [Hazlett]," in author's possession.

54. Albright, "Columbus Y. 'Bud' Heaslet"; Ericson, *The People of Nacogdoches County in the Civil War* (Lufkin, TX: Pineywood Printing, 1980), p. 109.

55. Albright, "Columbus Y. 'Bud' Heaslet"; State Police Roster; Columbus Y. Hazlett, #1443, Nacogdoches County, 1867 Voters' Registration, Secretary of State, both in ARIS/TSLAC.

56. W. J. Grayson, Compiled Military Service Records of Confederate Soldiers Who Served in Organizations from the State of Texas, RG 109, NA; Grayson, #405, Nacogdoches County, 1867 Voters' Registration, Secretary of State; Roster of Special Policemen, 1871–1872, Nacogdoches County, pp. 228–229, both in ARIS/TSLAC.

57. Roster of Special Policemen, 1871–1872, Nacogdoches County, pp. 228–229; Election Register, Nacogdoches County (1869–1873), Secretary of State; Election Returns, Nacogdoches County, 1871, all in ARIS/TSLAC; *Texas State Gazette* (Austin), February 5, 1872.

58. Ericson, *The People of Nacogdoches County*, pp. 165, 187; Parmelly, "Linn Flat Raid," Part 1. The dialogue is from Haltom, *History and Description*, p. 40.

59. Haltom, *History and Description*, p. 40; Ericson, *The People of Nacogdoches County*, p. 169; Parmelly, "Linn Flat Raid," Part 1.

60. *Clarksville Standard*, January 13, 1872, p. 2.

61. Ibid.

62. Haltom, *History and Description*, pp. 41–42.

63. Ibid., p. 39; Tise, *Texas County Sheriffs*, p. 387; Election Register, Nacogdoches County (1869–1873), Secretary of State, ARIS/TSLAC; Linda Sybert Hudson, "Richard David Orton," *NHT*, IV, p. 1174.

64. State Police Roster; Roster of Special Policemen, 1871–1872, Nacogdoches County, pp. 228–229, all in ARIS/TSLAC; Haltom, *History and Description*, p. 42–43; Parmelly, "Linn Flat Raid Spread Death, Fear, Despair," *Daily Sentinel* (Nacogdoches), July 21, 1960, Part 2, p. 1.

65. Haltom, *History and Description*, p. 43; Parmelly, "Linn Flat Raid," Part 2.

66. Ibid.; Campbell, "Scalawag District Judges," *Houston Review* 14 (1992), pp. 78, 80, 87.

67. *Houston Union* in *Clarksville Standard*, January 13, 1872, p. 2; *Tri-Weekly State Gazette* (Austin), January 29, 1872, p. 2.

68. JD to Williams, November 1, 1871, p. 580; JD to M. Priest, December 28, 1871, p. 405; JD to Thomas Williams, December 30, 1871, p. 419, all in AG LPB, ARIS/ TSLAC; EJD to Thomas H. Baker, December 12, 1871, p. 124, LPB, GP (EJD), ARIS/TSLAC.

69. JD to Priest, December 28, 1871, p. 405; JD to Williams, December 30, 1871, p. 419, both in AG LPB, ARIS/TSLAC; *Daily State Journal* (Austin), January 28, 1872, p. 2; *Tri-Weekly State Gazette* (Austin), January 29, 1872, p. 2; *Texas State Gazette* (Austin), February 5, 1872, p. 2.

70. *DSJ*, January 28, 1872, p. 2.

71. *Tri-Weekly State Gazette* (Austin), January 29, 1872, p. 2; *DSJ*, January 28, 1872, p. 2.

72. Ibid.; Campbell, "Scalawag District Judges," p. 87.

73. Roster of Special Policemen, 1871–1872, Rusk County, pp. 258–259, ARIS/ TSLAC; *Tri-Weekly State Gazette* (Austin), January 29, 1872, p. 2; *DSJ*, January 28, 1872, p. 2; *Texas State Gazette* (Austin), February 5, 1872, p. 2.

74. *Texas State Gazette* (Austin), February 5, 1872, p. 2.

75. Ibid.

76. *DSJ*, February 3, 1872, p. 2.

77. JD to Williams, February 10, 1872, p. 224, AG LPB; EJD to JD, February 19, 1872, pp. 305–306, LPB, GP (EJD), both in ARIS/TSLAC.

78. EJD to JD, February 13, 1872, pp. 305–306, LPB, GP (EJD), ARIS/TSLAC.

79. William A. Baker to Editors, *State Journal*, February 28, 1872, *DSJ*, March 8, 1872, p. 1. The *Tri-Weekly State Gazette*, January 29, 1872, p. 2; February 5, 1872, p. 2; February 7, 1872, p. 2, had earlier suggested that Davidson go to Nacogdoches County.

80. *The State of Texas v. Columbus Hazlett and William J. Grayson*, Case Nos. 1095 and 1108, District Court Records, Ralph Steen Library, Nacogdoches, Texas.

81. Ibid.; Milton Mast (Sheriff, Nacogdoches County) to Governor Richard B. Hubbard, July 31, 1877, in Columbus Hazlett Extradition Papers, Secretary of

State Records; Letter to Milton Mast, August 4, 1877, p. 164, LPB, GP (Richard B. Hubbard); Governor John Ireland, *The State of Texas v. William J. Grayson,* March 5, 1885, Executive Clemency Records, Secretary of State Records, ARIS/ TSLAC.

82. FLB to EJD, December 14, 1872, pp. 345–346, AG LPB, ARIS/TSLAC; *Report of the Adjutant General, 1872* (Austin: James P. Newcomb and Company, 1873), pp. 3–5.

83. L. H. McNelly (Captain) to EJD, January 5, 1873, GP (EDJ), ARIS/TSLAC; *Taranaki Herald* (New Plymouth, New Zealand), October 24, 1874, p. 2; Parsons and Little, *Captain L. H. McNelly,* pp. 116–118.

84. For the inquest see *Taranaki Herald,* April 8, 1885, pp. 2–3; April 17, 1885, p. 2.

85. 1850 United States Population Census, Spencer County, Indiana, p. 52; 1860 Spencer County, p. 215; 1880 Galveston County, Texas, p. 101; Britton Civil War Record (Indiana State Archives, Indianapolis); Christine Young, comp., *Marriage Records, Spencer County, Indiana, 1818–1855* (Thomson, IL: Heritage House, 1974), p. 9; *History of Texas Together with a Biographical History of the Cities of Houston and Galveston* (Chicago: Lewis Publishing Company, 1895), pp. 674–675; Marriage Records, Galveston County, vol. F, p. 91; 1880 United States Population Census, Custer County, Colorado, p. 256; *Galveston Daily News,* November 6, 1880, p. 4; Frank Britton's remains were taken to Evansville, Indiana, for interment in the Oak Hill Cemetery. *Rockport* [Indiana] *Journal,* November 4, 1880.

CHAPTER SEVEN

1. *Norton's Union Intelligencer* (Dallas), March 29, 1873, p. 1; *DSJ,* February 6, 1873, p. 2.

2. James B. Gillett, *Six Years with the Texas Rangers, 1875 to 1881* (Austin: Von Boeckmann-Jones Co., Publishers, 1921), p. 108; *Weekly Dispatch* (Lampasas), October 31, 1871, p. 2.

3. Lampasas *Dispatch,* November 9, 1872, p. 1 (courtesy of Jeffrey Jackson); *Flake's Semi-Weekly Bulletin,* April 24, 1872, p. 2; Alice J. Rhoades, "Lampasas, Texas," and "Lampasas County," both in *NHT,* IV, pp. 48–51.

4. *Texas Almanac For 1873,* pp. 208–210; F. M. Cross, *A Short Sketch-History from Personal Reminicences* [sic] *of Early Days in Central Texas* (Brownwood, TX: Greenwood Printing Company, 1910), pp. 30–31; Janet Valenza, "'Taking the Waters' at Texas's Health Spas," *SWHQ* 98 (January 1995), pp. 427–456; Valenza, *Taking the Waters in Texas: Springs, Spas, and Fountains of Youth* (Austin: University of Texas Press, 2000). Today, Lampasas has a population of approximately 7,100. The writer who located Lampasas in "South Western Texas" did not have a firm grasp of Texas geography.

5. JD to Sergeant L. C. Locke, January 28, 1871, p. 167; February 10, 1871, p. 274; March 2, 1871, p. 430; March 1, 1871, p. 545; March 11, 1871, pp. 559–560; March 20, 1871, p. 606, JD, Order, January 28, 1871, p. 172; JD to Private Thomas Lamb,

February 10, 1871, p. 272; all in SPLPB, No. 2 (January 3, 1871, to April 26, 1871), AGC, ARIS/TSLAC; *DSJ*, May 28, 1872, p. 3. The ten men ordered to report to Locke were Privates W. T. Rought, Levi Abel, Lewis Lane, J. L. L. Hollander, Thomas Lamb, E. F. Jones, Joseph F. Bond, John Franklin, John Valentine, and Charles C. King.

6. "Statement of S. T. Denson," in *DSJ*, January 25, 1873, p. 2; February 4, 1873, p. 2; "Report on the Condition of Affairs in Lampasas County, March 24, 1873," *Report of the AG for the Year 1873* (Austin: Cardwell & Walker, Printers, 1874), p. 128; *Flake's Semi-Weekly Bulletin* (Galveston), November 15, 1871, p. 2; December 20, 1871, p. 2; P. J. Rasch, "The Horrell War," *New Mexico Historical Review* 31 (July 1956), p. 223.

7. JD to EJD, March 21, 1871, p. 640; JD to Sheriff of Lampasas County, June 9, 1871, p. 265, both in SPLPB, ARIS/TSLAC.

8. JD to S. T. Denson (Sheriff, Lampasas County), April 15, 1872, p. 41; JD to Denson, September 4, 1872, p. 178; JD to William Lewis (District Judge, Lampasas), September 15, 1871, p. 228; JD to William Martin (Registrar, Lampasas County), September 30, 1871, p. 357, all in AG LPB, ARIS/TSLAC.

9. Lampasas History Book Committee, comp., *Lampasas County Texas: Its History and Its People* (Marceline, MO: Walsworth Publishing Company, 1991), p. 24 (hereafter cited as *LCT*); Rasch, "The Horrell War," pp. 223–231; Sonnichsen, *I'll Die Before I'll Run*, pp. 97–98.

10. John Duff Green, "Recollections," ed. Joan Green Lawrence, unpublished ms., pp. 49–50, 90–91 (courtesy of Jeffrey Jackson).

11. Gillett, *Six Years with the Texas Rangers*, p. 108. Later writers have followed a similar line in describing the Horrells. William MacLeod Raine, in *Famous Sheriffs and Western Outlaws* (Garden City, NJ: Garden City Publishing Company, Inc., 1929), although he referred to them as the "Harrolds," asserted that "they were cattlemen, well respected at Lampasas before they 'went bad,' though they were recognized as men quick on the draw when stirred to anger," p. 119. The most recent defense is "Fightin' Family," in Gra'Delle Duncan, *Texas Tough: Dangerous Men in Dangerous Times* (Austin: Eakin Press, 1990), pp. 73–77, who claims that they were "well known for their gun skills but generally were well liked and agreeable," p. 73.

12. John Nichols to J. Evetts Haley, May 15, 1927, J. Evetts Haley Collection (Nita Stewart Haley Memorial Library, Midland, TX), hereafter cited Nichols Interview; *LCT*, pp. 214–215; 1870 United States Agricultural and Population Census, Lampasas County, Texas, ARIS/TSLAC.

13. Nichols Interview; *LCT*, pp. 214–215; 1870 United States Agricultural and Population Census, Lampasas County, Texas, ARIS/TSLAC; Frederick Nolan, *The Lincoln County War: A Documentary History* (Norman: University of Oklahoma Press, 1992), p. 48. Nichols wrote that Tom and John's wife forced the Indians to retreat after Samuel was killed. When he listed the Horrell offspring, Nichols forgot Thomas.

14. *LCT*, pp. 214–215; 1870 United States Agricultural and Population Census, Lampasas County, Texas, ARIS/TSLAC; Rasch, "The Horrell War," p. 223; Nolan, *Bad Blood*, pp. 1–3. Although much has been written about the Horrells, its veracity is questionable. More importantly, what seems interesting about the description of the Horrells is that they are referred to as "old settlers" (by 1873 they had been in the state only fifteen or sixteen years). Yet individuals such as Governors E. J. Davis, E. M. Pease, and A. J. Hamilton, none of them born in Texas, had made their homes in the state at least a decade longer than the Horrells but are frequently labeled as carpetbaggers.

15. A collective biography of the Horrells that is interesting is Nolan, *The Lincoln County War*, pp. 467–468; and his *Bad Blood*.

16. *LCT*, 214–215; 1870 United States Agricultural and Population Census, Lampasas County, Texas, ARIS/TSLAC; Rasch, "The Horrell War," p. 223; Nolan, *Bad Blood*, pp. 1–3.

17. 1870 United States Agricultural and Population Census, Lampasas County, Texas, ARIS/TSLAC.

18. *LCT*, 214–215; Nolan, *Bad Blood*, pp. 1–3; Sonnichsen, *I'll Die Before I'll Run*, pp. 97–118; Rasch, "The Horrell War," pp. 223–231; Nichols Interview. Interestingly enough, three of the widows of these men came from the Grizzell family.

19. "Report on the Condition of Affairs in Lampasas County, March 24, 1873," p. 128; Nolan, *The Lincoln County War*, p. 48.

20. "Statement of S. T. Denson," in *DSJ*, January 25, 1873, p. 2; February 4, 1873, p. 2. Denson's statement was certified by the district court clerk, A. P. Anderson. Nichols stated that it was Mark, a "sort of a wild man" who "tried to paint the town up once while court was in session," who originated the difficulty with Denson. Nichols Interview. The Short brothers, born in Missouri, came to Texas with their parents. In 1861, Mark enlisted with the Twenty-seventh Brigade, Texas Militia, under E. S. C. Robertson of Lampasas County. Prior to this he had served in Captain A. B. Burleson's company of Texas Rangers. He was a stock raiser. His brother "Wash" never amounted to much. Nolan, *Bad Blood*, pp. 177–178; 1870 United States Population Census, Lampasas County, Texas; Muster roll of Captain A. B. Burleson, January 8, 1861; Muster roll of Captain R. Y. Cross, September 1861, both in Military Rolls, AGR, ARIS/TSLAC. Most writers relying upon later oral testimony argue that it was Mark who created the original difficulties for Denson. The contemporary material, including Denson's statement, points to Wash.

21. "Statement of S. T. Denson," in *DSJ*, January 25, 1873, p. 2; February 4, 1873, p. 2; Rasch, "The Horrell War," pp. 223–224; Nolan, *Bad Blood*, p. 17. In the Nichols Interview he contends that Samuel W. Denson, the sheriff's son, shot Wash Short around 1876. For background on Samuel see the 1870 United States Population Census, Lampasas County, Texas, p. 394.

22. "Statement of Thomas Sparks," in *DSJ*, January 25, 1873, p. 2; February 4, 1873, p. 2; *LCT*, p. 24; Nolan, *Bad Blood*, p. 17. According to the 1870 United States

Population Census for Lampasas County, Guinaty was, by 1873, a twenty-six-year-old Missouri-born wagoner who headed an extended household of eight other individuals, which included a wife and three young daughters. He was worth six hundred dollars of personal property.

23. FLB to Lt. A. P. Lee (Commander, Company M, Minute Men, Lampasas), January 23, 1873, p. 279, AG LPB; Special Order No. 2, January 24, 1873, AG, Special Orders (August 1870–April 1897), SP Records; Military Rolls, all in AGR, ARIS/TSLAC.

24. FLB to William Woods (Special State Agent, Frontier Forces), January 24, 1873, p. 287, AG LPB, ARIS/TSLAC. For those interested in such arcane matters, Woods received six dollars per diem and a mileage rate of ten cents a mile.

25. Rasch, "The Horrell War," p. 224; Nolan, *Bad Blood*, p. 18.

26. FLB to County Court of Lampasas County Through Thomas Pratt (Justice of the Peace, Precinct No. 1, Lampasas), February 4, 1873, p. 365, AG LPB, ARIS/TSLAC.

27. FLB to Sergeant J. M. Redmon, February 10, 1873, p. 482, AG LPB; Redmon to FLB, February 13, 28, 1873, SPC; FLB to E. H. Happe (Austin), February 12, 1873, p. 488, AG LPB, all in ARIS/TSLAC; Parsons, "Texas State Policeman Redmon in Lampasas," *The Brand Book* 23 (Winter 1984), p. 12.

28. The following information on Redmon is based upon "Cemetery Records of Cooke County, Texas" (Gainesville: Cross Timbers Genealogical Society, 1980): Marriage Records, 1849–1879, Cooke County, Texas; Service Record, Company D, McCord's Frontier Regiment; and letters from Redmon to Adjutant Generals Davidson and Britton in SPC (February 1872 to March 1873), all in ARIS/TSLAC; "Transcripts from the Office of the Adjutant General of Texas, 1870–1876," DBCFAH UTA; *DSJ*, April 8, 1872, p. 1; April 17, 1872, p. 4; June 3, 1872, p. 1; June 4, 1872, p. 1; June 7, 1872, p. 3. For Redmon's activities in Montague County see *Lockhart News-Echo*, April 27, 1872, p. 5. On Hardin, see Marohn, *The Last Gunfighter*, Metz, *John Wesley Hardin: Dark Angel of Texas*.

29. Governor's Proclamation, February 10, 1873, p. 1,080, Executive Record, 1870–1874, Secretary of State; Redmon to FLB, February 13, 17, 28, 1873, SPC; FLB to Happe, February 12, 1873, p. 488, AG LPB; FLB to Privates H. K. Street (Giddings), p. 461; M. L. Woolley (McDade), p. 462; William Williams (McDade), p. 463; J. M. M. Harris (Brenham), p. 464; John Downey (Brenham), p. 466; C. M. Jennings (Giddings), p. 467, E. S. Gantt (Burton), p. 468; G. A. Hall, p. 469; J. M. Brown (Giddings), p. 470; C. L. Bell (Brenham), p. 471, A. L. Roy (Giddings), p. 472, all dated February 10, 1873, FLB to George A. Hall, February 22, 1873, p. 574, all in AG LPB, all in ARIS/TSLAC; Parsons, "Texas State Policeman Redmon in Lampasas," p. 12.

30. FLB to E. H. Happe, February 12, 1873, p. 488, FLB to W. H. Evans, February 14, 1873, p. 517, both in AG LPB; Redmon to FLB, February 17, 28, 1873, SPC, all in ARIS/TSLAC; Parsons, "Texas State Policeman Redmon," pp. 13–14, suggests that John Salmon may have been the John Selman who killed John Wesley

Hardin in 1894. They were not the same person. On Salmon, see Christabel Hargett Cook, *Salmon and Related Families* (Phoenix: Apex Printing Corporation, 1983), p. 2; on Selman, see Metz, *John Selman, Gunfighter* (New York: Hastings House, 1966). Evans resigned April 21, 1873; no reason is listed.

31. Redmon to FLB, February 17, 28, 1873, SPC, ARIS/TSLAC; Parsons, "Texas State Policeman Redmon," pp. 13–14. Parsons only found Downey. Gantt was discharged on March 31, and Hall, who later joined McNelly's Washington County Volunteer Militia Company "A" as an occasional spy, died after being shot in a gunfight on April 2, 1878. Brown later became Lee County Sheriff and supervised the hanging of William "Wild Bill" P. Longley. C. L. Bell has sometimes been confused with C. S. Bell, who had a checkered career as a detective, spy, and literary contributor. On Brown, see Chuck Parsons, *James Madison Brown: Texas Sheriff, Texas Turfman* (Wolfe City, TX: Hennington Publishing Company, 1993), pp. 17–19, 73–82.

32. Redmon to FLB, February 28, 1873, SPC, ARIS/TSLAC.

33. Redmon to FLB, February 13, 28, 1873, SPC, ARIS/TSLAC; Parsons, "Texas State Policeman Redmon in Lampasas," p. 12.

34. Redmon to FLB, February 28, 1873, SPC, ARIS/TSLAC.

35. Redmon to FLB, February 13, 17, 1873, SPC, ARIS/TSLAC; Parsons, "Texas State Policeman Redmon," p. 13. Parsons wrote that the State Police roster listed a Jasper Biddy of Edinburg, not a Henry Biddy. Later, he claimed Biddy was not Henry Eddy of Austin. Norwood was discharged on April 7, 1873. No reason is listed for his discharge. William Waltz is lined out on the roster; State Police Roster, 1870–1873, ARIS/TSLAC.

36. Redmon to FLB, February 28, 1873, SPC, ARIS/TSLAC. Texas Ranger James B. Gillett later killed Dublin.

37. Redmon to FLB, February 17, 28, 1873, SPC, ARIS/TSLAC; Parsons, "Texas State Policeman Redmon," pp. 12–13.

38. Redmon to FLB, February 28, 1873, SPC, ARIS/TSLAC; Sheriff S. T. Denson to FLB, February 26, 1873, in *DSJ*, March 3, 1873, p. 3.

39. FLB to Thomas Williams, March 10, 1873, p. 36; FLB to A. Jessen (State Storekeeper), March 11, 1873, p. 45, both in AG LPB, ARIS/TSLAC; March 11, 1873 Account, Miscellaneous Ledger, 1873, Accounts, State Police Records, all in ARIS/TSLAC; "Report on the Condition of Affairs in Lampasas County, March 24, 1873," pp. 126–127.

40. FLB to EJD, March 24, 1873, pp. 196–201, AG LPB, ARIS/TSLAC; "Report on the Condition of Affairs in Lampasas County, March 24, 1873," pp. 126–127.

41. 1870 United States Population Census, Lampasas County, Texas, ARIS/TSLAC.

42. This sketch is based upon extensive manuscript material collected by Brice in preparation for a biography of Williams. There is some debate about Williams's name and background. His name was either Thomas Howard or Thomas G.

Williams. He had two children, Laura E. and Thomas G., by his first wife, Mattie G., who was also Missouri born in 1845. His brother, Samuel (also listed as Sanford or Sandford), served in the First Texas Cavalry (Union) during the Civil War but died in a New Orleans hospital just before Thomas enlisted. Angela Hosage to Brice, August 2, 1996, author's files. See also Crouch, "Captain Thomas Williams: The Path of Duty," in *The Human Tradition in Texas*, pp. 71–86.

43. Ibid.

44. Election Returns, 1872, for Caldwell, Gonzales, and Guadalupe counties, Texas, Secretary of State Records, ARIS/TSLAC.

45. Without citing every letter, we have thoroughly researched the State Police Letterpress Books, AG LPB, and the State Police Correspondence, all in AGR, ARIS/TSLAC. See also *DSJ*, December 14, 1872, p. 3; January 21, 1873, p. 3. The *Tri-Weekly Statesman* (Austin), December 17, 1872, praised Williams as a "competent and efficient officer," and while they condemned the "imaginary cause for such officers, we commend the appointment." p. 4. The text quotation is from Williams to EJD, November 23, 1872, GP (EJD), ARIS/TSLAC.

46. *DSJ*, March 19, 1873, p. 2; Rasch, "The Horrell War," p. 225.

47. *Lampasas Dispatch* quoted in *Houston Telegraph* (Daily Edition), March 15, 1873, p. 2.

48. FLB to EJD, March 24, 1873, pp. 196–201, AG LPB, ARIS/TSLAC; "Report on the Condition of Affairs in Lampasas County, March 24, 1873," pp. 126–127; Gillett, *Six Years*, p. 108, claims they arrived at about 3 p.m.

49. Nichols Interview. Nichols had been appointed sheriff in 1868 by General Joseph J. Reynolds, but he failed to qualify; Tise, *Texas County Sheriffs*, p. 319.

50. Nichols Interview; Gillett, *Six Years*, pp. 73–75; Nolan, *Bad Blood*, pp. 24–25; Sonnichsen, *I'll Die Before I'll Run*, pp. 98–99; Rasch, "The Horrell War," p. 225. Sonnichsen also makes much of the alleged "cowardice" of the black State Policeman, Private Samuel Wicks, but never mentions his name. In charge of the horses, he was "never in much danger, for at the first shot he mounted the fastest horse they had and split the wind down the Austin road." Tom Horrell attempted to shoot him but missed. "They say he went so fast the stake rope tied to the saddle stood straight out behind, and that he ruined a fine horse in his haste to get away from there." In Austin, he protested to his commander: "Captain, I thought you said this was a race horse. Why, Captain, he can't run for nothing," p. 99. Gillett followed a similar line when he wrote that "at the first crack of a pistol the negro police mounted his horse and made a John Gilpin ride for Austin," p. 109. In this case, both writers rely upon pure imagination. There is simply no contemporary evidence supporting this unheroic conduct of Wicks and most of this information is gratuitous, seemingly expected by the mores of the times. See the State Police Roster, 1870–1873, pp. 316–317, ARIS/TSLAC.

51. FLB to EJD, March 24, 1873, pp. 196–201, AG LPB, ARIS/TSLAC; *Norton's Union Intelligencer* (Dallas), March 29, 1873, p. 1; *Daily Democratic Statesman*

(Austin), March 20, 1873, p. 2; *DSJ*, March 17, 1873, p. 2; March 19, 1873, p. 2; "Report on the Condition of Affairs in Lampasas County, March 24, 1873," pp. 126–127; *LCT*, p. 24.

52. *Norton's Union Intelligencer* (Dallas), March 29, 1873, p. 1; *DSJ*, March 17, 1873, p. 2; March 19, 1873, p. 2.

53. FLB to EJD, March 24, 1873, pp. 196–201, AG LPB, "Roster of the State Police," pp. 316–317, AGR, ARIS/TSLAC; "Report on the Condition of Affairs in Lampasas County, March 24, 1873," pp. 126–127; *DSJ*, March 17, 1873, p. 2; March 26, 1873, p. 2; *Norton's Union Intelligencer* (Dallas), March 29, 1873, p. 1. The *San Antonio Daily Herald* called the Horrells and their hangers-on "a band of citizens" and stated that the reports came from a "portion of the police force engaged" in the altercation and thus "must be a one-sided" account. "No matter who was in fault, the whole thing is exceedingly unfortunate," the paper concluded, March 22, 1873, p. 4.

54. FLB to EJD, March 24, 1873, pp. 196–201, AG LPB; "Roster of the State Police," pp. 316–317, AGR, both in ARIS/TSLAC; "Report on the Condition of Affairs in Lampasas County, March 24, 1873," pp. 126–129; *DSJ*, March 26, 1873, p. 2; *Norton's Union Intelligencer* (Dallas), March 29, 1873, p. 1. The other members of the inquest group, along with Pratt, were G. T. Hill, W. J. Standerfer, R. W. Hill, Alexander J. Northington, W. W. East, and Louis Borho. They simply said that the policemen died by "gun and pistol shots."

55. Nichols Interview; *San Antonio Daily Herald*, March 25, 1873, p. 4; Gillett, *Six Years*, pp. 73–75; Sonnichsen, *I'll Die Before I'll Run*, p. 99.

56. FLB to Mrs. Marie E. Bates (Providence, RI), April 30, 1873, pp. 570–571, AG LPB, ARIS/TSLAC; *San Antonio Daily Herald*, March 25, 1873, p. 4; *LCT*, p. 24.

57. FLB to A. S. Kohner (Lampasas), April 10, 1873, p. 401; FLB to John Flattery (Galveston), April 21, 1873, p. 579; FLB to Mrs. Marie E. Bates (Providence, RI), April 30, 1873, pp. 570–571, all in AG LPB, ARIS/TSLAC; *San Antonio Daily Herald*, March 25, 1873, p. 4; *LCT*, p. 24. Interestingly enough, Britton admitted privately to A. S. Kohner that the "law does not make any provision for payment of such (medical) claims, and not having means at my command, I am unable to procure the services of a Physician here to visit Lampasas." Melville had pay amounting to $138 due him for services in the State Police. *San Antonio Daily Herald*, March 25, 1873, p. 4; *LCT*, p. 24. Even in death, the State Police created difficulties. The Lampasas County court agreed to pay the account of A. B. Hayunth & Brothers $9.90 for furnishing Melville with various items, but rejected requests by Doctors W. P. Beall and T. S. Denny for an additional sum for medical attendance upon Melville. If our calculations are correct, it cost the Lampasas citizens $963.40 for the Horrell/State Police imbroglio. The court petitioned the legislature for reimbursement as the expenses had all been incurred by the State Police; "Minutes of the Lampasas County Court," October 1, 1873, Vol. I, p. 5; January 28, 1874, p. 18; March Term 1874, pp. 28–29 (Lampasas County Courthouse).

58. FLB to EJD, "Report on the Condition of Affairs in Lampasas County, March 24, 1873", pp. 196–201, AG LPB, ARIS/TSLAC; *Report of the AG of the State of Texas For the Year 1873*, pp. 126–129; *Journal of the Senate, 13th Legislature* (Austin: John Cardwell, State Printer, 1873), March 25, 1873, pp. 351–355.

59. *DSJ*, March 19, 1873, p. 2; C. L. Douglas, *Famous Texas Feuds* (Dallas: The Turner Co., 1936), contended that when Britton appeared in Lampasas "he found plenty of help on hand. Even before his arrival two Minute Men companies had mobilized—the Lampasas County group under Lieutenant Lee, and the Burnet County organization under Sergeant W. H. Shelburne. In addition, Sheriff S. T. Denson had formed a small posse," p. 133.

60. William D. Shepherd (Chief Clerk, AG) to FLB (Lampasas), March 18, 1873, p. 144; March 21, 1873, p. 187; FLB to EJD, "Report on the Condition of Affairs in Lampasas County, March 24, 1873," pp. 196–201; FLB to Lieutenant Madison Wear (Lampasas), March 26, 1873, p. 237; March 28, 1873, p. 268; FLB to Private Rafael Martinez (Austin), March 27, 1873, p. 246; FLB to John Downey (Brenham), March 29, 1873, p. 280; FLB to G. A. Hall (Burton), March 29, 1873, p. 282, all in AG LPB, ARIS/TSLAC; *Report of the AG of the State of Texas for the Year 1873*, pp. 126–129; *DSJ*, March 22, 1873, p. 3.

61. FLB to John L. Peay (Sheriff, Williamson County), April 3, 1873, p. 339; FLB to Lieutenant John Alexander (Commander, Company O, Minute Men, Burnet), April 3, 1873, p. 331, both in AG LPB, ARIS/TSLAC.

62. *Lampasas Dispatch* quoted in *Houston Telegraph* (Daily Edition), March 15, 1873, p. 2.

63. EJD Proclamation, $3000 Reward, March 25, 1873, Executive Record, 1870–1873, p. 1,123, Secretary of State Records; FLB to S. T. Denson (Sheriff, Lampasas County), March 26, 1873, p. 242; FLB to R. W. Cates (Sheriff, Burnet County), March 26, 1873, p. 254; FLB to Redmon (Gainesville), April 10, 1873, p. 399, all in AG LPB, ARIS/TSLAC. State Police Captain A. C. Hill reported in early April that some of those who murdered Williams and his party still inhabited the brush and mountains around Stephenville (Erath County) and continued to "bid defiance to all authority." Hill to AG, April 2, 1873, p. 362, AG, LR, ARIS/TSLAC.

64. FLB to EJD, "Report on the Condition of Affairs in Lampasas County, March 24, 1873", pp. 126–129; *DSJ*, March 22, 1873, p. 3; March 26, 1873, p. 2; Rasch, "The Horrell War," p. 225.

65. *DSJ*, March 24, 1873, p. 2.

66. *Norton's Union Intelligencer* (Dallas), March 29, 1873, p. 1; *DSJ*, March 22, 1873, p. 3; *Daily Democratic Statesman* (Austin), March 23, 1873, p. 2; Rasch, "The Horrell War," p. 225. Later, Britton sent a four-dollar invoice of O. J. Murchison for feeding two mules used in bringing prisoners to Austin to Sheriff Denson as it was the county's responsibility. FLB to S. T. Denson (Sheriff, Lampasas County), April 9, 1873, p. 391, AG LPB, ARIS/TSLAC.

67. *DSJ*, March 24, 1873, p. 2.

68. *DSJ*, March 17, 1873, p. 2; April 10, 1873, p. 3; April 11, 1873, p. 3; April 12, 1873, p. 3; *Journal of the Senate*, March 25, 1873, p. 356; *Journal of the House of Representatives, 13th Legislature* (Austin: John Cardwell, State Printer, 1873), April 10, 1873, p. 596; Senate Bill No. 221, 13th Legislature, Regular Session, Records of the Legislature, ARIS/TSLAC.

69. *DSJ*, March 17, 1873, p. 2; *LCT*, p. 24.

70. *DSJ*, April 30, 1873, p. 2. Britton had sent at least one man to assist Sheriff Denson; FLB to Private Edward Labatte (Lampasas), April 12, 1873, p. 421, AG LPB, ARIS/TSLAC.

71. Rasch, "The Horrell War," pp. 226–227, 230; Sonnichsen, *I'll Die Before I'll Run*, pp. 100, 102–103.

72. *Daily State Gazette* (Austin), May 5, 1873, p. 2; *DSJ*, May 3, 1873, p. 2; *Weekly Democratic Statesman* (Austin), May 8, 1873, p. 2; Gillett, *Six Years*, pp. 110–111; Douglas, *Famous Texas Feuds*, p. 133.

73. *Daily State Gazette* (Austin), May 5, 1873, p. 2; *DSJ*, May 3, 1873, p. 2; *Weekly Democratic Statesman* (Austin), May 8, 1873, p. 2; Gillett, *Six Years*, pp. 110–111. On May 15, the *Weekly Democratic Statesman* (p. 1) reported that Martin (Mart) Horrell, the leader of the ' Lampasas raiders" who broke into the Georgetown jail, was dead, having died from wounds received on the night of the fracas. The *Daily State Gazette* (p. 2) noted on May 9 that they had been informed that William Horrell, one of the accused Lampasas murderers, died recently at Florence, from wounds received in making his escape during the Georgetown raid. "The ways of the transgressor are hard." A "sad chapter in the book of crime" in Texas, lamented the newspaper, and it was time the "volume was closed with some exemplary punishment, that will vindicate the integrity of the law and good name of the people." Both accounts are wrong about the death of a Horrell.

74. *Daily State Gazette* (Austin), May 5, 1873, p. 2.

75. *DSJ*, May 12, 1873, p. 2; July 28, 1873, p. 2. In late April, Adjutant General Britton informed Private John Downey, stationed in Brenham, and who had earlier been ordered to Lampasas, that it was not necessary for Downey to report to the town as it was "too late to be of service there." FLB to Downey, April 25, 1873, p. 478, AG LPB, ARIS/TSLAC.

76. Charles H. Porter (Lampasas) to EJD, July 6, 1873, GP (EJD), ARIS/TSLAC.

77. "A Subscriber" to Editor, *State Journal*, July 23, 1873, in *DSJ*, July 28, 1873, p. 2. The individual stated: "I am afraid to sign my name as my life would be greatly in danger."

78. Anonymous (Lampasas) to Edman [Edmund] Davis, July 30, 1873, GP (EJD), ARIS/TSLAC.

79. Military Rolls, AGR, ARIS/TSLAC; *Galveston Daily News*, September 14, 1873, p. 2; September 25, 1873, p. 2; October 5, 1873, p. 2. These stories were taken from the *Lampasas Dispatch*. On Sweet see Jeff Jackson, "Victim of Circumstance: Albertus Sweet Sheriff of Lampasas County, Texas, 1874–1878," *Quarterly of the*

National Association for Outlaw and Lawman History, Inc. 20 (July–September 1996), pp. 14, 16–21, hereafter cited as *NOLA*.

80. *Galveston Daily News*, September 25, 1873, p. 1, October 4, 1873, p. 1; October 5, 1873, p. 2; October 15, 1873, p. 1; *Lampasas Record*, June 29, 1933, p. 4.

81. *Lampasas Dispatch*, October 5, 1876, quoted in the *Houston Daily Telegram*, October 10, 1876, p. 3. The *Dispatch* also added that "many other circumstances and threats were proven which went to justify or mitigate the action" of the Horrells. (Actually, there was no one present to support the State Police version of the incident.) At last, the docket was clear of this disruption, which had "tended to keep up an anxiety and excitement all over the county." The *Dispatch* also noted that an 1875 killing by Charles Keith brought forth a verdict of second-degree murder. Keith was sentenced to ten years in the state penitentiary at Huntsville. "This is the first conviction for murder that has ever been had in this county since its organization, over twenty years ago," claimed the local newspaper, "although about fifty cases of murder have darkened the records of our court."

82. *Galveston Daily News*, October 10, 1876, p. 2; November 14, 1879, p. 4; Rasch, "The Horrell War," p. 231; Gillett, *Six Years*, pp. 112–113. Although he garbles the chronology, Sonnichsen, in *I'll Die Before I'll Run*, wrote that Merritt Horrell and Bill Bowen surrendered to answer charges for killing Williams. "Each was able to raise ten thousand dollars bond, so they must have had some pretty substantial friends," p. 104. There is no evidence that the bond was established at ten thousand. Sam Denson accosted Mart (who had been arrested in Clay County and returned to face charges before the district court) on a Lampasas street and pumped three bullets into him. Denson mounted his horse and escaped. *Galveston Daily News*, September 26, 1876, p. 2.

83. Sonnichsen, *I'll Die Before I'll Run*, pp. 100–109; Nichols Interview; Nolan, in *Bad Blood*, claimed that a "tradition maintains that one of the victims of the shootout in the saloon was related to the Higgins family and that the Horrell-Higgins feud began with that killing," p. 28; Jonnie Elzner, *Relighting Lamplights of Lampasas County, Texas* (Lampasas: Privately published, 1974), pp. 70–74. On Higgins see Bill O'Neal, *A Half Century of Violence in Texas: The Bloody Legacy of Pink Higgins* (Austin: Eakin Press, 1999); Jerry Sinise, *Pink Higgins, The Reluctant Gunfighter and Other Tales of the Panhandle* (Wichita Falls, TX: Nortex Press, 1973), pp. 23–43; Charles Adams Jones, "Pink Higgins, the Good Bad Man," *Atlantic Monthly* 154 (July 1934), pp. 79–89, which attempts to resuscitate Higgins's reputation but fails to do so. (He was an accomplished killer.) The dead man had been an innocent bystander.

84. Nichols Interview; Sonnichsen, *I'll Die Before I'll Run*, pp. 110–117; Sonnichsen, "Horrell-Higgins Feud," *NHT*, III, pp. 702–703; Gillett, *Six Years*, p. 117; *Lampasas Leader*, January 26, 1889, p. 1; "Elzner Notes," J. Evetts Haley Collection (Nita Stewart Haley Memorial Library, Midland, TX); Douglas, "Famous Texas Feuds," *Houston Press*, November 13, 1834, p. 1. Sonnichsen provides this

background: The Horrell brothers had been implicated in the robbery of a store and the murder of the storekeeper. A wounded horse had been traced to Mart's place, and one of their followers had turned state's evidence. Thus, they were imprisoned when shot down in cold blood, presumably by friends of the storekeeper, pp. 116–117. Dan W. Roberts wrote that the Horrells were put in jail about one hundred miles north of Lampasas and were safe as long as the Rangers were around. But when they left Lampasas, a mob organized, "overpowered the sheriff, entered the jail and shot the Horrel [sic] to death. The ugly crime was never righted by law." Dan W. Roberts, *Rangers and Sovereignty* (San Antonio: Wood Printing & Engraving Co., 1914), pp. 169–170. Of course, Roberts could have said the same thing about the killing of the four State Policemen. Jeff Jackson, in "Vigilantes: The End of the Horrell Brothers," *NOLA* 16 (April–June 1992), pp. 13–19, suggests, with much documentation, that the Horrell brothers may have been innocent of this particular murder, although the evidence is certainly murky; J. B. Cranfills, *Dr. J. B. Cranfills Chronicle: A Story of Life in Texas* (New York: Fleming H. Revell Company, 1916), pp. 221–228.

EPILOGUE

1. *Journal of the House of Representatives of the State of Texas: Being the Session of the Thirteenth Legislature Begun and Held at the City of Austin, January 14, 1873* (Austin: John Cardwell, State Printer, 1873), pp. 32–33.

2. Ibid., 33.

3. Ibid., 34.

4. *Senate Journal, 1873*, pp. 53, 59, 76, 84–85, 100, 114–115, 118–120, 125, 151–152, 164; *House Journal, 1873*, pp. 45, 55, 59, 68, 92–93, 97, 112.

5. *Senate Journal, 1873*, pp. 263–264, 273, 298–299; *House Journal, 1873*, pp. 190, 266, 330, 395, 405, 529; *DSJ*, February 10, 1873, p. 2.

6. *House Journal, 1873*, pp. 11, 55, 67, 92–93, 111, 143, 208–209, 466, 490, 640, 654; *Senate Journal, 1873*, pp. 56, 71, 84, 87, 91, 388–389, 392, 459, 463, 478, 497–498, 559, 568; *Daily Democratic Statesman* (Austin), March 30, 1873, p. 2.

7. EJD to M. D. K. Taylor (House Speaker), April 16, 1873, pp. 44–49, LPB GP (EJD); FLB to EJD, April 18, 1873, GP (EJD), both in ARIS/TSLAC; Also in *House Journal, 1873*, pp. 701–704.

8. Ibid.

9. Ibid. Davis also pointed out that in two counties the public records had been destroyed, in two others the courthouses burned, and finally, in another, the cattle record had been stolen.

10. Ibid.

11. Ibid.

12. Ibid.

13. *Daily Democratic Statesman* (Austin), March 30, 1873, p. 2; April 15, 1873, p. 2; April 20, 1873, p. 2; April 28, 1873, p. 2; *Senate Journal, 1873*, pp. 497, 568; *House Journal, 1873*, pp. 704–705.

14. *Houston Union* quoted in *DSJ*, March 19, 1871, p. 1.

15. Statistical data compiled by Erik Larson, Senior Programmer Analyst, Integral Systems, Incorporated, from information found in Texas State Police Rosters, ARIS/TSLAC.

16. *AG Report, 1872*, p. 12; *DSJ*, April 11, 1873, p. 2; Hardin, *The Life of John Wesley Hardin*, pp. 61–63; Marohn, *The Last Gunfighter*, pp. 28–29; EJD to J. B. Cope (JP, Bastrop), September 6, 1871, p. 225, LPB, GP EJD), ARIS/TSLAC; *Flake's Daily Bulletin*, March 3, 1871, p. 2; *Navasota Times* quoted in *Dallas Herald*, March 11, 1871, p. 1; May 27, 1871, p. 4; *DSJ*, December 14, 1872, p. 3. The myth persists that Hardin murdered two other black State Policemen, Green Paramore and John Lackey. They were, in fact, Special Policemen, not State Policemen; see Parsons and Little, *Captain L. H. McNelly*, p. 97. It is interesting to note that Hardin's brother, Joseph, briefly served in the State Police in the Erath County area; A. C. Hill (Captain) to AG, April 2, 1873, H-276, p. 362, Summary of Letters, AG LR, ARIS/TSLAC.

17. *San Antonio Herald* in *Flake's Daily Bulletin*, April 12, 1871, p. 5. The slaying of another horse thief is recounted in *Houston Daily Union*, November 21, 1870, p. 2.

18. *Daily Herald* (San Antonio), March 6, 1871, p. 2; *DSJ*, December 17, 1870, p. 2; December 20, 1870, p. 2; January 27, 1873, p. 2.

19. Z. Norton (Judge, 29th Judicial District) to EJD, December 16, 1871, GP (EJD), ARIS/TSLAC; James Smallwood, *The History of Smith County, Texas: Born in Dixie, Smith County Origins to 1875* (2 vols.; Austin: Eakin Press, 1999), I, pp. 299–300; *DSJ*, June 8, 1871, p. 1 (for earlier problems); *Daily Democratic Statesman* (Austin), April 15, 1873, p. 2. An older view is expressed in Sid S. Johnson, *Some Biographies of Old Settlers: Historical, Personal and Reminiscent* (Tyler: Sid S. Johnson, Publisher, 1909), pp. 319–322.

20. D. M. Prendergast to Editors *Statesman*, April 12, 1873, in *Daily Democratic Statesman* (Austin), April 15, 1873, p. 2.

21. EJD to Sergeant Green R. Cessna, July 31, 1871, p. 139; EJD to Judge F. P. Wood, September 8, 1871, p. 239, both in LPB, GP (EJD), ARIS/TSLAC; *DSJ*, September 23, 1870, p. 1; July 11, 1871, p. 2; *Flake's Daily Bulletin*, November 18, 1870, p. 1; July 22, 1871, p. 1; September 3, 1871, p. 2; September 15, 1871, p. 4; September 28, 1871, p. 4; *Houston Daily Telegraph*, September 19, 1871, p. 4.

22. *St. Louis Republican*, June 12, 1876, p. 4 (courtesy of Chuck Parsons).

23. Ibid.

Essay on Sources

Until Carl H. Moneyhon's *Texas After the Civil War: The Struggle of Reconstruction* appeared in 2004, twenty-first-century Texas had no objective general history of Reconstruction. Numerous theses, dissertations, monographs, and books produced over the past three decades attempted to explain various facets of the postwar experience, but none surveyed the composite picture. Three historiographical essays provided guidance: Edgar P. Sneed, "A Historiography of Reconstruction in Texas: Some Myths and Problems," *Southwestern Historical Quarterly* 72 (April 1969), pp. 435–448; Merline Pitre, "A Note on the Historiography of Blacks in the Reconstruction of Texas," *Journal of Negro History* 66 (Winter 1981), pp. 340–348; and Barry A. Crouch, "'Unmanacling' Texas Reconstruction: A Twenty-Year Perspective," *Southwestern Historical Quarterly* 93 (January 1990), pp. 275–302.

In addition, overviews in collected editions have furnished insight into Reconstruction Texas. Ralph A. Wooster, in "The Civil War and Reconstruction in Texas," which appeared in *A Guide to the History of Texas*, edited by Light Townsend Cummins and Alvin R. Bailey Jr. (New York: Greenwood Press, 1988), pp. 37–50, discusses considerable material but is not comprehensive. Randolph B. Campbell has attempted to interpret the Reconstruction era as part of a three-decade continuum, in "Statehood, Civil War, and Reconstruction, 1846–76," in *Texas Through Time: Evolving Interpretations*, edited by Walter L. Buenger and Robert A. Calvert (College Station: Texas A&M University Press, 1991), pp. 165–196.

Campbell has been a prolific Reconstruction scholar. His work *Grass-Roots Reconstruction in Texas, 1865–1876* (Baton Rouge: Louisiana State University Press, 1997), focuses upon six Texas counties (the essays previously appeared in different historical journals), attempting to explain Texas after the war. The State Police are only briefly mentioned. His accounts, however, of local personnel have supplied historians of Texas with valuable information about who appointed them and their background. Campbell's "Carpetbagger Rule in Reconstruction Texas: An Enduring Myth," *Southwestern Historical Quarterly* 97 (April 1994), pp. 587–596, convincingly demonstrates that this group of interlopers had minimal influence in postwar Texas.

Campbell's investigation of district judges and local politicos is also important for understanding the State Police and their activities. See especially "The District Judges of Texas in 1866–1867: An Episode in the Failure of Presidential Reconstruction," *Southwestern Historical Quarterly* 93 (January 1990), pp. 357–377; "Grass Roots Reconstruction: The Personnel of County Government in Texas, 1865–1876," *Journal of Southern History* 58 (February 1992), pp. 99–116; "A Moderate Response: The District Judges of Dallas County During Reconstruction, 1865–1876," *Legacies: A History Journal for Dallas and North Central Texas* 5 (1993), pp. 4–12; "Scalawag District Judges: The E. J. Davis Appointees," *Houston Review* 14 (1992), pp. 75–88.

A number of books have appeared about the Texas postwar experience. Dale Baum's *The Shattering of Texas Unionism: Politics in the Lone Star State During the Civil War Era* (Baton Rouge: Louisiana State University Press, 1998) devotes two chapters to Reconstruction: "From the Dollar Oath to Military Registration, 1865–1868" and "The Stillbirth of Two-Party Politics: The 1869 Gubernatorial Race." This contest is also detailed in "Chicanery and Intimidation in the 1869 Texas Gubernatorial Race," *Southwestern Historical Quarterly* 97 (July 1993), pp. 37–54. He also dissects the secession vote in "Pinpointing Apparent Fraud in the 1861 Texas Secession Referendum," *Journal of Interdisciplinary History* 22 (Autumn 1991), pp. 201–212.

It is important to provide background concerning the era which authors are writing about, but it must be said that few modern writers of Texas history have discussed the State Police. We have surveyed and used a vast number of sources in this study, in fact most of the unpublished and published works that have focused upon Texas Reconstruction, but our major concentration has been upon the manuscript material in the Texas State Archives and assorted local repositories. The papers relating to the State Police in these varied archives are incredible. Amazingly, these vast sources have remained relatively untouched by historians over the years. Obviously, they are the foundations of the current work.

A conventional bibliography would have served little purpose here. The preface delineates the State Police historiography and demands that a new milieu of Texas history during the immediate decade after the Civil War begin to take shape, preferably not in past norms. Therefore, this study has based its foundation, premise, and interpretation upon the vast array of original documents available. From the State Police records to the Chief of Police/Adjutant General Letterbooks (some thirteen or fourteen volumes of five hundred pages each), abundant and voluminous sources abound. In addition, it is futile to attempt to list all the information gleaned from the Adjutant General materials and the policemen themselves, because they are so extensive that their listing would be almost endless. The governors' records also provide a wonderful insight into the workings of the state Reconstruction government and activities of the State Police.

Although the notes to this work indicate some reliance upon secondary sources, particularly where county background is necessary and essential, we have also visited a number of the counties discussed in the text and have scoured their courthouses and local historical societies for additional information. The State Police, as earlier noted, have almost never received a "fair" hearing before the Texas historical board, and the precise reason for that evaluation is that previous investigators never bothered to mine the rich archives. The manuscript record relating to the State Police is momentous, varied, and surprisingly complete. This should not surprise anyone knowledgeable about the available sources for Reconstruction Texas.

In addition to primary materials, we have extensively canvassed the newspapers of Texas, both Democratic (conservative) and Republican (radical), to supplement the manuscript sources of the State Police. Although we attempted to be judicious in using papers of every political bent, the *Daily State Journal*, the administration's organ, consistently carried more information about the State Police and their activities, good and bad, than did any other newspaper. Moreover, the legislature published several investigations of the declaration of martial law in Hill and Walker counties. There are also published interviews of those involved in the Limestone/Freestone County imbroglio. Finally, we have included in the appendix a complete roster of State Police members.

Although until recently no modern study existed of how the Democrats/Conservatives responded to Reconstruction, and their abiding hatred of the State Police, a brilliant analysis of their attitudes and philosophy, which extends back into the Governor E. J. Davis era, is Patrick George Williams, "Redeemer Democrats and the Roots of Modern Texas, 1872–1884" (Ph.D. diss., Columbia University, 1996), and his *Beyond Redemption: Texas Democrats After Reconstruction* (College Station: Texas A&M University Press, 2007). Williams has dissected the contradictions among the Democrats of their disputes about homesteads, land, railroads, and, most of all, their desire to remove African Americans from Texas politics in a deft and searching manner. The Democrats opposed centralization in every manner as they demonstrated in their opposition to Davis and Republican philosophy.

Most historians of Texas have ignored the philosophical conundrum, but the point is that the practice of the state's prewar and postwar administration was to rely upon local or county administration. The Republicans realized this was not a healthy situation, that the diffusion of power among the county populace had created problems for the state ever since it had become a member of the United States. But this conflict between the two parties, whatever their origins before the war, continued into Reconstruction. The Democrats, of course, assumed direction shortly after the conflict and diffused power among the lower echelons (district, county, local, and precinct), but they adamantly refused to deal with violence on the basic level.

With Moneyhon's *Texas After the Civil War*, there now exists a survey of Reconstruction that places the Lone Star State among other Southern states that experienced the same process. Previously, overviews through county studies have been only marginally successful. Until the past three decades, most of the writings were favorable to the Democrats, or former Confederates, however one wants to define them. Unfortunately, this interpretation neglected what the Republicans attempted to do in establishing a different type of program that included everyone. Texas was a rather unique case. From the end of the war until the advent of Governor E. J. Davis's administration, initially the United States Army focused upon violence. With the election of James W. Throckmorton in 1866, internal conflict was ignored, with the focus on the frontier. Davis changed the emphasis of the state administration and concentrated on violence in the interior.

Appendix

ROSTER OF THE STATE POLICE

Information on the State Police roster includes the individual's name, rank, age, race, district, residence/post office address, commission, and remarks. Remarks include dates of commission, qualification, promotion, dismissal, discharge, resignation, reinstatement, and transfers. An asterisk (*) indicates that the information was taken from the 1870 U.S. census for Texas.

ABLE, LEVI (pvt.); 30*; W; Dist. 1; Lampasas; Corsicana; comm. 11/9/70; qual. 11/10/70; disc. 6/28/71; reinst. 9/1/71; dropped 9/1/71 did not report.

ADAMS, J. H. (sgt./lt.); 35; W; Dist. 7; Hempstead; comm. 12/5/72; qual. 12/5/72; prom. from sgt. 1/24/73.

ADAMS, WILEY (pvt.); 26*; B; Dist. 3; Carthage; comm. 9/11/71; qual. 9/11/71; disc. 11/10/71.

ADAMS, WILSON (pvt.); 28; W; Dist. 2/3; Troupe, Tyler, Smith Co.; comm. 4/13/71; qual. 5/5/71; disc. 6/27/71.

ADKINS, LECK; 24; W; Dist. 4; comm. 10/5/71; qual. 10/5/71; disc. 11/30/71.

ALBRICH, WILLIAM (pvt.); Dist. 1; comm. 7/11/70; comm. declined.

ALDERETTE, MARTIN C. (pvt.); 32; M; Dist. 5/Sub; Ysleta, Franklin P.O., El Paso Co.; comm. 3/20/71; qual. 4/8/71; disc. 6/27/71; reinst. 3/21/72.

ALEXANDER, E. M. (capt.); 37*; W; Dist. 2; Clarksville, Red River Co.; comm. 7/7/70; qual. 7/25/70; disc. 6/15/72; reinst. as lt. 8/1/72.

ALEXANDER, FRED (pvt.); W; Dist. 1; Waco, McLennan Co.; comm. 11/12/70; dismiss. 11/30/70.

ALEXANDER, JAMES (pvt.); Dist. 1; comm. 7/27/70; comm. never accepted; cancelled 11/15/70.

ALEXANDER, JOSEPH (pvt.); 40; W; Dist. 3; Homer; comm. 8/12/71; qual. 9/21/71; resign. 12/30/71.

ALEXANDER, SIMON (pvt.); B; Dist. 4; Austin; comm. 6/1/71; qual. 6/1/71.

ALLEN, CHARLES T. (pvt./sgt.); 23; W; Dist. 4; Cameron; comm. 6/16/71; qual. 6/16/71; disc. 6/28/71; reinst.; prom. to sgt. 8/1/71; disc. 10/3/71.

AMACKER, M. M. (pvt.); W; Dist. 2; Clarksville; comm. 6/10/71; qual. 6/10/71; disc. 6/28/71; reinst. 9/1/71; disc. 11/30/71.

AMASON, HIRAM (pvt.); 31; W; Dist. 3; Center; comm. 9/12/71; qual. 9/12/71; disc. 11/30/71.

ANDERSON, CALVIN (pvt.); B; Dist. 3; Calvert, Robertson Co.; comm. 8/1/70 [8/20/70]; comm. declined; dismiss. 3/1/71.

ANDERSON, COTTON; 24; B; Dist. 4; Marlin; comm. 7/15/70; qual. 7/21/70.

ANDERSON, E. M. (pvt.); B; Dist. 3/7; Montgomery, Montgomery Co.; comm. 10/6/70; qual. 10/6/70; resign. 9/30/71.

ANDERSON, GEORGE; Dist. 1; Dallas; comm. 6/13/71; cancelled 6/28/71 not qual. in time.

ANDERSON, S. A. (pvt.); W; Dist. 2; Jefferson; comm. 5/4/71; cannot qual.

ANDERSON, WILLIAM H. (pvt.); 30; W; Dist. 1; Dallas; comm. 5/24/71; qual. 5/24/71; disc. 9/30/72.

ANDREWS, G. R. (pvt.); 21; W; Dist. 4; Groesbeck; comm. 10/10/71; qual. 10/10/71; disc. 11/30/71.

ANGLER, J. C. (pvt.); 24; W; Dist. 4; Groesbeck; comm. 10/10/71; qual. 10/10/71; disc. 11/30/71.

ARCH, HENRY C.; B; Dist. 4; Webberville; comm. 10/30/72; qual. 10/30/72; disc. 12/14/72.

ARGENT, A. (pvt.); known service Sept. – Oct. 1872.

ARIAS, JULIAN [JULIEN] (pvt.); 48; M; Dist. 5/Sub; Socorro, El Paso Co.; comm. 7/7/70; qual. 7/25/70; disc. 8/25/71; reinst. 9/19/71; disc. 11/30/71.

ARMSTRONG, E. P. (pvt.); Dist. 6; Giddings; qual. 7/9/72; disc. 10/5/72 [Rio Grande Expedition].

ARMSTRONG, GEORGE (pvt.); W; Dist. 2; Paris; comm. 8/5/71; qual. 8/17/71; disc. 2/15/72.

ARMSTRONG, J. W.; 34; W; Dist. 4; Comanche; comm. 11/27/72; qual. 11/27/72.

ARMSTRONG, JAMES L. (pvt.); 31; Dist. 1; Hog Eye, Bastrop Co.; comm. 8/9/70; resign. 8/24/70.

ARNEL, M. (pvt.); Dist. 6; Giddings; qual. 7/9/72; disc. 10/5/72 [Rio Grande Expedition].

ARNOLD, LEWIS T. (pvt.); W; Dist. 4; Circleville; comm. 6/16/71; qual. 6/16/71; disc. 10/21/71; trans. to Bell Co.

ARWARK, JOHN (pvt.); W; Dist. 1; Waco, McLennan Co.; comm. 2/4/71; disc. 4/21/71.

ARWINE, DANIEL (pvt.); 41; W; Dist. 1; Fort Worth; comm. 8/29/71; qual. 8/29/71; disc. 10/31/71; reinst. 5/20/72.

ATKINS, JOHN L.; Dist. 5; San Elizario; comm. 3/18/72; qual. 4/1/72; disc. 10/25/72; re-comm. 1/4/73.

ATKINS, P. B. (pvt.); Dist. 3; qual. 10/14/71; disc. 11/30/71.

ATKINSON, JOHN G. (lt.); known service Apr. – Sept. 1872.

AUSTIN [ALLISTER], WILLIAM (pvt.); 24; B; Dist. 3; Crockett; comm. 9/11/71; qual. 9/22/71; disc. 11/30/71.

AYNESWORTH, A. F. (pvt.); 27*; W; Dist. 1; Austin; comm. 1/23/71; revoked 2/18/71.

AYNESWORTH [AINESWORTH], G. L. (pvt.); W; Dist. 1; Austin; comm. 1/23/71; special comm.; revoked 2/18/71.

BABB, JOHN S. (pvt.); 52*; W; Dist. 1; Decatur; comm. 11/20/71; qual. 11/20/71; disc.
7/31/72.

BADER, FREDERICK (pvt./sgt.); 26*; W; Dist. 1/5; San Antonio; comm. 7/26/70;
qual. 8/4/70; prom. to sgt. 12/1/70; prom. from sgt. 9/21/72 [11/2/72].

BAGBY, W. H. (pvt.); 21; W; Dist. 2; Clarksville; comm. 8/12/71; qual. 9/18/71; disc.
11/30/71.

BAILEY, F. M.; 26; Dist. 1; Decatur; comm. 10/20/71; qual. 10/20/71; unauthorized &
not sustained. Appt. by A. C. Hill.

BAINS, W. W. (pvt.); W; Dist. 3; Pittsville, Fort Bend Co.; comm. 9/1/70 (special
appt.); special instructions; revoked 11/5/70.

BAKER, ALDEN H. (pvt.); 24; W*; Dist. 4; Indianola, Calhoun Co.; comm. 8/12/70;
declined 9/20/70; cannot take oath.

BAKER, DAVID P. (pvt.); 24; W; Dist. 6; comm. 11/27/71; qual. 1/12/72.

BAKER, MILTON A. (pvt.); 28*; B*; Dist. 3; Houston, Harris Co.; comm. 8/9/70;
dismiss. 9/22/70 for disobedience of orders.

BAKER, O. B. (pvt.); Dist. 2; Red River Co.; comm. 7/22/70; comm. declined 8/12/70.

BAKER, WILLIAM H. (sgt./lt.); 25; W; Dist. 1/4/6; Lockhart, Caldwell Co.; Rockport,
Refugio Co.; comm. 7/7/70; trans. to 4th Dist; qual. 7/9/70; resign. 12/6/70; reinst.
2/13/71 [2/14/71] without loss of pay; prom. from sgt. 5/1/71; dismiss. 12/17/71; reinst.
2/1/72 for special duty for 2 months.

BALDWIN, JACOB H. (pvt.); 25; W*; Dist. 4; Columbus, Colorado Co.; comm.
7/23/70; dismiss. 10/3/70.

BALLANTINE, GEORGE W. (lt./capt.); 29*; W; Dist. 4/6; Waco; Brownsville;
comm. 6/1/71; qual. 6/1/71; prom. to capt. 7/17/71 [7/19/71]; trans. to Brownsville,
Cameron Co.; disc. 3/15/72.

BALLARD, JOHN (pvt.); B; Dist. 2; Jefferson; comm. 9/11/71; qual. 9/11/71; resign.
11/12/71.

BARCENA, PRIMITIVO (pvt.); 26; M; Dist. 6; Brownsville; comm. 11/25/72; qual.
11/25/72.

BARKER, CHARLES (pvt.); 24; W*; Dist. 1; Waco; Travis Co.; comm. 7/12/70; dismiss. 11/5/70 for disobedience of orders.

BARNETT, GRANSON (pvt.); 30; B; Dist. 1; Dresden; comm. 8/25/71; qual. 8/25/71;
disc. 11/10/71 by A. L. Edward.

BARRERO, E.; 28; W; Dist. 6; Conception; comm. 9/23/72; qual. 9/23/72.

BARRETT, ANDREW (pvt.); Dist. 1; comm. 8/18/71; qual. 8/18/71; disc. 10/9/71 by G.
W. Smith for inefficiency.

BARROW, M. J. (pvt.); Dist. 3; Hempstead, Austin Co.; comm. 8/20/70; appt. cancelled 11/15/70; never accepted.

BARTHOLM, A. J.; Dist. 6; Brownsville; comm. 10/16/72; qual. 10/16/72; resign.
11/15/72.

BASTIAN, HENRY (pvt./sgt.); 25 [20]; W; Dist. 1/4; Austin; comm. 11/5/70; qual.
11/5/70; disc. 6/30/72; qual. 12/9/72; prom. to sgt. 2/1/73; resign. 3/6/73.

BAWCOM, J. C. (pvt.); 38; W; Dist. 5; Burnet; comm. 6/5/72; qual. 6/26/72; resign. 2/28/73.

BEAKLEY, JEHU; Mountain City; comm. 4/6/72; qual. 4/6/72; resign. 1/6/73.

BEAKLEY, WRIGHT; 22*; W; Mountain City; comm. 8/18/72; qual. 8/18/72; dropped from rolls 2/28/73.

BEAMAN, CHARLES (pvt.); W; Dist. 4; Austin; comm. 11/27/71; qual. 11/27/71; disc. 8/31/72.

BECK, J. C. (pvt.); Dist. 6; San Antonio; qual. 7/15/72; disc. 8/31/72 [Rio Grande Expedition].

BEDELL, B. E. (pvt.); Dist. 6; Hempstead; qual. 6/4/72; disc. 9/30/72 [Rio Grande Expedition].

BELL, C. L. (pvt.); Dist. 6/4; Brenham; qual. 6/29/72; disc. 10/5/72; re-comm. 11/16/72; dismiss. 3/12/73 [Rio Grande Expedition].

BELL, CALVIN; 46*; B*; Dist. 6; Albuquerque; comm. 6/1/72; declined.

BELL, GENERAL (pvt.); 29; B; Dist. 1; Waco, McLennan Co.; comm. 7/26/70; killed 2/71 while on duty.

BELL, WILLIAM; Dist. 6; Eagle Pass; comm. 3/19/73; qual.

BENNETT, J. A. N. (pvt.); 25; W; Dist. 2; Quitman; comm. 9/22/71; qual. 9/22/71; disc. 11/1/71.

BENNETT, O. H. (pvt.); 50; Dist. 4; Yorktown, DeWitt Co.; comm. 7/26/70; disc. 10/1/70; reinst. 12/30/70; disc. 3/14/71.

BERRY JOHN F. (pvt.); 21; W*; Dist. 2; Boston; qual. 9/4/71; resign. 9/1/72.

BESSERER, WILLIAM (pvt.); 19; W; Dist. 1; Austin; comm. 9/3/70; disc. 3/18/71.

BIDDY, JASPER; Dist. 6; Edinburg; comm. 10/24/72; qual. 10/24/72.

BIGAR, ISOM (pvt.); 25; B; Dist. 3; Shelbyville; comm. 9/20/71; qual. 9/20/71; disc. 10/31/71.

BILLINGSLEY, W. B. (pvt.); 54; Dist. 1; Bastrop; comm. 8/1/70; appt. revoked 12/28/70.

BILLSON, WILLIAM (pvt.); W; Dist. 1; Austin, Travis Co.; comm. 7/15/70; dismiss. 10/20/70.

BIRDSELL, L. (pvt.); W; Dist. 1; Fredericksburg, Gillespie Co.; comm. 11/12/70; dismiss. 2/6/71; reinst. 2/14/71; disc. 3/29/71.

BIRMINGHAM, EDWARD (pvt.); 26; W; Dist. 2; Paris, Lamar Co.; comm. 4/20/71; qual. 5/10/71; disc. 5/31/71.

BLACK, CLEM (pvt.); B; Dist. 3; Carthage; comm. 9/11/71; qual. 9/11/71; disc. 11/15/71.

BLACK, W. W. (pvt.); 41; W; Dist. 5/4; Lodi, Sutherland Springs, Wilson Co.; comm. 7/23/70; qual. 8/4/70; disc. 4/19/71; reinst.; disc. 4/30/72.

BLACKSHER, W. R. (pvt.); Dist. 3; comm. 9/9/71; qual. 9/9/71; disc. 10/12/71.

BLAKELY, THOMS M. (pvt.); 34; W; Dist. 4/7; Richmond; Austin [mistake – belongs to Wharton Co.]; comm. 8/8/71; qual. 9/16/71; disc. 11/30/71; trans. to Fort Bend Co.

BLOOD, C. D. (pvt.); Dist. 1; Denton; comm. 8/18/71; qual. 8/18/71; disc. 9/30/72.

BLUMENTRITT, LOUIS (pvt.); 31; W; Dist. 4; Austin; comm. 9/16/72; qual. 9/16/72; dismiss. 3/24/73 with loss of all pay.

BOID, ELBERT (pvt.); Dist. 3; comm. 9/15/71; qual. 9/15/71; disc. 11/30/71.

BOLDRIDGE, BEN F. (sgt.); 31*; W; Dist. 4/7; Huntsville; Millican, Brazos Co.; comm. 7/13/70; qual. 7/13/70; resign. 3/72.

BOLT, JOHN C.; W; Dist. 4/5; Austin; San Antonio; comm. 6/6/71; qual. 6/6/71; trans. to Bexar Co. [clerk]; disc. 6/28/71.

BOND, JOSEPH F. (pvt.); 29; W; Dist. 1/4; Lampasas, Lampasas Co.; comm. 9/22/70; qual. 9/22/70; disc. 6/28/71; reinst. 9/1/71; disc. 9/1/71.

BOND, VIRGIL A. (sgt.); 29; Dist. 2; McKinney, Collin Co.; comm. 7/11/70; dismiss. 10/27/70 for drunkenness.

BONN, FREDERICK A.; 25; W; Dist. 6; Corpus Christi; comm. 8/10/71; qual. 8/17/71; disc. 10/14/71.

BONNET, J. W. (pvt.); known service Mar. – Apr. 21, 1873.

BONNET, WILLIAM (pvt.); 24; W; Dist. 5; San Antonio; comm. 8/28/72; qual. 9/10/72.

BOOKMAN, A. W. (pvt.); 30; B; Dist. 3/7; Courtney, Grimes Co.; comm. 4/24/71; qual. 4/29/71; disc. 10/14/71.

BOONE, B. H.; 33*; W; Dist. 7; Wharton; comm. 8/1/71; qual. 8/12/71; dismiss. 9/9/71.

BOOTHE, HENRY [see LEFTAGE, HENRY] (pvt.); B; Dist. 4; Hochheim; comm. 8/20/70; disc. 10/1/70; disc. annulled; disc. 1/11/71; reinst. 1/11/71.

BOOTHE, ZACHARIAH (pvt.); Dist. 3; comm. 8/1/70; appt. cancelled – never accepted.

BORHAS, CHARLES (pvt.); 36; W; Dist. 5; San Antonio; comm. 5/23/71; qual. 5/30/71; disc. 12/20/71.

BORNEFELD, J[ULIUS] A. (pvt.); 26; W; Dist. 6; Victoria; comm. 8/22/72; qual. 9/3/72; disc. 10/31/72.

BOSTICK, JOHN H. (pvt.); 29; Dist. 3; Palestine, Anderson Co.; comm. 7/16/70; re-sign. 11/31/70.

BOWERS, WINN (pvt./lt.); 40; B; Dist. 2; Clarksville, Red River Co.; comm. 7/7/70; qual. 7/23/70; dismiss. 1/9/71; reinst. as pvt. 8/3/71 [8/1/71]; disc. 11/30/71.

BOYD, W. T. (pvt.); 28*; W; Dist. 4; Austin; comm. 6/1/71; qual. 6/1/71; disc. 6/30/71 [clerk].

BOYLES, W. P. (pvt.); Dist. 3; Bryan, Brazos Co.; comm. 11/9/70; appt. cancelled 12/28/70.

BOYNTON, G. S. (pvt.); 34; Dist. 2; Corsicana, Navarro Co.; comm. 8/5/70; dismiss. 2/6/71; comm. returned 2/24/71.

BOZARTH, J. J. (pvt.); 25; W; Dist. 4/6; comm. 2/22/72; qual. 2/22/72; disc. 8/12/72; reinst.; resign. 9/18/72.

BOZARTH, J. T. (pvt.); Dist. 6; Giddings; qual. 6/27/72; disc. 8/12/72; reinst.; disc. 10/5/72 [Rio Grande Expedition].

BRADLEY, F. H. (pvt.); W; Dist. 2/4; Paris; Austin; comm. 8/7/71; qual. 8/7/71; trans. to Lamar Co.

BRADY, E. W. (lt.); W; Dist. 2; Paris; comm. 7/1/71; qual. 7/1/71; resign. 1/6/72; re-appt. 3/1/73.

BRADY, T. H. (pvt.); W; Dist. 5; San Antonio; comm. 6/8/71; qual. 6/8/71; disc. 6/28/71.

BRANTLEY, G. A.; 27; Dist. 1; Dallas; comm. 9/29/71; qual. 9/29/71; disc. 7/31/72.

BRANTLEY, JOHN L. (pvt.); W; Dist. 3/2; Athens, Henderson Co.; comm. 8/6/70; qual. 8/15/70; resign. 8/13/71.

BRENTANO, C. B. (pvt.); W; Dist. 2; Jefferson; qual. 8/15/71; dropped – never reported.

BRIDGES, M. V. (pvt.); 30; W; Dist. 1/4/5; Ft. Mason; Ledbetter; comm. 5/2/71; qual. 5/9/71; disc. 6/28/71.

BRIGGS, EDWARD W. (pvt.); W; Dist. 4/1; Waco, McLennan Co.; comm. 1/12/71; qual. 1/13/71; killed 5/71.

BROWN, A. C. (pvt.); 21; W; Dist. 1; Denton; comm. 11/25/71; qual. 11/25/71.

BROWN, F. M.; 24; W; Dist. 4; Comanche; comm. 11/28/71; qual. 11/28/71.

BROWN, JAMES M. (pvt.); W; Dist. 4; Giddings; comm. 8/18/72; qual. 8/18/72; dismiss. 3/8/73.

BROWN, JOEL; Dist. 3; Center, Shelby Co.; comm. 4/26/71; removed from state.

BROWN, R. C. (pvt.); Dist. 6; Fayetteville; qual. 7/4/72; disc. 10/5/72 [Rio Grande Expedition].

BROWN, THOMAS J. (pvt.); 37; B; Dist. 2/3; Marshall, Harrison Co.; comm. 3/21/71; 8/12/71; cancelled 6/14/71 – never having qual.; qual. 9/13/71; disc. 12/20/71.

BROWN, WILLIAM (pvt.); W; Dist. 4; Mountain City; comm. 8/18/72; qual. 8/18/72.

BROWNE, H. M. (pvt./sgt.); W; Dist. 4/6/7; Hallettsville, Lavaca Co.; Texana; comm. 10/1/70; qual. 19/3/70; promoted from pvt. 4/1/71; disc. 4/30/71 [disc. annulled]; reinst.; trans. to Jackson Co. 5/15/71; disc. 1/15/72.

BROWNING, JAMES T. (pvt./sgt.); W; Dist. 3/7; Hempstead, Austin Co.; comm. 8/20/70; qual. 9/1/70; prom. to sgt. 12/1/70; resign. 2/14/71; reinst. verbally by J. D.; resign. 12/23/71.

BRUCE, W. E. (pvt.); Dist. 4; Comanche; comm. 12/10/72; qual.

BRUMLY, J. S.; 34; W; Dist. 1; Stephenville; comm. 11/27/72; qual. 11/27/72.

BRYAN, JAMES D. (pvt.); 24; W; Dist. 1; Austin, Travis Co.; comm. 9/22/70; dismiss. 9/30/70.

BUASS [BUAAS], JOHN L.; 52*; W; Dist. 4; Austin; comm. 9/1/72; qual. 9/1/72; disc. 11/13/72.

BUCKELEW, P. W. (pvt.); Dist. 3; Brenham; comm. 7/15/70; resign. 4/1/71.

BUCKLEY, B.; Dist. 5; San Antonio; comm. 2/19/73; qual. 3/10/73.

BUCKMASTER, SAM A. (pvt.); Dist. 2; McKinney, Collin Co.; Greenville, Hunt Co.; comm. 9/6/70; appt. cancelled 11/15/70 – never having accepted.

BURKE, CHARLES A. (pvt./sgt.); W; Dist. 1/4; Austin; comm. 1/18/71; qual. 1/18/71; promoted from pvt. 4/1/71; dropped.

BURKE, WILLIAM (sgt./lt.); 33; W; Dist. 4/6; Brownsville, Cameron Co.; comm. 8/11/70; qual. 9/1/70; promoted from sgt. 5/1/71.

BURKHART, ALEX C. (pvt.); 39; W; Dist. 7; Matagorda; comm. 4/18/72; qual. 4/27/72; disc. 9/7/72.

BURLAND, D.; 26; W; Dist. 4; Austin; comm. 2/12/73; qual. 2/12/73.

BURLESON, A. B. (sgt.); W; Dist. 4; Austin; comm. 7/1/72; qual. 7/1/72.

BURLESON, JOHN C.; W; Dist. 4; Austin; comm. 8/12/72; cannot qualify.

BURNES, S. D.; Dist. 7; Dodge Station; comm. 1/17/73; qual. 2/3/73.

BURNS, PETER (pvt.); 26; W*; Dist. 3; Galveston; comm. 7/23/70; comm. cancelled 11/15/70.

BURNS, T. A. (pvt.); 33; W*; Dist. 1; McCulloch Co.; Ft. Mason; Lockhart, Caldwell Co.; comm. 8/8/70; resign. 4/7/71.

BURNS, T. W.; Dist. 3; comm. 11/12/70; never reported; cancelled.

BUSBY, C. V. (pvt.); 26; W; Dist. 4/6; Goliad, Goliad Co.; comm. 8/13/70; qual. 8/13/70; resign. 4/30/72.

BUSBY, NATHAN (pvt.); Dist. 4; comm. 1/20/72; qual. 2/3/72; dropped from rolls 2/28/73.

BUSCH, LOUIS A. (pvt.); 31; W; Dist. 6; Indianola; comm. 8/22/72; qual. 8/29/72; dismiss. 9/21/72; reinst.; disc. 10/31/72.

BUSHCHICK, HUGO (pvt.); 41*; W; Dist. 4/6; Clinton, DeWitt Co.; comm. 1/25/71; qual. 2/21/71; disc. 11/30/71.

BUTLER, JOHN (pvt.); B; Dist. 1

BUTLER, JOHN (2nd) (pvt.); B; Dist. 4; Austin; comm. 5/10/71; qual. 5/10/71; disc. 7/31/71.

BUTLER, JOHN (pvt.); W; Dist. 2; Marshall, Harrison Co.; comm. 3/22/71; dismiss. 4/21/71.

BUTLER, LEANDER G. (pvt.); 38; W; Dist. 6; Oakville; comm. 5/12/71; qual. 5/22/71; disc. 6/24/71.

CABARSER [CABASOS], CHRISTOPHER (pvt.); 24; Dist. 6; Albuquerque; comm. 7/6/72; disc. 9/30/72.

CAMERON, LAWSON R. (pvt.); 53*; W*; Dist. 3/8; Jasper Co.; comm. 8/1/70; resign. 5/18/71.

CAMPBELL, COLIN (sgt./lt.); 44; W; Dist. 4/6; Helena, Karnes Co.; comm. 12/17/70; qual. 12/17/70; resign.; reinst. 2/14/71; leave of absence 7/1 to 8/31/71; resign. 10/31/71.

CAMPBELL, G. W. (pvt.); 38; Dist. 1/2; Bastrop; comm. 7/12/70; trans. to 2nd Dist. (Weatherford, Parker Co.); dismiss. 10/12/70 for not obeying orders to proceed to Weatherford on 10/27/70.

CANFIELD, W. S. (pvt.); W; Dist. 2.

CANNEDY, D. D. (pvt.); Dist. 2; McKinney, Collin Co.; Greenville, Hunt Co.; comm. 9/6/70; dismiss. 9/12/71.

CANNON, GEORGE (pvt.); W; Dist. 1; comm. 7/23/70; comm. uncalled for and cancelled 9/22/70.

CANO, E. (pvt.); W; Dist. 6; Uvalde, Uvalde Co.; comm. 2/3/71; qual. 2/3/71; disc. 12/15/71.

CANON, GEORGE (pvt.); 26; B; Dist. 1/4; Belton; Austin; comm. 5/10/70 [1/1/71] [comm. revoked 1/15/71]; qual. 5/10/71; trans. to Bell Co.; returned to Austin; disc. 10/24/71.

CARLISLE, C. C. (pvt.); Dist. 1; comm. 7/23/70; comm. uncalled for and cancelled 9/22/70.

CARO, M. S.; Dist. 6; Rio Grande City; comm. 10/25/72; qual. 10/25/72; resign. 1/28/73.

CARR, JAMES A. (sgt.); 31 [41]; Dist. 4; Laredo, Webb Co.; comm. 8/11/70; resign. 1/9/71.

CARREON, JUAN JOSE (pvt.); 37; M; Dist. Sub/5; El Paso, San Elizario, El Paso Co.; comm. 1/23/71; qual. 2/7/71; disc. 8/25/71.

CARROLL, A. D. (pvt.); W; Dist. 4; comm. 1/1/71.

CARROLL, ROBERT (pvt.); B; Dist. 3; disc. 10/31/71; appt. by Capt. Farrow; no oath; no comm.

CARROLL, W. C. (sgt.); W; Dist. 2; Clarksville, Red River Co.; comm. 9/6/70; declined 9/22/70.

CARSON, THOMAS; W; Dist. 1; Corsicana; comm. 8/5/72; qual. 8/5/72; disc. 10/5/72.

CARTER, J. Q. A. (pvt.); 42; W; Dist. 1; Red River City [Grayson Co.]; comm. 9/21/71; qual. 9/27/71; disc. 1/23/73.

CARTER, REUBEN (pvt.); 23*; B*; Dist. 3; Austin Co.; comm. 7/15/70; resign. 4/1/71.

CASANOVA, JESUS J. (pvt.); 27*; M; Dist. 5; qual. 12/23/72.

CASTELLO [COSTELLO], RICHARD (pvt.); Dist. 4/1; Waco; comm. 12/21/70; qual. 12/21/70; disc. 7/20/71; reinst. 8/1/71; disc. 1/31/72.

CASWELL, C. B. (pvt.); 32; W; Dist. 6; Goliad; comm. 9/21/72; qual. 10/1/72; disc. 2/28/73.

CATLIN, J. H. (pvt.); 25; W; Dist. 3; Travis, Austin Co.; comm. 7/15/70; dismiss. 12/29/70.

CAVALLO, PEDRO (pvt.); Dist. 1; San Antonio; comm. 7/26/70; resign. 8/26/70.

CESSNA, GREEN K. (pvt./sgt.); 31; W; Dist. 3/8; Sandy Point, Brazoria Co.; Liberty; comm. 10/11/70; qual. 10/18/70; promoted to sgt. 2/14/71; disc. 7/14/71.

CHALMERS, ALEXANDER; B; Dist 4; Austin; comm. 3/18/73; qual. 3/18/73.

CHAPMAN, J. S. (pvt.); Dist. 6; Hempstead; qual. 6/4/72; disc. 10/5/72 [Rio Grande Expedition].

CHERRY, WESLEY (pvt.); 33*; W; Dist. 4; Austin; comm. 1/29/73; qual. 1/29/73; To draw pay from 1/15/73; Commenced service at that date and subsequently commissioned and qualified. Killed at Lampasas 3/14/73.

CHURCH, FRANCIS H. (pvt.); W; Dist. 4; Bryan; comm. 8/12/71; qual. 8/17/71.

CLARDY, U. P.; W; Dist. 4; Mountain City; comm. 8/20/71; qual. 8/20/71; disc. 10/22/71.

CLARK, F. H.; 33; W; Dist. 6; Banquete; comm. 9/14/72; qual. 9/14/72.

CLARK, V. J.; 32; W; Dist. 6; Corpus Christi; comm. 9/14/72; qual. 9/14/72; disc. 12/15/72.

CLARK, WRIGHT (pvt.); 28; Dist. 2; Sulphur Springs; comm. 9/4/71; qual. 9/4/71; resign. 4/30/72.

CLEWIS, LEWIS (pvt.); 40; W; Dist. 2; Emory, Rains Co.; comm. 1/10/71; qual. 2/15/71; resign. 11/30/71; reinst. 4/15/72.

CLINTON, JOHN (sgt.); Dist. 1; New Braunfels; comm. 7/26/70; comm. declined 8/13/70.

CLOUGH, JUDSON (pvt.); Dist. 3; Lookout, Madison Co.; comm. 11/12/70; dismiss. by letter 2/1/71.

COFFEY, H. H. (pvt.); 21; W; Dist. 2; Sulphur Springs; comm. 6/6/72; qual. 6/6/72; resign. 2/12/73.

COFFEY, JOHN S. (pvt./lt.); 24; W; Dist. 2/1; Bright Star, Hopkins Co.; McKinney; comm. 7/11/70; qual. 8/1/70; comm. declined; promoted to lt. 11/1/70 [10/28/70]; dismissed 2/1/71 [2/24/71] for disobedience of orders; reinst. 3/13/71; dismiss. 9/15/72.

COFFEY, THOMAS J. (pvt.); 31; W*; Dist. 2; Daingerfield, Titus Co.; comm. 7/12/70; resign. 10/31/70.

COLE, BENJAMIN; 22*; B*; Dist. 8; Cold Spring; comm. 10/15/72; qual. 10/29/72.

COLLINS, C. C.; Dist. 3; Homer; Appt. by Farrow without oath; no comm. received; disc. 10/31/71.

COLLINS, JOHN (pvt.); 54; B; Dist. 2/4; Hempstead, Austin Co.; comm. 7/9/70 [declined on account of agent].

CONNALLY [CONLEY], JAMES (pvt.); W; Dist. 4/6; Uvalde, Uvalde Co.; comm. 2/3/71; qual. 2/3/71; dismiss. 7/5/71.

COOK, C. C. (pvt.); 40*; W*; Dist. 3; Middleton, Leon Co.; comm. 8/9/70; comm. revoked 1/4/71.

COOK, JOHN; W; Dist. 4; Austin; comm. 8/4/71; appt. cancelled.

COOPER, ISAIAH; Dist. 1; Corsicana; comm. 3/12/73; qual. 3/12/73; disc. 3/25/73.

COOPER, THOMAS (pvt.); 27; B; Dist. 2; Jefferson; comm. 8/23/72; qual. 9/11/72; disc. 12/9/72.

COOPER, WILLIAM (pvt.); 32; B; Dist. 3; Wallisville, Chambers Co.; comm. 7/9/70; qual. 7/28/70; dismiss. 5/17/71.

COTTON, ANDERSON (pvt.); 24; B; Dist. 1; Waco; Marlin (Rock Dam), Falls Co.; comm. 7/16/70 [7/15/70].

COUILLARD, ANTOINE (pvt.); 31; W; Dist. 1; Waco; comm. 7/18/70; comm. cancelled 8/6/70.

COWLING, JAMES (pvt.); W; Dist. 4; Austin; comm. 6/13/71; qual. 6/13/71; dropped to date 8/31/71.

COX, FRANK (pvt.); 25; B; Dist. 1; Hillsboro; comm. 8/25/71; qual. 8/25/71; disc. 10/7/71 by W. Smith for inefficiency.

COX, J. W. (pvt.); 47; W*; Dist. 4; Clinton, DeWitt Co.; comm. 7/13/70; removed 2/13/71.

COX, TALBOT (pvt.); B; Dist. 2/4; Bryan; Clarksville, Red River Co.; comm. 8/5/70; 8/10/71; comm. uncalled for and cancelled 9/22/70; qual. 8/15/71; disc. 12/15/71.

CRAMER, THEODORE E. (pvt.); 37; W; Dist. 1; Lockhart, Caldwell Co.; comm. 8/2/70; resign. 9/30/70 (verbally); comm. returned 10/8/70.

CREARY, ED (lt.); W; Dist. 7; Houston; comm. 9/4/72; qual. 9/4/72; resign. 1/9/73.

CROOM, SHADE (pvt.); 36*; B*; Dist. 2; Fort Bend Co.; comm. 8/9/70; comm. uncalled for and cancelled 9/22/70.

CROSBY, W. L. (pvt.); W; Dist. 4; Austin; comm. 12/12/71; qual. 12/12/71; resign. 1/16/72.

CROSS, HAYWOOD (pvt.); 35*; B; Dist. 1; Seguin, Guadalupe Co.; comm. 7/27/70; dismiss. 8/18/70 for horse stealing.

CROWDER, J. A. (pvt.); 23; W; Dist. 2; Bright Star, Hopkins Co.; comm. 8/9/70; qual. 8/30/70; resign. 1/3/72.

CROWSON, T. J. (pvt.); W; Dist. 4; Bryan; comm. 9/15/71; qual. 9/15/71; disc. 12/15/71.

CUELLAR, FRANCISCO (pvt.); 57; Dist. 4; Carrizo, Zapata Co.; comm. 7/11/70; dismiss. 11/30/70.

CUNEY, N. W. (lt.); Dist. 3; Bryan, Brazos Co.; comm. 7/8/70; appt. declined.

CUNEY, PHILLIP M. (pvt.); 27; W; Dist. 3/7; Iron's Creek, Austin Co.; comm. 1/20/71; qual. 2/10/71; disc. 5/17/71.

CURRAN, WILLIAM (pvt./sgt.); W; Dist. 1/4; Austin; Giddings; comm. 3/1/71; qual. 3/1/71; promoted to sgt. 3/1/71; dismiss. 7/17/71; reinst.; dismiss. 8/17/71; reinst. 8/1/72; resign. 8/31/72.

CUSACK, FRANCIS (lt./capt.); W; Dist. 2; Jefferson; comm. 5/1/72; qual. 5/1/72; resign. 4/7/73.

DAFFAN, JOHN; 23; W; Dist. 3; Brenham; comm. 2/19/72; H & TC RR.

DAFFIN, L. A.; 26; W; Dist. 3; Giddings; comm. 4/22/71; Spec. H & TC RR.

DAMON, M. A. (pvt.); known service Sept. – Oct. 1872.

DANIELS, JAMES M.; 47; W; Dist. 4; Austin; comm. 2/13/73; qual. 2/14/73; killed at Lampasas 3/14/73.

DANSON, J. M.; W; Dist. 3; Center, Shelby Co.; comm. 10/14/70; refused to qual.

DARK, J. N.; Dist. 8; Hardin; comm. 1/17/73; qual. 3/6/73; disc. 4/1/73.

DAVIDSON, HUGH (pvt.); Dist. 3; comm. 11/12/70; never reported – cancelled.

DAVIS, GEORGE (pvt.); W; Dist. 1/4; Austin; Waco, McLennan Co.; Weatherford; comm. 1/24/71; qual. 1/24/71 [1/30/71]; trans. to Travis Co.; Trans. to Parker Co.; dropped 12/31/71; not heard from since 9/71.

DAVIS, JAMES (pvt.); Dist. 3; Crockett, Houston Co.; comm. 1/7/71; qual. 1/18/71; dismiss. 3/1/71; reinst. 3/27/71.

DAVIS, ROBERT L. (pvt.); Dist. 6; Albuquerque; comm. 6/1/72; qual. 6/1/72; resign. 7/31/72.

DAVIS, S. WESLEY (pvt./sgt.); 39; W; Dist. 1; Denton; comm. 10/25/71; qual. 10/25/71; promoted from pvt. 3/73; qual. 3/10/73; re-promoted to sgt.

DAVIS, T. J. (pvt.); W; Dist. 3/7; Wharton, Wharton Co.; comm. 1/28/71; qual. 1/28/71; disc. 5/17/71.

DAVIS, W. W. (sgt.); 34; W; Dist. 6; Albuquerque; comm. 3/28/72; qual. 4/6/72; disc. 9/27/72; disc. revoked; resign. 10/31/72.

DEAL, G. W.; W; Dist. 2; Paris, Lamar Co.; comm. 3/73; qual. 3/24/73; disc. 4/22/73.

DEATON, JOHN; 35; W; Dist. 3; Gilmer; comm. 9/25/71; could not qualify.

DECKER, W. S.; W; Dist. 4; Austin; comm. 12/7/72; qual. 12/7/72; dropped 2/28/73.

DEFREYE, CHARLES E. L.; 31; W; Dist. 4; Brownsville; comm. 3/24/71; cancelled 4/8/71.

DELGADO, MARCELLO (pvt.); M; Dist. 4/6; Brownsville, Cameron Co.; comm. 7/11/70; qual. 8/14/70; disc. 10/14/71; re-comm. 9/28/72.

DELGADO, VICTOR (pvt.); M; Dist. 6; Goliad; comm. 3/4/72; qual. 3/25/72; disc. 4/9/73.

DESMOND, EDWARD (pvt.); 21*; W; Dist. 2/3/7; Huntsville, Walker Co.; comm. 3/1/71; qual. 3/1/71; disc. 5/31/71.

DIGNOWITY, A. J. (pvt.); 26; Dist. 4; Helena, Karnes Co.; comm. 8/5/70; ordered to Victoria; comm. revoked 9/2/70.

DIGNOWITY, A. W. (pvt.); 24; W; Dist. 1; San Antonio, Bexar Co.; comm. 7/12/70; dismissed for neglect of duty 8/9/70.

DILLON, A. C. (pvt.); W; Dist. 1; Kosse; McLennan Co.; comm. 11/12/70; never reported – cancelled.

DIXON, F. M.; W; Dist. 3; San Augustine, San Augustine Co.; comm. 10/14/70; recommendation withdrawn and cancelled.

DODSON, B. H. (pvt.); Dist. 2; Bright Star, Hopkins Co.; comm. 7/11/70; comm. declined.

DOLAN, PAT (pvt.); 24; W; Dist. 1; San Antonio; comm. 7/26/70; resign. 8/26/70.

DONAHO, HENRY (pvt.); 28*; B; Dist. 3/8; Huntsville, Walker Co.; Woodville, [Cold Spring, Tyler Co.]; comm. 3/1/71; qual. 3/1/71; disc. 4/15/71; reinst. 5/1/71; dismiss. 6/27/71; reinst. 8/10/71; resign. 9/30/71 [trans. to Tyler Co.].

DONNELLY, MARTIN (pvt.); W; Dist. 1; Waco, McLennan Co.; comm. 11/12/70; resign. 12/5/70.

DONOGHUE, THOMAS (pvt.); W; Dist. 4; Austin; comm. 3/1/72; qual. 3/1/72; resign. 5/31/72.

DONOHO, ROBERT (pvt.); 21; W; Dist. 2; Boston; comm. 9/1/71; qual. 9/1/71; disc. 10/31/71.

DONOVAN, BARTHOLOMEW (pvt.); 27; W; Dist. 4; Austin; comm. 7/15/71; qual. 7/15/71; resign. 11/23/71; reinst. 5/13/72; resign. 7/12/72.

DONOVAN, HENRY J. (pvt./sgt.); W; Dist. 2; Austin; Paris; comm. 8/3/71; qual. 8/3/71; promoted from pvt. 3/1/72 [9/1/71]; disc. 6/15/72; trans. to Lamar Co.

DONOVAN, JOHN R.; Dist. 6; Austin; qual. 7/9/72; disc. 8/10/72 [Rio Grande Expedition].

DORAN, THOMAS H. (pvt./sgt.); 27; W; Dist. 1/4; Austin; comm. 9/8/71; 2/22/73; qual. 9/8/71; promoted to sgt. 4/1/72; resign. 6/30/72; reinst.; disc. 11/1/72; qual. 2/22/73; disc. 4/3/73; trans. to Travis Co.

DORMAN, JOHN K.; Dist. 6; Austin; qual. 7/9/72; disc. 8/10/72 [Rio Grande Expedition].

DOUGLASS, NATHAN (pvt.); Dist. 1; known service Jan. 1871.

DOW, JOHN (pvt.); 23; Dist. 1/3; Houston, Harris Co.; comm. 7/23/70; comm. returned 10/28/70 from dead letter office as unclaimed letter.

DOWNEY, JOHN (pvt.); 37; W; Dist. 4; Brenham; comm. 9/13/72; qual. 9/13/72; disc. 10/21/72; reinst.

DOYLE, HUGH (pvt.); 22*; W*; Dist. 1; comm. 7/12/70; comm. declined.

DOYLE, JOHN; 27; W; Dist. 3; Groesbeck; comm. 4/22/71 [Spec. H & TC RR].

DRAKE, SAM (pvt.); 21; B; Dist. 1; Spring Hill; comm. 9/13/71; qual. 9/13/71; disc. 11/30/71.

DRAKE, W. E.; W; Dist. 4; Austin; comm. 8/15/71; qual. 8/15/71; disc. 9/71.

DUKE, E. P. (pvt.); 26; W; Dist. 2/3; Starrville; Jefferson; comm. 3/21/71; qual. 5/19/71; cancelled 6/28/71; not qual. in time – error – qual.; trans. to Marion Co.

DUNBAR, E. M.; 22; W; Dist. 1; Denton; comm. 11/1/72; qual. 11/1/72; resign. 4/17/73.

DUNCAN, TURNER (pvt.); Dist. 2; Jefferson; comm. 2/16/72; qual. 2/16/72; disc. 5/15/72.

DUNLAP, WILLIAM H. (pvt.); W; Dist. 3/7; Pittsville, Fort Bend Co.; comm. 7/15/70; qual. 7/15/70; disc. 10/21/72.

DUNN, GEORGE (pvt.); W; Dist. 4; Austin; qual. 3/1/72; disc. 6/21/72.

DUNN, L. E. (pvt.); W; Dist. 3; Montgomery, Montgomery Co.; comm. 10/6/70; resign. 2/6/71.

DURHAM, W. S. (pvt./lt.); W; Dist. 3/8; Woodville, Tyler Co.; comm. 12/28/70; 2/3/73; qual. 1/14/71; promoted to sgt. 2/1/71; resign. 5/31/71; reinst. 8/1/71; promoted to lt. 2/3/73; qual. 2/3/73.

DURRETT, T. H. (pvt.); 31; W; Dist. 3; Nacogdoches; comm. 8/12/71; qual. 9/11/71; disc. 12/15/71.

DWIRE, JOHN M. (pvt.); 37; W; Dist. 3; San Augustine, San Augustine Co.; comm. 11/1/70; dismiss. 3/6/[71] for incompetency and unfitness.

DYE, J. K. P. (pvt.); 27; W; Dist. 3; Larissa; comm. 9/11/71; qual. 6/13/72; disc. 10/5/72 [Rio Grande Expedition].

EARLEY, B. F. (pvt.); Dist. 6; Brenham; qual. 3/1/70; dismiss. 7/14/71; reinst. 8/15/71; resign. 10/31/71.

EARNEST, JOHN W. (pvt.); 23; W; Dist. 1/2; Sherman, Grayson Co.; comm. 3/1/71 [Spec. H & TC RR].

EASTON, T. B.; 30; W; Dist. 3; comm. 4/22/71.

EDDINS, HARD; 28; W; Dist. 1; Galveston; comm. 1/20/71 [Henderson; special].

EDDY, HENRY; 40; W; Dist. 4; Austin; comm. 1/11/73; qual. 1/11/73.

EDGAR, JOHN (pvt.); Dist. 4; Uvalde, Uvalde Co.; comm. 2/4/71; resign. 4/5/71.

EDICK, GEORGE W. (pvt.); 26*; W; Dist. 1; comm. 7/25/70; cancelled 11/15/70.

EDWARDS, H. L. (pvt./lt.); Dist. 1; Corsicana; comm. 9/20/71; qual. 9/20/71; promoted to lt. 10/15/71; disc. 4/1/72.

EDWARDS, JULIEN E. (pvt.); Dist. 1; comm. 8/20/71; qual. 8/20/71; disc. 11/30/71.

EDWARDS, SAMUEL (pvt.); Dist. 3; Millican, Brazos Co.; comm. 9/1/70; resign. 4/10/71.

EEDS, JAMES (pvt.); Dist. 3/7; Madisonville, Madison Co.; comm. 3/3/71; qual. 3/3/71; disc. 6/12/71.

ELDER, WILLIAM F. (pvt.); W; Dist. 4/6; Helena, Karnes Co.; comm. 10/1/70; qual. 1/21/71; disc. 6/27/71; reinst. 7/25/71; disc. 1/31/72.

ELGIN, A. W. (pvt.); 20; W; Dist. 1/6; Lockhart, Caldwell Co.; comm. 10/3/70; qual. 10/6/70; disc. 11/16/71.

ELKINS, J. J.; Dist. 7; Montgomery; comm. 6/14/71; cancelled 6/28/71; not qualified in time.

ELKINS, R. S. (pvt.); 37; W; Dist. 1; Mountain City, Hays Co.; comm. 9/22/70.

ELLETT, INNES (pvt.); 22; W; Dist. 2; Clarksville, Red River Co.; comm. 8/9/70; qual. 8/18/70; resign. 5/10/71.

ELLINGTON, J. M. (pvt.); 23; W; Dist. 3; Center; comm. 9/14/71; qual. 9/14/71; disc. 11/30/71.

ELLIOTT, R. H. (pvt.); 32; W; Dist. 4; Austin; qual. 1/1/72; disc. 6/21/72; reinst.; disc. sustained.

ELLIS, CHARLES E (pvt.); 35*; W*; Dist. Sub; San Elizario, El Paso Co.; comm. 7/7/70; comm. declined 7/22/70.

EMANUEL, EDGAR (pvt.); 33; Dist. 3; Cotton Gin, Freestone Co.; comm. 8/1/70; disc. 5/10/71.

ENDERLE, GEORGE; 36*; W*; Dist. 5; San Antonio; comm. 5/23/71; cancelled – not qualified in time.

ESCAMINA, PABLO (pvt.); Dist. 6; Laredo; comm. 8/2/72; qual. 8/2/72 [Rio Grande Expedition].

ESTAPA, LEON (pvt.); 25; M; Dist. 4/6; Edinburg, Hidalgo Co.; comm. 7/11/70; qual. 8/3/70 [oath sent back 7/31/70].

EVANS, JONATHAN (pvt.); 40; Dist. Sub; El Paso, El Paso Co.; comm. 7/7/70; disc. 4/30/71.

EVANS, W. H.; 38; W; Dist. 4; Austin; comm. 10/31/72; qual. 10/31/72; resign. 3/21/73.

EVANS, WILLIAM E. (sgt.); 24; Dist. 1; Belton, Bell Co.; comm. 7/29/70; resign. 2/4/71.

EVERHART, SAMUEL V. (sgt.); 35; Dist. 3; Galveston; comm. 7/16/70; dismiss. 9/5/70.

EVERLING [EBERLING], WILLIAM (pvt.); Dist. 4; Laredo, Webb Co.; comm. 9/1/70 [8/20/70]; never accepted – appt. cancelled.

FALVY, JOHN (pvt.); W; Dist. 1; Fredericksburg, Gillespie Co.; comm. 11/12/70; dismiss. 2/6/71; reinst. 2/14/71; disc. 3/29/71.

FARLEY, J. C. (pvt.); 27; W; Dist. 1; comm. 7/13/72; qual. 7/25/72; resign. 3/12/73.

FARROW, GEORGE W. (lt./capt.); 24; W; Dist. 3/7; Houston; Bryan City, Brazos Co.; comm. 7/7/70; 7/23/71; promoted to capt. 11/1/70; qual. 7/25/71; resign. 12/19/71; reinst.; resign. 11/4/72.

FAULK, JAMES E. (pvt.); 22; W; Dist. 1/2; Corsicana, Navarro Co.; comm. 3/25/71.

FAULK, WESLEY (pvt.); Dist. 2/3; Canton, Van Zandt Co.; comm. 1/10/71 [1/16/71]; qual. 1/19/71; resign. 9/11/71.

FAUNTLEROY, J. B. (pvt.); Dist. 6; Hempstead; qual. 6/29/72; disc. 7/31/72 [Rio Grande Expedition].

FERGUSON, ALEXANDER (pvt.); 29; W; Dist. 7; Galveston; comm. 8/20/72; qual. 8/26/72; disc. 9/30/72.

FERGUSON, J. A. (pvt.); 26; W; Dist. 3; Hemphill; comm. 9/19/71; qual. 9/19/71; disc. 10/31/71.

FERGUSON, ROBERT (pvt.); 34; W; Dist. 1; Denton; comm. 10/30/71; qual. 10/30/71.

FESSLER, ANTHONY; Dist. 6; comm. 8/1/71; dropped 11/1/71 – never qualified.

FISCH, LOUIS F.; 28; W; Dist. 1; Montague; comm. 3/18/73; qual. 3/18/73.

FISHER, HENRY (pvt.); B; Dist. 1; Austin; comm. 10/1/70.

FLAHERTY, DENNIS; Dist. 1; Denton; comm. 3/10/73; qual. 3/10/73.

FLEMING, B. P. (pvt.); 21; Dist. 2; Lone Star; comm. 9/28/71; qual. 9/28/71; disc. 12/15/71.

FLINT, FRANK (pvt.); Dist. 1; comm. 8/18/71; qual. 8/18/71; disc. 9/21/71.

FLORES, RICARDO (pvt.); Dist. 6; Brownsville; comm. 10/7/72; qual. 10/7/72.

FLORES, VICENTE (pvt.); 56; Dist. 4; Laredo, Webb Co.; comm. 9/1/70.

FONTAINE, JACOB; B; Dist. 4; Austin; comm. 11/1/72; qual. 11/1/72; disc. 11/30/72.

FOOTE, EMORY (pvt.); 33; W; Dist. 6; Indianola; comm. 9/1/71; qual. 9/1/71; resign. 7/10/72.

FOREMAN, A. J. (pvt.); W; Dist. 4/7; Madisonville; Austin; comm. 8/8/71; qual. 8/8/71; dismiss. 9/12/71; trans. to Madison Co.

FOREMAN, GEORGE B. [R.] (pvt.); 24; Dist. 3; Alto, Cherokee Co.; comm. 7/29/70; dismiss. 9/24/70 without pay.

FOREMAN, WILLIAM T.; Dist. 1; Denton; comm. 3/10/73; qual. 3/10/73.

FORREST, EDWARD; 22; W; Dist. 3; Ledbetter; comm. 3/20/71; cancelled 3/25/71.

FOSTER, E. D. (pvt.); 30; W*; Dist. 2; Quitman; comm. 9/11/71; qual. 9/11/71; resign. 11/30/71.

FOSTER, WILLIAM (pvt.); 47; Dist. 2; Corsicana, Navarro Co.; comm. 8/5/70; dismiss. 2/6/71; comm. returned 2/24/71.

FOWLER, RICHARD; 22*; W; Dist. 4; Lampasas; comm. 3/22/73; qual. 3/22/73.

FOWLES, JOHN S.; 27; Dist. 2; Mount Pleasant; comm. 9/12/71; qual. 9/12/71; resign. 10/5/71.

FRANKLIN, GREEN (pvt.); Dist. 3; Robertson Co.; comm. 8/1/70; appt. cancelled 11/15/70 – never accepted.

FRANKLIN, JOHN (pvt.); 39; W; Dist. 1/3; Polk Co.; Lampasas; comm. 9/17/70; trans. to 3rd Dist. from 1st Dist.

FRAZELLE, JAMES C.; Dist. 2; Bonham, Fannin Co.; comm. 3/25/71; cancelled – dropped from date of appt. 5/12/71.

FRAZIOR, EBENEZER (pvt.); 31; Dist. 2; Linden; comm. 9/5/71; qual. 9/5/71; disc. 10/3/71.

FREDERICK, HOWARD (pvt.); W; Dist. 2; comm. 10/19/70; cancelled having never accepted.

FRENCH, A. H. (lt.); 35; W; Dist. Sub/5; El Paso, El Paso Co.; comm. 7/7/70; qual. 7/20/70; disc. [resigned] 1/31/72; re-comm. 10/25/72; disc. 12/13/72.

FRIES, JOHN P. (pvt.); 22; W; Dist. 6; Eagle Pass; comm. 5/1/71; qual. 5/13/71; dismissed 6/22/71.

FRITH, HENRY; 23*; W; Dist. 4; Groesbeck; Austin; Qual. 3/1/72; resign. 6/30/72; reinst.; resign. 1/5/73.

FRITZ [FRITTZS], HENRY W. (pvt.); 29*; W; Dist. 1/4; Austin, Travis Co.; comm. 2/8/71; qual. 2/8/71; orderly died (consumption) 12/24/71.

FULLER, DANIEL (pvt.); 65; W; Dist. 4/6; Helena, Karnes Co.; comm. 12/21/70 [12/26/70]; qual. 12/31/70; disc. 1/25/72; reinst.

FULLER, FRANK D. (sgt.); Dist. 4; Point Isabel; comm. 7/7/70; comm. declined 8/9/70.

GALAN, FRANCISCO; 36; W; Dist. 5; San Antonio; comm. 11/21/72; qual. 11/23/72.

GALES, MOSES (pvt.); W; Dist. 1; Madisonville; comm. 10/1/70; resign. 11/30/70.

GALLANT, L. J. (lt.); 26; W; Dist. 2; Marshall, Harrison Co.; comm. 7/8/70; resign. 8/18/70.

GANN, JAMES D. (pvt.); 28*; W; Dist. 1/3; Homer, Angelina Co.; comm. 1/12/71 [1/13/71]; qual. 1/13/71; resign. 12/7/71.

GANNON, WILLIAM (sgt.); 18; Dist. 1; Uvalde Co.; comm. 7/8/70; comm. declined 7/11/70.

GANTT, E. S. (pvt.); 24; W; Dist. 4/6; Burton; comm. 2/21/72; qual. 2/21/72; suspended 2/13/73; disc. 4/1/73; detached temporarily from his proper station [Rio Grande Expedition].

GARCIA, LEON (pvt.); W; Dist. 1; Mountain City, Hays Co.; comm. 1/28/71.

GARDINER, C. A. (pvt.); Dist. 7; Madisonville; comm. 6/13/71; qual. 6/13/71; disc. 6/28/71.

GARLAND, FRANK (pvt.); W; Dist. 3/4/7; Kosse, Limestone Co.; Houston; comm. 11/12/70; qual. 11/12/70; trans. to Harris Co.

GARLAND, THOMAS LAW (pvt.); W; Dist. 1/2; Weatherford, Parker Co.; comm. 1/21/71; qual. 2/9/71; disc. 6/20/71.

GARLAND, W. E. (pvt.); Dist. 7; Galveston; comm. 4/1/72; qual. 4/1/72; resign. 2/15/73.

GARRETT, JOHN D.; Dist. 7; comm. 8/19/72; qual.; appt. cancelled 9/10/72.

GARZA, CHRISTOBAL [CRISTOBAL] (pvt.); 37; M; Dist. 4/6; Rio Grande City; comm. 7/11/70; qual. 7/30/70; disc. 6/27/71.

GARZA, JULIO (pvt.); 30; M; Dist. 4/5; Lodi, Wilson Co.; Sutherland Springs; comm. 7/29/70; qual. 8/4/70.

GARZIA, GUADALUPE (pvt.); 27; W; Dist. 1; San Antonio, Bexar Co.; comm. 2/7/71; resign. 4/14/71.

GATLIFF, JAMES (pvt.); Dist. 1; Burnet; comm. 7/26/70; comm. declined 9/17/70.

GATLIN, L. G. (pvt.); Dist. 6; Burton; qual. 7/3/72; disc. 9/30/72 [Rio Grande Expedition].

GEARHART, WILLIAM (pvt.); W; Dist. 1; Waco, McLennan Co.; comm. 1/24/71; resign. 3/8/71.

GEFFERS, WILLIAM (pvt.); 25; W; Dist. 4; Bastrop; comm. 9/15/71; qual. 9/16/71; disc. 12/15/71.

GIBBS, THEODORE; 21*; B; Dist. 4; Austin; comm. 11/22/72; qual. 11/22/72.

GIBSON, RUBEN (pvt.); 50; B; Dist. 8; Woodville; comm. 9/19/71; qual. 9/19/71; disc. 12/15/71.

GIDEON, J. M. (pvt.); 26*; W*; Dist. 1; Mountain City, Hays Co.; comm. 3/1/71.

GIESENSCHLAG, CHRIST; Dist. 6; Burton; qual. 6/1/72; disc. 9/30/72 [Rio Grande Expedition].

GILBERT, PHILLIP (pvt.); 24; W; Dist. 3/8; Huntsville, Walker Co.; Woodville, Tyler Co.; comm. 8/1/70; 3/1/71; qual. 8/12/70; dismiss. 10/7/70 by JD; reinst.; resign. 5/10/71.

GILDER, J. L. (pvt.); 24; W; Dist. 8; Woodville; comm. 9/3/71; qual. 9/3/71; disc. 10/12/71.

GILLESPIE, CHARLES (pvt.); Dist. 3; Brenham [On duty with Capt. McNelly hunting after Ed Peirce and others August 1 to September 18, 1870].

GILLSON, WILLIAM (pvt.); Dist. 1; Austin; comm. 7/16/70.

GIROUX, JOSEPH (pvt.); 22; W; Dist. 2/3/4; Crockett; Marshall, Harrison Co.; Ledbetter; Marion Co.; comm. 8/18/70 [8/17/70]; qual. 8/26/70 [8/21/70]; dismiss. 1/16/71; reinst. 4/1/71; disc. 11/25/71 (teaching school).

GIRRAND, AUGUSTIN; Dist. 6; Brownsville; comm. 2/1/73; qual. 2/4/73; to receive pay from 2/1/73; evidence of qualification furnished Gen'l. Britton and allowed.

GLASENAPP, GEORGE V. (sgt.); known service Sept. 19 – Nov. 1871.

GOODE, BENJAMIN E. (pvt.); 32; W; Dist. 1/2; Sherman, Grayson Co.; comm. 7/11/70; qual. 8/4/70; disc. 12/15/71.

GOODE, JR., HENRY; W; Dist. 4; Austin; comm. 2/22/73; qual. 2/22/73 [badge #40].

GOODE, SR., WILLIAM; W; Dist. 4; Austin; comm. 1/22/73; qual. 1/22/73; on police duty 1/12/73; on frontier duty 1/24/73 to 2/5/73; on police duty to 3/9/73; frontier duty 3/10/73.

GOODJOHN, F. H.; Dist. 2; Jefferson; comm. 3/11/73; qual. 3/20/73.

GOODNER, FRANK M. (pvt.); Dist. 5; New Braunfels; disc. 1/5/73;

GOODWIN, JAMES W. (pvt.); 25; W; Dist. 3; Cresswell; comm. 8/12/71; qual. 9/7/71; disc. 12/15/71.

GOODWIN, WILLIAM (pvt.); W; Dist. 3/4/6; Pleasanton, Atascosa Co.; comm. 11/12/70 [12/12/70]; 8/4/71; qual. 11/12/70; disc. 6/20/71; appt. cancelled; trans. to 4th Dist.

GOOLSBEE, HEROD (pvt.); Dist. 8; comm. 9/12/71; qual. 9/12/71; disc. 12/15/71.

GORDON, WILLIAM (pvt.); 40*; W*; Dist. 4; LaGrange, Fayette Co.; comm. 7/11/70; comm. uncalled for and cancelled 9/22/70.

GOSSLER, J. J. (pvt.); 45; W; Dist. 4; LaGrange; disc. 10/3/71.

GRAHAM, SAM T. (pvt.); B; Dist. 3; qual.; disc. 10/31/71; appointed by Capt. Farrow; no oath; no comm.

GRANGER, C. C.; Dist. 4; comm. 6/20/72; qual.; returned from post office unclaimed.

GRAVES, GEORGE (pvt.); W; Dist. 1; Kosse; McLennan Co.; comm. 11/12/70; dismiss. 2/27/71 for drunkenness and general inefficiency.

GRAY, HARDY (pvt.); 46; B*; Dist. 3; Owensville, Robertson Co.; comm. 8/1/70; dismiss. 3/1/71.

GRAY, JOHN H.; 25; W; Dist. 3; Columbus; Harrisburg; comm. 6/10/71 [BBB and C RR].

GRAYSON, FRANK (pvt.); 28; B; Dist. 2; Jefferson; comm. 5/4/71; qual. 5/16/71; resign. 6/30/71.

GREEN, BOLIVAR (pvt.); 46*; W; Dist. 4/6; Brownsville; Austin; comm. 6/16/71; qual. 6/16/71; disc. 6/28/71; reinst.; trans. to Cameron Co.; disc. 2/28/72.

GREEN, GEORGE W. (pvt.); B; Dist. 3/5; Hearne, Robertson Co.; comm. 2/25/71; qual. 3/1/71; resign. 9/30/71.

GREEN, JAMES (lt.); 47; B; Dist. 3; Galveston; Houston, Harris Co.; comm. 7/22/70; appt. cancelled 7/25/70; re-appt. 9/1/70; resign. 10/31/70.

GREEN, T. E. (pvt.); Dist. 4; comm. 8/14/71; qual. 9/1/71; disc. 12/20/71.

GREEN, W. B.; Dist. 3; comm. 4/26/72; removed from state.

GREEN, WILLIS (pvt.); Dist. 3; Marshall; qual. 9/1/71; disc. 12/20/71.

GREENLEAF, LEONIDAS; 35; W; Dist. 2; Jefferson; comm. 12/11/72; qual. 1/3/73.

GREGORY, A. M. (pvt.); B; Dist. 2; Jefferson; comm. 10/11/71; qual. 10/11/71; disc. 12/20/71.

GRIFFIN, F. M. (pvt.); Dist. 6; Long Point; qual. 6/20/72; disc. 10/5/72 [Rio Grande Expedition].

GRIFFIN, T. F. (pvt.); 23; W; Dist. 3; comm. 9/19/71; qual. 9/19/71; disc. 10/31/71.

GRIGG, WILLIAM; 35; W; Dist. 1; Decatur; comm. 8/25/71; qual. 8/25/71; killed 10/12/71 in a house of ill fame.

GRIGSBY, T. A. (pvt.); Dist. 2; Bonham, Fannin Co.; comm. 7/11/70; disc. 3/23/71.

GRIMES, M. H. (pvt.); W; Dist. 3; Mount Enterprise; comm. 8/10/71; qual. 8/10/71; resign. 2/1/73.

HACKWORTH, J. W. (pvt.); Dist. 6; Brenham; qual. 6/28/72; disc. 10/5/72 [Rio Grande Expedition].

HACKWORTH, STEPHEN A. (pvt.); 30; W; Dist. 3; Brenham, Washington Co.; comm. 7/16/70 [resign. 8/28/70].

HALE, JOHN W. (pvt.); 26; W; Dist. Sub/5; El Paso, El Paso Co.; comm. 1/23/71; qual. 2/6/71; disc. 6/27/71.

HALEY, J. M. (pvt.); 22; W; Dist. 6; Texana; comm. 8/4/70; qual. 8/12/70; resign. 2/5/72.

HALEY, J. W. (pvt.); Dist. 6; Hempstead; qual. 6/29/72; disc. 10/5/72 [Rio Grande Expedition].

HALEY, JAMES (pvt.); W; Dist. 4; Austin; comm. 8/7/71; qual. 8/7/71; dropped 8/16/71.

HALL, G. A.; Dist. 4; Burton; comm. 11/29/72; qual. 11/29/72.

HALL, GEORGE; 30*; B; Dist. 3; Center; qual.; disc. 10/31/71; appt. by Capt. Farrow; no oath; no comm.

HALL, JERRY (pvt.); 30*; B; Dist. 1; Lampasas, Lampasas Co.; comm. 2/18/71.

HALL, W. T. (pvt.); 40; W; Dist. 7; Wharton; comm. 8/1/71; qual. 8/12/71; resign. 4/30/72.

HANKINS, CLABE; B; Dist. 4; Austin; comm. 1/30/73; qual. 2/1/73; disc. 4/8/73 with loss of all pay.

HANKS, M. F. (pvt.); 21; W; Dist. 8; Woodville; comm. 8/31/71; qual. 8/31/71; disc. 9/28/71 for drunkenness and conduct unbecoming an officer.

HANNA, A. J. (pvt.); Dist. 4; Bagdad; comm. 4/12/72; qual. 4/13/72; resign. 6/20/72.

HANNAY, ROBERT E. (pvt.); Dist. 6; Hempstead; qual. 6/4/72; disc. 9/30/72 [Rio Grande Expedition].

HANSOM, JACOB (pvt./sgt.); 25; Dist. 4; Corpus Christi, Nueces Co.; comm. 9/1/70 [8/20/70]; promoted to sgt. 1/30/71; disc. 3/23/71.

HANSON, JACOB (pvt.); 28; W; Dist. 6; Santa Gertrudis; comm. 9/9/72; qual. 9/9/72; resign. 1/31/73.

HAPPE, E. H. (pvt.); 29; W; Dist. 4; Austin; qual. 2/14/72.

HARCROW, D. L.; Dist. 1; Corsicana; comm. 2/7/73; qual. 2/12/73; disc. 2/28/73.

HARDIN, JOHN G.; Dist. 4; Comanche; comm. 11/1/72; qual. 11/1/72.

HARLAN, WILL (pvt.); 24; B; Dist. 1; Corsicana; comm. 8/20/71; qual. 8/20/71; disc. 10/9/71 by G. W. Smith.

HARLEY, ALEX (pvt.); B; Dist. 1; comm. 7/23/70 [not accepted].

HARN, SAMUEL D. (sgt.); 23; W; Dist. 3/4; Burton; Navasota, Grimes Co.; comm. 7/8/70; qual. 7/14/70; dismiss. 10/31/70; reinst. 6/1/71; disc. 12/2/71; reinst. 12/3/71; disc. 1/31/72; reinst.; disc. 4/17/72.

HARPER, JACKSON; 27*; B; Dist. 4; Onion Creek; comm. 10/1/70; qual. 10/1/70; disc. 6/28/71; reinst. with leave of absence 9/1/71; never reported back.

HARPER, W. H. (pvt.); 22; W; Dist. 2; Charleston; comm. 5/17/71; qual. 6/6/71; disc. 6/28/71.

HARRIS, ISAAC (pvt.); 46; B; Dist. 1; Dresden; comm. 9/13/71; qual. 9/13/71; disc. 11/30/71.

HARRIS, J. C. (pvt.); W; Dist. 4; Austin; comm. 3/15/72; qual. 3/15/72; deserted.

HARRIS, J. W. M.; 31*; W*; Dist. 4; Brenham; comm. 11/16/72; qual. 12/26/72; dropped from rolls 2/28/73.

HARRIS, JOSEPH P.; 29; W; Dist. 7; Columbus; comm. 11/16/72; qual. 11/25/72; resign. 1/22/73.

HARRISON, A. M. (pvt.); Dist. 3; Woodville, Tyler Co.; comm. 7/11/70; declined 11/4/70.

HARRISON, CAPTAIN (pvt.); 24; B; Dist. 1; Waco, McLennan Co.; comm. 8/17/70; dismissed 12/31/70

HARTWELL, ALBERT (pvt.); 21; W; Dist. 3; Wallisville, Chambers Co.; comm. 7/9/70; dismissed 3/12/71.

HARWOOD, JOSEPH (pvt.); 22; Dist. 6; Albuquerque; comm. 7/6/72; qual. 7/8/72; disc. 8/31/72.

HASDORFF, WILLIAM G. (pvt.); 28; W; Dist. 4/6; Victoria, Victoria Co.; comm. 8/16/70 [8/16/71]; qual. 8/16/71; dismissed.

HASKINS, M. T.; Dist. 2; comm. 8/29/71; resign. 10/31/71.

HASKINS, ROBERT F. (capt.); 32; W; Dist. 4/6; Helena, Karnes Co.; Clinton; comm. 12/1/70; qual. 12/1/70; resign. 8/31/72.

HATCHEL, J. C. (pvt.); 21; W; Dist. 2; comm. 9/2/71; qual. 9/2/71; disc. 10/31/71.

HAWKINS, THOMAS (pvt.); 31; W; Dist. 1; Dresden; comm. 9/10/71; qual. 9/10/71; disc. 11/30/71.

HAYNES, J. W.; Dist. 3; Madisonville; comm. 3/1/71; disc. 5/4/71.

HAYNES, PETER (pvt.); 22; B; Dist. 4/6; Albuquerque, Gonzales Co.; comm. 8/1/70;

8/13/70; qual. 9/8/70; dismiss. 12/1/70; reinst. 3/1/71 without loss of pay; disc. 6/27/71; reinst.; resign. 1/30/73.

HAYNIE, GEORGE E. (sgt.); 24 [23]; W; Dist. 1; Austin; Bastrop; comm. 7/7/70; resign. by telegram 10/5/70.

HAYS, JOHN C.; Dist. 2; Parker Co.; comm. 10/8/70 [cannot qual.].

HAZLIT, COLUMBUS Y. (pvt.); 23; W; Dist. 3; Nacogdoches; comm. 9/22/71; qual. 9/22/71; disc. 12/20/71.

HEAD, JOHN W. (pvt.); 27; W; Dist. 3; San Augustine; comm. 9/11/71; qual. 9/11/71; disc. 12/15/71.

HEATON, THOMAS (pvt.); W; Dist. 4/5; Austin; New Braunfels; comm. 6/14/71; qual. 6/14/71; disc. 11/15/71.

HECK, R. D. (pvt.); 21; W; Dist. 4; Giddings; comm. 2/22/72; qual. 2/22/72; resign. 5/18/72.

HEINEMANN, JOHN (sgt.); Dist. 4/6; Corpus Christi; comm. 7/9/70; 2/17/72; comm. declined 7/28/70; qual. 3/4/72; disc. 8/21/72.

HEINEN, HENRY JOSEPH (pvt.); Dist. 1; Comfort, Kerr Co.; comm. 7/23/70 [papers not delivered]; comm. declined.

HEINEN, JOHN (pvt.); 23; W; Dist. 1/5; Bandera City, Bandera Co.; comm. 7/30/70 [8/1/70]; qual. 8/13/70; disc. 2/13/71; reinst. 4/19/71; resign. 5/28/71.

HEINZ, EDMUND (pvt.); 38; Dist. 1; Bastrop, Bastrop Co.; comm. 7/12/70; resign. 9/21/70 to take effect 9/30/70.

HELM, JACK (capt.); 30; W; Dist. 4; Clinton, Concrete, DeWitt Co.; comm. 7/13/70; resign. [9/21/70]; resignation accepted 11/30/70.

HEMPHILL, S. G. (pvt.); W; Dist. 1; Austin, Travis Co.; comm. 1/16/71; S. P. comm. revoked 1/22/71.

HENDERSON, JOHN (pvt./sgt.); Dist. 4/6; Corpus Christi, Nueces Co.; comm. 12/7/70 [12/10/70]; qual. 1/10/71; disc. 6/27/71; reinst. 7/22/71; promoted from pvt. 8/1/72.

HENRY, ED A. (pvt.); 22; W; Dist. 3; Livingston, Polk Co.; comm. 8/10/70 [ordered to Woodville, Tyler Co. 1/21/71]; disc. 3/1/71.

HENRY, WILLIAM (pvt.); Dist. 3; San Augustine, San Augustine Co.; comm. 11/1/70; dismiss. 3/6/71 for incompetency.

HILL, A. C. (sgt./lt./capt.); 46 [45]; W; Dist. 1; Denton; comm. 7/25/71; qual. 7/27/71; promoted from sgt. 2/1/72 to lt.; promoted from lt. 8/1/72 to capt.

HILL, GEORGE (pvt.); Dist. 6; Brownsville; comm. 2/24/72; qual. 3/12/72.

HILL, JOHN; 50; W; Dist. 4; San Marcos; comm. 10/30/72; qual. 11/1/72.

HILLYARD, GEORGE W. (pvt.); 23; Dist. 1; Waco; San Antonio; Falls Co.; comm. 7/16/70 [7/15/70]; appt. revoked 1/6/71; reinst. and dropped 4/30/71.

HILT, HENRY (pvt.); W; Dist. 1; Fredericksburg, Gillespie Co.; comm. 11/12/70; dismiss. 12/10/70; reinst.; dismiss. 3/6/71 for worthlessness and improper conduct.

HINZIE, MARTIN; Dist. 3; Hearne, Robertson Co.; comm. 4/10/71 [Spec. Int. R. R. policeman].

HOBBS, GABRIEL (pvt.); 44*; W*; Dist. 2; Quitman; comm. 9/22/71; qual. 9/22/71; disc. 11/1/71.

HOBSON, GEORGE W. (pvt.); Dist. 3; Kosse; comm. 11/12/70; dismiss. by letter 2/1/71.

HODGES, THOMAS (pvt.); 38; B; Dist. 4/1; Bastrop; comm. 8/9/70; qual. 8/12/70; resign. 12/6/71.

HOEHN, JOHN M. (pvt.); W; Dist. 1; San Antonio; comm. 1/26/71; disc. 4/15/71.

HOFFMAN, ANTON (pvt.); W; Dist. 2; Jefferson; comm. 10/11/71; qual. 10/11/71; disc. 12/20/71.

HOFFMAN, L. J. (pvt.); 29; W*; Dist. 1; Waco, McLennan Co.; comm. 7/11/70; appt. revoked 9/22/70; dismiss. for accepting appt. as marshal.

HOGAN, MICHAEL (pvt.); 28; W; Dist. 1/4; Weatherford; Waco; Austin; comm. 4/24/71; qual. 5/1/71; disc. 6/27/71; trans. to Travis Co.; qual. 5/6/72; trans. to Parker Co.

HOGES, T. C. (pvt.); 32; W; Dist. 4; Bremond [Bryan]; comm. 9/15/71; qual. 9/15/71; disc. 12/15/71.

HOHMANN, CHRISTIAN (pvt.); 31; W*; Dist. 1; New Braunfels, Comal Co.; comm. 7/8/70; appt. revoked 12/19/70.

HOLBERT, JAMES T. (pvt./lt.); 30; W; Dist. 2; Mount Pleasant; Quitman, Titus Co.; comm. 7/9/70; qual. 7/23/70; disc. 2/15/71; reinst. without loss of pay 3/10/71; disc. 3/16/72; reinst.; promoted from pvt. 4/1/72; resign. 4/30/72; comm. as lt. 12/2/72; qual. as lt. 12/3/72.

HOLLAND, O. C. (pvt.); W; Dist. 1; Waco, McLennan Co.; comm. 11/12/70; resigned.

HOLLAND, S. M. (pvt.); known service Aug. 1 – Aug. 18, 1872.

HOLLANDER, J. J. L. (pvt.); W; Dist. 1; Corsicana; Lampasas; comm. [1/21/71]; 1/26/71; qual. 1/21/71; resign. 6/5/71; reinst. 9/11/71; disc. 1/341/72.

HOLLIDAY, LUCIUS (pvt.); 28; B; Dist. 4; Austin; comm. 9/1/72; qual. 9/1/72; resign. 10/19/72.

HOLMAN, JOHN C.; 36*; W*; Dist. 1/2; Fort Worth; comm. 4/20/71; cannot qual. – cancelled 6/27/71.

HOOKS, THOMAS W. (pvt.); 29; W; Dist. 2; Boston, Bowie Co.; comm. 8/6/70; qual. 8/22/70; disc. 9/29/71.

HOOPER, WILLIAM (pvt.); 35*; W; Dist. 1; Hill Co.; comm. 7/23/70; dismiss. 11/30/70.

HOPKINS, C. O. (pvt.); W; Dist. 4; Uvalde, Uvalde Co.; comm. 12/1/70; disc. 7/31/71.

HORNUNG, AUGUST (pvt.); 21; W*; Dist. 1; Castroville, Medina Co.; San Antonio; comm. 7/29/70 [7/28/70]; resign. 8/12/70.

HOSEMAN, JOSEPH (pvt./sgt.); W; Dist. 4; Bastrop; comm. 7/12/70; qual. 7/15/70; promoted from pvt. 1/1/71 to sgt.; disc. 12/20/71; reinst. 2/14/72; deserted en route to Nacogdoches.

HOUSTON, JAMES (pvt.); W; Dist. 1; Waco, McLennan Co.; comm. 1/24/71; resign. 3/18/71.

HOUSTON, JAMES (pvt.); 52; W; Dist. 4; Groesbeck; comm. 12/13/72; qual. 12/26/72 [badge #26].

HOWARD, G. W. (pvt.); 36; W; Dist. 2/3; Troupe, Tyler, Smith Co.; comm. 4/13/71; qual. 5/5/71; disc. 6/28/71.

HOWELL, THOMAS (pvt.); W; Dist. 4; Austin; comm. 8/10/71; qual. 8/10/71; resign. 9/30/71.

HUBRICH, CHARLES; W; Dist. 3; Austin Co.; comm. 3/20/71; appt. revoked 4/30/71; revocation cancelled.

HUDDLESTON, T. W.; Dist. 2; White Oak; comm. 9/9/71; qual. 9/9/71; resign. 9/26/71.

HUDSON, R. B. (pvt.); 49; W*; Dist. 4; Clinton, DeWitt Co.; comm. 8/13/70; resign. 9/30/70.

HUDSON, WILLIAM (pvt.); W; Dist. 1; Caldwell, Burleson Co.; comm. 7/15/70 [7/12/70]; comm. declined.

HUDSON, ZACHARIAH (pvt.); W; Dist. 1; Denton; comm. 3/18/72; qual. 3/18/72; disc. 10/31/72.

HUEBNER, FRANK L. (pvt.); 23; W; Dist. 5/1; San Antonio; comm. 3/13/71; qual. 3/13/71.

HUFFMAN [HOFFMAN], BENJAMIN F. (sgt.); Dist. 3; Bryan, Brazos Co.; comm. 11/12/70; dismiss. 3/8/71.

HUGES, JAMES W.; Dist. 3; comm. 8/12/71; returned from Crockett unopened.

HUNE, HENRY C. (pvt.); 46; W; Dist. 4/6; Brownsville; comm. 5/6/71; qual. 5/13/71; disc. 6/28/71; reinst. 7/22/71; resign. 2/1/72.

HUNNICUTT, M. P. (capt.); 43; W; Dist. 1; Waco, McLennan Co.; comm. 7/7/70; appt. revoked 9/1/70.

HUNTER, JOHN M. (pvt.); 25; W; Dist. 3/4; Ledbetter; Circleville; Austin; comm. 3/20/71; qual. 3/23/71; dropped 4/6/71; reinst.; disc. 9/18/71 [9/14/71]; reinst.; trans. to Travis Co.; disc. 10/3/71 [10/23/71].

HUNTER, WALLIS L. (pvt.); 32*; W; Dist. 1/2; Weatherford, Parker Co.; comm. 10/8/70; qual. 10/14/70.

HURLEY, PATRICK H. (pvt.); 24*; W*; known service May, 1872.

HURLEY, WILLIAM (pvt.); W; Dist. 1; Lampasas, Lampasas Co.; comm. 2/10/71.

HUTCH, EDWARD M. (pvt.); 29; W; Dist. 1; Corsicana; Denton; comm. 3/1/72; qual. 2/14/72; resign. 7/18/72; comm. 2/4/73; qual. 2/4/73.

HUTCHISON, GEORGE H. (pvt.); Dist. 1; Corsicana; Denton; comm. 3/20/72; qual. 3/20/72.

HYNES, DOMINIC (pvt.); 24*; W; Dist. 4; Austin; comm. 6/9/71; qual. 6/9/71; dismiss. 7/17/71.

INGENHUTT, THOMAS; 31; W; Dist. 5/1; Boerne, Comfort, Kendall Co.; comm. 1/10/71 [1/17/71]; qual. 1/19/71; resign. 10/1/71.

INGRAM, W. J. (pvt.); Dist. 2; comm. 11/10/72; qual. 11/10/72; disc. 3/28/73.

INNESS, JOHN W.; Dist. 1; qual. 10/20/71; resign. 11/7/71.

IRISH, B. M. (pvt.); W; Dist. 3; Center, Shelby Co.; comm. 10/14/70; qual. 10/14/70; resign. 6/22/71.

IRWIN, S. S. (pvt.); 46; W; Dist. 2/3; Troupe, Tyler, Smith Co.; comm. 4/13/71; qual. 5/5/71; resign. 6/5/71.

JACKSON, CHARLES (pvt.); W; Dist. 2; Marshall, Harrison Co.; comm. 10/19/70; cancelled – never having accepted.

JACKSON, HARPER (pvt.); 26*; B; Dist. 1; Onion Creek; comm. 10/1/70.

JACKSON, HENRY (pvt.); W; Dist. 1; Kosse; comm. 12/1/70; disc. 12/3/71.

JACOBS, GEORGE W. (pvt.); 47; W*; Dist. 4; Yorktown, DeWitt Co.; comm. 7/26/70; returned comm. and declined 8/17/70.

JAMES, DANIEL (pvt.); 22*; B*; Dist. 2; Jefferson; comm. 2/16/72; qual. 2/16/72; disc. 5/29/72; re-comm. 6/23/72; disc. 2/10/73.

JAMES, HENRY (pvt.); 31; B; Dist. 1; San Antonio; New Braunfels, Comal Co.; comm. 9/3/70; trans. to 4th Dist. "Eagle Pass"; resign. 1/7/71.

JANES [JAYNES], JOHN W. (pvt.); Dist. 3; Madisonville; comm. 3/1/71; qual. 3/1/71.

JASPER, MUNGER (pvt.); 27; B; Dist. 1; Dresden; comm. 8/25/71; qual. 8/25/71; disc. 12/13/71.

JENNINGS, C. M.; W; Dist. 4; Giddings; comm. 1/17/73; qual. 1/23/73; disc. 2/28/73 [badge #442].

JENNINGS, G. A. (pvt.); 45; W; Dist. 1; Fort Worth; comm. 8/23/71; qual. 8/23/71; resign. 8/26/72.

JENNINGS, HENRY (pvt.); 21; W; Dist. 1; Fort Worth; comm. 8/29/71; qual. 8/29/71; disc. 12/20/71.

JENNINGS, J. F. (pvt.); W; Dist. 1; Decatur; comm. 5/20/72; qual. 5/30/72.

JESSEN, ADELBERT (sgt.); 28*; W; Dist. 4; Austin; comm. 10/14/71; qual. 10/14/71; resign. 3/12/73.

JOHNSON, CHARLES; B; Dist. 7; Houston; comm. 3/5/73; qual. 3/10/73.

JOHNSON, CLAIBORNE (pvt.); 53*; B; Dist. 3; Madison Co.; comm. 8/9/70; resign. 11/15/70.

JOHNSON, J. A.; W; Dist. 4; Mountain City; comm. 8/20/71; qual. 8/20/71.

JOHNSON, R. D. (pvt.); 21; B; Dist. 2/3; Tyler, Smith Co.; comm. 10/19/70; qual. 10/31/70; dropped 12/6/71.

JOHNSON, W. A. (pvt./sgt.); 23; W; Dist. 4; Austin; comm. 6/1/72; qual. 6/1/72; promoted to sgt. 1/24/73.

JOHNSON, WILLIAM (pvt.); B; Dist. 2; Bowie Co.; comm. 7/11/70; never accepted – comm. cancelled.

JONES, A. J.; 34*; W; Dist. 4; Lampasas; comm. 3/22/73; qual. 3/22/73.

JONES, ADOLPHUS (pvt.); Dist. 1; Blanco; comm. 3/1/71; declined.

JONES, AUGUST (pvt.); Dist. 1; Blanco; comm. 3/1/71; declined.

JONES, BARTON [BURTON] (pvt.); 30; B; Dist. 4/7 [care of F. B. Franks, Wharton, Wharton Co.]; comm. 9/1/70; qual. 9/12/70; disc. 1/30/71.

JONES, E. Z. (pvt./sgt.); W; Dist. 1/4; McLennan Co.; Eagle Pass, Maverick Co.; comm. 7/11/70; revoked 8/6/70 for not complying with orders to report; reinst. as pvt. 1/10/71 [1/11/71]; dismiss. 1/30/71; trans. to 4th Dist.

JONES, EMANUEL (pvt.); B; Dist. 4; Belton; Austin; comm. 5/1/71; qual. 5/1/71; trans. to Travis Co.; disc. 10/24/71.

JONES, EMMET; Dist. 4; Austin; comm. 3/6/73; qual. 3/7/73; resign. 3/27/73.

JONES, FRANKLIN (pvt.); W; Dist. 4; Eagle Pass, Maverick Co.; comm. 12/1/70; appt. cancelled 12/15/70.

JONES, NELSON P.; W; Dist. 6/7; Yorktown; comm. 8/12/71; 3/18/72; cancelled 11/1/71 – never qual.; qual. 3/18/72; disc. 11/15/72.

JONES, PATRICK (pvt.); Dist. 3; comm. 11/12/70; dismiss. 11/30/70.

JONES, ROBERT (pvt.); 19 [20]; B; Dist. 1/4; Austin; comm.; 7/29/70 [7/28/70]; 4/19/71; 11/20/72; qual. 4/19/71; orderly appointment cancelled; reinst.; disc. 2/28/72; qual. 11/20/72; disc. 2/7/73; reinst. 3/1/73; disc. 3/31/73.

JONES, SOLOMON (pvt.); B; Dist. 3/7; Huntsville, Walker Co.; comm. 12/12/70; qual. 12/19/70; disc. 6/28/71.

JONES, WALTER; Dist. 7; Hempstead; comm. 2/17/73; qual. 2/17/73.

JONES, WILLIAM E. (sgt.); 29; W; Dist. 4; Gonzales, Gonzales Co.; comm. 10/3/70; promoted from pvt. 12/1/70; resign. 1/9/71.

JONES, WILLIAM H. (pvt.); W; Dist. 1/4; Waco; Austin; comm. 12/13/70; qual. 12/13/70; trans. to Travis Co.; disc. 6/27/71.

JOYCE, ROBERT F. (sgt.); 35; W; Dist. 5; Fort Concho; comm. 1/17/72; qual. 1/17/72; resign. 2/28/72.

JUNG, CHARLES (pvt.); 31; W; Dist. 5; Fredericksburg; comm. 8/5/72; qual. 8/21/72; disc. 2/1/73.

KARNS, HENRY L (pvt.); W; Dist. 1; comm. 2/10/71; comm. cancelled 2/15/71.

KEATING, PAUL W. (pvt.); Dist. 1; comm. 10/10/71; qual. 10/10/71; disc. 11/30/71.

KEEL, C. B. (pvt.); 45*; W*; Dist. 3; Crockett; comm. 9/5/71; qual. 9/5/71; disc. 12/15/71.

KEESEE, JAMES C. (pvt.); 24*; W*; Dist. 4; Washington Co.; comm. 8/14/71; qual. 8/19/71; disc. 12/15/71.

KEESEE, THOMAS (pvt.); 30*; W*; Dist. 3/4; Burton, Chappell Hill, Washington Co.; comm. 7/15/70; 8/14/71; resign. 12/4/70; reinst. without loss of pay; appt. cancelled 2/28/71; qual. 9/13/71; dismiss. 2/8/72; reinst. 5/1/72; resign. 6/24/72.

KEITH, WILLIAM; 58; W; Dist. 1; Stephenville; comm. 11/27/72; qual. 11/27/72.

KELLEY, MARTIN (pvt.); 48; W; Dist. 1; Corpus Christi; comm. 8/15/71; qual. 9/8/71; resign. 11/30/71.

KELLNER, EMIL (lt./capt.); 33; W; Dist. 1; New Braunfels, Comal Co.; comm. 7/7/70; qual. 7/9/70; promoted to capt. 5/1/71; resign. 1/6/73.

KELLY, WILLIAM (pvt.); 32; W; Dist. 1/4; Austin; comm. 5/3/71; qual. 5/3/71; resign. 6/16/71.

KELSO, A. A. (pvt.); W; Dist. 4/6; Uvalde, Uvalde Co.; comm. 2/3/71; qual. 2/3/71; resign. 11/30/71.

KELSO, JOHN R. (pvt./sgt.); W; Dist. 4/6; Huntsville, Walker Co.; Uvalde, Uvalde Co.; comm. 2/3/71; qual. 2/3/71; promoted to sgt. 4/1/71; resign. 1/12/72.

KEMPFER, JOHN (pvt.); W; Dist. 1/4; Austin, Travis Co.; comm. 1/1/71; qual. 1/1/71; disc. 11/21/71 [orderly].

KENEDY, PATRICK (pvt.); 24; W; Dist. 4; Belton; Austin; comm. 7/15/71; qual. 7/15/71; trans. to Bell Co.; disc. 9/28/71 for disobedience of orders by superior officer.

KENNEDY, JOSEPH (pvt.); B; Dist. 1; Waco, McLennan Co.; comm. 7/16/70 [7/17/70]; dismiss. 1/6/71.

KENT, DAVID (pvt.); 35; W; Dist. 1; San Antonio, Bexar Co.; comm. 7/12/70; 1/16/71; comm. declined; re-appt. 1/16/71; dismiss. 1/27/71 with loss of all pay and allowances.

KERBER, CHARLES; Dist. 5; San Elizario; comm. 9/1/71; cancelled 11/1/71 – never qual.

KIMBROUGH, A.; 32; W; Dist. 1; Dallas; comm. 8/13/71; qual. 8/13/71; disc. 12/20/71.

KINEHAN, JOHN (pvt.); W; Dist. 5; San Antonio; comm. 4/27/72; qual. 4/27/72; promoted from pvt. 12/7/72 [12/1/72]; resign. 1/31/73; returned badge #75 and comm.

KING, C. H. (pvt.); 25; W; Dist. 1; Ft. Mason, Mason Co.; comm. 11/12/70; dismiss. 2/6/71.

KING, CHARLES E. (pvt.); 24; W; Dist. 1; Lampasas, Lampasas Co.; comm. 1/16/71; comm. revoked 1/22/71; retained as regular policeman; resign. 4/26/71.

KING, SIMPSON (pvt.); 29; B; Dist. 1/4; Lexington; Austin; Burleson Co.; comm. 7/16/70 [7/12/70]; qual. 8/12/70; disc. 3/29/71; disc. revoked 4/6/71; trans. to Travis Co.; disc. 6/28/71; reinst. 9/1/71; trans. to Burleson Co.; disc. 12/15/71.

KINNEY, THOMAS; Dist. Sub; San Elizario, El Paso Co.; comm. 1/23/71; declined.

KIRBY, JARED E. (pvt.); Dist. 6; Hempstead; qual. 6/29/72; disc. 10/5/72 [Rio Grande Expedition].

KIRCHNER, F. R. (pvt.); 31 [32]; Dist. 1; San Antonio; comm. 7/26/70 [delivered 8/2/70]; resign. 8/12/70.

KIRK, A. M. (pvt.); 21; W; Dist. 8; Woodville; comm. 8/31/71; qual. 8/31/71; disc. 10/6/71.

KIRK, J. M. (pvt.); 49; W; Dist. 3/8; Woodville, Tyler Co.; comm. 10/11/70; qual. 10/15/70; disc. 3/28/71 [4/1/71]; reinst. 8/29/71; disc. 10/31/71; reinst.; resign. 9/8/72 [re-appt. and trans. to Tyler Co.].

KIRK, JAMES; 23; W; Dist. 4; Austin; qual. 2/12/72; disc. 5/9/72; charged but not convicted as a horse thief.

KIRKSEY, ISAAC; 23; W; Dist. 3; Shelbyville; comm. 9/18/71; qual. 9/18/71; disc. 10/31/71.

KIRNAN, FRANK (pvt.); 23; Dist. 1; Travis Co.; comm. 7/8/70; dismiss. 8/7/70.

KLEID, PETER (pvt.); 25; W; Dist. 1; San Antonio; comm. 7/26/70; resign. [dismiss.].

KOCH, MARTIN (pvt.); W; Dist. 4; Fayetteville, Fayette Co.; comm. 3/16/71; qual. 4/8/71; resign. 9/19/71.

KOGLER, GEORGE (pvt.); W; Dist. 2/4; Austin; Paris; comm. 8/3/71; qual. 8/3/71; trans. to Lamar Co.; resign. 12/10/71.

KRATZ, HUGO (pvt.); 34*; W; Dist. 4; Austin; comm. 6/1/72; qual. 6/1/72; resign. 7/31/72.

KRATZER, FREDERICH (pvt.); W; Dist. 1/4; Bremond; Kosse; McLennan Co.; comm. 11/12/70; qual. 11/12/70; dismiss. 11/30/70; reinst.; resign. 8/12/71 [11/30/71]; reinst.; trans. to Robertson Co.

KRAUSE, RUDOLPH (pvt./sgt.); 37; W; Dist. 1/5/6; Brownsville; San Antonio; temporarily in San Antonio, Bexar Co.; comm. 2/13/71; qual. 2/27/71; promoted to sgt. 5/1/71; trans. to Bexar, 5th Police Dist.

KUHN, JOSEPH (pvt.); W; Dist. 4; Oak Hill; comm. 6/1/72; qual. 6/1/72; dropped 2/28/73.

LABBAITE [LABATTE], EDMUND A.; 55*; W; Dist. 4; Lampasas; comm. 3/22/73; qual. 3/22/73.

LACEY, IRWIN (pvt.); 28*; B; Dist. 3; Palestine, Anderson Co.; comm. 7/16/70; qual. 7/23/70; dismiss. 11/3/70 [11/30/70]; dismissal revoked; reinst.; dismiss. 9/30/71.

LACY, ASA P. (lt.); 27*; W*; Dist. 1; Gillespie Co.; comm. 7/8/70; comm. declined 7/27/70.

LAFRANCE, PAUL C.; W; Dist. 4; Austin; comm. 8/3/71; qual. 8/3/71; disc. 10/10/71.

LAMAR, CHARLES (pvt.); 35; W; Dist. 1; New Braunfels, Comal Co.; Waco; comm. 7/16/70 [7/15/70]; resign. 10/31/70.

LAMB, THOMAS (pvt.); B; Dist. 1; Lampasas; comm. 1/7/71; dismiss. 1/31/71; reinst. without loss of pay; resign. 3/15/71.

LAMKIN, ROM (pvt.); 36; W; Dist. 4; Bryan; comm. 9/11/71; qual. 9/11/74; disc. 11/30/71.

LANCASTER, F. B. (pvt.); W; Dist. 1/4; LaGrange, Fayette Co.; comm. 2/23/71; qual. 2/24/71; disc. 6/27/71.

LANDROS, E. C. [LANDROZ, C.] (pvt.); Dist. 1; qual. 10/20/71; resign. 11/7/71.

LANDS, JACK [JOHN] (pvt.); 38; B; Dist. 3; Brenham, Washington Co.; comm. 7/16/70; resign. 8/3/70.

LANE, ADDISON (pvt.); 33*; W*; Dist. 3; comm. 9/11/71; qual. 8/18/71; disc. 10/31/71.

LANE, LEWIS A. (pvt.); W; Dist. 1/4; Lampasas, Lampasas Co.; comm. 1/21/71; qual. 1/21/71; disc. 11/15/71; reinst. [discharge sustained].

LANE, THOMAS J. (pvt.); 27 [28]; W; Dist. 1/4; Bryan; Lockhart, Caldwell Co.; comm. 1/7/71; 8/12/71; disc. 4/6/71; reinst.; re-appt. 8/12/71; trans. to Brazos Co.; disc. 1/20/72.

LANGFORD, W. A. (pvt.); 28*; W; Dist. 1; Georgetown, Williamson Co.; comm. 12/7/70; declined.

LANGHAMMER, CHARLES (pvt.); 26; W; Dist. 3/7; Cat Springs, Austin Co.; comm. 1/20/71; qual. 2/8/71; disc. 5/17/71.

LANGLEY, EDMUND D. (pvt.); W; Dist. 4; Austin; comm. 7/1/71; qual. 7/1/71 for two months only; disc. 7/31/71; reinst. 9/1/71; disc. 11/15/71; reinst. 1/1/72.

LATCHEM, JOHN P. (pvt.); 51*; W*; Dist. 3; Sabine Pass; comm. 1/21/71; disc. 4/12/71.

LAURENCE, CHARLES H. (pvt.); Dist. 4; Giddings; comm. 10/4/72; qual. 10/6/72; resign. 2/1/73.

LAWRENCE, GEORGE W.; B; Dist. 4; Austin; disc. 2/19/73.

LEAL, BENIGNI [BENINO]; 25*; W*; Dist. 6; Hidalgo; comm. 10/12/72; qual. 10/28/72.

LEAL, MIGUEL; 44*; W*; Dist. 6; Eagle Pass; comm. 2/18/73; qual. 3/10/73.

LECKY, JOHN F.; 27; W; Dist. 4; Austin; comm. 5/13/72; qual. 5/13/72; disc. by T. H. Doran – allowing prisoner to escape.

LEE, C. G. (pvt.); 40*; W*; Dist. 2; Paris, Lamar Co.; comm. 7/11/70; disc. 3/14/71.

LEE, GEORGE (pvt.); 39; W; Dist. 1; Perryville, Bastrop Co.; comm. 9/21/70; appt. revoked 11/3/70.

LEE, LEROY (pvt.); Dist. 4; Giddings; comm. 9/27/72; qual. 9/27/72; disc. 11/1/72.

LEFTAGE [LEFTRIDGE], HENRY [alias Henry Boothe] (pvt.); 37*; B; Dist. 4/6; Clinton, Hochheim, DeWitt Co.; comm. 8/13/70; qual. 8/20/70; disc. 10/1/70; disc. annulled; disc. 1/11/73; reinst.

LEIFESTE, FRITZ R. (pvt.); 26; W; Dist. 1/4/5; Fort Mason; comm. 5/2/71; qual. 5/11/71; disc. 6/28/71.

LEMMONS, VAL (pvt.); Dist. 3; Travis, Austin Co.; comm. 7/15/70; appt. revoked 1/5/71.

LEONARD, PATRICK (pvt.); 38 [30]; W; Dist. 4/6; Corpus Christi, Nueces Co.; Austin; comm. 12/7/70; qual. 12/19/70; trans. to Travis Co.; resign. 7/15/71.

LEWIS, D. H. (pvt.); 21; W; Dist. 3; Center; comm. 9/18/71; qual. 9/18/71; disc. 10/31/71.

LEWIS, FRANK; 42*; B*; Dist. 2/3; Gilmer, Upshur Co.; comm. 3/21/71; cancelled 6/24/71 never having qualified.

LEWIS, JOHN (pvt.); 23 [25]; B; Dist. 7; Anderson; comm. 11/12/71; 10/15/72; qual. 11/16/71; disc. 12/31/71; qual. 10/23/72.

LEWIS, LAFAYETTE (pvt.); 23; W; Dist. 3; Center; comm. 9/18/71; qual. 9/18/71; disc. 10/31/71.

LEWIS, MOSES (pvt.); 37; B; Dist. 3; Galveston, Galveston Co.; comm. 7/8/70; dismiss. 8/29/70.

LEWIS, W. W. (pvt./sgt.); 32; B; Dist. 2; Jefferson; comm. 5/4/71; qual. 5/17/71; promoted from pvt. to sgt. 3/1/72; disc. 6/15/72.

LIECK, AUGUST (sgt.); 38; Dist. 1; San Antonio; comm. 7/15/70; dismiss. 11/30/70 for not complying with order to take post at Bastrop.

LINDENBURG, AUGUST (pvt.); 28 [25]; Dist. 4; Hallettsville, Lavaca Co.; comm. 8/13/70; comm. returned 10/31/71.

LINSMEYER, STEPHEN (pvt.); 37; Dist. 1; San Antonio, Bexar Co.; comm. 7/23/70; appt. revoked 8/9/70 for neglect of duty.

LITTIG, A. W.; 38; W; Dist. 3; Houston; comm. 4/22/71 [Spec. H & TC RR].

LOCK, L. C. (pvt./sgt.); 33*; W; Dist. 4; Lampasas, Lampasas Co.; Belton; Austin; Mountain City, Hays Co.; comm. 10/1/70; qual. 10/1/70; promoted to sgt. 2/1/71; disc. 7/11/71; reinst.; disc. 11/15/71; reinst. as per 2/8/72; disc. 4/4/73 with loss of pay due.

LOCKE, WILLIAM K (pvt.); Dist. 7; Hempstead; comm. 1/11/73; qual. 1/20/73.

LOCKWOOD, CHARLES E. (pvt.); W; Dist. 3/4; Austin; comm. 6/13/71; qual. 6/13/71; dropped 9/30/71; trans. to Cherokee Co.

LOGAN, DAVID H. (pvt.); 22; W; Dist. 4; Groesbeck; qual. 10/18/71; disc. 10/26/71.

LOGAN, JOHN (pvt.); 25; W; Dist. 3; Marshall; comm. 9/19/71; qual. 9/19/71; disc. 1/15/72.

LOGGINS, WILLIAM D. (pvt.); 33; W; Dist. 3; comm. 9/11/71; qual. 9/11/71; disc. 10/31/71.

LONG, A. N. (pvt.); 39*; W; Dist. 4/6; Uvalde, Uvalde Co.; comm. 2/3/71; qual. 2/3/71; disc. 1/15/72.

LONG, AMBROSE B. (pvt.); Dist. 2; Paris, Lamar Co.; comm. 9/6/70; appt. cancelled 11/15/70 never having accepted.

LONG, J. L. (pvt.); W; Dist. 3; Rusk, Cherokee Co.; comm. 1/26/71; resign. 3/21/71.

LONG, TOBIAS; 49*; W*; Dist. 6; comm. 8/5/72; returned comm.

LOONEY, TIMOTHY (pvt.); W; Dist. 3/7; Columbia; Galveston; comm. 5/1/71; qual. 6/14/71; disc. 6/10/71; reinst.; disc. 9/12/71; trans. to Brazoria Co.

LOPEZ, EVARISTO (pvt.); 35; Dist. 4; Laredo, Webb Co.; comm. 9/1/70 [8/20/70]; dismiss. 3/3/71 for want of energy in discharge of duties.

LORENZ, J. A. (pvt.); 31; W*; Dist. 6; Helena; comm. 5/10/71; qual. 5/10/71; disc. 7/25/71.

LOVEALL, JACOB H. (pvt.); W; Dist. 1/4; Austin; Weatherford; comm. 6/10/71; qual. 6/10/71; trans. to Parker Co.; dismiss. 7/17/71.

LOWELL, ROBERT; Dist. 4; Matagorda; comm. 8/13/70.

LOWENBEIN, F. A. (pvt.); W; Dist. 4; Austin; comm. 10/30/72; qual. 10/30/72; disc. 11/12/72.

LOWERY, MICHAEL (pvt.); W; Dist. 4; Giddings (convict camp); Austin; comm. 6/17/71; qual. 6/17/71; resign. 1/3/72; trans. to McLennan Co.

LUCAS, FRANK (pvt.); 26; Dist. 3; Calvert, Robertson Co.; comm. 8/1/70; dismiss. 10/31/70.

LUFKIN, JOEL A. (pvt./sgt.); W; Dist. 1/3; Palestine, Anderson Co.; Corsicana, Navarro Co.; comm. 8/1/70; qual. 8/11/70; promoted to sgt. 2/1/71 [1/1/71]; disc. 1/20/72.

LUMKINS, FREDERICK (pvt.); 36; B; Dist. 3; Brenham, Washington Co.; comm. 7/16/70 [resign. 8/13/70].

LUSK, GEORGE; 25*; W*; Dist. 3/4; Centreville; comm. 4/20/71; cancelled 6/24/71 never having qual.

LUSK, T. C. (pvt.); Dist. 4/6; Brenham; qual. 6/29/72; disc. 10/5/72; re-comm. 11/16/72; dismiss. 3/12/73; reinst. 4/4/73 [Rio Grande Expedition].

MABRY, JAMES R.; 28; W; Dist. 2; Clarksville; comm. 9/2/71; qual. 9/2/71; resign. 2/27/72.

MACKEN, PATRICK (pvt.); Dist. 1; Waco [comm. uncalled for].

MACKEY, DICK; Dist. 1; comm. 9/10/71; qual. 9/10/71; disc. 10/9/71 by G. W. Smith.

MACOMBER, H. A. (pvt.); 34; W; Dist. 1; Corsicana; McDade; comm. 9/6/71; qual. 9/6/71; disc. 4/30/72.

MAHONEY, LAWRENCE; 25; W; Dist. 4; Waco; Bastrop; Austin; comm. 6/17/71; qual. 6/17/71; resign. 7/31/71; trans. to McLennan Co.

MAKEMSON, J. K. (pvt.); W; Dist. 1; Georgetown, Williamson Co.; comm. 12/7/70; declined.

MANGER, PHILLIPP (pvt.); 24*; W; Dist. 5; New Braunfels; comm. 9/5/72; qual. 9/7/72; resign. 11/30/72.

MANGOLD, JOHN (pvt.); 30; W; Dist. 1/5; Kerrville, Kerr Co.; comm. 7/30/70 [8/1/70]; qual. 8/23/70; resign. 5/10/71.

MANNING, WENTWORTH (pvt./sgt.); W; Dist. 2/3; Canton, Van Zandt Co.; comm. 7/22/70; qual. 8/8/70; promoted to sgt. 4/1/71; resign. 9/12/71.

MARCHAL, FERDINAND (pvt.); 31; W; Dist. 4; Austin; comm. 9/6/71; qual. 9/8/71; disc. 11/5/71; reinst. 1/1/72; resign. 3/16/73.

MARIA, PABLO; 31; M; Dist. 5; San Elizario; comm. 8/3/70; qual. 9/5/70; disc. 8/25/71; reinst. 9/19/71.

MARSHALL, A. A.; Dist. 3; Athens; comm. 9/12/71; cannot qual.

MARSHALL, J. J.; Dist. 4; comm. 8/12/71; declined.

MARSHALL, WALTER (pvt.); 49; B; Dist. 3/7; Galveston; Richmond; comm. 7/23/70; qual. 8/17/70; disc. 5/17/71.

MARTIN, AUGUST; Dist. 5; comm. 8/5/72; declined.

MARTIN, C. A. (pvt.); 24; W; Dist. 1; Mountain City, Hays Co.; comm. 12/23/70.

MARTIN, ERNST; 35; W; Dist. 5; Fort Mason; comm. 1/2/73; qual. 1/2/73 [badge #136].

MARTIN, J. P. (pvt.); known service Aug. 1872.

MARTIN, JAMES C. (pvt.); 25; W; Dist. 1/4; Onion Creek; Lampasas Co.; comm. 12/23/70; qual. 12/23/70; disc. 11/16/71; reinst. 3/26/72; resign. 3/14/73.

MARTIN, JOHN H.; Dist. 6; Victoria; comm. 2/5/73.

MARTIN, JOSEPH L. (pvt.); Dist. 3; Huntville, Walker Co.; comm. 11/21/70; removed 2/14/71; comm. returned 3/10/71.

MARTIN, THOMAS G. (pvt./sgt./lt./capt.); 30; W; Dist. 1/4; Mountain City, Hays Co.; comm. 8/10/70 [7/10/70]; qual. 8/10/70 [7/10/70]; promoted to sgt. 11/1/70; promoted to lt. 2/4/71 [2/1/71]; promoted to capt. 11/1/72; resign. 12/11/72.

MARTIN, WILLIAM (pvt.); 20; W; Dist. 3/7; Huntsville, Walker Co.; comm. 1/7/70 [10/7/70]; qual. 10/7/70; disc. 5/31/71.

MARTINEZ, RAFAEL (pvt.); 30; W; Dist. 5; Boerne; comm. 8/5/72; qual. 8/23/72 [badge #393].

MCALLISTER, JOSEPH (pvt.); 26; W; Dist. 2; Jefferson; comm. 5/4/71; qual. 5/17/71; resign. 6/30/71.

MCCARTER, J. D. P. (pvt.); W; Dist. 3; Mount Enterprise; comm. 8/19/71; qual. 8/19/71.

MCCLENDON, ROBERT L. (pvt.); 21; W; Dist. 3; Homer; qual. 9/30/71; disc. 10/31/71.

MCCULLOCH [MCCULLOUGH], NED (pvt.); 36; B; Dist. 2; Bonham, Fannin Co.; comm. 7/11/70; qual. 8/13/70; disc. 6/27/71.

MCDONALD, ARTHUR (pvt.); W; Dist. 4; Austin; comm. 5/15/72; qual. 5/15/72; resign. 6/30/72.

MCFARLAND, S. E. (pvt.); 29; W; Dist. 1; Austin, Travis Co.; comm. 8/1/70; 10/30/72; dismiss. 11/28/70; reinst. 12/10/70; resign. 12/31/70; qual. 10/30/72.

MCGEE, S. W. (pvt.); Dist. 8; qual. 10/25/71; disc. 12/8/71.

MCGOWN, ANDREW H. (pvt.); 46*; W*; Dist. 3; Milam, Sabine Co.; comm. 7/30/70 [8/1/70]; qual. 9/8/70; resign. 6/4/71.

MCGOWN, G. W. (pvt.); 21; W; Dist. 3; Milam; comm. 9/19/71; qual. 9/19/71; disc. 5/1/72.

MCGUIRE, JAMES (pvt./sgt.); W; Dist. 2/4; Austin; comm. 4/19/71; qual. 4/19/71; promoted to sgt. 5/1/71; trans. to Police Clerk 7/1/71.

MCKELVY, GEORGE R. (pvt.); 25; B; Dist. 3/7; Columbia, Brazoria Co.; comm. 2/12/71; qual. 3/11/71; disc. 8/9/71.

MCKEW, JOSEPH (pvt.); 22*; W*; Dist. 4; Corpus Christi; comm. 3/22/71.

MCKNIGHT, JAMES W. (pvt.); known service Jan. – May 1872.

MCMURRY, HIRAM; 26*; W*; Dist. 1; Denton; comm. 3/15/73; qual. 3/15/73.

MCNELLY, LEANDER H. (capt.); 24; W; Dist. 3/4; Burton, Brenham, Washington Co.; comm. 7/12/70; qual. 7/12/70; detached temporarily from his proper station [Rio Grande Expedition].

MEIR, A.; W; Dist. 4; Austin; comm. 8/15/71; qual. 8/15/71; cancelled 11/1/71 – never qual.

MEJIA, PABLO (pvt.); 31; Dist. Sub; San Elizario, El Paso; comm. 8/3/70.

MELVILLE, ANDREW (pvt.); 25; W; Dist. 4; Austin; comm. 2/17/73; qual. 2/18/73; died 4/10/73 of wounds received at Lampasas on 3/14/73 [badge #425].

MENEFEE, W. H.; 40; W; Dist. 1; Dallas; comm. 11/14/72; qual. 11/25/72.

MERTH, C. C.; 58; W; Dist. 6; Victoria; comm. 11/18/72; qual. 11/21/72; resign. 12/31/72.

METCALF, W. R.; Dist. 5; Fort Concho; comm. 5/25/72; cancelled 7/3/72 – not qual. in time.

MEYER, JOHN; Dist. 7; Houston; comm. 8/12/71; appli. cancelled – never qual.

MEYER, JOSEPH; Dist. 5; Ysleta; comm. 9/1/71; cancelled 11/1/71 – never qual. declined.

MEYERS [MYERS], D. W.; Dist. 7; Montgomery, Tyler Co.; comm. 2/25/71; qual. 3/1/71; disc. 5/16/71.

MEYERS, WILLIAM; Dist. 1; comm. 9/1/71; qual. 9/1/71; disc. 11/10/71 by H. L. Edwards.

MILLER, A. R.; 28; W; Dist. 5; Round Mountain; comm. 10/31/72; qual. 11/5/72.

MILLER, CHAUNCEY (pvt.); B; Dist. 4; Austin; comm. 9/12/71; qual. 9/13/71; disc. 10/31/71.

MILLER [MULLER], G. FREDERICK (pvt.); 25; W; Dist. 4; Bastrop; comm. 9/15/71; qual. 9/16/71; disc. 12/15/71.

MILLER, N. J. (pvt./sgt.); 27; W; Dist. 1/5; Pedernales; Burnet Co.; comm. 7/26/70; qual. 8/6/70; promoted from pvt. 9/1/72.

MILLER, WILLIAM (pvt.); 25; W; Dist. 1; Bastrop; comm. 1/1/71; resign. 3/10/71.

MILLICAN, J. W.; 38; W; Dist. 4; Comanche; comm. 11/27/71; qual. 11/27/71.

MILLIGAN, J.; Dist. 2; Jefferson; comm. 3/11/73.

MILLSAPS, JACOB (pvt.); 48; W*; Dist. 2; Cow Hill; comm. 9/11/71; qual. 9/11/71; disc. 1/25/72.

MILROY, JOHN; W; Dist. 1/4/6; Brownsville; Waco, McLennan Co.; comm. 1/24/71; qual. 1/30/71; disc. 6/27/71; reinst. 7/22/71; disc. 10/14/71; trans. to 4th Dist.

MILSTEAD, P. G. (pvt.); 31; W; Dist. 4; Groesbeck; comm. 10/7/71; qual. 10/7/71; disc. 12/20/71.

MITCHELL, ALLEN (pvt.); 28; B; Dist. 1/4; Eagle Pass, Maverick Co.; comm. 9/28/70; dismiss. 12/21/70.

MITCHELL, J. N. (pvt.); Dist. 4; Texana, Jackson Co.; comm. 8/13/70; cancelled 11/15/70 – never accepted.

MITCHELL, WILLIAM J. (pvt.); 24; B; Dist. 1; Austin; comm. 9/5/70 [on duty at Austin]; appt. revoked 12/31/70.

MOCK, P. L. (pvt.); W; Dist. 4/6; Uvalde, Uvalde Co.; comm. 2/3/71; qual. 2/3/71; resign. 5/13/71.

MOHIER, L. J.; Dist. 3; Palestine; comm. 3/21/72; declined.

MOLES, JAMES B.; 23; B; Dist. 4; Austin; comm. 1/11/73; qual. 1/11/73; disc. 2/18/73; reinst. 3/18/73.

MONTGOMERY, HENRY R. (pvt.); 25; Dist. 1; Belton, Bell Co.; Travis Co.; comm. 7/12/70 [with Sgt. Evans]; resign. 9/17/70.

MONTGOMERY, JOHN (pvt.); B; Dist. 4; Austin; comm. 10/1/72; qual. 10/1/72; disc. 11/15/72.

MOODY, HENRY (pvt.); 40*; W*; Dist. 1/2; Cedar Grove, Kaufman Co.; comm. 1/10/71; qual. 1/19/71; resign. 1/8/72.

MOONEY, THOMAS (pvt.); 24; W; Dist. 4; Austin; qual. 2/10/72; disc. 8/22/72.

MOORE, IRVING (pvt.); W; Dist. 4; Austin; Palestine; comm. 10/8/71; qual. 10/8/71; disc. 5/31/72.

MOORE, MATTHIAS [MATHIAS] (pvt.); Dist. 2; Canton, Van Zandt Co.; comm. 7/22/70 [dead].

MOORE, NATHANIEL (pvt.); 40*; W; Dist. 1/4; Austin, Travis Co.; comm. 3/11/71; qual. 3/11/71; disc. 8/15/71; re-comm. 10/19/72; disc. 11/21/72.

MOORE, WILLIAM E.; Dist. 4; comm. 1/10/71; never qual.; comm. returned.

MOORMAN, CHARLES; 23; W; Dist. 2; Clarksville; comm. 1/22/73; qual. 2/3/73.

MORELAND, WESLEY; 23; B; Dist. 2; Clarksville, Red River Co.; comm. 10/19/70; cancelled 11/15/70 never having accepted.

MORGAN, O. E. (pvt.); W; Dist. 4; Austin; comm. 8/3/71; qual. 8/3/71; resign. 12/5/71; trans. to Bell Co.

MORGAN, W. J. (pvt.); 32; W; Dist. 1; Milford; comm. 9/16/71; qual. 9/16/71; disc. 11/10/71 by H. L. Edwards.

MORRILL, W. C. (pvt.); 27; W; Dist. 1; Sherman; comm. 8/26/71; qual. 8/26/71; disc. 12/31/71.

MORRIS, J. C. (pvt.); Dist. 4; Burton; comm. 2/20/71; qual. 2/20/71; disc. 8/9/71; reinst.; disc. 10/10/71.

MORRIS, JAMES (pvt.); B; Dist. 1; comm. 7/26/70; comm. uncalled for and cancelled 9/22/70.

MORROW, J. H. (pvt.); W; Dist. 4; Austin; comm. 10/1/72; qual. 10/1/72.

MORTON, WALTER H. (pvt./sgt.); 29; W; Dist. 2; Sulphur Springs; comm. 9/11/71; qual. 9/11/71; promoted to sgt. 6/1/72; resign. 2/28/73.

MOSBY, SAMUEL W.; 30; W; Dist. 4; Austin; comm. 12/6/72; qual. 12/6/72; disc. 1/12/73.

MOSELY, JAMES W. (pvt.); Dist. 2; comm. 5/13/71; cancelled 6/24/71 never having accepted.

MOUNTS, JOSEPH H. (pvt.); 29; W; Dist. 1; Denton; comm. 9/9/72; qual. 9/9/72; resign. 10/31/72.

MOY, W. B. (pvt.); 21; W; Dist. 8; comm. 9/3/71; qual. 9/3/71; disc. 12/15/71.

MURCHISON, K. B. (pvt.); Dist. 3/4; Millican; comm. 2/25/71; qual. 3/1/71; disc. 6/26/71.

MURCHISON, WILLIAM M. (pvt.); 34*; W*; Dist. 3; Crockett, Houston Co.; comm. 8/1/70; appt. revoked 12/31/70.

MURPHY, JACK K.; Dist. 4; comm. 8/14/71; qual. 9/1/71; disc. 12/31/71.

MURPHY, JORDAN (pvt.); 45*; B; Dist. 3; Crockett; comm. 9/15/71; qual. 9/15/71; disc. 12/15/71.

MURPHY, MICHEL (pvt.); Dist. 3; Brenham, Washington Co.; comm. 8/11/70; appt. cancelled 12/5/70.

MURPHY, PAT [THOMAS] (pvt.); 28; Dist. 4; Corpus Christi, Nueces Co.; comm. 8/20/70; Thomas Murphy qual. but not recognized; oath returned 9/22/70 as recommendations were for Pat Murphy.

MURPHY, THOMAS (pvt.); 25; W; Dist. 6; Corpus Christi; comm. 8/1/71; qual. 8/10/71; disc. 2/17/72.

MUSGROVE, E. G. (pvt.); 23; W*; Dist. 2; Winnsboro; comm. 9/13/71; qual. 9/13/71; disc. 3/29/73 with loss of all pay.

MYERS, WILLIAM (pvt.); Dist. 2/3; Henderson, Rusk Co.; comm. 3/21/71; cancelled 6/28/71 – not qual. in time.

NAGLE, PIERCE (pvt.); 22; W; Dist. 1/4; Waco; Eagle Pass, Maverick Co.; comm. 7/11/70; resign. 12/21/70; reinst. and trans. to 4th Dist.; dismiss. 1/30/71 [deserted].

NAIL, ALLEN (pvt.); Dist. 7; Columbus; comm. 6/12/71; cancelled 6/28/71 – not qual. in time [Error, he was appt. by order and performed duty and qual. but oath reached office 7/12/71].

NASH, JIM (pvt.); 30; W; Dist. 5; Camp Colorado, Coleman Co.; comm. 10/21/72; qual. 10/21/72.

NEATHERLIN, JAMES M. (pvt.); 34; B; Dist. 6; Pleasanton; comm. 9/1/71; qual. 9/6/71.

NEELY, J. B. (pvt.); 28; W; Dist. 4; Bryan; comm. 9/5/71; qual. 9/5/71; disc. 12/15/71.

NELSON, RICHARD (pvt.); 28; B; Dist. 3; Galveston; comm. 8/4/70 [declined 8/28/70].

NEWMAN, JAMES W. (pvt.); 23; W*; Dist. 3; Calvert, Robertson Co.; comm. 8/1/70; dismiss. 10/31/70.

NICHOLS, JOHN (pvt.); W; Dist. 1; Lampasas, Lampasas Co.; comm. 2/10/71; resign. 5/1/71.

NICHOLS, S. M. (pvt.); 43; W; Dist. 7; Sempronius; comm. 8/15/72; qual. 8/29/72.

NICHOLS, WILLIAM (pvt.); W; Dist. 4; Austin; comm. 9/1/72; qual. 9/1/72; resign. 10/19/72.

NORDHAUS, ALEXANDER (pvt.); 36; Dist. 1; San Antonio; comm. 7/25/70; comm. cancelled 7/25/70.

NORWOOD, MORRIS (pvt.); 26; B; Dist. 1; New Braunfels; Mountain City, Hays Co.; comm. 7/27/70.

NORWOOD, SAMUEL; 23; B; Dist. 4; Austin; comm. 1/23/73; qual. 1/24/73; disc. 4/8/73 with loss of all pay; rept. to George W. Paul, Kerrville.

NUEGENT, WILLIAM S.; 21; W; Dist. 1; Denton; comm. 10/23/71; qual. 10/23/71; appointment by A. C. Hill; appointment unauthorized and not sustained.

NUGENT, ED; 23; W; Dist. 2; Clarksville; comm. 8/12/71; qual. 9/21/71; resign. 9/21/71.

NUGENT, THOMAS L. (sgt.); Dist. 1; Austin; comm. 1/1/71; disc. 3/12/71.

NUNN, W. L. (pvt.); 23; W; Dist. 4; Bryan; comm. 9/13/71; qual. 9/13/71; disc. 12/15/71.

OAKLEY, WALTER H. (pvt./sgt.); 28; W; Dist. 1/4; Waco, McLennan Co.; Austin; McKinney, Collin Co.; Weatherford, Parker Co.; comm. 12/1/70; qual. 12/1/70; promoted to sgt. 2/4/71 [2/1/71]; trans. to Parker Co.; deserted 9/1/71.

OATS, JACKSON (pvt.); 24; B; Dist. 1; Dresden; comm. 8/25/71; qual. 8/25/71; disc. 12/13/71.

O'BRYAN, T. [F.] (pvt.); W; Dist. 4; Uvalde, Uvalde Co.; comm. 2/3/71; qual. 2/3/71; resign. 3/20/71.

OHLENBERGER, F. (pvt.); 35*; W*; Dist. 4; Columbus, Colorado Co.; comm. 7/23/70; dismiss. 11/24/70; reinst. 12/10/70 without loss of pay; dismiss.; comm. returned 3/10/71.

OHLER, WILLIAM (pvt.); Dist. 4; Corpus Christi, Nueces Co.; comm. 8/20/70; declined having been appt. inspector 9/12/70.

OLIVAREZ, CIRIACO; Dist. 6; Carrizo; comm. 3/28/72; qual. 11/5/72; to be allowed pay from date of qual.

OLIVER, WILLIAM JOHNSON; W; Dist. 1; comm. 1/24/71 [Special].

ONEAL, ROBERT L. (pvt.); 30*; W*; Dist. 4; Matagorda, Matagorda Co.; comm. 8/13/70; disc. 2/16/71 [2/15/71].

ORTEGA, PERFETO (pvt.); 42; M; Dist. Sub/5; San Elizario, El Paso Co.; comm. 7/7/70; qual. 7/20/70; disc. 8/25/71; reinst. 9/19/71.

ORTON, JAMES (pvt.); B; Dist. 2/3; Marshall, Harrison Co.; comm. 10/19/70; qual. 10/18/70; dismiss. 3/1/71 for incompetency and dereliction of duty; reinst.; disc. 6/30/71.

O'SHAUGHNESY [SHAUGHNESSY], JOSEPH P.; 30*; W*; Dist. 6; Brownsville, Cameron Co.; comm. 2/24/72; qual. 3/2/72; disc. 9/15/72; reinst. 11/15/72.

O'TOOLE, PATRICK (pvt.); W; Dist. 3/7; Huntsville; Lookout; Madison Co.; comm. 11/12/70; qual. 11/12/70; dismiss. 3/1/71 [3/7/71]; reinst.; disc. 6/13/71.

OWENS, S. A. (pvt.); 29; W; Dist. 3; Center; comm. 9/12/71; qual. 9/12/71; disc. 10/31/71.

OWENS, W. J. (pvt.); W; Dist. 3; Mount Enterprise; comm. 8/14/71; qual. 8/14/71.

PACKARD, CLARK; Dist. 3; Hearne, Robertson Co.; comm. 4/10/71 [Spec. Int. R.R. policeman].

PARIS, E. V. (pvt.); 26; B; Dist. 2; Emory, Rains Co.; comm. 12/12/70; qual. 9/13/71.

PARKER, ABRAM (pvt.); B; Dist. 3/8; Beaumont; comm. 1/21/71; qual. 2/22/71; dismiss. 5/17/71.

PARKER, EDWARD (pvt.); W; Dist. 2; Austin, Travis Co.; comm. 2/1/71; disc. 4/30/71.

PARKER, J. F. (sgt.); Dist. 1; comm. 7/23/70; comm. cancelled for drunkenness 8/1/70.

PARKER, L. J. (pvt.); 26; W; Dist. 1/5; Burnet Co.; Pedernales; comm. 7/23/70; qual. 8/6/70.

PARKERSON, EDWARD (pvt.); W; Dist. 4/6; Uvalde, Uvalde Co.; comm. 2/3/71; qual. 2/3/71; resign. 6/10/71.

PASCHAL, WILLIAM (pvt.); Dist. 1; Waco, McLennan Co.; comm. 7/16/70 [7/15/70]; comm. declined 7/19/70.

PASKINS, M. T.; Dist. 2; comm. 8/29/71; disc. [resigned] 10/31/71; appt. by J. D.

PASSONS, FRANK (pvt.); 38; W; Dist. 3; Palestine; comm. 9/11/71; qual. 9/11/71; disc. 8/3/72.

PATRICK, J. H. (pvt.); 28*; W; Dist. 3/7; Madison; comm. 8/9/70; qual. 8/30/70; disc. 10/31/70; reinst. 8/24/71; disc. 12/31/71.

PATTERSON, F. M (pvt.); 23; W; Dist. 2; Clarksville; comm. 8/12/71; qual. 9/2/71; disc. 12/20/71.

PATTON, THOMAS L (pvt./sgt./lt.); 41; W; Dist. 4/6; Helena, Karnes Co.; comm. 10/1/70; qual. 10/1/70; disc. 6/27/71; reinst. 7/25/71; promoted to sgt. 4/1/72; promoted to lt. 4/10/73.

PAUL, JOHN W. (pvt.); Dist. 3; Calvert, Robertson Co.; comm. 8/1/70; dismiss. 3/1/71.

PAYTON, W. H. (pvt.); 38; W; Dist. 4/6; Clinton, DeWitt Co.; comm. 3/20/71; qual. 4/3/71; disc. 6/27/72.

PEIL [PIEL], MARTIN (pvt.); Dist. 1; comm. 10/10/71; qual. 10/10/71; disc. 11/31/71 [10/31/71]; re-comm. 9/1/72; disc. 9/30/72.

PELHAM, WILLIAM; Dist. 4; Onion Creek; comm. 7/1/71; qual. 7/1/71; received no pay; cannot qual.

PENNINGTON, HUGH; 40*; W; Dist. 3/4; Brenham; Chappell Hill; Austin Co.; comm. 7/15/70; qual. 7/15/70; disc. 6/27/71.

PERKINS, ANDREW (pvt.); 32; B; Dist. 1; San Antonio, Bexar Co.; comm. 7/26/70; dismiss. 2/25/71 for drunkenness and interference with a police officer in San Antonio.

PERKINS, WILLIAM (pvt.); W; Dist. 1/3/4; Bremond; Kosse; Weatherford; comm. 3/24/71; qual. 3/25/71; trans. to Robertson Co.; trans. to Parker Co.; re-trans. to Bremond; resign. 8/12/71.

PERRY, JAMES E. (pvt.); 27; W; Dist. 4; Pleasanton, Atascosa Co.; comm. 1/10/71.

PETER, PHILIP; 32; W; Dist. 5; Fredericksburg; comm. 2/12/73; qual. 2/19/73 [badge #178].

PETERS, NIC (pvt.); W; Dist. 5; San Antonio; comm. 6/5/71; qual. 6/5/71; disc. 6/28/71.

PETTY, JAMES E. (pvt.); 27; W; Dist. 6; Pleasanton; comm. 1/10/71; qual. 1/17/71; disc. 6/28/71.

PHILLIPS, W. C. (pvt.); W; Dist. 6; Albuquerque; comm. 9/1/72; qual. 9/1/72.

PINNER, M. M. (pvt.); W; Dist. 1; Denton; disc. 2/28/73.

POPE, WILLIAM J. (pvt.); 33; W; Dist. 7; Willow Hole; comm. 8/15/71; qual. 9/16/71; disc. 12/20/71.

PORTER, JAMES B. (pvt.); 50; W; Dist. 7; Anderson; comm. 9/6/72; qual. 9/22/72.

POWELL, BIRD (pvt.); 34; W; Dist. 1; Stephenville; comm. 11/27/72; qual. 11/27/72.

PRATHER, RAISIN (pvt.); W; Dist. 1; Gidding; Austin; comm. 4/4/71; qual. 4/4/71; resign. 11/4/71; trans. to Washington Co.

PRICE, CALVIN; B; Dist. 4; Austin; comm. 2/14/73; qual. 2/19/73; resign. 3/8/73 [badge #184].

PRICE, DAVID (pvt.); 40; W; Dist. 4; Middleton; comm. 4/12/71; qual. 9/8/71; disc. 5/15/72.

PRICE, JOHN; W; Dist. 7; Houston; comm. 2/22/73; promoted to sgt. 3/10/73.

PRIESTLEY, JOSEPH L. (pvt.); Dist. 6; Burton; qual. 6/3/72; disc. 9/30/72 [Rio Grande Expedition].

PRITCHETT, W. T. (lt.); Dist. 1; Waco, McLennan Co.; comm. 8/29/70; started for Tennessee on leave of absence 2/6/71; leave extended to 3/31/71; never came back and dropped as a deserter 3/31/71.

PRUITT, JOHN T.; W; Dist. 4; Onion Creek; comm. 8/18/72; qual. 8/18/72.

PURVIS, ROBERT (pvt.); Dist. 4; comm. 8/14/71; qual. 9/1/71.

QUAYLE, WILLIAM H. (pvt.); known service Aug. 25 – Sept. 1871.

QUEAN, TURNER (pvt.); known service May 1–15, 1872.

RABB, CHRISTOPHER (pvt.); W; Dist. 4; Austin (Wheatville); comm. 6/21/72; qual. 6/21/72; disc. 8/22/72.

RAFFERTY, PATRICK (pvt.); 34; W; Dist. 1; Austin, Travis Co.; comm. 1/13/71; 8/15/72; comm. revoked 1/22/71; retained as a regular policeman; disc. 4/30/71; qual. 8/16/72; disc. 11/15/72; reinst.; dismiss. 3/11/73; reinst. 3/18/73.

RAGLAND, HENRY (pvt.); 27*; W; Dist. 4/6; Victoria, Victoria Co.; comm. 8/13/70 [8/13/71]; qual. 11/1/71.

RAINS, ISAAC (pvt.); Dist. 1; comm. 8/20/71; qual. 8/20/71; disc. 11/10/71 by H. L. Edwards.

RAINS, L. C. (pvt.); 20*; W*; Dist. 2; Emory; qual. 10/18/71; resign. 4/30/72.

RAMSEY [RUMSEY], ALFRED (pvt.); 24; W; Dist. 1; comm. 1/10/71; comm. revoked with loss of pay 1/24/71.

RAMSEY, R. J. M. (pvt.); 22; W; Dist. 3; Carthage; comm. 9/11/71; qual. 9/11/71; disc. 11/30/71.

RATTAN, VOLNEY (pvt.); 38; W; Dist. 2; Cooper; qual. 9/19/71; disc. 1/25/72; re-comm. 6/6/72; disc. 3/31/73.

RAWLEY, PATRICK (pvt.); 25*; W; Dist. 2; Marshall, Harrison Co.; comm. 10/19/70; dismiss. 12/29/70.

RAWSON, E. D.; W; Dist. 4; Waco; Austin; comm. 6/19/71; qual. 6/19/71; disc. 7/20/71; trans. to Parker Co.

RAY, J. H.; 30; W; Dist. 1; Fort Worth; comm 8/25/71; qual. 8/25/71; dismiss. 8/25/71.

REDMON, JOHN M. (pvt./sgt./lt.); 32 [34]; W; Dist. 1/2; Gainesville, Cooke Co.; comm. 1/20/71; qual. 2/11/71 [2/16/71]; disc. 6/27/71; reinst. 8/1/71; promoted to sgt. 6/1/72; promoted to lt. 3/6/73.

REDMON, LAFAYETTE (pvt.); 26*; B; Dist. 3; Center; disc. 10/31/71; appt. by Capt. Farrow; no oath; no comm.

REESE, HENRY B. (pvt.); 28; W; Dist. 1; Dallas; Denton; comm. 9/22/71; qual. 9/22/71; disc. 10/31/71; reinst. 2/24/72; dismiss. 6/21/72.

REESER, MANUEL (pvt.); Dist. 6; Albuquerque; comm. 6/1/72; qual. 6/26/72; disc. 9/30/72.

REICHENSTEIN, LOUIS (pvt.); W; Dist. 4; Austin; comm. 1/13/71 [6/13/71]; qual. 1/13/71 [6/13/71]; disc. 10/20/71; trans. to Bell Co.

REID, WARREN (pvt.); 35; B; Dist. 3/4; Centreville, Leon Co.; comm. 10/29/70; 10/19/71; qual. 10/29/70; disc. 5/23/71; reinst.; disc. 11/30/71.

RHODES, J. B. (pvt.); 46; W; Dist. 3; Carthage; comm. 9/14/71; qual. 9/14/71; disc. 12/20/71.

RICE, GEORGE (pvt.); known service Sept. – Oct. 1872.

RICE, JAMES H. (pvt.); 27; W; Dist. 4/6/7; Hallettsville, Lavaca Co.; Texana; comm. 8/4/70; 9/15/71; qual. 8/12/70; appt. revoked 12/1/70; disc. 12/1/70; reinst. 12/29/70; trans. to Jackson Co. 5/15/71; qual. 9/27/71; resign. 12/6/71.

RICHARDSON, DAVID; W; Dist. 7; Galveston; comm. 4/2/73; qual. 4/2/73.

RICHARDSON, HARRY (pvt.); Dist. 3; Calvert; comm. 8/1/70.

RICHARDSON, HENRY (pvt.); 30; B; Dist. 2/3; Athens, Henderson Co.; comm. 8/6/71; qual. 8/15/71; disc. 12/20/71.

RICHARDSON, LEWIS (pvt.); 45*; B; Dist. 3; Grimes Co.; comm. 1/18/71; dismiss. 3/7/71.

RICKER, H. A.; 35; W; Dist. 3; Hearne; comm. 4/22/71 [Spec. H & TC RR].

ROACH, SAM D. (pvt.); 33*; W*; Dist. 2; Lamar Co.; comm. 7/11/70; declined 8/4/70.

ROBERTS, A. G. (pvt.); 30; W; Dist. 3; San Augustine; comm. 9/8/71; qual. 9/8/71; disc. 10/31/71.

ROBERTS, JONES (pvt.); Dist. 4; Austin; comm. 7/1/71; qual. 7/1/71; disc. 11/1/72.

ROBINSON, J. W. (pvt.); Dist. 1; comm. 7/18/70; cancelled 11/15/70 – never accepted.

ROBINSON, JOHN H. (pvt.); 26; W; Dist. 2; Quitman; comm. 9/22/71; qual. 9/22/71; resign. 2/15/72.

ROBINSON, LAWSON (pvt.); Dist. 7; Huntsville; comm. 10/15/72; qual. 10/16/72.

ROGERS, HENRY O. (pvt.); 40; W; Dist. 4; Austin; comm. 9/4/72; qual. 9/4/72; re-sign. 12/11/72.

ROGERS, HIRAM (pvt.); 56; B; Dist. 3; Columbia, Brazoria Co.; comm. 7/8/70; appt. revoked 12/29/70.

ROGERS, WALLACE (pvt.); 23; B; Dist. 3/4; LaGrange, Fayette Co.; comm. 7/11/70; appt. revoked 8/29/70 being a cripple.

RONBECK, JULIAN; W; Dist. 5; New Braunfels; comm. 8/20/72; qual. 8/20/72; re-sign. 10/17/72.

ROONEY, P. H. (pvt.); W; Dist. 4; Onion Creek; comm. 4/24/72; qual. 4/24/72.

ROSALE, SYLVESTER (pvt.); 22; Dist. 4; Clinton, DeWitt Co.; comm. 7/13/70; dismiss. 10/1/70.

ROSS, J. L.; Dist. 4; comm. 1/11/73.

ROSS, PRIMUS; 45; B; Dist. 7; Huntsville; comm. 12/28/72; qual. 11/13/72.

ROUTT, W. T. (pvt.); W; Dist. 1; Lampasas, Lampasas Co.; comm. 1/28/71; resign. 4/26/71.

ROWLAND, J. J. (pvt.); 30; W; Dist. 1/4; Lampasas; comm. 5/1/71; qual. 5/6/71; disc. 6/28/71; reinst. 9/1/71; disc. 9/1/71.

ROY, A. L. (pvt.); W; Dist. 4/6; Giddings; comm. 7/8/72; qual. 7/8/72; disc. 10/5/72; reinst.; trans. to Bastrop Co.; dropped 2/8/73; reinst. 3/1/73 [Rio Grande Expedition].

RUBENDALL, HENRY E. (pvt.); 21; Dist. 3; Columbia, Brazoria Co.; comm. 8/5/70; disc. 8/29/70.

RUCKABY, RICHARD; Dist. 1; Dallas; comm. 6/13/71; cancelled 6/28/71 not qual. in time.

RUCKER, ANTHONY (pvt.); 53; B; Dist. 1; Waco; Austin; comm. 7/16/70 [7/15/70]; qual. 7/16/70; disc. 6/27/71.

RUSH, H. R. (pvt.) [30]; W; Dist. 4; Bastrop; Austin; comm. 8/3/71; qual. 8/4/71; resign. 11/30/71; trans. to Bastrop Co.

RUSKA, H. V. (pvt.); 25; W; Dist. 1; Corsicana; comm. 9/15/71; qual. 9/15/71; disc. 10/9/71 by G. W. Smith for drunkenness.

RUSSELL, GEORGE; Dist. 4; comm. 8/10/71; resign. 9/30/71.

RUSSELL, T. H.; Dist. 1; comm. 10/10/71; qual. 10/10/71; disc. 11/30/71.

RYAN, H. C.; Dist. 6; comm. 9/1/71; declined.

RYAN, H. M.; known service Sept. 15 – Oct. 15, 1872.

RYAN, JAMES (pvt.); Dist. 7; Navasota; comm. 7/10/72; qual. 7/10/72.

RYAN, JOHN C. (pvt.); 28; Dist. 3; Bryan City, Brazos Co.; comm. 7/23/70; dismiss. 9/30/70 for robbery.

SALINAS, ANDRES (pvt.); 40*; W*; Dist. 4; Hidalgo; comm. 7/11/70; comm. declined 8/8/70.

SALINAS, AUGUSTUS; 36; M; Dist. 6; Rio Grande City; comm. 10/28/70; qual. 10/15/72; resign. 3/26/73.

SALMON, GEORGE G.; 20; W; Dist. 4; Austin; comm. 3/5/73; qual. 3/5/73; disc. 4/8/73 with loss of all pay [badge #405].

SALMON, JOHN; W; Dist. 4; Austin; comm. 2/3/73; qual. 2/4/73.

SAMMON, EDWARD W. (pvt.); 46*; W; Dist. 3; Mount Enterprise; comm. 8/14/71; qual. 8/14/71.

SAMMON, JULIUS J. (pvt.); 19*; W; Dist. 3; Mount Enterprise; comm. 8/14/71; qual. 8/14/71.

SANDERS, THOMAS D. (pvt.); Dist. 3; Bryan; comm. 8/20/70; never accepted; appt. cancelled 11/15/70.

SANDERS, WILLIAM (pvt.); Dist. 1/3; Houston Co.; comm. 7/23/70; comm. returned and cancelled.

SANDS, ANDREW; 24*; B*; Dist. 2; Clarksville; comm. 3/10/73.

SAPP, P. W. (pvt.); Dist. 6; Hockley; qual. 6/5/72; disc. 10/5/72 [Rio Grande Expedition].

SAUNDERS, L. D. (pvt.); 22; W; Dist. 3; Rusk; comm. 9/11/71; qual. 9/21/71; disc. 12/15/71.

SCHERTZ, JOHN E. (pvt.); Dist. 5; New Braunfels; comm. 9/6/72; qual. 9/2/72; disc. 1/10/73.

SCHMERBER, JOSEPH (pvt.); 26; W; Dist. 6/4; Eagle Pass; comm. 4/13/71; qual. 4/19/71; dismiss. 6/22/71; reinst.; disc. 10/5/72.

SCHMIDT, CHARLES (pvt.); 45*; W*; Dist. 7; Columbus; comm. 6/12/71; cancelled 6/28/71 not qual. in time [error; he was appt. by order and performed and qualified but oath reached office 7/12/71].

SCHMIDT, EDWARD (pvt.); 22, 24, [23]; W; Dist. 1/5; Comfort, Kendall Co.; Blanco; comm. 8/11/70 [8/10/71] [8/30/70]; 3/1/71; 5/1/71; comm. returned 8/26/70; dismiss. 11/30/70; qual. 5/6/71; disc. 6/28/71; reinst. 9/14/71; resign. 7/23/72.

SCHOBEY, GEORGE W. (pvt.); 43*; W; Dist. 4; Austin; comm. 9/1/71; qual. 9/1/71; disc. 10/21/71.

SCHUBERT, LOUIS H. (lt.); 27; W; Dist. 3; Marshall; comm. 9/12/71; qual. 9/12/71; disc. 12/31/71; dropped 2/15/72; sent to penitentiary.

SCHUTZE, OTTO; Dist. 3; Austin; comm. 3/20/71; cancelled 3/25/71.

SCHWARTZ, HENRY (pvt.); 33; Dist. 3; Galveston; comm. 8/4/70; appt. revoked 11/1/70.

SCOLES, ROBERT; Dist. 3; Galveston; comm. 12/16/70; declined 12/21/70.

SCOTT, CHARLES; W; Dist. 7; Houston; comm. 11/18/72; qual. 11/18/72; application revoked.

SCOTT, JACK (pvt.); 33; W; Dist. 1; Dallas; comm. 8/13/71; qual. 8/13/71; disc. 12/31/71.

SCOTT, PATRICK (pvt.); W; Dist. 4; Austin; comm. 1/1/72; qual. 1/1/72; disc. 5/31/72; reinst.; disc. 8/21/72; reinst. 9/1/72; disc. 10/31/72.

SCREWBY, JOHN E.; Dist. 5; New Braunfels; disc. 1/10/73.

SCRUGGS, JAMES P. (pvt.); W; Dist. 3; Mount Enterprise; comm. 8/10/72; qual. 8/20/72; resign. 3/31/73.

SHANKS, CYRUS (pvt.); 29*; B*; Dist. 3; Navasota, Grimes Co.; comm. 8/4/70; re-sign. 11/15/70.

SHELDON, R. G. (pvt.); 27; W; Dist. 4/6; Indianola; comm. 5/9/71; qual. 5/31/71; disc. 6/28/71.

SHELTON, J. C. (pvt.); known service Apr. 13, 1872 – May 1872.

SHELTON, JAMES K; Dist. 4; Bagdad; comm. 4/12/72; qual. 4/13/72; disc. 6/30/72.

SHERIFF, THOMAS (sgt./lt.); 26; W; Dist. 3/4/7; Richmond [Pittsville], Fort Bend Co.; Rusk; comm. 7/8/70; qual. 7/14/70; promoted to sgt. 11/1/70; trans. to 7th Dist.; disc. 9/30/71.

SHIELDS, MILTON J.; 24; W; Dist. 1; Decatur; comm. 10/20/71; qual. 10/20/71; appt. by A. C. Hill; unauthorized and not sustained.

SHOTWELL, ALFRED J. (pvt.); 39*; B; Dist. 8; Liberty; comm. 7/30/71; qual. 7/30/71; re-appt. 3/8/72.

SHOWMAN [SHOUREMAN], CHARLES (pvt.); Dist. Sub; El Paso; comm. 7/7/70; comm. declined 7/31/70.

SICKOLD [SECKHOLTZ], JACOB (pvt.); 29 [28]; W; Dist. 1/5; New Braunfels, Comal Co.; comm. 7/30/70; qual. 8/6/70; disc. 8/31/71; comm.; qual.

SIERA [SIERRA], ANTONIO; 31*; W*; Dist. 6; Eagle Pass; comm. 2/18/73; qual. 3/6/73; resign. 4/18/73.

SIMMONS, C. C. (pvt.); 28; W; Dist. 4/6; Clinton, DeWitt Co.; Goliad; comm. 8/13/70; qual. 8/23/70; resign. 4/1/72.

SIMON [TIMON], HUGH (sgt.); Dist. 4; Corpus Christi, Nueces Co.; comm. 8/11/70; comm. declined 9/12/70.

SKIPWITH, G. J.; 45; W; Dist. 7; Houston; comm. 2/22/73; qual. 2/22/73.

SLADE, WILLIAM C. (sgt.); 33; W; Dist. 3/4/7; Bellville, Austin Co.; Richmond; Columbia; comm. 7/9/70; qual. 7/16/70 [ordered to Richmond 1/24/71]; resign. 7/31/71.

SLATLER [SLATTER], DANIEL; Dist. 2; Linden, Davis [Cass] Co.; comm. 3/21/71; cancelled 6/24/71 – never having qual.

SMALLEY, JIM (pvt.); 24*; B; Dist. 2; Marshall, Harrison Co.; comm. 10/18/70; killed while on duty 1/22/71.

SMITH, A. M. (pvt.); 21; W; Dist. 3; Center, Shelby Co.; comm. 10/24/70; resign. 4/27/71.

SMITH, ALFRED (pvt.); 37; B; Dist. 3; Bryan, Brazos Co.; comm. 7/11/70; dismiss. 10/31/70 [amended to "resignation accepted"].

SMITH, GEORGE W.; Dist. 1; Corsicana; comm. 8/22/71; qual. 8/22/71; resign. 10/15/71; no pay allowed.

SMITH, H. E. (pvt.); W; Dist. 1/4; McKinney; Waco, McLennan Co.; Austin; comm. 1/24/71; 1/24/73; qual. 1/30/71; disc. 1/13/73; reinst. 1/13/73; qual. 1/30/73; trans. to Austin, Travis Co.; trans. to Parker Co.

SMITH, JACOB (pvt.); Dist. 1; comm. 7/23/70; comm. uncalled for and cancelled 9/22/70.

SMITH, JAMES (pvt.); 30; W; Dist. 1; Sherman; comm. 9/1/71; qual. 9/1/71; disc. 10/31/71; reinst. 2/17/72; resign. 4/1/72.

SMITH, JOHN (pvt.); Dist. 1; comm. 10/10/71; qual. 10/10/71; resign. 2/10/72; reinst.; disc. 5/31/72.

SMITH, JOHN E. (pvt.); 29*; W*; Dist. 3; Crockett, Houston Co.; comm. 8/1/70; dismiss. 12/29/70.

SMITH, JOHN M. (pvt.); 26; Dist. 1/4; Clinton, DeWitt Co.; Belton, Bell Co.; comm. 7/12/70; comm. declined and returned; cancelled; reinst. and trans. to 1st Dist. 8/28/70; dismiss. 9/13/70.

SMITH, ROBERT (pvt.); 34; W; Dist. 1; Denton; comm. 8/12/72; qual. 8/12/72; disc. 2/28/73.

SMITH, THOMAS J. (pvt.); 30; W; Dist. 1/4; Bastrop, Bastrop Co.; comm. 2/20/71; qual. 2/22/71; resign. 7/20/71.

SNIVELY, JOSEPH; W; Dist. 7; Huntsville, Walker Co.; comm. 3/1/71; cancelled 6/24/71 – never having qual.

SNOWBALL, JAMES; W; Dist. 4; Houston; comm. 1/29/73; qual. 1/29/73; resign. 2/8/73.

SOUTH, BESTER (pvt.); Dist. 3; Bryan, Brazos Co.; comm. 11/9/70; dismiss. 3/7/71.

SPARKS, BAILEY (pvt.); 24; B; Dist. 3; Houston, Harris Co.; comm. 7/13/70; dismiss. 9/22/70 for disobedience of orders.

SPEARS, JAMES D. (pvt.); 32 [23]; W; Dist. Sub/5; El Paso; comm. 1/23/71; qual. 2/11/71; disc. 6/27/71.

SPEIGHTS, J. H. H. (pvt.); 21; W; Dist. 3; Milam; comm. 9/19/71; qual. 9/19/71.

SPEIGHTS, WILLIAM M. (pvt./sgt.); 46 [50]; W; Dist. 3; Milam, Sabine Co.; comm. 8/1/70; 9/16/71; appt. revoked 12/10/70; qual. 9/16/71; died 5/17/72.

SPENCER, A. W.; 35; W; Dist. 3; Houston; comm. 4/22/71 [Spec. H & TC RR].

SPICER, GEORGE; Dist. 6; Eagle Pass; comm. 3/19/73; qual. 4/8/73.

STAFFORD, WILLIAM F.; W; Dist. 1/4; Austin (clerk); comm. 5/1/71; qual. 5/1/71; trans. 5/1/71 as clerk AG's office.

STAKES, E. T. (lt.); W; Dist. 2/3; Marshall; Crockett; comm. 10/14/70 [10/6/70] [10/17/70]; qual. 10/14/70; qual. 10/16/70; resign. 12/19/71.

STANFIELD, JOHN C. (pvt.); 38; W; Dist. 4; Somerset, Lavaca Co.; comm. 1/10/71; dismiss. 3/13/71.

STANLEY, FLEM (pvt.); 32; B; Dist. 3; Shelbyville; comm. 9/20/71; qual. 9/20/71; disc. 10/31/71.

STANLEY, JAMES W. (pvt.); W; Dist. 3; Crockett; comm. 9/15/71; qual. 9/15/71; returned from P. O. unopened; returned 10/7/71; care of A. T. Monroe; disc. 12/15/71.

STANLEY, S. J. (pvt.); W; Dist. 3; Crockett; comm. 9/15/71; qual. 9/15/71; disc. 12/15/71.

STANLEY, W. G. (pvt.); Dist. 3; Crockett; comm. 10/6/71; qual. 10/6/71; disc. 12/15/71.

STAPLETON, PATRICK (pvt.); W; Dist. 2/4; Austin; Paris; comm. 8/4/71; qual. 8/4/71; trans. to Lamar Co.; resign. 12/10/71.

STEEN, ROBERT (pvt.); B; Dist. 3; Freestone Co.; comm. 8/1/70; dismiss. 11/30/70; reinst. 12/1/70; killed 4/27/71.

STEINHEIL, THADDEUS (pvt.); 29*; W; Dist. 1/5; Fredericksburg, Gillespie Co.; comm. 10/1/70; qual. 10/4/70; disc. 3/29/71; reinst. (disc. by mistake); resign. 7/12/72.

STEPHENS, GEORGE (pvt.); B; Dist. 1; Hill Co.; comm. 7/23/70; dismiss. 11/30/70.

STEVENS, ANDREW M. (pvt.); Dist. 6; Brownsville; comm. 10/7/72; qual. 10/7/72; resign. 2/13/73.

STEWART, J. ALBERT (pvt.); W; Dist. 4; Oak Hill; comm. 10/19/72; qual. 10/19/72; resign. 3/10/73.

STEWART, J. O.; 29; W; Dist. 1; Sherman; comm. 8/26/71; qual. 8/26/71; killed by Loss Kimble 6/1/72.

STILL, J. M.; Dist. 2; comm. 8/29/71; disc. 10/31/71; appt. by J.D.

STOKES, JOHN F. (pvt.); 28; W; Dist. 4; Austin; comm. 4/30/72; qual. 5/3/72; disc. 11/13/72.

STONE, ALFRED (pvt.); 23*; W*; Dist. 2; Red River Co.; comm. 7/11/70; comm. declined 7/26/70.

STONE, GEORGE (pvt.); W; Dist. 4/6; Uvalde, Uvalde Co.; comm. 2/3/71; qual. 2/3/71; resign. 5/13/71.

STONE, J. C. (pvt.); W; Dist. 1/2; Weatherford, Parker Co.; comm. 1/24/71; qual. 1/24/71; disc. 6/20/71.

STONE, W. B. (pvt.); 26; W; Dist. 2; Clarksville; comm. 5/20/72; qual. 6/6/72.

STOUT, JOHN; 30; W; Dist. 2; Bonham; comm. 3/10/73; qual. 4/2/73.

STRAWDER [SHAWDER], WILLIAM A. (pvt.); 24; B; Dist. 3/4/8; Woodville; Cold Spring; Polk Co; Eagle Pass, Maverick Co.; comm. 9/22/70; qual. 9/22/70; dismiss. 6/27/71; reinst. 8/10/71; disc. 12/20/71; re-comm. 9/4/72 [appt. cancelled by Ed Creary, Lt. S.P.]; trans. to Tyler Co.; trans. to 3rd Dist.

STREET, H. K.; 45*; W; Dist. 4; Evergreen via Giddings; comm. 10/22/72; disc. 2/18/73.

STRICKLAND, GEORGE (pvt.); 28; Dist. 6; Ecleto; comm. 5/14/71; qual. 5/14/71; disc. 7/25/71; reinst. 2/1/72; resign. 8/9/72.

SUGDEN, JOHN (pvt.); W; Dist. 4/6; Uvalde, Uvalde Co.; comm. 2/3/71; qual. 2/3/71; disc. 1/15/72.

SULLIVAN, DAN; W; Dist. 1 [RR; Special].

SULLIVAN, JOHN L. (pvt.); Dist. 4/6; Helena; comm. 4/12/71; qual. 6/16/71; cancelled 6/24/71 never having qual.; reinst. 7/25/71 having qual. and performed duty; resign. 11/30/71.

SULLIVAN, PATRICK (pvt.); W; Dist. 2/3; Marshall, Harrison Co.; comm. 10/19/70; qual. 10/19/70; dismiss. 10/31/70; dismiss. 11/1/70 for having allowed William Parrish, prisoner, to escape; reinst; disc. 6/27/71.

SUMMERS, WILLIAM (pvt.); 22; B; Dist. 1; Waco, McLennan Co.; comm. 7/12/70; resign. 12/22/70.

SWANN, WILLIAM E. (pvt.); Dist. 6; Leesburg; comm. 6/1/72; qual. 6/10/72; disc. 2/19/73.

SWEARINGEN, S. W. (pvt.); 27; W; Dist. 4/6; Oakville, Live Oak Co.; comm. 3/20/70; qual. 3/23/70; disc. 6/27/71; reinst. 7/25/71; disc. 6/30/72; reinst.; disc. 2/19/73.

SWENSON, AUGUST (pvt.); W; Dist. 4/6; Uvalde, Uvalde Co.; comm. 2/3/71; qual. 2/3/71; disc. 10/15/71.

TABOR, WILLIAM H. (pvt.); Dist. 3; Tyler Co.; comm. 2/25/71; appt. revoked 3/31/71; reinst. by recommendation of Sen. Baker; disc. 4/72.

TALLEY, RILEY (pvt.); Dist. 2/3; Canton, Van Zandt Co.; comm. 1/10/71; qual. 1/10/71; resign. 8/31/71.

TARPLEY, SAM S. (pvt.); 25; W*; Dist. 2; Plano, McKinney, Collin Co.; comm. 9/6/70; dismiss. 3/6/71 for failure to proceed to McKinney.

TATUM, B. R. (pvt.); 23; W; Dist. 3; Center; comm. 9/4/71; qual. 9/4/71; disc. 12/15/71.

TAYLOR, DAN (pvt.); B; Dist. 7; Navasota; comm. 5/1/71; qual. 5/1/71; disc. 12/20/71; reinst. 7/1/72; removed 8/10/72.

TAYLOR, G. E.; Dist. 4; comm. 8/14/71; qual. 9/1/71; disc. 12/20/71.

TAYLOR, J. H. (pvt.); W; Dist. 4; Austin, Travis Co.; comm. 1/16/71; S.P. comm. revoked 1/22/71.

TAYLOR, JAMES R. (pvt.); 34; W; Dist. 4; Yorktown, DeWitt Co.; comm. 8/13/70; disc. 10/1/70 by J.D.

TAYS, JAMES A. (pvt.); Dist. 5; El Paso; comm. 3/21/72; qual. 4/13/72.

TEAGUE, PETER (pvt.); 20*; B; Dist. 7; Navasota; comm. 5/1/71; qual. 5/1/71; disc. 10/14/71.

TEMPLE, CHARLES (pvt.); Dist. 1; comm. 10/10/71; qual. 10/10/71; disc. 11/30/71.

TEMPLETON, L. A. J. (pvt.); 51; W; Dist. 2/3; Tyler, Smith Co.; Troupe; comm. 4/13/71; qual. 5/5/71; disc. 6/28/71.

TENN, PETER (pvt.); B; Dist. 1; Austin; comm. 10/1/70; cancelled 2/8/71.

TERRELL, ALFRED B.; Dist. 6; Santa Gertrudis; comm. 9/25/72; qual. 9/25/72; disc. 12/31/72.

TERRELL, MONROE; 26; B; Dist. 6; Eagle Pass; comm. 10/20/72; qual. 10/20/72.

TERRY, JAMES; 32; W; Dist. 1; Houston; comm. 1/20/71 [Gal. Houston; Special].

THAYER, CHARLES H. (sgt.); 31; W; Dist. 4; Navasota; comm. 5/1/72; qual. 5/15/72; resign. 6/22/72.

THIELL, WILLIAM H. (pvt./sgt.); 32; W; Dist. 1; Denton; comm. 10/23/71; qual. 5/8/72; promoted from pvt. 3/1/73; appt. by A. C. Hill, appt. unauthorized and not sustained; re-comm. 5/20/72.

THOMAS, J. M. (pvt./sgt.); 28; W; Dist. 2; Jefferson; comm. 10/18/70; qual. 10/18/70; promoted to sgt. 5/1/71; resign. 8/26/71; reinst. by J.D.; disc. 11/30/71.

THOMPSON, CHARLES (pvt.); W; Dist. 7; Harrisburg; comm. 5/31/72; qual. 6/1/72; appli. revoked from date of comm.

THOMPSON, CHARLES (pvt.); W; Dist. 4; Austin; comm. 8/4/71; qual. 8/4/71; dismiss. 8/31/71.

THOMPSON, CHARLES (pvt.); 23; B; Dist. 4/6; Indianola, Calhoun Co.; comm. 3/1/71; qual. 3/27/71; disc. 6/27/71.

THOMPSON, GEORGE (pvt.); 22; B; Dist. 1; Corsicana; comm. 8/20/71; qual. 8/20/71; disc. 10/9/71 by G. W. Smith.

THOMPSON, JOHN (pvt.); W; Dist. 1; Waco; comm. 12/1/70; trans. to 4th Dist.

THOMPSON, JOHN (pvt.); W; Dist. 7; Antioch; comm. 12/1/70; qual. 12/1/70; disc. 4/30/71; reinst.; disc. 6/27/71.

THOMPSON, JOHN (pvt.); Dist. 1; comm. 9/10/71; qual. 9/10/71; disc. 11/10/71 by H. L. Edwards.

THOMPSON, STEPHEN (pvt.); W; Dist. 1/4/7; Antioch, Lavaca Co.; Waco; comm. 12/1/70; trans. from 1st Dist.; qual. 12/1/70; trans. to 4th Dist. 1/23/71; disc. 4/30/71; disc. annulled; reinst.; disc. 6/27/71.

THORN, F. W. R. (pvt.); B; Dist. 1; Austin; comm. 10/1/70; dismiss. 12/1/70.

TINSLEY, EDWARD W. (pvt.); Dist. 3; Grimes Co.; comm. 7/12/70; comm. declined.

TIVYMAN, R. G.; Dist. 2; Tyler, Smith Co.; comm. 3/21/71; appt. withdrawn 4/3/71.

TODD, SHADRICK; 31*; B; Dist. 4; Austin; comm. 10/29/72; qual. 10/29/72.

TOM, JOHN (pvt.); Dist. 6; Burton; qual. 7/10/72; disc. 10/5/72 [Rio Grande Expedition].

TRACY, W. H.; 38; W; Dist. 4; Austin; comm. 9/9/71; qual. 9/9/71; cancelled appt. – not recognized.

TRAMMEL, GILES (pvt.); B; Dist. 3/4; Springfield, Limestone Co.; comm. 8/2/70; qual. 8/23/70; disc. 5/10/71; reinst.; disc. 6/30/72.

TRAMMEL, MERRICK (pvt.); 35; B; Dist. 3/4; Springfield, Limestone Co.; comm. 8/1/70; qual. 8/1/70; disc. 5/10/71; reinst.; disc. 6/30/72.

TRAWEEK, S. T.; W; Dist. 4; Lampasas; comm. 3/22/73; qual. 3/22/73.

TREVINO, JESUS; Dist. 6; San Diego; comm. 9/24/72; qual. 9/24/72.

TRIMBLE, GEORGE (pvt.); 24 [26]; B; Dist. 2; Clarksville; comm. 8/29/71; 2/6/73; qual. 8/29/71; disc. 5/1/72; qual. 2/18/73; disc. 2/28/73.

TRIMBLE, W. C. (pvt.); 33; W; Dist. 3; Jacksonville; comm. 8/12/71; qual. 9/11/71; disc. 12/20/71.

TRUELOVE, JOHN A. (pvt.); 29; W; Dist. 1/2; Gainesville, Cooke Co.; comm. 1/20/71; qual. 2/16/71; disc. 6/27/71; reinst. 8/1/71; disc. 6/1/72.

TRUITT, CHARLES (pvt.) B; Dist. 4; Bryan; comm. 8/10/71; qual. 8/15/71; disc. 10/24/71.

TUMLINSON, JOSEPH (pvt.); 58; W*; Dist. 4; Yorktown, DeWitt Co.; comm. 7/13/70; disc. 4/30/71.

TUNSTALL, WILLIAM V. (pvt.); 42; W; Dist. 3/4; Crockett, Houston Co.; Rusk, Cherokee Co.; comm. 3/29/71; qual. 3/29/71; appt. revoked 6/30/71 with loss of all pay; previous remarks as to pay cancelled; reinst. 8/4/71; disc. 7/3/72.

TURNER, THEODORE E. (pvt.); 28; W; Dist. 1; Waco; comm. 7/16/70 [7/15/70] [dismiss.].

TYGARD, J. L.; 24; W; Dist. 3; Houston; comm. 4/22/71 [Spec. H & TC RR].

VALENTINE, JOHN (pvt.); W; Dist. 1/4; Lampasas, Lampasas Co.; comm. 2/3/71; qual. 2/3/71; resign. 12/31/71; reinst; disc. 5/31/72.

VAN NORMAN, S. S. (sgt.); Dist. 1; Austin; comm. 1/1/71.

VAN PATTEN, EUGENE; 26; W; Dist. Sub/5; El Paso, El Paso Co.; comm. 1/23/71; qual. 2/11/71; disc. 6/27/71.

VAN WEY, D. C. (pvt.); 31; W; Dist. 2; Clarksville; comm. 4/20/71; qual. 5/8/71; disc. 2/15/72.

VASQUEZ, THOMAS (pvt.); Dist. 4; Brownsville, Cameron Co.; comm. 7/11/70; comm. declined 8/10/70.

VAUGHAN, J. M. (pvt.); 45; W; Dist. 2; Sulphur Springs; comm. 6/7/72; qual. 6/7/72.

VAUGHN, M. J. (pvt.); 52; W; Dist. 2; Paris; comm. 8/29/71; qual. 8/29/71; disc. 12/20/71.

VEGA, GEORGE F. B. (pvt.); 35; W; Dist. 4; Brownsville, Cameron Co.; comm. 9/21/70; dismiss. 1/23/71; comm. returned 3/10/71.

VELA, APOLONIO (pvt.); Dist. 6; San Diego; comm. 9/24/72; qual. 9/24/72.

VELA, CECILIO (pvt.); 50; W*; Dist. 4; Starr Co.; comm. 7/11/70; resign. 2/6/71.

VICKERY, VANCE; Dist. 8; Woodville; comm. 9/18/71; qual. 9/18/71; disc. 9/19/71.

VILLANUEVA, MAURICIO (pvt.); 25; M; Dist. 4/6; El Sauz, Hidalgo Co.; comm. 8/11/70; qual. 9/7/70; disc. 6/27/70.

VILLAREAL, J. M.; Dist. 6; Brownsville; comm. 10/7/72; qual. 10/7/72; resign. 2/2/73.

VILLAREAL, JOSE MARIA; Dist. 6; Carrizo; comm. 10/27/72; qual. 10/27/72.

VIRLON [VIRLOW], THOMAS (pvt.); W; Dist. 1; Austin, Travis Co.; comm. 1/14/71.

WADE, JAMES W. (pvt.); 44; W*; Dist. 3; Pittsville, Fort Bend Co.; comm. 8/12/70; dismiss. 9/28/70 on several complaints.

WADSWORTH, W. B. (pvt.); 29; W; Dist. 7; Matagorda; comm. 4/18/72; qual. 5/1/72; resign. 8/8/72.

WALKER, P. B.; Dist. 1; McKinney; comm. 8/12/71; comm. returned from P.O. unopened.

WALLACE, B. R. (pvt.); 43; W; Dist. 3; San Augustine; comm. 9/8/71; qual. 9/8/71; disc. 12/15/71.

WALLACE, JAMES T.; W; Dist. 3; Iron Mountain; comm. 8/12/71; qual.; declined.

WALLER, H. B. (pvt.); 21; W; Dist. 6/7; Hempstead; comm. 2/17/73; qual. 6/5/72; disc. 10/5/72; qual. 2/20/73 [Rio Grande Expedition].

WALSH [WALCH], JOHN [1st] (pvt.); W; Dist. 1/4; Austin; comm. 4/20/71; qual. 4/20/71; resign. 12/31/71 [printer].

WALSH [WALCH], JOHN [2nd] (pvt.); W; Dist. 4; Austin; comm. 5/5/71; qual. 5/5/71; resign. 12/4/71; trans. to Bell Co.

WALSH, PATRICK J. (pvt.); 23; W; Dist. 1; Waco; comm. 11/9/70; resign.

WALTZ, WILLIAM; 27; B; Dist. 4; Austin; comm. 1/23/73; qual. 1/24/73; resign. 3/4/73.

WARD, CHARLES (pvt.); W; Dist. 3/7; Madisonville; Kosse; comm. 11/12/70; qual. 11/12/70; disc. 5/15/71; reinst.; disc. 12/20/71.

WATERS, E. (pvt.); known service Aug. – Sept. 1872.

WATSON, JAMES T. (pvt.); 49; W; Dist. 4; Bagdad; comm. 9/6/71; qual. 9/19/71; resign. 12/15/72.

WATTS, HENRY (pvt.); 21; B; Dist. 1; Corsicana; comm. 8/25/71; qual. 8/25/71; resign. 10/9/71.

WATTS, TAYLOR (pvt.); 21; B; Dist. 1; comm. 8/20/71; qual. 8/20/71; disc. 10/7/71 by G. W. Smith.

WEAR, MADISON (sgt./lt.); W; Dist. 4; Austin; Brenham; comm. 9/11/72; qual. 12/13/72; promoted to lt. 2/18/73.

WEATHERLY, EDWIN (pvt.); 25; Dist. 4; Travis Co.; Belton, Bell Co.; Clinton, De-Witt Co.; comm. 7/12/70; trans. to 1st Dist.; resign. 9/17/70.

WEAVER, GEORGE W. (pvt.); 69; W*; Dist. 3; Center, Shelby Co.; comm. 8/1/70; comm. revoked 9/6/70; for being too old to do duty.

WEBB, E. H.; W; Dist. 4; Mountain City; comm. 8/20/71; qual. 8/20/71; disc. 10/22/71.

WEBB, W. H. (pvt.); W; Dist. 3; Huntsville, Walker Co.; comm. 2/1/71; disc. 3/15/71.

WEIR, A. (pvt.); W; Dist. 4; Austin; comm. 8/15/71; qual. 8/15/71; disc. 9/71.

WENDLER, C. F. (sgt./lt.); 34; W; Dist. 1/4/5; Boerne, Kendall Co.; comm. 7/16/70; qual. 7/16/70; promoted to lt. 5/1/71; trans. to 4th Dist.; trans. annulled.

WERNER, AUGUST (pvt.); W; Dist. 3/4; Ledbetter; Bastrop; Kosse, Limestone Co.; comm. 11/12/70; qual. 11/12/70; resign. 2/11/71; reinst.; trans. to Bastrop Co.; dismiss. 6/22/71; reinst. 8/7/71; killed 8/18/71.

WEST, CHARLES M. (pvt.); Dist. 3; Hearne, Robertson Co.; comm. 4/10/71 [Spec. Int. RR policeman].

WHEAT, JAMES (pvt.); 34*; W*; Dist. 2; Paris, Lamar Co.; comm. 12/1/70; qual. 1/3/71; disc. 3/29/73 with loss of all pay.

WHEELER, JEFF L. [F.] (pvt.); 39; W; Dist. 3; Homer, Angelina Co.; comm. 1/20/71; qual. 3/1/71; disc. 6/27/71; reinst. 9/14/71 by G. W. Farrow; disc. 2/28/72.

WHEELER, PETER (pvt.); B; Dist. 1; comm. 7/23/70; comm. cancelled 9/22/70.

WHELAN, PATRICK (pvt.); 30; W; Dist. 6/4; Corpus Christi, Nueces Co.; comm. 12/7/70; qual. 12/19/70; resign. 7/31/71.

WHIPPLE, A. W. (pvt.); 24; Dist. 3; Navasota, Grimes Co.; comm. 7/13/70; dismiss. 10/31/70.

WHIPPLE, THOMAS; Dist. 3; Paris; comm. 1/24/73; declined and comm. returned.

WHITE, F. M. (pvt.); 20; Dist. 4; Texana, Jackson Co.; comm. 8/13/70; comm. cancelled 9/6/70 [not being of age to hold office] under age 20.

WHITE, FRED (pvt.); Dist. 1; known service Mar. 1, 1871 – Mar. 31, 1871.

WHITE, JOHN (pvt.); 25; W; Dist. 1; comm. 9/17/70; deserted 1/31/71.

WHITE, P. J. (pvt.); 34; Dist. 2; Sulphur Springs; comm. 9/4/71; qual. 9/4/71; resign. 4/30/72.

WHITE, S. F. (pvt.); 25; W; Dist. 4; Austin; comm. 12/12/72; qual. 1/1/73; disc. 2/13/73.

WHITESIDE, JOHN (pvt.); Dist. 3; comm. 11/12/70; never reported; cancelled.

WHITNEY, J. FRANK (pvt.); W; Dist. 8; Navasota; comm. 8/22/71; qual. 8/22/71; disc. 10/31/71; reinst.; disc. 12/31/71.

WICKS, SAMUEL; 54; B; Dist. 4; Austin; comm. 1/23/73; qual. 1/24/73 [Rept. to George W. Paul, Kerrville].

WIGGINS, HUGH L. (pvt.); 26; W; Dist. 1/4; Waco, McLennan Co.; Cameron; comm. 7/16/70 [7/15/70]; qual. 7/18/70; resign. 11/8/71.

WILCOX, GEORGE (pvt.); 25; W; Dist. 1/4; Travis Co.; Waco, McLennan Co.; Clinton, DeWitt Co.; comm. 7/12/70; disc. 10/1/70.

WILKERSON, ED (pvt.); 35*; B; Dist. 1; Austin, Travis Co.; comm. 7/12/70; comm. declined.

WILLIAMS, ANDREW (ANDY) (pvt.); 35; B; Dist. 3/1; Waco; trans. to Springfield, Limestone Co.; comm. 7/16/70 [7/15/70]; resign. 4/4/71; trans. to Limestone Co. (3rd Dist.).

WILLIAMS, B. H. (pvt.); 22; W; Dist. 6; Lockhart; comm. 8/1/71; qual. 8/10/71; disc. 2/5/72.

WILLIAMS, CHARLES C. (sgt.); W; Dist. 4; Austin; comm. 6/1/71; qual. 6/1/71; trans. to AG's clerk; dropped from rolls 2/28/73.

WILLIAMS, F. M. (pvt.); Dist. 3; Rusk; qual. 10/7/71; disc. 10/30/71.

WILLIAMS, GEORGE W. (pvt.); Dist. 2; Wood Co.; comm. 12/12/70 [recalled].

WILLIAMS, J. F. (pvt.); 28; W; Dist. 2; Paris; comm. 8/29/71; qual. 8/29/71; disc. 12/20/71.

WILLIAMS, JOHN (pvt.); 23; Dist. 3; Waco; Pittsville, Richmond, Fort Bend Co.; comm. 7/16/70 [died 9/2/70 at Richmond].

WILLIAMS, JOHN (pvt.); Dist. 1; Fort Worth; comm. 10/2/71; qual. 10/2/71; disc. 3/15/72.

WILLIAMS, JOHN H. (pvt.); known service Sept. 1871 – Feb. 1872.

WILLIAMS, JOHN W (pvt.); W; Dist. 1; San Saba, San Saba Co.; comm. 2/4/71.

WILLIAMS, T. J. (pvt.); 29; W; Dist. 1; Fort Worth; comm. 8/29/71; qual. 8/29/71; disc. 10/31/71.

WILLIAMS, T. S. (pvt.); Dist. 3; Rusk; qual. 10/14/71; disc. 11/30/71.

WILLIAMS, THOMAS (lt./capt.); 25 [26]; W; Dist. 1/4; Lockhart, Caldwell Co.; Bastrop; Austin; comm. 7/7/70; qual. 7/9/70; resign. 1/7/71; reinst. 7/17/71; resign. 4/11/72; reinst. as capt. 12/16/72; killed at Lampasas 3/14/73.

WILLIAMS, WILLIAM; 26; B; Dist. 4; McDade; comm. 12/28/72; qual. 1/13/73 [badge #81].

WILLSON, JOHN W. (pvt.); Dist. 4; Oakville, Live Oak Co.; comm. 1/1/71; resign. 3/31/71.

WILSON, CYRUS M. (pvt.); W; Dist. 1; Kosse; McLennan Co.; comm. 11/12/70; never reported – cancelled.

WILSON, J. W. (pvt.); Dist. 1; comm. 8/21/71; qual. 8/21/71; disc. 12/13/71; reinst. 2/24/72; reported by C. D. Blood as directed 1/72.

WILSON, MACK (pvt.); B; Dist. 1/4; Austin; comm. 5/10/71; qual. 5/10/71; dismiss. 6/1/71.

WILSON, P. A. (pvt.); 29; W; Dist. 1; Dresden; comm. 9/13/71; qual. 9/13/71; disc. 12/13/71.

WILSON, SAMUEL H.; W; Dist. 3; Huntsville, Walker Co.; comm. 10/7/70; dismiss. 1/9/71 with loss of all pay.

WINFIELD, MARTIN (pvt.); W; Dist. 4; Austin; comm. 6/10/71; qual. 6/10/71; disc. 7/30/71.

WIPFF, JOHN M. (pvt.); 38; W; Dist. 6; Eagle Pass; comm. 4/13/71; qual. 4/19/71; disc. 10/15/72.

WISOFF, MICHAEL (pvt.); B; Dist. 4; Eagle Pass; comm. 4/13/71.

WOFFORD, JOE (pvt.); Dist. 3; Crockett; comm. 9/15/71; 8/22/71; disc. 12/15/71.

WOOD, J. H. (pvt.); 25; W; Dist. 1; Ft. Mason, Mason Co.; comm. 11/12/70; dismiss. 2/6/71.

WOOD, JAMES P (pvt.); 27; W*; Dist. 2; Linden; comm. 9/5/71; qual. 9/5/71; disc. 6/30/72.

WOOD, R. C. (pvt.); Dist. 6; Hempstead; qual. 6/4/72; disc. 9/30/72 [Rio Grande Expedition].

WOODRIDGE, STROTHER (pvt.); 36; B; Dist. 1; Seguin, Guadalupe Co.; comm. 8/13/70; dismiss. 11/4/70 for allowing prisoner Neighbors to escape.

WOODS, JOHN; Dist. 5; El Paso; comm. 9/1/71; cancelled 11/1/71 – never qual.

WOOLLEY, M. L. (pvt.); 28; W; Dist. 4; McDade; comm. 6/3/72; qual. 6/3/72; resign. 2/18/73.

WREN, WILLIAM W.; 30; W; Dist. 4; Austin; comm. 2/17/73; qual. 2/18/73; comm. cancelled and returned 4/22/73.

WRIGHT [WIGHT], ALEXANDER; 38*; W*; Dist. 2; Greenville; comm. 1/17/72; declined.

WRIGHT, DANIEL (pvt.); Dist. 7; Navasota; comm. 8/23/71; qual. 8/23/71; disc. 12/15/71.

WRIGHT, J. M. (pvt.); 34; W; Dist. 3; Gilmer; comm. 6/26/71; qual. 6/26/71.

WRIGHT, W. W. (pvt.); 41; W; Dist. 3; Buena Vista; comm. 9/11/71; qual. 9/11/71; disc. 12/15/71.

WULFING, ROBERT (lt.); Dist. 1; Sisterdale, Kendall Co.; comm. 8/13/70; comm. declined 8/19/70.

WYNNE, MITCHELL; 33; B; Dist. 7; Huntsville; comm. 10/15/72; qual. 10/21/72.

WYSE, J. M.; Dist. 3; comm. 4/22/71 [Spec. H & TC RR].

YANCEY, FAYETTE (pvt.); 35*; B; Dist. 4/7; Columbus; comm. 7/23/70; qual. 8/1/70; disc. 9/5/71.

YARBROUGH, W. J. (pvt.); Dist. 4; Groesbeck; comm. 10/7/71; qual. 10/7/71; disc. 12/15/71.

YORK, MILTON (pvt.); Dist. 4; Giddings; comm. 1/20/72; qual. 2/1/72; resign. 8/17/72.

YOUNG, J. M. H. (pvt.); Dist. 6; Hempstead; qual. 6/5/72; disc. 7/31/72 [Rio Grande Expedition].

YOUNG, W. J. (pvt.); 26; W; Dist. 4/6; Albuquerque, Gonzales Co.; comm. 8/13/70; qual. 9/5/70; dismiss. 12/1/70; reinst. 3/1/71 without loss of pay; resign. 6/10/71.

YOUNG, WILLIAM (pvt.); 28; W; Dist. 5; Fort Davis; comm. 9/1/71; qual. 9/11/71; disc. 12/15/71.

YREGOYEN, CRESANO (pvt.); 31; M; Dist. Sub/5; El Paso, El Paso Co.; comm. 1/23/71; qual. 2/6/71; disc. 6/27/71.

ZAPATA, CLEMENTE (pvt.); 56; M; Dist. 4/6; Carrizo; Zapata; comm. 7/11/70; qual. 10/25/70; resign. 5/8/71.

ZINSMEYER, STEPHEN (pvt.); 37; Dist. 1; San Antonio; comm. 7/23/70 [dismiss. 8/9/70] for neglect of duty.

ZORB, A. (pvt.); 38; W; Dist. 4; LaGrange, Fayette Co.; comm. 7/23/70; qual. 7/23/70; dropped 7/1/71 [insane].

Index

Page numbers in **boldface** indicate illustrations. Texas State Police is abbreviated as TSP.

CPSIA information can be obtained
at www.ICGtesting.com
Printed in the USA
FSOW01n0045110116
15490FS